COME UP
HIGHER

COME UP
HIGHER

PAUL L. COX
Editor

LIBERTYVILLE, ILLINOIS

Manuscript Editor: Ginny Emery
Cover Designer: Laura Sebold
Concept for Cover: Brodie Budd
Book Layout: Mary Anne Pfitzinger

Published by This Joy! Books—A Division of Three Cord Ministries, Inc.
1117 So. Milwaukee Ave, Suite A4, Libertyville, IL 60048—www.thisjoybooks.com.

ISBN-13: 978-0-9821835-8-8
First printing, 2010
Printed in the United States of America

Dedicated to
Pastor Patti and Mike Velotta of
Calvary Way International Fellowship in Libertyville, Illinois.
Thank you, Mike and Patti, for demonstrating in word and action your love for Donna and me and Aslan's Place. My journey of going higher has been so much easier because of your friendship.

Contents

Contents

Contents

Why Pray
Generational Prayers?

PAUL L. COX

I must admit that I have frequently asked myself, "What is so important about praying written generational prayers?" After all, at the point of placing our trust in the Lord Jesus Christ, we are saved. *What more needs to be done?* I am not the only one who asks this question. Over the years, many have suggested that we should not have to pray written prayers, even that praying them is unbiblical.

Others have also questioned whether we should repent for generational issues. I have been told, sometimes in hateful ways, that this also is unbiblical and certainly not necessary. Many would say that "the work was finished at the cross of Christ and nothing else needs to be done. The matter is settled. We already have all we need. No more praying about generational issues is necessary."

Now, here is the crux of the issue. For twenty years, I have ministered to hundreds of people. Through generational praying and leading others to pray written prayers, I have seen believers transformed by the power of the Lord. This transformation has led to a deeper level of intimacy with Jesus Christ and new levels of freedom. So, how do I reconcile this apparent contradiction between the finished work of the Cross and what I have seen in ministry over the past twenty years? The Bible is our ultimate authority, not our experience. At any point where experience and the Bible disagree, the Bible wins. I believe that and I practice that. *So, what does the Bible say?*

Here are the fundamentals. We are saved by grace.

For by grace you have been saved through faith, and that not of yourselves; it is the gift of God, not of works, lest anyone should boast. For we are His workmanship, created in Christ Jesus for good works, which God prepared beforehand that we should walk in them. (Ephesians 2:8–10)

Our works, in our Christian life, verify that we really are saved.

Thus also faith by itself, if it does not have works, is dead. But someone will say, "You have faith, and I have works." Show me your faith without your works, and I will show you my faith by my works. You believe that there is one God. You do well. Even the demons believe—and tremble! But do you want to know, O foolish man, that faith without works is dead? (James 2:17–20)

Having established that we are saved by grace and our works verify our salvation, what part do we play in this process? Some argue that we have no part. It is true that salvation is the work of Christ alone. Even our coming to faith is made possible by the drawing of the Holy Spirit. The book of Romans clearly indicates that sanctification is a process; it is accomplished through the working of Christ in us, transforming us through the power of the Holy Spirit. So the question must be asked again, "Do we have any responsibility in our transformation from glory to ever-increasing glory?"[1]

I believe the answer is yes. We do have a responsibility in our transformation from glory to ever-increasing glory. Look at Philippians 2:12–13:

Therefore, my beloved, as you have always obeyed, not as in my presence only, but now much more in my absence, work out your own salvation with fear and trembling; for it is God who works in you both to will and to do for His good pleasure.

The key phrase to examine is "work out your own salvation." What does this mean? It certainly does not mean work for your salvation. Scripture is clear that salvation comes through faith and not through works. We must understand what this "[working] out your own salvation" means.

This issue is foundational to what I do in ministry, the reasoning behind publishing a book on prayers. If there is no scriptural mandate for this kind of ministry, then pursuing it is error. With this in mind I would like to give an extended quote from the *Baker Exegetical Commentary on the New Testament*. I am aware that it is a little tedious and will take some concentration on the part of the reader! However, if the importance of a believer's part in maturing, in "[working] out your own salvation" cannot be settled, then this book is meaningless! With this in mind, here is a section from the theological discussion of Philippians 2:12–13.

> But, the Biblical concept of salvation is not thus restricted to justification; more commonly what is in view includes God's redemptive work in its totality. Thus, while in a very important sense, we have already been saved (Ephesians 2:5, 8; Titus 3:5), in another sense, we are yet to be saved (Romans 5:9–10; 1 Corinthians 3:15, 5:5; 2 Timothy 4:18). Calvin rightly claims "that salvation is taken to mean the entire course of our calling, and that this term includes all things by which God accomplishes that perfection, to which He has determined us by His free election." Because salvation in its entire scope necessarily includes the manifestation of righteousness in our lives, it follows that our activity is integral to the process of salvation; we can never afford to forget the juxtaposition between verse 9 ("not of works") and verse 10 ("for good works") in Ephesians 2. In the particular context of Philippians 2, the out workings of the believer's personal salvation take the form of corporate obligations within the Christian community: the duty of seeking the good of others.
>
> For those who admit the soteriological[2] thrust of the passage, the tendency is to define verse 12 by means of verse 13 (or verse 13 by means of verse 12), that is, to tone down human activity by appealing to divine grace (or vice versa). One may, for example, so emphasize the truth that God does not force us to act against our will, that as a result, grace is restricted to little more than spiritual aid: "God will help us along, but it's really up to us." Conversely, fear of legalism may lead us to a more or less passive understanding of sanctification: "Our responsibility is simply to rest in God's grace, to let Him work in us." The text itself, by its very juxtaposition of those two emphases, cries out loudly against any such attempts at resolution. And the point here is not merely that both the human and the divine are stressed, but that in one and the same passage,

we have what is perhaps the strongest Biblical expression of each element.

Note first Paul's concern with human activity. Although several New Testament verses place considerable emphasis on the role of human responsibility in salvation (cf. esp. 2 Peter 1:10 [NASB], "for as long as you practice these things, you will never stumble"), none puts it so bluntly as Philippians 2:12. The very choice of the verb *katergazomai* is notable. Chrysostom explained this compound form as indicating "with great effort, with great care"; though the evidence speaks against seeing such a nuance in the verb itself, we should not completely overlook the fact that this ancient Greek speaker perceived the term as emphatic. Bauer's "achieve, accomplish" brings us closer to the distinctive nuance of the verb; he rightly places Philippians 2:12 under the second heading, "bring about, produce, create." It is impossible to tone down the force with which Paul here points to our conscious activity in sanctification. The thought should give us pause: our salvation, which we confess to be God's from beginning to end, is here described as something that we must bring about.

For all that, our dependence on divine activity for sanctification is nowhere made as explicit as here. To begin with, God's work is viewed as having a causal relation to our working (*gajr,* gar, for); our activity is possible only because of divine grace. Second, the syntax is emphatic: Paul says not merely "God works" *(ho theos energei)* but "the One Who works, the working is God" *(theos . . . estin ho energon . . . to energein).* Third, the divine influence is said to extend not only to our activity but to our very wills—a unique statement, though the idea is implied in other passages (e.g., John 1:13; Romans 9:16). Calvin comments: "There are, in any action, two principal parts, the will, and the effective power. Both of these [Paul] ascribes to God; what more remains to us to glory in?" Fourth, the apostle reinforces our dependence on God's sovereignty with a concluding reference to "his good pleasure," a distinctly theological term used to describe *divine grace.*

The point is that, while sanctification requires conscious effort and concentration, our activity takes place not in a legalistic spirit, with a view to gaining God's favor, but rather in a spirit of humility and thanksgiving, recognizing that without Christ we can do nothing (cf. John 15:5), and so He alone deserves the glory.

God's working in us is not suspended because we work, nor our working suspended because God works. Neither is the relation strictly one of cooperation as if God did His part and we did ours so that the conjunction or coordination of both produced the required result. God works and we also work. But the relation is that because God works, we work. All working out of salvation on our part is the effect of God's working in us. . . . We have here not only the explanation of all acceptable activity on our part, but we also have the incentive to our willing and working. . . . The more persistently active we are in working, the more persuaded we may be that all the energizing grace and power is of God.[3]

Let me summarize this excerpt. First, it is Christ who works in us both in salvation and in transforming us after salvation. Second, we have a part in bringing our salvation to completion. Third, our part is in the context of the church, the redeemed body of Christ.

What is stated in logical form in Philippians is illustrated in story form in the book of Joshua. The Lord clearly states that the land of Israel has been given to the children of Israel.

Moses My servant is dead. Now therefore, arise, go over this Jordan, you and all this people, to the land which I am giving to them—the children of Israel. Every place that the sole of your foot will tread upon I have given you, as I said to Moses. (Joshua 1:2–3)

Verse three delineates an important condition for receiving this gift. The land which has been totally given to them must be possessed by them. Joshua 1:3 says, "Every place that the sole of your foot will tread upon I have given you, as I said to Moses." The children of Israel have a part in possessing the land. They cannot simply cross over the river Jordan, set up camp, and wait for the coming of the Lord. They must possess their possessions. How do they do this? They must "walk" out their responsibility. "Every place that the sole of your foot will tread upon I have given you!"

In other words, they must come against the strongholds in the land, take them down, and possess the land. This is a picture of the Christian life. We come into the Promised Land, that is, the Kingdom of God, through the blood of Christ. The word Jordan actually means "to spread judgment."

As we walk through the River Jordan, judgment does not touch us because it has been held back by the power of the Lord. We enter into the land and begin to take down, through the power of God, the strongholds in our lives. God does his part and we do our part. Our part includes the use of spiritual disciplines as well as being intentional about getting all the deliverance from the old nature that we can. That is where generational prayers come in.

I understand from personal experience that those who do not believe in generational deliverance or in praying written generational prayers will not be satisfied by any reasoning or evidence. After I had been ministering deliverance for several months as a Baptist pastor, several of the deacons came to me to express their concerns. Some of our discussions became very intense! Finally, one deacon said to me, "Well, if this is really true, then where is the fruit?" The point was well taken. To show him the fruit, I scheduled a Sunday evening service where several people who had been significantly helped by prayers for generational deliverance gave testimonies of what the Lord had done. The evening was very powerful. For over two hours, person after person came to the microphone and shared how the Lord had touched their lives. The testimonies were particularly meaningful because I had ministered to some of these people for nine years before I started praying for deliverance. Clearly it was the ministry of deliverance that had made a difference!

After the service, that same deacon came to me and said, "I do not care what all those people say, I do not believe in this ministry." At the following deacon's meeting, the debate continued. Finally, in frustration, I said to the board, "If you do not want me to help these people, then you help them!" I was shocked by their responses. They all raised their hands and said, "We can't." Here was the real heart of the issue. Those who do not believe in this ministry not only do not believe in it, but they also have no answers or alternative solutions to offer believers who continue to be in pain. Their only answer is their own personal biblical and theological response to the concept of praying for people.

All of this should not be a surprise to anyone who knows the Bible. Jesus also encountered religious people who came against his healing and deliverance ministry. One of the most shocking Scriptures in the Bible is the account of the raising of Lazarus from the dead.

Now when He had said these things, He cried with a loud voice, "Lazarus, come forth!" And he who had died came out bound hand and foot with graveclothes, and his face was wrapped with a cloth. Jesus said to them, "Loose him, and let him go." Then many of the Jews who had come to Mary, and had seen the things Jesus did, believed in Him. But some of them went away to the Pharisees and told them the things Jesus did. Then the chief priests and the Pharisees gathered a council and said, "What shall we do? For this Man works many signs. If we let Him alone like this, everyone will believe in Him, and the Romans will come and take away both our place and nation." And one of them, Caiaphas, being high priest that year, said to them, "You know nothing at all, nor do you consider that it is expedient for us that one man should die for the people, and not that the whole nation should perish." Now this he did not say on his own authority; but being high priest that year he prophesied that Jesus would die for the nation, and not for that nation only, but also that He would gather together in one the children of God who were scattered abroad. Then, from that day on, they plotted to put Him to death. (John 11:43–53)

What is so shocking? Here is Jesus raising someone from the dead. Think of the joy of Lazarus and the joy of those who loved him; but the religious people do not see this. They can only see their own agendas and beliefs. Truth is not the issue! Their only response to the raising of Lazarus from the dead was to plot Jesus' death.

The deacon's meetings at my Baptist church finally culminated in congregational meetings. The debate seemed endless! Finally, I decided I had to leave the church. I can remember a conversation right after the meeting. I turned to a friend and said, "All I have ever wanted to do in ministry is to help others. Now that I am finally able to really help people, the deacons won't let me." I walked away crushed. But the Lord was not finished with me or with the ministry of deliverance. His heart is to see his people set free. In obedience, I have followed his calling on my life. Years later, the fruit is evident. The Lord has been faithful. Yes, there is resistance, but lives are being changed.

This book is really a reporting of the journey of ever-unfolding revelation of the tactics of the enemy to destroy the lives of individuals.

However, the emphasis is not on what the enemy has done and is doing, but on the freedom that is possible through taking back of the land of our inheritance. Victory has been secured at the cross of Jesus Christ. It is time now for you to possess your possessions. Receive it. Walk in it. Establish it.

Notes:

1. 2 Corinthians 3:18.

2. Study of salvation.

3. Moises Silva, *Philippians*, 2nd ed., Baker Exegetical Commentary on the New Testament (Grand Rapids, MI: Baker Academic, a division of Baker Pubishing Group, 2005). Used by permission.

Renunciation of
Sins in the Family Line

PAUL L. COX

You have probably heard it said that a journey begins with the first step. So it was with the book, *Prayers for Generational Deliverance*. The only difference is that I did not know I was beginning a journey that would include over forty prayers!

In the middle 1990s, I was in Dallas, Texas, praying for a twenty-one-year-old man who had deteriorated to such a low level because of mental anguish that a psychiatrist had prescribed three different types of medication. He was extremely depressed and although he had previously functioned at a high intellectual level, he was no longer able to do much more than exist. The high doses of medication had alleviated his despair, but the payback was a life of passivity. In reality, he could no longer function.

As I walked him through a generational deliverance, I could see his countenance change. It was clear that the Lord was doing a wonderful work in his life! After over two full days of ministry, it seemed that his hope was returning. I was almost finished with the prayer when I had a sudden inclination to turn to Romans 1. I felt he was to turn that passage into a prayer. As he strolled through the passage, I was stunned to see the change taking place in him. It was as if I were hearing this very familiar Scripture for the first time. That young man was transformed. The last I heard about him, his medication had been drastically reduced, and he was able to live a much more content life.

I realized the Lord had given me a key to healing. With the help of others, I wrote down the prayer based on Romans 1. I now had the first prayer in the book, *Prayers for Generational Deliverance*. I was so excited that I contacted friends in Alaska and shared what had happened. They were equally excited because the Lord had just given them the same passage and had also instructed them to turn it into a prayer. The Lord had confirmed what I had felt instructed to do in Dallas.

The "Renunciation of the Sins in the Family Line" is an extraordinary revelation, for within the prayer is a listing of sins that sweeps over the full landscape of the fallen human condition. Within its phrases there is repentance for idolatry, sexual immorality, ingratitude to God, depravity, wickedness, murder, jealousy, transgressions of the tongue, and rebellion against the ways of the Lord.

No prayer in this manual has been prayed more and translated into more languages. The depth of its significance is often visible when a person going through deliverance struggles for extended periods of time as he simply tries to renounce the ancestral sins in his family line.

The journey began with one prayer, but there were to be more! The Lord really does want to change us "from glory to glory."

The Prayer: Renunciation of the Sins in the Family Line

✠ As a member of this family line, I repent for all of those who suppressed the truth by their wickedness.

✠ I repent for all those who, although they knew God, neither glorified him as God nor gave thanks to him because their thinking was futile and their foolish hearts were darkened.

✠ I repent for all those who became fools and exchanged the glory of the immortal God for images made to look like mortal man, birds, animals, and reptiles.

✠ I repent for the sinful desires of my ancestors who gave their hearts to sexual impurity for the degrading of their bodies with one another.

�֍ I repent for all those who exchanged the truth of God for a lie and worshipped and served created things rather than the Creator, Who is forever praised.

✖ I repent for the shameful lusts of my ancestors and for the women who exchanged natural relations for unnatural ones.

✖ I repent for the men in my family line who abandoned natural relations with women and were inflamed with lust for one another, men who committed indecent acts with other men and received in themselves the due penalty for their perversion.

✖ I repent for those who did not think it worthwhile to retain the knowledge of God, and therefore they were turned over to a depraved mind to do what ought not to be done.

✖ I repent for all those who have been filled with every kind of wickedness, evil, greed, and depravity, and for all those who were full of envy, murder, strife, deceit, and malice.

✖ I repent for all those who were gossips, slanderers, God-haters, insolent, arrogant, and boastful, for all those who invented ways of doing evil, who were disobedient to their parents, who were senseless, faithless, heartless, and ruthless.

✖ I repent for those who although they knew God's righteous decree that those who do such things deserve death, they not only continued to do these very things but also approved of those who practiced them.

CHAPTER THREE

The Inertia Prayer

JOANNE TOWNE

In 2001 I was assisting Paul Cox in prayer for a woman with a severe dissociative disorder caused by multigenerational occult ritual abuse. No matter what we did in prayer that day, she would circle back to some other demonically controlled second heaven captivity. It caused the session to be defeating for her and frustrating for us. On the long drive home, I asked the Lord why things were more complicated and difficult for some people than for others. *How could we help those with severe issues to gain their freedom with less difficulty?*

As I drew closer to home, I began to have thoughts about ships and planes and how they stayed on their courses. I thought I was just tired and ignored it. The next morning, as I awakened to a vision of a gyroscope being drawn in white light, I realized that the Lord was answering my prayer. He had prompted the thoughts about ships and planes the day before.

I went to the encyclopedia and looked up the word *gyroscope*. I read that a *gyroscope* (or *gyro*) is a device that uses rotation to bring a stable direction in space, and this stability causes a vehicle to be fixed on its set course.[1] As I began to realize that God was explaining a spiritual principle to me, I continued to read.

The gyro consists of a spinning ball, called a rotor, and a support system. Once the rotor is set in motion, the gyro resists any attempt to change its direction or rotation. It's the principle behind the spinning tops of children and is known as *gyroscopic inertia*. Gyroscopic inertia is defined as "the tendency of a spinning body to resist the attempt to change its axis of rotation."[2] This property of spinning bodies is widely used in flight and navigation instruments to provide heading or course information that will be unaffected by air turbulence or heavy seas. Ships use a gyrocompass to find true north. Magnetic forces do not affect the gyro, however it must be protected from vibrations, impacts, and jolts.

As I continued reading, the gyro was described as "a wheel within a wheel." I remembered how Ezekiel described the workings of wheels of the four living creatures. In Ezekiel 1:15–21 and 10:9–17, his picture of these wheels is consistent with a gyroscope's appearance and function. I realized that God was revealing a spiritual principle to me that could be understood by the physics of the gyroscope.

To understand the spiritual principles and the resulting prayer the Lord gave me, I need to explain some basic principles of physics that are foundational to what the Lord was showing me.

According to the online encyclopedia *Wikipedia*:

The principle of inertia is one of the fundamental principles of classical physics which is used to describe the motion of matter and how it is affected by applied forces." In simple terms, inertia means "A body in motion tends to remain in motion; a body at rest tends to remain at rest." In common usage, however, people may also use the term "*inertia*" to refer to an object's "amount of resistance to change in velocity" (which is quantified by its mass), and sometimes its momentum, depending on context e.g., "this object has a lot of inertia."[3]

The strength of the inertia (stability and resistance to change of movement) depends on the distribution of the weight of the rotor and the speed of its spin. Regardless of how the support moves about, the axis of the gyroscope resists change and points in one set direction. A gyroscope has a north–south wheel and an east–west wheel within itself.

The greater the weight (or mass) at the rims of the wheels, the greater the inertia. That is why a rotating bicycle wheel produces more inertia than a pencil point that spins on itself. For example, the earth spins around its axis, an imaginary line that connects the North and South Poles. The gyroscopic inertia produced by the spin, causes the north axis of the earth to continually point to the North Star as the earth rotates in its orbit around the sun.

There are, however, influences that can create a shift of axis direction in a body set in gyroscopic inertia. In physics, the mass of a body determines the momentum of a body at a given velocity. In astronomy, inertia will break down near supermassive objects such as black holes and neutron stars because of the high gradient of the gravitational fields around such objects. Therefore, when a greater force is imposed on a given body, the jolt of a greater magnetic or gravitational pull can cause a change of axis direction on the body. Therefore, when an object's inertia is changed, its velocity (direction and speed) also changes.

As I began to understand the physical principles of inertia, I became aware of spiritual parallels. In Ezekiel, chapter one, the size and nature of the wheels indicate that they create a tremendous amount of inertia. Verse 18 says, "As for their rims, they were so high they were awesome; and their rims were full of eyes, all around the four of them."[4] This indicates a great weight (mass) in the wheels with the capacity to create powerful inertia. When I understood the physics principles and saw that the function and shape of the wheels Ezekiel saw were gyroscopic, I realized that the Lord was saying that the Holy Spirit's function, when joined to our spirits, works like the principle of a gyroscope. Ideally, the Holy Spirit would exert a continuous, uninterrupted effect on the life of every believer.

God's intention is to create a powerful inertia that sets us on a fixed set course of covenantal blessings, fulfilled divine purpose, and destiny. Godly inertia would keep us in constant alignment with the authority of the throne of God and allow continual divine intervention and influence from the third heaven in our daily lives.

However, the Lord explained to me that forces, those jolts and interrupting forces mentioned earlier, can affect this principle of inertia even in believers. Just as in physics where a body shifts in axis direction when a greater mass is imposed on it, believers can be thrown off God's intended course because of jolts created by demonically strategized trauma or by the greater magnetic/gravitational pull of strongholds, unbelief, traditions, doctrines of men, legalism, and other ungodly strategies.

Inertia can be a powerful positive force if one's alignment is toward the Kingdom of God and his divine authority and rule. If the believer's course is set and fixed on the divine will and purposes of God, this godly inertia results in fruitfulness and experienced blessings. If, however, a believer is pulled off of that original course through traumas, he is left without the power to move toward God's purposes and even without the will to resist the opposing force.

The Lord explained to me that ungodly inertia is created when a believer is plagued by powerful forces that resist change. These resistant forces, which were created by serial traumas, take believers off the set course of blessing and provision intended by God.

Just as the earth would be knocked out of its orbit around the sun by an extremely large gravitational force or impact, Satan, the enemy, deploys forces of havoc against a believer, especially in early life stages. This creates an "axis shift" that can cause one to be repeatedly knocked out of alignment with the Spirit of God's authority, influence, and agenda. The demonic then attempts to keep its place as a "fixed star" in the axis of life of the traumatized believer. This holds the believer under the captivity and influence of a demonic dimension in the second heaven. Just as a strong inertia might force a planet into another orbit or create enough imbalance to cause its axis to point towards another star and away from true north, or the Kingdom of God, an ungodly inertia, initiated by the kingdom of darkness, causes consequences in believers that result in constant unresolved issues and a continual lack of godly movement.

This captivity is expressed on earth by various afflictions, hardships, inabilities, and mental or corporate strongholds. The demonic influence is further strengthened as captives become territorially aligned to the demonic dimensions on the earth, below this earth, and in the second heaven. Captives are not only dealing with the results of their captivity, but they are also territorially attached: gates are shut, barring escape from demonic influence.

The traumas that created the jolt in a believer's life cause mental strongholds, generational captivities, and heart issues; they result in demonic influences that continue to hold minds and thoughts captive, giving the enemy a legal foothold to imprison wounded victims within their dark spiritual territory. Just as believers are called to be ambassadors on earth, bringing the manifestation of the influence of heaven to earth, Satan attempts to set up his embassy in the life of the believer and hold him captive to his rule and authority. This keeps a believer functionally more aligned to the forces of the kingdom of darkness than to the Kingdom of God and keeps him in a continual battle from which he constantly struggles to get free. This struggle for freedom is not limited to individuals; it can also be territorial.

People held under ungodly inertia or influence often say that they feel "stuck." Some synonyms for inertia include: "inactivity, powerlessness, lifelessness, and passivity." A man may become inactive from a lack of incentive, but one who is inert is restrained by something in his constitution or his habits which operates like a weight holding him back from exertion; it implies some defect of mental or physical constitution.[5]

The earth's dependence upon the sun is an analogy of how inertia works in a believer's life. Gravitational properties and inertia keep the earth orbiting around the sun. In proper orbit, the earth receives just the right amount of light and heat needed to sustain life. Inertia also holds the earth on a set course, fixed to true north, the polestar Polaris. If another object or force would create a greater gravitational pull and knock the earth off course, it would lose its ability to maintain every life function that depends upon the sun. Just as the earth needs light and heat from the sun to sustain life, the believer needs blessings and provision from the Lord to maintain his life functions (heart, spirit, soul, and body) and to maintain his course (purpose).

Godly inertia is constantly maintained by the mass, the weight of God's glory, in a believer's life. God's glory is not to be an abstract positional ideal but a concrete reality that is emotionally, mentally, and functionally realized through the thoughts and outworkings of the Holy Spirit within each believer. The manifestations of godly inertia in a believer's life include a pure and blameless heart sprinkled from an evil conscience, sincere faith, a reverent and worshipful spirit, a heavenly mind-set, ownership of salvation's benefits, and acknowledged citizenship in heaven. A believer's course is maintained by the Lord's gravitational pull, the perfect love of God, and the Holy Spirit's influence and power.

If another celestial object, the demonic, with greater magnetic pull (because of traumas, strongholds, enforced generational curses, idolatries, wrong doctrine, etc.) comes along, this demonic influence can begin to create enough "gravitational" pull to move the believer off his intended orbit (his calling, purpose, blessings, authority), and pull him into a demonic orbit, thereby taking the believer captive. Like a black hole, the demonic creates a gravitational pull to its own "star." This dimensional captivity results in "ungodly inertia" that keeps the believer in captivity to the demonic realm and influence. This spiritual captivity keeps the believer from God's intended blessings and from fulfilling his God-designed purpose and influence on earth.

Is there such a thing as dimensional captivity? Is there any scriptural reference to it? Nehemiah 1:9 says, "Though some of you were cast out to the farthest part of the heavens, yet I will gather them from there, and bring them to the place which I have chosen as a dwelling for My name." Deuteronomy 30:4–5 states,

> *If any of you are driven out to the farthest parts under heaven, from there the LORD your God will gather you, and from there He will bring you. Then the LORD your God will bring you to the land which your fathers possessed, and you shall possess it. He will prosper you and multiply you more than your fathers.*

Deuteronomy 9:1–2 says,

> *Hear, O Israel: You are to cross over the Jordan today, and go in to dispossess nations greater and mightier than yourself, cities great and fortified up to heaven, a people great and tall, the descendants of the Anakim, whom you know, and of whom you heard it said, 'Who can stand before the descendants of Anak?'*

Interestingly, this verse is talking about life after crossing the Jordan (the Christian life) indicating that these are issues those in Christ will face as they take their respective lands for the Lord. The Hebrew word for fortified here is *batsa*[6] meaning to be fenced, to be clipped off like grapes, to be isolated, inaccessible by height or fortification, to withhold. This indicates the characteristics of strongholds and the resulting captivity. Remember, believers are supposed to be in rulership over the second heaven; this is the battle we are continually engaged in. Who will have rule, the church or the enemy? Satan will do whatever he can to see to it that we, both individually and collectively as a church, do not rule. He frustrates us individually with so many tumults and afflictions that taking nations is seemingly impossible.[7]

The Lord revealed to me that a believer can take authority for those under the enemy's captivity by removing them from ungodly inertia and the consequential territorial alignments. By restoring a person to his proper alignment to God's throne and to the divine order of the third heaven suggested in Ezekiel 1:22–28, the person is restored to the Holy Spirit's gyroscopic influence. This brings godly inertia resulting in divine movement, breakthrough, and renewed stability. The person is reinstated to a position of true ambassadorial authority with his full God-given rights as a citizen of heaven.

This prayer is often effective when people have prayed everything they have known to pray because it addresses the second heaven captivity, not just the resulting "earthly" effects of the captivity (such as sickness, poverty, afflictions, etc.). People will sometimes feel a tugging or a pulling when this prayer is prayed. They often feel the ungodly inertia of dimensional captivity being broken off.

Please also understand that though we can stand in the gap for people under of the captivity of inertia, their ability to maintain individual freedom is still their own responsibility and is best maintained through seeking discipleship. I have found that removing captives from demonic territorial influence enables them to break strongholds that seemingly would not move before. Additional deliverance is possible because the ungodly inertia is now broken. This results in increasingly proper alignment to third heaven influence and continued godly movement into their proper course.

The Prayer: Changing Inertia

�incross✝ I pray protection for myself, my family, and my household. I command that no astral projections, remote viewing, remote sensing, telluric energies, demonic spiritual fields, (e.g., ley lines) or witchcraft can in any way empower, influence, or have any adverse affect on me.

✝ Father God, I agree with your purposes to remove all ungodly inertia and the influence of all demonic territorial captivity in my life. Lord, please remove all strongholds, idolatries, afflictions, generational curses, traditions, false teachings, and doctrines caused by any person, place, Satan, or his demons, above and below this earth. I break all ungodly ties between me and any ungodly dimension.

✠ I ask the Holy Spirit of the true and living God to release from captivity all parts of me—heart, spirit, soul, and body—from these territories. Lord please remove any giftings, callings, resources, blessings, and purposes from captivity.

✠ I thank you Lord for now realigning me to your throne.

I declare that I will be aligned to:

✠ The Spirit of the Lord and all his characteristics, attributes, and benefits including the Spirit of wisdom and understanding, the Spirit of counsel and might, the Spirit of knowledge, and the fear of the Lord.

✠ My seated position in the heavenly places with the Lord Jesus Christ and to the all-seeing God, El Rai, and his direction for me.

✠ The voice and power of the Almighty, El Shaddai, and to the Word of God, both the *rhema* Word and the living *Logos*, the Lord Jesus Christ, and to the protection and authority of the Lord of Hosts.

✠ The grace, authority, rule, and dominion of the throne of God and to his right hand, and to his Kingdom purposes and divine order.

✠ The name of the Lord Jesus Christ that is above every other name in every dimension of the heavens, the earth, and below the earth.

✠ The fire of his presence, his sanctifying, purifying, and revelatory attributes, and to all reproductivity and creativity purposed through him for me.

✠ All the covenant promises and blessings given to Abraham and fulfilled in God the Father's Seed, the Lord Jesus Christ.[8]

✠ Please restore me to the image of Yahweh's glory and honor and to every Kingdom purpose, calling, and gifting. Please permanently align me to a position where I am seated with the Most High God in his most holy place.

✠ I now thank you Lord that the Spirit of the living God brings a permanent godly inertia and that I am now properly aligned to the throne of God and will never again be moved from this position by any ungodly force above, below, or on this earth.

Notes:

1. *Wikipedia.* s.v. "Gyroscope," http://en.wikipedia.org/wiki/Gyroscope.

2. *Wikipedia.* s.v. "Inertia," http://en.wikipedia.org/wiki/Inertia.

3. *Wikipedia.* s.v. "Inertia," http://en.wikipedia.org/wiki/Inertia.

4. James Strong, Enhanced Strong's Lexicon 2.0 (Woodside Bible Fellowship, 1995).

5. *Wikipedia.* s.v. "Inertia," http://en.wikipedia.org/wiki/Inertia.

6. James Strong, *Enhanced Strong's Lexicon* 2.0 (Woodside Bible Fellowship, 1995).

7. See Ephesians 3:10; Colossians 1:16.

8. You may appropriate the Abrahamic covenant promises here as you would like.

CHAPTER FOUR

Prayer to
Dismantle the Powers

PAUL L. COX

As a Baptist pastor, I was familiar with God and Satan, and angels and demons; that was the extent of my understanding of the spiritual world. I was content with this view of spiritual reality. However, the Lord was ready to stretch me. One afternoon I was discussing spiritual issues with a therapist friend of mine when I thought to myself, "I think I really do have a handle on deliverances and the spiritual world." With that thought came a response. "Paul, why do you think the spiritual world is so simple?" Then came a question, "How complex is the physical world?" I knew the Lord was talking to me! "Well, Lord the physical world is very complicated! The universe seems to extend out forever. Besides that, scientists have found smaller and smaller particles in the atom." I was not ready for his response. "Then why do you think the spiritual world is so simple?" My *Heaven Trek* adventure was continuing[1]. I was going to learn about other spiritual beings.

Many spiritual beings are mentioned in the Bible that are rarely discussed. Some of these beings are called *powers*. It was now time for me to learn about these powers. My training in discerning powers was to begin.

What does the Bible say about powers? Scriptural references include:

For I am convinced that neither death nor life, . . . nor any powers, . . . will be able to separate us from the love of God. (Romans 8:38–39, NIV)

Far above all rule and authority, power and dominion. (Ephesians 1:21, NIV)

For our struggle is not against flesh and blood, but against the rulers, against the authorities, against the powers of this dark world. (Ephesians 6:12, NIV)

For by him all things were created: things in heaven and on earth, visible and invisible, whether thrones or powers or rulers or authorities. (Colossians 1:16, NIV)

And having discerned the powers and authorities, he made a public spectacle of them, triumphing over them by the cross. (Colossians 2:15, NIV)

It saves you by the resurrection of Jesus Christ, who has gone into heaven and is at God's right hand—with angels, authorities, and powers in submission to him. (1 Peter 3:21–22)

My awareness of the powers began several years ago. During a trip to Argentina, I began to feel a new electrical type of anointing and to experience some very strong sensations on my body. While I am well-accustomed to my gift of discernment taking the form of unusual sensations, this was different. Initially I thought it was really strange, but life was about to become even stranger.

Needing some cash, I went to a local ATM machine, put in my card, and expected to receive my money. Instead, my card was returned and the display indicated that the machine was out of order. I went to a second location and tried again; once again the display read, "Out of Order." Then I went the third machine; it was out of order, too. *Once could be a normal event, twice a strange coincidence, but three times?* It was becoming apparent that something significant was happening. *But what?*

After we arrived home from Argentina, I went to the Northwest Airlines ticket counter at LAX to deal with a problem with a flight to Minnesota. Again, I felt all this "righteous energy" on me. As I approached the Northwest Airlines computer terminals, every computer stopped functioning. The Northwest employees worked desperately to get their equipment working. I overhead one employee say, "This has never happened before!" My wife commented, "This isn't funny anymore." Suddenly, all of the computers came back online except the one directly in front of me. Since it would not reboot, the agent had to use another computer to print my ticket. Interestingly, this happened again on another flight back from Minneapolis.

Additionally, I began experiencing episodes where streetlights went out as I drove by. (Others have reported experiencing this phenomenon as well.) I would set off the theft prevention detectors in stores, not only when I left a store, but also when I entered. I also had difficulties with digital watches. Whenever powers showed up, the display on my watch would go blank. When the display returned, I noticed that the watch had lost time!

Investigating the reality of powers, it was helpful and interesting to note these definitions of and uses of the word *powers*.

In Greek, the word for powers is *dynameis*.

- *Strong's Exhaustive Concordance of the Bible*: dunamis (doo'-nam-is) force (literally or figuratively); specially, miraculous power (usually by implication, a miracle itself)

- KJV translations of *dunamis* are ability, abundance, meaning, might (-ily, -y, -y deed), (worker of) miracle (–s), power, strength, violence, mighty (wonderful) work

- *Theological Dictionary of the New Testament* (TDNT): to be able, to be capable (II: 284)

From this, it's clear that powers have something to do with "force," with the ability or power to do something.

Continuing to investigate powers, I felt the Lord say that these created beings were responsible for managing electromagnetic fields. I thought— if this is correct—then a compass would respond to their presence. So, I tested the idea. On discerning the powers, I placed a compass on the sites where I sensed their presence. The compass needle moved every time. There was definitely something electromagnetic in those spots. After enough trials, I knew by induction that I could actually prove the presence of an electromagnetic spiritual being in a particular place.

The Scriptures about the powers and definitions of power dovetailed with the most basic knowledge about electromagnetism as an energy or power behind all ability and capability to do anything. According to *Wikipedia*,

> the electromagnetic force is the one responsible for practically all the phenomena encountered in daily life, with the exception of gravity. All the forces involved in interactions between atoms can be traced to the electromagnetic force acting on the electrically charged protons and electrons inside the atoms. This includes the forces we experience in "pushing" or "pulling" ordinary material objects, which come from the intermolecular forces between the individual molecules in our bodies and those in the objects. It also includes all forms of chemical phenomena, which arise from interactions between electron orbitals.[2]

All this seems to support the idea that powers are beings that are connected with electromagnetic fields.

In his book, *Body Electric*, Robert O. Becker, MD, examines the impact of magnetic fields on the human body. His extensive research includes the following observations and/or conclusions:

> All living things . . . share the common experience of being plugged into the electromagnetic fields of earth, which in turn vary in response to the moon and the sun.[3]

> Wever concluded that this frequency in the micro pulsations of the earth's electromagnetic field was the prime timer of biocycles. . . . Every creature is hooked up to the earth electromagnetically system.[4]

> Studies of the pineal gland have shown it to be "more than the vaguely defined 'third eye' of the mystics. It produces melatonin and serotonin, two neurohormones that . . . directly control all of the biocycles." . . . "Very small magnetic fields influence the pineal gland."[5]

> A study to determine any correlation between the disturbances in the earth's field caused by magnetic storms on the sun and human behavior showed increased admissions to a VA psychiatric

hospital as well as behavioral changes among the patients already hospitalized. Becker states, "We suspected that the earth's normal field played a major role in keeping the DC system's control of bodily functions within normal bounds."[6]

At the end of the nineteenth century, geophysicists found that the earth's magnetic field varied as the moon revolved around it. . . . Most preliterate cultures reckoned their calendar time primarily by the moon.[7]

About every eight days [due to] the sun's rotation . . . the earth's field is slightly changed in response to the flip-flop in polarity. (An interesting correlation to the seven-day week, with a new week beginning every eighth day.)[8]

Correlations have been discovered between activity in the sun's magnetic field and major flu epidemics, the growth of *Escherichia coli* in our intestines, and the severity of symptoms in patients suffering from neurological disorders. "Life's geometric coupling to heaven and earth is apparently more like a web than a simple cord and socket. . . . We might suspect, therefore, that many creatures would use magnetic information for their sense of place.[9]

The existence of magnetic sensors in such diverse creatures as bacteria, bees, and birds . . . suggests that a magnetic sense has existed from the very beginning of life.[10]

From a study of Scriptures (Ephesians 1:15–23, Ephesians 4:8, and Colossians 2:13–15), we learn these truths:

- Christ has supremacy over the powers.

- Christ's power and authority is cosmic in scope.

His name alone, and not his name in addition to others, is sufficient for a successful confrontation with the powers of evil . . . Christ's power and authority is exceedingly superior to all 'powers' indeed, every name that is named.[11]

- The "captives" of Ephesians 4:8 (NIV) are very likely the "enemies" of Ephesians 1:21.

- Jesus Christ has disarmed the powers.

The Lord was showing me some of the basic principles of the universe and that magnetism is an essential part. So I asked the question, do righteous and unrighteous powers control and supervise magnetic fields? Based on my observations, I believe the answer is yes. I have repeatedly noted that whenever I sense the presence of these righteous or unrighteous powers, I can stand in front of a person with a compass in my hand and the needle invariably moves right over the area where I can feel something.

It appears to me that the enemy has been perverting the magnetic fields, which has resulted in a lot of mental disorders as well as physical problems. My theory is that Satan may be perverting the magnetic fields and disrupting godly balance, and the result has been mental disorders and physical problems.

There is another interesting observation. *Why does the enemy draw people to worship the sun, moon, and stars? Why would he do that? Could it be that by focusing worship away from the Creator God, the enemy empowers the unrighteous powers to negatively affect the magnetic fields of the earth?* If so, the kingdom of Satan is enhanced so that he can disrupt and distort the perfect Creation of God. This strategy falls right into line with the second law of thermodynamics, a universal law of decay that tells us that material things are not eternal. We are all in the process of dying physically, and the universe is winding down.

Since the Lord began to teach me about powers, the Lord has shown in ministry sessions that there are gradations of powers. There seem to be either righteous or unrighteous powers around each person. There are also powers around land areas and even powers that are in charge of the earth and other planets.

We have discerned that powers around individuals usually show up in sets of four, and observations by those who can see in the spirit include the following comments. The powers:

- Look like the monolith in *2001 Space Odyssey* or appear like black slabs or monoliths, sheer blackness

- Appear as a pyramid on the head of the person

- Seem similar to Stonehenge

- Have connections similar to electrical equipment like TV cables; the connectors look like cords and boxes on a person

- Appear as frozen metal (which would indicate superconductors)

- Seem to have magnets rotating in a circular motion around the person

So what can we do? As with any other scheme of the enemy, we can pray and ask God to prevail. In this case, we ask God to disconnect us from the ruler of the air—from the second heaven.[12] We have carefully built a prayer from Galatians 4:3-7, 9-10, and Colossians 2 to dismantle the powers.

As people have prayed this prayer, the results have been amazing. A friend who was suffering from a chronic lung disease had been told by his doctor that he would not get better. After prayer to dismantle the powers (and ministry by others), he returned to the doctor who conducted the usual test. The doctor returned with the results stating, "This is impossible, but you have improved." He continued to improve and is no longer tested for this disorder.

We have seen the Lord heal depression by dealing with the unrighteous powers. Not too long ago *Scientific American* printed a small article noting that depressed people become joyful while they are in the magnetic tube for an MRI. This is an absolute confirmation of what we have found! I believe during MRIs, the incorrectly aligned magnetic fields are temporarily aligned. As the Lord removes the unrighteous powers, he can restore his righteous powers, then what he intended in Creation is realized!

At the conclusion of the prayer, people have discerned:

- Magnets slowly melting

- Reversed rotation and reversed polarity

- A disconnection taking place and a cord being yanked out

- A cable snapping out

- The pyramid on top shot up and away

- A rushing into the person of new "anointing"

- The sensation of an electrical storm over the room like fields of power shooting out

- Orange and blue electrical sparks

One final testimony. I was ministering at a church in the midwestern United States, and a friend of ours revealed to me that she had discovered a lump in her breast. We were all very concerned and began to pray. I felt one of the strongest manifestations of powers I had ever felt. I looked at my watch and it had gone blank. We continued to pray and asked the Lord to remove the unrighteous powers. The spiritual energy in the room was almost overpowering. The next day she went to the doctor, and the lump was not there! God had healed her!

The Prayer: Dismantle the Powers

I declare that once I was a child in slavery under the elemental spirits of the world. But when the time had fully come, God sent his Son, born of a woman, born under law, to redeem me who was under the law that I might receive the full rights of a son.[13] Because I am a son, God sent the Spirit of his Son into my heart, the Spirit who calls out, "Abba, Father." So I am no longer a slave, but a son, and since I am a son, God has made me also an heir.

I repent for myself and my ancestors for all current and generational religious activities, and for the belief in and practice of all human philosophies and traditions, including any ungodly reliance on the law.

I now command that all ungodly powers leave and that all magnets, capacitors, cylinders, tubing, antennas, and any other device they have placed on me leave and go to the feet of Jesus.

I ask, Father, that you will remove all dominions, rulers, and thrones that are aligned with these powers.

I renounce and repent for the ungodly magical belief in the four basic elements of the creation—earth, air, fire, and water.[14]

Lord, please bring all magnetic fields influencing me into correct alignment and balance. Father, please send your fire to consume all the evil associated with these powers.

✠ Lord, please return to me everything the enemy has stolen.

✠ I now declare that I am seated with Christ in heavenly places and that the enemy is under my feet. I now ask, Father, that you release me into my generational birthright.

Notes:

1. Paul L. Cox, *Heaven Trek* (Hesperia, CA: Aslan's Place, 2007). An earlier version of this chapter was first published in Heaven Trek.

2. *Wikipedia*, s.v. "Electromagnetism," http://en.wikipedia.org/wiki/Electromagnetism.

3. Robert O. Becker and Gary Selden, *The Body Electric*, 1st edition (New York: Harper Paperbacks, 1998), 243.

4. Ibid., 249.

5. Ibid., 249.

6. Ibid., 244–245.

7. Ibid., 246–247.

8. Ibid., 247–248.

9. Ibid., 250.

10. Ibid., 253.

11. Clinton E. Arnold, *Powers of Darkness* (Downers Grove, IL: InterVarsity Press, 1992), 107–108.

12. The Apostle Paul relates his experience of being caught up into the third heaven, the dwelling place of God. From this Scripture we extrapolate that the first heaven is the universe we perceive, and the second heaven is the location of the enemy.

13. Note that as a man part of the bride of Christ, so a woman can be a son who receives the inheritance of the firstborn son.

14. Asian cultures add natural resources such as metals in their list of basic elements.

CHAPTER FIVE

Prayer to
Dismantle the Roots of Rebellion

PAUL L. COX

I was in the air on an American Airlines flight, again, traveling home from a ministry trip to Germany and Switzerland. My ears were ringing, and I wondered if I were suffering from an inner ear medical condition called tinnitus. The ringing did not stop after I arrived home. Day after day, the ringing continued. Nights seemed worst. Sleep would arrive delayed by the constant sound.

On the fortieth day of ringing, I was in Deland, Florida, training a small group in a local church. I shared my frustration with the ringing and begged for any insight that might alleviate the unending assault. Some intercessors in the group shared how they had prayed against a witchcraft stronghold in a nearby town. Comparing notes, we were astonished to realize that their prayer confrontation had been on same day the ringing began in my ears. I counted the days of ringing, and it had been exactly forty days.

Revelation began flowing! A stark realization occurred. I was actually hearing witchcraft. The ringing in my ears was witchcraft! That revelation began to lead to understanding. It was time to construct a prayer.

It was clear that first I had to understand the nature of witchcraft. By definition, *divination* (or *witchcraft*) is "the art or practice that seeks to foresee or foretell future events or discover hidden knowledge by the interpretation of omens or by the aid of supernatural powers."[1] The word is first used in the Bible in Genesis 44:5, when Joseph sent his steward to retrieve the cup Joseph had planted in Benjamin's sack. The steward is told to say to Joseph's brothers that the cup was used for divination. The *New Bible Dictionary* defines this biblical word *divination* as the attempt to discern events that are distant in time or space and that consequently cannot be perceived by normal means.[2] It is possible that the word can have a "righteous" sense as one might speak of a prophet having clairvoyant gifts without thereby approving all forms of clairvoyance.[3] Except in these rare contexts, where seeing the future is clearly from God, divination and witchcraft are strictly condemned by Scripture.[4]

Magic and divination are attempts to find out information from superhuman powers. More precisely, magic is used to compel a god to do what one wishes, and divination is used to secure information about issues and events that are not readily known to the person who practices this art. The word magic is derived from the word *magus*, a priestly class in ancient Persia. In magic, it is believed that one can get in touch with the "gods" and these "gods" can be influenced to bring benefit to the magician or diviner.

Divination can be divided into two categories, internal and mechanical. The internal divination consists of a trancelike state of a shaman. The mechanical facets of witchcraft include using material objects like sand, entrails of a sacrifice, or tea leaves. The Bible mentions several types of witchcraft or divination:

- *Rhabdomancy*—Sticks or arrows were thrown into the air and omens were deduced from their position when they fell. Hosea 4:12, Ezekiel 21:21.

- *Hepatoscopy*—Examination of the liver or other entrails of a sacrifice was supposed to give guidance. Probably shapes and markings were classified, and the priest interpreted them. Ezekiel 21:21.

- *Teraphim*—Images of dead ancestors were used to predict the future, which is a form of spiritualism. 1 Samuel 15:23, Ezekiel 21:21; Zechariah 10:2.

- *Necromancy*—Necromancy was getting information from the dead. Deuteronomy 18:11; Leviticus 19:31, 20:6; 1 Samuel 28:8; 2 Kings 21:6; 1 Chronicles 10:13; and Isaiah 8:19–20.

- *Astrology*—Astrology was making predictions based on the position of the sun, moon, and planets in relation to the zodiac and to the positions of one another.

- *Hydromancy*—Hydromancy was seeing "divination" pictures in water. Genesis 44:5, 15 [5]

In a remarkable passage, Samuel expands our understanding of witchcraft. Saul once again was disobedient to the will of the Lord. Because Saul has not obeyed the Lord in eliminating all of the sheep, Samuel has some words to say to Saul!

So Samuel said: "Has the LORD as great delight in burnt offerings and sacrifices, as in obeying the voice of the LORD? Behold, to obey is better than sacrifice, and to heed than the fat of rams. For rebellion is as the sin of witchcraft." (1 Samuel 15:22–23)

So, witchcraft is the same as rebellion. But how?

Rebellion is "opposition to one in authority." [6] The Hebrew word *mâriy* is derived from the word *marah* meaning "to be contentious, be rebellious, be refractory, be disobedient towards, be rebellious against." [7] The word is most used in terms of "rebellion" against the ways commanded by God. What, then, is the connection between witchcraft and rebellion?

Over the years, I have read several explanations of why witchcraft is the same as rebellion. Frankly, the explanations, although interesting, have not been satisfying. The Lord was about to show us something new. I was ministering to a person and felt impressed to place my hand just off the left ear. I was surprised to feel anointing, but more surprised when I moved my hand a little further away from the ear and could discern witchcraft. Then I suddenly had the revelation from the Lord. In generational rebellion, we give the enemy the right to take anointing off of us. When that happens, that anointing is transformed into witchcraft. That witchcraft is then sent against us! Witchcraft really is the same as rebellion!

Further revelation was to come. After showing many different discernment training schools what the Lord had taught me, I thought, *"If indeed someone is stealing anointing from us and shifting it into witchcraft, then who is that 'someone'?"* As I felt under the flow of witchcraft, I was surprised that indeed I did feel something. As I felt the spiritual outline of that entity, I realized it was a "spiritual force." Spiritual forces are mentioned in Ephesians 6:12:

For our struggle is not against flesh and blood, but against the rulers, against the powers, against the world forces of this darkness, against the spiritual forces of wickedness in the heavenly places. (Ephesians 6:12, NASB)

It is my belief that these beings are in some way "interdimensional" because Scripture tells us that they war in "heavenly places." I sense these fallen "spiritual forces" pervert the anointing of the Lord, corrupting that anointing, and changing it into witchcraft.

A full day of discussion had taken place. The prayer was written and we prayed the prayer. I waited to see a difference, but there was no change. *Had we missed the mark?* As I went to bed that night, my ears were still ringing. *Could I live like this?* As I escaped my sleep the next morning, I was aware of something different. There was no more ringing. The prayer had worked!

The Prayer: Dismantling the Roots of Rebellion

✠ In the name of the Lord Jesus Christ, I repent for all generational idolatry.

✠ I repent for all personal and generational rebellion, stubbornness, and disobedience that have contributed to witchcraft in my life and in my generational line.

✠ I repent for all envy and jealousy of the minds, physical bodies, and personalities of others.

✠ I repent for any worship of myself and any need of personal recognition.

✠ I repent for all envy and jealousy of the spiritual giftings and capacities of others.

✠ I repent for myself and for those in my generational line who did not guard the gates of the spiritual and physical senses.

✠ I repent for choosing my will above the will of the Lord.

✠ I choose to owe no one anything but to love one another.

✠ I choose to cast off the work of darkness and to put on the armor of Light, the Lord Jesus Christ, and to make no provision for the flesh, to fulfill its lusts.

✠ I choose to walk only according to the grace and anointing God has given to me.

✠ I choose to walk in unity with my brothers and sisters in the Lord.

✠ I choose to follow Christ, living a life of love, preferring others above myself.

✠ I choose to yield and surrender my personal rights so that I might serve the Lord wholeheartedly.

✠ I choose to be devoted to one another in brotherly love and to honor one another above myself. I will never be lacking in zeal, but will keep my spiritual fervor, serving the Lord. I will be joyful in hope, patient in affliction, and faithful in prayer. I will share with God's people who are in need. I will practice hospitality. I will bless those who persecute me. I will rejoice with those who rejoice and will mourn with those who mourn. I will live in harmony with other believers. I will not be proud, but I will associate with people of low position. I will not be conceited. I will not repay evil for evil. I will have regard for good things in the sight of all men. I will live at peace with everyone. I will not take revenge on others.

✠ Lord, please now remove all ungodly spiritual beings and devices that have been empowered by my idolatry, rebellion, and jealousy, and the idolatry, rebellion, and jealousy of my ancestors.

✖ Lord, will please disconnect me from any evil network, and I break all ungodly ties between the abode of the enemy and myself.

✖ Lord, please remove the generational tree of the knowledge of good and evil.

✖ Lord, please break the cords of death that entangle me, the torrents of destruction that overwhelm me, the cords of Sheol that are coiled around me, and the snares of death that confront me.

✖ Lord, I now take back any godly anointing, energy, authority, finances, and health given away and perverted because of my sin and my ancestors' sin.

✖ Lord, will you set me as a seal upon your heart and as a seal upon your arm, for your love is stronger than death.

✖ I declare that you, Lord Jesus Christ—I declare that the Lord, Jesus Christ, is the Lord over all.[8]

Notes:

1. *Merriam-Webster's Collegiate Dictionary*, Eleventh Edition (Springfield, MA: Merriam-Webster, 2003), s.v. "Divination".

2. *New Bible Dictionary* (Leicester, England: InterVarsity Press, Universities and Colleges Christian Fellowship, 1996), s.v. "Divination".

3. Ibid.

4. Leviticus 19:26; Deuteronomy 18:9–14; 2 Kings 17:17, 21:6; 1 Samuel 6:2; Isaiah 44:25; Ezekiel 21:22.

5. D. R. W. Wood, *New Bible Dictionary*, electronic edition (Leicester, England: InterVarsity Press. Universities and Colleges Christian Fellowship, 1996), s.vv. "Rhabdomancy," "Hepatoscopy," "Teraphim," "Necromancy," "Astrology," "Hydromancy."

6. *Merriam-Webster's Collegiate Dictionary*, Eleventh Edition (Springfield, MA: Merriam-Webster, 2003), s.v. "Rebellion."

7. W. E. Vine, Merrill F. Unger, and William White, Jr., *Vine's Complete Expository Dictionary of Old and New Testament Words* (Nashville, TN: Thomas Nelson, 1996), s.vv. "*mâriy*," "Marah."

8. Prayer based on Genesis 2; Deuteronomy 4:15–20; 1 Samuel 15:23; Psalm 18; Ezekiel 8:1–6; John 17; Romans 12:3, 10–19; 13; Ephesians 1:22; 4:12–13.

Prayer of Renunciation—Soul

PAUL L. COX

A friend who wasn't doing well called from the northern part of our state and asked if I would fly north and pray for him. Upon arriving at his house, I immediately discerned that a geometric plane was splitting him in half from his head to his feet. As I reached out to put my hand against that plane, I felt a shift of pressure on my hands as I moved against it. Because of my discernment, I knew that this plane had an evil attachment. Since this was the first time I'd ever discerned[1] an evil plane, I wasn't sure what to do, so I simply asked the Lord to correct the problem. My friend was immediately better. *So, what was this?*

After discerning this first plane, new revelation about planes began to come during ministry sessions; others rapidly confirmed what I was receiving. As I've mentioned before, revelation is progressive. It usually begins with a simple impression, like my discernment of an evil plane. Additional revelations, adding complexities, always build upon the original simple thought or discernment. These new revelations always come in the context of the body of Christ. When we gather together, others tell what they discern. Repeated confirmations verify that truth is being revealed.[2] Often, a person will see something without knowing that others have already seen the same thing. This continual testing assures that what I am receiving from the Lord is accurate.

In a gathering shortly after I felt the first plane, a second geometric plane was discovered running from right to left (or left to right) on a person's waist. Another geometric plane was located splitting the person from head to toe on the person's side. Finally, a cut was found splitting the brain from right to left (or left to right) from the area of the eyes. At first, I believed these planes cut a person into nine sections, however it has recently become clear that the planes divide a person into twelve sections. One day, when planes showed up again during ministry, a medical professional told me that similar planes are used in the field of medicine to identify different sections of the body. I did some investigation and sure enough, the terms medium plane, lateral plane, transverse plane and coronal plane describe anatomical planes in the human body. The only difference between my discernment and the standard definitions was that instead of discerning the coronal plane splitting the front part of the head from the back part of the head, I have seen it dividing the eyes from the top part of the brain. *What did this all mean?*

I was about to find out. I was invited with Arthur Burk to join Dr. Tom Hawkins in Virginia to pray for several people with Dissociative Identity Disorder (DID). Some twelve of us were together one day when the Lord brought to my consciousness what I had learned about these sections of the body. As I started showing the group what I had learned, revelation began flowing! Somehow, these twelve planes are connected to domains. The Lord revealed that there were twelve domains.[3] Each domain has 144,000 cubes. Each cube is made up of five parts. *Could this be the DNA of the soul?*

More revelation came. Each cube seemed to have different colors. The domains seemed to have names: Love, Peace, Understanding, Faith, Will, Wisdom, Joy, and Secret Place.

At present, we do not know the names for the other domains. The six sides of the cube appear to contain or represent different categories: land, body of Christ, government, generations, time, and commerce.

On the way to the airport after the meeting with Dr. Tom Hawkins, a friend and I were discussing what we had learned. Suddenly I felt a shift in my body. I asked him what he saw in the Spirit. He said that I had just passed through a territorial spirit, and it had shifted my domains. I have no clue why that happened; perhaps somehow the enemy still had some generational right to attack me. Over the years this happens less frequently. Perhaps something has changed!

Believing that, in reality, everything is more complicated than it seems, I do not yet understand all the implications of the domains. I do know that as people ask Jesus to cleanse the domains and invite his lordship over them, something happens. Once, my daughter Christy came to me saying she felt "out of sorts." I discerned that the domains were out of alignment and asked the Lord to put all the domains into correct alignment. Immediately she felt better.

It is my belief that the enemy can take parts of the cubes into the dimensions.[4] Perhaps this is a key in understanding dissociation. In prayer, after asking for a return of these parts, we have seen some measure of integration.[5] Again, "nothing is always!" This kind of prayer is only a partial solution. *Could Psalm 86:11b indicate a similar integration?* "Unite my heart to fear Your name" (NASB). In Hebrew the "heart" is the non-material part of a person and includes a person's spirit and soul. Unite is the Hebrew word *yāhad* and means "to join, unite, be joined, be united." The text certainly means to "unite" one's heart to the ways of the Lord, but I wonder if it also means "knitting" a divided heart together as one.

This prayer is very short! However, it took me, Dr. Tom Hawkins, Arthur Burk, and nine others an entire day to formulate this prayer. The answers to this prayer have been significant. May the Lord use it to bring you into greater freedom.

The Prayer: Renunciation of Soul

✠ I transfer ownership of all that I am and all that I have to the Lord Jesus Christ of Nazareth. I now ask you, Lord, to cancel all legal right for evil influence and activity in every domain of my being.

✠ I declare the lordship of Jesus Christ over every domain of my person including above me and below me, to the left and to the right, and to the front and to the back. Lord, release me from the evil power of all these domains and return to me any part of me that has been taken to any ungodly dimension.

✠ I now apply the blood of Christ, the refiner's fire, and the launderer's soap[6] to the passageways between the domains, so that the anointing of the Lord may flow freely through me.

Notes:

1. Discernment is the use of the five senses to know what is happening in the spiritual world.

2. 2 Corinthians 13:1.

3. We use the word domain simply as a way of expressing what is discerned. Although we first thought there were nine domains, we now believe there are twelve. I have used the new number in the text.

4. *See* chapter 7, p. 42–54.

5. Integration: A process where various alters of a personality of a person who has DID are integrated into the host personality.

6. Malachi 3:2.

CHAPTER SEVEN

Prayer of
Renunciation—Physical Body

PAUL L. COX

Ten years had passed since the first time I prayed for someone to be delivered. There was no prayer manual. I was ministering in the southern part of New Jersey in a log cabin house. Suddenly, an "urgency" came upon me! Three of us went upstairs into an office, and I started writing. The Lord distilled all I had learned in ten years and poured it into one simple prayer. It was the first prayer that we wrote in a group! Then an intercessor from Minnesota called and told me to add something to the prayer. She had no idea we were working on a prayer! Little did I know that it was the first of over forty prayers. The journey had begun.

In many ways, this prayer is a simple version of many prayers that developed later. This prayer has become a foundational work that the Lord has continued to develop into more complex understandings about the nature of the spiritual world.

I would like to dissect this prayer to help convey an understanding of its intent. I won't give a complete interpretation of each concept as that would require another book! Hopefully, there will be enough information to comprehend the prayer's purpose.

- *Evil Operator*—An operator is a mathematical function that causes other mathematical functions. Our world is built on math. The enemy knows this and corrupts the original design of God. In speaking of foundational matters in terms of math, it is essential to ask the Lord to go back to the "basics" and correct what happened at the Fall. In prayer times, we have also asked the Lord to bring $E = mc^2$ into correct alignment in places where it may have been turned upside down, backwards, or reversed by the enemy. We have also prayed and asked the Lord to bring all equations in the body back into correct created order.

• *Vibration[1] of the superstrings*—Below is an article about the dimensions briefly explaining superstring theory. We are made up of sound, which is vibration. Each of us is a sound that the Lord sings! The enemy corrupts our original sound and makes us discordant.

• *Zygote*—The union of the male sperm and female egg in the womb.

• *DNA*—deoxyribonucleic acid. The DNA strand makes up the molecular basis of heredity. The DNA is constructed as a double helix.

• *Covalent bonding*—A chemical bond shared by electrons. For example, H_2O is the bonding of two hydrogen atoms with one oxygen atom. In 1 Corinthians 10:20 Paul writes, "Rather, that the things which the Gentiles sacrifice they sacrifice to demons and not to God, and I do not want you to have fellowship with demons." There is an implication by the Apostle Paul that one actually becomes joined to the demonic. One meaning of the word *fellowship* is partnering. It is a joining that can affect a person and his generational line. This would indicate a spiritual covalent bonding. It is interesting to note that covalent bonding is best broken by fire and soap.[2] I have discerned the "furnace" many times, but I have not discerned the soap.

• *Spiritual Interferon*—Interferons are proteins released by the body in response to infections to help kill viral growth. They are an important part of the immune system. A shot can also be given as a shot to counteract a virus.

As you read the prayer you will notice the mention *dimensions*. This term is often used in mathematics and physics but may not be familiar to you as a biblical term. Following is a introductory explanation of dimensions.

Dimensions and Spiritual Realities

PAUL L. COX

Introduction

In recent years, the media has discovered quantum physics, string theory, and the dimensions. Many television programs and movies include mathematical and scientific terms and concepts. Novelists are jumping into the action by incorporating these concepts into their story lines. All this is being done in an attempt to understand life apart from God. If we are to accept what those in the media say, quantum physics and string theory will help us deal correctly with life choices so that our lives will be better. There is no reason to bring a living God into the discussion. Instead of rejoicing in the Creator of this marvelous complex universe, we are led away from the Creator to simply view these extraordinary concepts as another way of seeing the world and as further evidence that man can find the ultimate reasons for life without dealing with the concept of a personal God.

For years, the Lord has been showing our prayer teams that the dimensions are an important part of our daily lives. We have found dimensions that are clearly in the realm of the living God, and dimensions that lie under the influence of the enemy. All of this information has collided with our daily lives and is exploding all over the place. What was once a "far out" deliverance observation is now accepted as valid in everyday conversation. What was once a topic of science fiction is now making the front covers of scientific journals as fact.

All of this has tremendous spiritual ramifications. The unseen is now being discovered. Language is being developed to interpret these concepts as part of a reality that excludes God. New Agers are jumping in, trying to "spiritualize these new scientific and mathematical concepts" so that men and women can ascend into higher levels of consciousness in this dimensional "universe." Of course, none of this includes a personal God who loves us and died on the cross for our sins.

Does the Church have a part in this discussion? I think so, for these concepts are all "biblical." The Word of God can open up for us the true understanding of the reality of a multilayered universe created by the living and true God. Understanding what the Word says brings new levels of freedom.

In God's Word, we continue our journey to being changed from "glory to ever increasing glory."

My goal in this chapter is to expand our understanding of the wonderful Creation of our Lord. I certainly do not understand everything in this article and don't want to pretend in any way that I do. I pray that my readers will simply receive this as a "first draft" of exploring "new worlds." The article includes some scientific information, an attempt to envision what the dimensions might look like, and finally, some practical applications to prayer ministry. The Bible is our beginning point.

What the Bible Says

In Ephesians 2:6 (NIV), the Apostle Paul wrote "and God raised us up with Christ and seated us with him in the heavenly realms in Christ Jesus." In this passage, the actual Greek word for "heavenly places" is only one word *epouranios*, meaning "heavenlies, the heavenly regions." The plural gives us the evidence that there is more than one heaven. Genesis 1:1 states that "God created the heavens and the earth." Harris in the *Theological Wordbook of the Old Testament*, states that "the heavens [are] the abode of God."[3] The heavens are frequently described in figurative language as having windows (Genesis 7:11; 2 Kings 7:2; Malachi 3:10). Could these be what we call "portals," which are entrances into dimensions? Other biblical passages speak of the "heavens."

There is no one like the God of Jeshurun, who rides the heavens to help you, and in His excellency on the clouds. (Deuteronomy 33:26)

He bowed the heavens also, and came down with darkness under His feet. (2 Samuel 22:10)

For all the gods of the peoples are idols, but the LORD made the heavens. (1 Chronicles 16:26)

43

You alone are the LORD; You have made heaven, the heaven of heavens, with all their host, the earth and everything on it, the seas and all that is in them, and You preserve them all. The host of heaven worships You. (Nehemiah 9:6)

He alone spreads out the heavens, and treads on the waves of the sea. (Job 9:8)

If God puts no trust in His saints, and the heavens are not pure in His sight. (Job 15:15)

When He prepared the heavens, I was there, when He drew a circle on the face of the deep. (Proverbs 8:27)

Indeed My hand has laid the foundation of the earth, and My right hand has stretched out the heavens; when I call to them, they stand up together. (Isaiah 48:13)

Oh, that You would rend the heavens! That You would come down! That the mountains might shake at Your presence. (Isaiah 64:1)

He who builds His layers in the sky, and has founded His strata in the earth; Who calls for the waters of the sea, and pours them out on the face of the earth—the LORD is His name. (Amos 9:6)

The burden of the word of the LORD against Israel. Thus says the LORD, who stretches out the heavens, lays the foundation of the earth, and forms the spirit of man within him. (Zechariah 12:1)

When He had been baptized, Jesus came up immediately from the water; and behold, the heavens were opened to Him, and He saw the Spirit of God descending like a dove and alighting upon Him. And suddenly a voice came from heaven, saying, "This is My beloved Son, in whom I am well pleased." (Matthew 3:16–17)

And [Stephen] said, "Look! I see the heavens opened and the Son of Man standing at the right hand of God!" (Acts 7:56)

For we know that if our earthly house, this tent, is destroyed, we have a building from God, a house not made with hands, eternal in the heavens. (2 Corinthians 5:1)

Nevertheless we, according to His promise, look for new heavens and a new earth in which righteousness dwells. Therefore, beloved, looking forward to these things, be diligent to be found by Him in peace, without spot and blameless. (2 Peter 3:13–14)

The Bible declares that we are seated with Christ in heavenly realms or places. Elsewhere in Scripture, we also see the mention of heavenly places or realms *(emphasis added by author)*.

*Blessed be the God and Father of our Lord Jesus Christ, who has blessed us with all spiritual blessings in **heavenly places** in Christ.* (Ephesians 1:3)

*Which he worked in Christ when He raised Him from the dead and set Him at His right hand in the **heavenly places**.* (Ephesians 1:20)

*And [He has] raised us up together, and made us sit together in **heavenly places** in Christ Jesus.* (Ephesians 2:6)

*To the intent that now the manifold wisdom of God might be made known by the church to the principalities and powers in the **heavenly places**.* (Ephesians 3:10)

I believe these places are what physicists and mathematicians call *dimensions*.

String Theory and the Dimensions

An Associated Press article[4] dated August 15, 2001, tells of the discovery that the speed of light has not been constant over the last fifteen billion years. This confirms what physicists believe about string theory. This theory supports the view that the universe is made up of anywhere between ten to twenty-six dimensions. These dimensions are curled or folded, which makes it impossible to detect them in everyday life. So where are these dimensions and why do physicists believe they exist? The answer lies in a theory called "string theory."

String theory is an attempt to create a "Theory of Everything"—a theory that unifies the electroweak force, the strong nuclear force, and the force of gravity. In this view, these forces once thought to be separate forces were recognized as one force in the 1990s.

The basis of the theory is that all matter is composed of strings. The strings themselves are the smallest possible particles, with a length of 10^{-33} cm and no width or height. Strings can be opened or closed. Closed strings have the shape of a circle or oval and open strings have ends. A string occupies one single point in space-time at any one time. Its path through time can be shown in a space versus time graph and is called a world sheet. The superstring theory can describe the three forces: electroweak, strong nuclear, and gravitational.

One problem with string theory is that it only works in ten to twenty-six dimensions. If there is any other number of dimensions, mathematical anomalies appear. The question then has to be asked, where are the other six (or more) dimensions? In normal life, there are only four dimensions: the three dimensions of length, width, and depth, plus the fourth dimension, time. The Kaluza-Klein theory shows that it is possible for a dimension to be "curled" up into an extremely tiny ball (10^{-31} cm long), which we could obviously not detect. In string theory, this is what has happened to the other six dimensions. It is theorized that they curled up just after the big bang. It is possible that if some variables in the big bang were different, some or all of these extra dimensions could have expanded. What would such a universe look like? Obviously, our four-dimensional perception cannot imagine it, but the possibility of it happening remains.

Originally, there were five separate string theories, and each one worked in a different situation. In 1994, these were unified into a single "M-theory." M-theory may hold true in eleven dimensions, one more than the ten originally theorized. The theory has not been fully fleshed out. Much advancement still needs to be made. It may be that "F-Theory" (*F* for father) will emerge, a string theory that involves the presence of strings in ten, eleven or twelve dimensions. We are still far from the ultimate Theory of Everything.

The discovery of extra dimensions would show that the entirety of human experience has left us completely unaware of a basic and essential aspect of the universe. It would forcefully argue that even those features of the cosmos that we have thought to be readily accessible to human physical senses need not be.[5] Strings are but one ingredient in string theory, not *the* ingredient.[6] Another ingredient might be branes, or membranes, which are theoretical objects with two or more spatial dimensions.

The revelation of other ingredients besides strings in string theory does not invalidate or make obsolete earlier work any more than the discovery of the tenth spatial dimension did. Research shows that if the higher-dimensional branes are much more massive than strings, as had been unknowingly assumed in previous studies, they have minimal impact on a wide range of theoretical calculations.[7] The grand expanse of the cosmos—the entirety of the space-time of which we are aware—may itself be nothing but an enormous brane. Ours may be a brane world;[8] higher-dimensional branes need not be tiny, either, and because they have more dimensions than strings do, a qualitatively new possibility opens up.[9] If we have a large two-brane, we envision a large two-dimensional surface that exists within the three large space dimensions of common experience.[10] A three-brane has three dimensions, so if it were large—perhaps infinitely large—it would fill all three big spatial dimensions.[11] Might we, right now, be living within a three-brane world?[12]

So, if we live in a three-brane world, there is an alternative explanation for why we're not aware of the extra dimensions. It is not necessarily that the extra dimensions are extremely small. They could be big. We don't see them because of the way we see. We see because of the electromagnetic force, which is unable to access any dimensions beyond the three we know about. Like an ant walking along a lily pad, completely unaware of the deep waters lying just beneath the visible surface, we could be floating within a grand, expansive, higher-dimensional space, limited by our physical dependence upon electromagnetic force—eternally trapped within our dimensions. And, within the brane world scenario, there is the possibility that the extra dimensions could be much larger than once thought.[13]

An Imaginative Journey

How do you imagine what it would look like to live in different dimensions? Since our only frame of reference is in three dimensions plus time, it is difficult to conceptualize life in those heavenly places. But, that's where we are to live; in fact, we are already seated with Jesus Christ in the "heavenly places."[14] Indeed this is the spiritual world that we have heard so much about in our Christian walk. What is it like there? What can happen there? Let's try and imagine.

Michio Kaku has written on string theory and tells us that if a surgeon lived in the tenth dimension, he could do surgery in the third dimension without cutting.[15] How is this possible? We need to understand more about these dimensions.

Rob Bryanton, a musician and theorist from Canada has written an interesting book called *Imagining the Tenth Dimension*. Perhaps this is a starting point for us to understand the realities of other dimensions. Here, in both my words and direct quotations from his book, is a summary of Bryanton's "Quick Tour of Ten Dimensions."[16]

The first dimension is length, "any straight line joining two points."[17] The second dimension is width, a line coming off of that line, like a *Y*.[18] The third dimension is depth. In 1884, Edwin Abbott, a mathematician wrote *Flatlanders: A Romance of Many Dimensions*. In order to help us to understand what it would look like to live in the third dimension, he describes people living in a two-dimensional world. Boynton summarizes it as follows:

> What would a three dimensional creature such as ourselves look like to a two dimensional flatlander? . . . A Flatlander viewing one of us passing through his Flatland World might see ten small objects representing our toes, which would become two larger objects which would grow and shrink and grow again as the Flatlander's viewpoint travelled pass our feet and up our legs. . . .

> An ant marching from left to the right side of a newspaper page could be thought of as a flatlander walking along in a two dimensional world. What if we want to help that ant get to his destination sooner, so we fold the newspaper to make it meet in the middle? Suddenly, the ant is able to finish his cross-paper trek much more quickly and go on his way.

When we folded the paper, we took the representation of a two-dimensional object and moved it through the third dimension.[19]

This is what we would call "folding space-time. The fourth dimension is time, having three dimensional spaces anywhere in time. The fifth dimension offers a multitude of choices at any given time. These choices could be influenced by others, our choice, and chance. In the sixth dimension, ". . . if we could fold the fifth dimension through the sixth dimension, we would be able to jump from one [possible] world to another without having to travel the long way back in time and forward again."[20]

The seventh dimension joins all the possible universes to all the possible outcomes at the other end and treats the entire package as a single point. The seventh dimension takes the concept of all the possible beginnings and their links to all the possible conclusions for viewing them simultaneously, as if it were a single point. A point in the seventh dimension represents infinity.[21] Bryanton notes, "Interestingly, the number seven appears in a number of our world's spiritual systems and mystical writings as the presentation of infinity/eternity or heaven, or the highest level of spiritual awakening."[22]

He says that the eighth dimension would be "the multiplicity of timelines that when perceived as a whole, represent some other completely different universe that would have been generated by some other set of initial conditions. In the ninth dimension, one imagines an infinite number of infinities. One could pop in and out of these infinities."[23]

The tenth dimension treats "as a point every possible beginning and end of all the possible universes generated by all the possible big bangs."[24] . . . "Imagine the tenth dimension as the uncut fabric from which is constructed all possible universes, all possible beginnings and endings, all possible branches within all possible time lines, but without the nuances added by the geometries of the dimensions below."[25]

The Dimensions and Current Applications

OK, now we must ask, so what? What does this have to do with my everyday life? I find it difficult enough to live in four dimensions, yet alone try to think about other dimensions.

Actually, what goes on in other dimensions seems to be connected with what happens in our four-dimensional world. During the past seventeen years, the Lord has instructed me to have individuals break all ungodly ties between themselves and the dimensions. I would have them break all ungodly ties between themselves and the fifth dimension, the sixth dimension, the seventh dimension, and so forth. Experientially, this has been very powerful. Often individuals have had difficulty trying to articulate the "breaking" phrases of the prayer. Many have reported feeling a sense of freedom after doing this. Exactly what is happening? It would seem that somehow these links to the ungodly dimensions have affected them.

I have also noticed that when I feel sick, I can feel the dimensions shifting. Additionally, I have discerned ungodly lines linking a physical problem and the dimensions. These lines appear to keep on going, and I believe they are lines into the dimensions where, somehow, evil is affecting the person. Perhaps a better understanding of the dimensions will result in higher level of healing for those who are suffering from illnesses.

It's an interesting development, the way these scientific theories from theoretical physics have spilled over into popular culture. Currently, the feeling that one can "tap into" other dimensions by choice and change the course of one's life is moving, via New Age influence, into mainstream thinking. Of course, this is all to be done without any dependence on the living God. Here is the humanistic reasoning: "According to quantum physics, particles are not particles at the subatomic level. Instead, they are waves of probabilities. . . . It is the act of observing those probability waves which collapses them into one specific state. If subatomic particles are collapsed out of their indeterminate wave function only when we observe them, doesn't it follow that we, as observers, are therefore creating our physical reality through the act of observation? . . . It is those subatomic particles that create the atoms and molecules of our universe.[26] . . . [Therefore,] "each of us is an observer, and each of us is creating our own unique reality."[27]

Bryanton asks, "If our reality is created by the act of observation, what happened before there was an observer, or has there always been something that we would call an observer? . . . But one may ask, if all of these other realities exist, why do we not see them?"[28] The answer would be that all the other possibilities are eliminated once we begin observing our current state.

Here is what is being proposed. We create our own reality. If our reality is not good, then we need to become an "observer" of another reality, which we can then bring into our current reality, thus changing what life is like. Bryanton suggests,

> The current space-time we are in and agree upon as being "reality" is our version of the fourth dimension, our "reality" is specifically selected from a list of other physically incompatible different-initial-conditions universes at the seventh dimension, and all of those physically incompatible universes exist simultaneously at the tenth dimension. . . .[29] [At the beginning,] all potential physical realities remained possible within the wave function, and at that point, the observer turned their attention upon our universe and collapsed the quantum wave function into the reality we see around us, complete with the impression that time had actually extended out for billions of years prior to that. . . . It could also be possible that the universe didn't actually exist until one second ago. . . . [Only] when the observer turned their attention upon our universe and collapsed the probability wave function into what we now perceive as our reality, complete with a history which each of us believes we remember.[30]

Here is the dangerous part. We who are believers would say that the Lord God is the observer. Those opposed to a personal God could say, no, we are gods, and we can therefore become the observers who create our own reality. Perhaps, this all sounds rather farfetched. While that is true, I have recently read a popular novel proposing exactly this kind of scenario and stating that we can choose who to become.

As believers, we want the Lord's will in our lives. We believe and expect him to do great works in us and through us. This is the reality we want to see. We desire for his will to be done on earth, through us, just as it is in heaven.

It appears that we can travel into the dimensions. The Lord often tells us in our discernment training schools to "Come up higher." Perhaps, this is the Lord's way of telling us that we can travel higher into the dimensions. Many of us have experienced this. Those who are seers have reported seeing different things in different dimensions. In Revelation 4, the Lord tells John to "come up here."

During countless prayer sessions, I have recorded what others have reported about the dimensions. It seems that there are dimensions that are available to the believer and dimensions that are controlled by the enemy. It may also be true that there are dimensions in the earth, under the earth, and above the earth.

In the dimensions controlled by the enemy, we have found that those who suffer from Dissociative Identity Disorder may have "parts" that are trapped in those dimensions. We have also found parts trapped around the throne of Satan. Other parts seem to be trapped in voids between the dimensions. As mentioned before, perhaps diseases and physical and mental disorders are rooted in the dimensions. Chains may be tied to a certain dimension. Addictions and phobias may be tied to certain ungodly dimensions. Occult activity, witchcraft, and sorcery may be located in specific dimensions. Astral projection and shape shifting may take place in certain ungodly dimensions. It is interesting that Nimrod built a tower[31] whose top went into the "heavens." Perhaps he attempted to access and travel in the ungodly dimensions—and succeeded.

What about righteous dimensions? The list of possible activities in the righteous dimensions is long. Here's what we have discovered. Please note that this is very subjective and perhaps speculative, but interesting, nevertheless!

- Maleness and femaleness may be in separate dimensions.

- Different spiritual giftings may be in different dimensions. Prophetic gifting may be in one dimension, teaching in another, etc.

- Rest or levels of rest may be in different dimensions.

- The heavenly Tabernacle seems to be a multidimensional structure.

- Different disciplines of learning may be in different dimensions, i.e., math in one dimension, science in one dimension, arts in another dimension.

- Sounds, colors, and vibrations may be in different dimensions.

- Finances may be in one or more dimensions.

- Plans for our lives may be in one or more dimensions.

- Sleep may be in a dimension. Perhaps this is where dreams are released.

Some years ago, I was with four other people and the Lord took us on a journey through several dimensions. The Lord has given us many of these experiences. Perhaps you are also ready to join the Lord in traveling in the heavenly places. This is a composite of what I felt and others saw.

This time I am with four others. We are moving through this darkness, but again there is peace. It is important to continue moving forward. The word is given, "Being changed from glory to glory." I feel my body almost going through a metamorphosis. It seems to be stretched, added to (and I don't mean more weight), strengthened. I have the sensation of moving up and forward As we move forward, the brighter it becomes. I even ask the Lord for sunglasses. This seems appropriate, because then I see in the distance angels walking up and down a staircase (not Jacob's ladder) to the place where the light and glare originates. At the bottom of the staircase, angels are waiting for us. In the hands of one is a letter. He hands it to me. The angels do not speak to me, yet I hear the words, "We have been waiting for you." Then the words, "Here are your orders, your commission; this is what is for today. Follow me." As we're walking, I see a bright sword given to me, along with a strong shield. There was some dimensional shifting going on, but it was not evil. When I would look behind, I saw that where we had been was now dark. I know that God wants all of us to go forward. It is important. I hear the words, "You are not to go back! It's time for new things!" Then we are moving up another staircase. I find us at the fifteenth dimension. Here, there are giftings, lots of giftings. Something is about to happen. We are presented with a book. It is very old—and very cold. Even though it appears thick, it is not that heavy. It smells like a refrigerator smell. We see other books. One person receives the description that these books have come out of cold storage. They were there for preservation. I get the distinct telling that these manuals have not been used very much since the time of Paul of Tarsus. We are told to command doubt to leave and go to the feet of Jesus! The books are instruction manuals for teaching, leading, and equipping. They come with apostolic authority. There are more gifts. Wow! What an anointing! Hot coals are placed in our right hands. We get the Scripture of Isaiah 54:16. "Behold, I have created the blacksmith who blows the coals in the fire, and who brings forth an instrument for his work; and I have created the spoiler to destroy." We seem to know that Isaiah has been here before. The anointing is so strong! There are new callings here and new authority. The Kingdom of God is here. There are a lot of gifts—music, instruments, dance, tambourines, songs, banners, and parchments.

When the *Star Trek: The Next Generation* was released, I went with my son and a few friends to see the movie. As I was enjoying the movie, I felt waves of the power of God coming over me. I looked around and wondered if anyone else knew God was there in a manifested way. I started to shake and realized that I would have difficulty walking out of the theater. As the movie ended, I had to have help exiting the theater and was shaking so violently that someone had to drive me the one-hour trip home. I have often contemplated what that experience was all about. As I was writing my book, *Heaven Trek*, I realized that the Lord was speaking in a dramatic way to me. Even as the theme of *Star Trek* is "to boldly go where no man has gone before,"[32] the Lord was saying to me, "Do you dare to go where I want you to go?" It is the Lord who invites each one of us to "come up higher" on a never-ending heaven trek through the dimensions.

Many years have passed since writing this prayer of *Renunciation for the Physical Body*; it has become one of the most used prayers in our arsenal. In the summer of 2008, my son, Brian Cox, came on staff and started doing individual prayer ministry. Although I had personally trained him and he had walked alongside me every step of the way through my own spiritual growth in generational prayer ministry, he had to "come up to speed" in actually doing generational prayer. Often, when he began a prayer session by asking for a memory or dream, the person was unable to provide anything relevant. Early on, the Holy Spirit guided him to have the person pray the *Prayer of Renunciation for the Physical Body* and suddenly the person would have a memory. He has consistently seen this happen. It seems the Lord continues to open up new avenues of insights!

The Prayer: Renunciation—Physical Body

✠ Lord, please reverse the work of the evil operator[33] who changed the vibration[34] of the superstrings affecting the DNA[35] of the zygote in the womb. Holy Spirit, please now hover over the original DNA in the zygote,[36] so that the superstrings will now resonate[37] only with the Holy Trinity. Lord, as you do this will you remove any evil matter,[38] evil vibrations, evil oscillation,[39] evil frequencies,[40] evil tones,[41] and evil colors. Lord, please do this in my generational line all the way back to Adam.

✠ Lord, now move me from the virtual reality created by the enemy to your reality. Lord, take me out of the prison that I am in and set me free. Remove all deception and denial that makes me believe that my current perception is reality. Lord, bring all programming back to nothing and reformat it so that the programming reflects the image and nature of Jesus Christ.

✠ Lord, please do this in every dimension.[42]

✠ Lord, please break all ungodly covalent bonding and any other chemical bonding.[43]

✠ Lord, please seal all of your work with spiritual interferon.[44]

Prayer Breaking Ungodly Ties
between a Person and the Dimensions[45]

✠ I repent and renounce for any in my family line who went into the second heaven to get information and power from the enemy. Lord Jesus, please take any part of me out of the second heaven and close and seal all ungodly doors, gates, or portals.

✠ Lord Jesus, please stop all ungodly dimensional shifting as it relates to me and my family line.

�incross Lord, please remove me from any black holes or vortexes, or out of any voids between dimensions.

✖ Lord, please remove me from being trapped in infinity[46] and from any ungodly constant or unending cycles.

✖ Lord, please remove from me any ungodly repeating patterns, any ungodly device, deposit, attachment, agreement, or entities from those dimensions, black holes, vortexes, or from any voids between dimensions.[47]

✖ In the name of Jesus Christ, on behalf of myself and my family line, I repent and renounce and break all ungodly ties between me and my family line and the first dimension,

Between me and my family line and the second dimension,[48]

Between me and my family line and the third dimension.

✖ I break all ungodly ties between me and my family line and the fourth dimension.[49]

✖ Lord please put me and my family line and time and space back in right alignment.

✖ I break all ungodly ties between me and my family line and the fifth dimension.

✖ The sixth dimension, the seventh dimension, the eighth dimension, the ninth dimension, the tenth dimension, the eleventh dimension,[50] and . . . twelfth, etc., and all dimensions through eternity.

✖ Lord, where it affects me and my family line, would you break all ungodly agreements between dimensions and all ungodly linkages between dimensions. Please remove any evil spirits energizing these ungodly connections and agreements.

Lord, please return anything good that was stolen or given away and close and seal all ungodly doors.

Lord Jesus, please open up the godly dimensions that lead to you and the revelation of your purposes in my life.

Notes:

1. See *Heaven Trek* by Paul L. Cox on vibrations.
2. Malachi 3:2.
3. Gleason Archer, R. Laird Harris, and Bruce Waltke, *Theological Wordbook of the Old Testament* (Chicago, IL: Moody Publishers, 1980).
4. Associated Press, "Speed of light may not have been constant after all". *USA Today,* August 15, 2001, http://www.usatoday.com/news/science/astro/2001-08-15-speed-of-light.htm.
5. Brian Greene, *The Fabric of the Cosmos: Space, Time, and the Texture of Reality* (New York: Vintage, 2005), 19.
6. Ibid., 385.
7. Ibid., 386.
8. Ibid., 386.
9. Ibid., 387.
10. Ibid., 387.
11. Ibid., 387.
12. Ibid., 388.
13. Ibid., 402.
14. Ephesians 2:6
15. Rob Bryanton, *The End of the World, Death, and the Tenth Dimension* (Facebook post, December 14, 2007), http://www.facebook.com/topic.php?uid=2583565632&topic=4103.
16. Rob Bryanton, *Imagining the Tenth Dimension.* (Victoria, BC, Canada: Trafford Publishing, 2006), 10.
17. Bryanton, 7.
18. Bryanton, 8, 9.
19. Bryanton, 11.
20. Bryanton, 13–16; direct quote, 17.
21. Bryanton, 18.

Notes (continued):

22. Bryanton, 20.

23. Bryanton, 23.

24. Bryanton, 25.

25. Bryanton, 26.

26. Bryanton, 29.

27. Bryanton, 30.

28. Bryanton, 30.

29. Bryanton, 32.

30. Bryanton, 33.

31. Genesis 11:4.

32. *Wikipedia.* s.v. "Where no man has gone before," http://en.wikipedia.org/wiki /Where_no_man_has_gone_before.

33. Mathematical function.

34. A quivering or trembling motion.

35. Deoxyribonucleic acid. Any of various nucleic acids localized in cell nuclei. The basic building blocks of life. The basis of heredity in many organisms.

36. The cell formed by the union of two gametes. The developing individual is produced from such a cell—the beginning of life.

37. Vibration, to relate harmoniously.

38. The substance of which a physical object is composed.

39. Variation, fluctuation, movement.

40. The number of sound waves per second produced by a sounding body or the number of oscillations per second of electromagnetic waves.

41. A sound of a definite vibration or pitch.

42. A position in time or space.

43. A chemical bond formed by shared electrons. In 1 Corinthians 10:20, Paul taught that a believer would actually be joined with demonic powers if he became involved in the table of fellowship of pagan deities.

44. Interferon—a protein released by the body in response to infections to help kill viral growth. An important part of the immune system.

45. Prayer by David Brown.

46. Infinity is an endless loop.

47. As you pray about a dimension, listen for what the Lord reveals; it may be something like "I sense witchcraft in that dimension," or it could be a knowing that there is a specific evil entity to dismiss. Sometimes, more prayer is needed about what was revealed. Ask, "What does this mean? What do you want us to know about this?" Pray until there's a sense of release and then move on. Sometimes, there is a sense of evil being drained off but nothing beyond that, so you just go to the next dimension and see what the Lord reveals about that one.

48. This is a continuation of the prayer for God to break ungodly ties between you and the dimensions.

49. The fourth dimension is time, and the other dimensions are aspects of space.

50. Sometimes the person praying is led to shift from numbering dimensions and to go to the, "and all dimensions through eternity" after eleven dimensions, but sometimes numbering the dimensions continues into the twenties before shifting.

Replace Double-Mindedness
with the Mind of Christ

PAUL L. COX

While I was in Argentina, I had the privilege of meeting Jim Goll. As Donna and I sat in a van with him after a conference meeting with Ed Silvoso, Jim began prophesying over us. He said that the Lord would take us to different places in the world and would begin equipping us by blessing us with the anointings on different land areas around the world. Since that prophetic word, I have been aware that as I have traveled to certain land areas, specific revelation has come. Could it be that specific revelation would have only come by being on "that" land? If so, there must be something, then, about the land of Minnesota.

Rochester, Minnesota, is a major center of intellectualism in the United States and the home of the Mayo Clinic. While I teaching a school on the land in Minnesota, I received the revelation about the two "spiritual" brains, one on either side of a person's head. These "spiritual" brains actually appeared like grey matter and seemed to be connected to the base of the physical brain by tentacles and a tube. A clear liquid and small particles that looked like seeds were inside the tube. The Lord spoke to us and gave us the word double-mindedness. A spiritual scroll came and the pastor received information about a declaration over the city. We couldn't see the relationship between the spiritual brain and the scroll until it was understood that the Lord wanted to come against intellectualism in the city.

As we pondered the scroll, the Holy Spirit spoke the words "Greek philosophy." It was then that we realized that much of science and math is built on Greek philosophy, which has its roots in magic. We were told that there is a statue of Apollo in the Mayo Clinic. We also learned that Mayo Clinic was one of the primary sources for information that was used to support abortion in the *Roe v. Wade* decision, including the idea that life does not begin at conception. One Supreme Court judge serving on the bench when the *Roe v. Wade* decision was made was from the Rochester area.

Sometime later, while I was in Big Lake, Minnesota, the Lord gave additional information about this double-mindedness to a group of twenty intercessors who had come for a day of waiting on the Lord. The "spiritual" exterior brain on the right side of each person seems to be connected with religious thinking and the exterior brain on the left side of the head seems to be connected with intellectualism based on Greek thinking and human logic.

Because our culture is immersed in the Greek mind-set, it is difficult to perceive other ways of seeing the world. As a seminary student, I was more exposed to the Greek mind-set than the Hebrew mind-set. I was instructed to read Plato, Aristotle, and Augustine as if their philosophical views of the world were correct. With no other frame of reference, I simply believed what I was taught. My church experience reinforced what I was being taught at seminary. It was all about the mind. Sermons were intellectual events to stimulate the mind. I lived in a world of ideas. Not only was experience discounted, but it was also preached against. We had to be careful about experiences as they were too subjective. I was shocked when I discovered that the Bible depicts a much different view.

I remember clearly sitting in a seminary class as the professor taught us about the word *to know*. We were instructed that *yada*, the Hebrew word *to know*, was to know intellectually. Why would I not believe this? A seminary professor had taught it! A few years ago I was shocked to realize the extent of my misunderstanding. *Yada* essentially means "to discern, as through the five senses." This root occurs [in every stem form] 944 times in the Old Testament and expresses a multitude of shades of knowledge gained by the senses. Its closest synonyms are *bin*, to discern, and *nākar*, to recognize.[1]

Some might argue that this is an Old Testament view of God and not a New Testament one. To counter the argument that *yada* describes a relational knowing, consider Philippians 3:10. In Philippians 3:10, the Apostle Paul expresses his desire about Christ, "that I may know Him and the power of His resurrection, and the fellowship of His sufferings, being conformed to His death." I had previously believed that the Apostle Paul was writing here about an "intellectual" knowing. This is not the case. *Tyndale Bible Dictionary* defines the Greek word *ginōskō* as follows:

> The word "know" or "knowledge" occurs more than sixteen hundred times in the Bible. The specific connotation of the word group provides insight into the basic messages of both the OT and the NT. The Hebrew view of man is one of differentiated totality—the heart, soul, and mind are so interrelated that they cannot be separated. "To know" thus involves the whole being and is not simply an action of the mind. The heart is sometimes identified as the organ of knowledge (cf. Psalm 49:3; Isaiah 6:10). The implication is that knowledge involves both will and emotions. It is in light of this connotation that the OT uses "to know" as an idiom for sexual intercourse between husband and wife. The Jew's concept of knowledge is beautifully illustrated in Isaiah 1:3: "Even the animals—the donkey and the ox—know their owner and appreciate his care, but not my people Israel. No matter what I do for them, they still do not understand" (NLT). Israel's failure lay not in ritual behavior but in refusal to respond in loving obedience to the God who has chosen her. Only the fool refuses to respond to this revelation. Thus the person who does not respond in obedience obviously has an incomplete knowledge of the Lord. "To know God" involves relationship, fellowship, concern, and experience."[2]

Therefore, the mind of Christ *knows* not only with the mental faculties or reason, but also with the emotions and the will. Further, the mind of Christ supersedes the human mind, emotions, and will and rises above the limitations of physical grey matter to apprehend reality experientially through the mind of the spirit, joined in loving union with God. Our relationship to Jesus Christ is not just a logical understanding. It is, in reality, an "intimate" relationship in which we know our Lord by our minds and by our experiences.

The Apostle Paul reminds us in Philippians 2:5–8 that the mind of Christ is not necessarily a cognitive mind but a mind of obedience through relationship.

Let this mind be in you which was also in Christ Jesus, who, being in the form of God, did not consider it robbery to be equal with God, but made Himself of no reputation, taking the form of a bondservant, and coming in the likeness of men. And being found in appearance as a man, He humbled Himself and became obedient to the point of death, even the death of the cross.

How does this apply to *double-mindedness*? The word double-minded is mentioned three times in Scripture:

I hate the double-minded, but I love Your law. (Psalm 119:113)

For let not that man suppose that he will receive anything from the Lord; he is a double-minded man, unstable in all his ways. (James 1:7–8)

Draw near to God and He will draw near to you. Cleanse your hands, you sinners; and purify your hearts, you double-minded. (James 4:8)

The double-minded person operates in doubt and not in faith. There is a trust issue with God. An intellectual understanding of God that is not based on a personal experiential relationship with the Lord is not stable. The logical mind easily wavers with circumstances and can be persuaded by deceptive reasoning. However, if one trusts in God and operates in trust, then his hope is sure in the goodness of the Lord. Trust is, of course, based upon and supported by the truths in the Word of God. Ultimately, by trusting in God and his promises, one can rest easily because he has experienced the continual faithfulness of the Lord.

The Prayer: Replace Double-Mindedness with the Mind of Christ

✖ In the name of the Lord Jesus Christ, I confess my doubt and the doubt in my generational line. I confess that this doubt has made me unstable and has given me double-mindedness. I confess that the source of this double-mindedness has been pride in my life and in my generational line. I also repent for all intellectualism, ungodly reasoning, logic, and humanism. I repent of caring more about man's approval rather than God's truth.

✖ I repent of my own self-effort and pride. In humility, I receive your love, God, and your mercy and your grace.

✖ I choose to be no longer conformed to the pattern of this world but to be transformed by the renewing of my mind so that I might prove what is the good and acceptable and perfect will of God.[2]

✖ I will do nothing out of selfish ambition or vain conceit, but I will walk in humility, considering others better than myself.

✖ I choose to resist the devil. I choose to submit myself to God as my Lord and Master and to draw near to him. Lord, please wash my hands and purify my heart.

✖ Father, thank you for giving me the mind of Christ, so I will be like him, becoming like a servant.

Notes:

1. Bruce K. Waltke, Robert Laird Harris, Gleason Leonard Archer, *Theological Wordbook of the Old Testament*, Electronic Edition (Chicago: Moody Press, 1999, 1980), citation 848.

2. "Ginōskō" taken from *Tyndale Bible Dictionary*, edited by Philip W. Comfort, Ph.D. and Walter A. Elwell, Ph.D. (Wheaton, IL: Tyndale House Publishers, Inc., Copyright © 2001). Used by permission of Tyndale House Publishers, Inc. All rights reserved.

3. Romans 12:1–2.

Janteloven Prayer

PAUL L. COX

The Jante Law is a concept that was created by the Norwegian/Danish author Aksel Sandemose in his novel, *A Fugitive Crosses His Tracks*.[1] In this novel, Aksel portrays a small Danish town, Jante, which is based on his own native town of Nykobing Mors.

Talking about cultural differences in any way that might be construed as discriminatory is touchy, even though many of these differences have been recognized for decades and have been passed down to us through our own generational lines. The Apostle Paul noted negative cultural traits in Titus 1:12. "One of them, a prophet of their own, said, 'Cretans are always liars, evil beasts, lazy gluttons.'" The Apostle Paul observed that one of Crete's own, a prophet, characterized the Cretans as liars, evil beasts, and slow bellies. Several commentaries believe this man to be Epimenides, who lived about 538 years before Christ. He evidently was from Cnossos and is mentioned by Plato. The terms "lie like a Cretan" and "When was there ever an upright Cretan?" were mentioned by Plutarch. The Cretans were dealing with the same character deficiencies during the days of Paul, nearly six hundred years later. Obviously, such cultural characteristics would be strongholds in the lives of Cretans who came to Christ, so Paul goes on to tell how to confront such strongholds.[2]

Things haven't changed. New believers still need to confront cultural strongholds that oppose God's truth. Probably every people group has characteristics that become strongholds or patterns of thinking within their own culture. The Scandinavians, for example, have similar cultural tendencies. While Cindy Jacobs of Generals of Intercession was visiting Norway, an intercessor named Laura Zavala, who had been praying in Norway, came to her. She handed Cindy a list of "laws" that most Scandinavians are aware of, cultural assumptions that govern their society. "Cindy," she said, "these represent one of the major strongholds that hinder many Scandinavians from coming into their fullness as believers."

Cindy took the list in hand and read it. At first, she could hardly grasp that the laws could be true. Pondering this, she asked her translator, Janaage Torp, if he would read them aloud to the conference attendees, while Cindy asked them if they were true. Here is the list:

1. You shall not think that you are special.

2. You shall not think that you have a good standing.

3. You shall not think that you are smart.

4. Don't fancy yourself as being better than anyone else.

5. You shall not think that you know more than anyone else.

6. You shall not think that you are more important than anyone else.

7. You shall not think that you are good at anything.

8. You shall not laugh.

9. You shall not think that anyone cares about you.

10. You shall not think that you can be taught.

To Cindy's amazement, heads began to nod up and down. Yes, these were laws that dictated social and moral standards in Scandinavia. All of a sudden, a number of things that she had noticed during the trip to Norway began to make sense.

Cindy strongly felt in her heart that the Jante Law represented a system of thinking that developed, through the years, into strongholds that kept the people of Scandinavia from fulfilling their highest calling. Of course, not everyone has subjected themselves to these laws. The truth of God's Word sets people free without, perhaps, a conscious realization of what is taking place in them.

In thinking further, it dawned on Cindy that not only Scandinavia, but also places where the people of Scandinavia have settled have been affected culturally by the Jante Law. In the United States, the Upper Midwest has been strongly influenced by Scandinavian settlers with Jante convictions. Other states, regions, and neighborhoods have also been affected by these beliefs.

Janteloven laws can have many effects. They would put a lid on worship when shouting louder than others is seen as speaking up too much in public. Also, they would stop the giving of "honor to whom honor is due," because that would be acting as if someone were more important than another. The apostles and the five-fold ministry cannot rise up because they might fancy themselves to be better than others.

We have also found that people from almost every culture may be victims of unexamined cultural beliefs, patterns, and traits that perpetuate iniquities and cause them to continue to be passed down the family line.

The Prayer: Renunciation of the Janteloven and Scandinavian Iniquities

I break, shatter, cut off, dissolve, and destroy the iniquity that says I am not special.

I break, shatter, cut off, dissolve, and destroy the iniquity that says that I do not have the same standing as others.

I break, shatter, cut off, dissolve, and destroy the iniquity that says that others are smarter than me.

I break, shatter, cut off, dissolve, and destroy the iniquity that says others are better than me.

I break, shatter, cut off, dissolve, and destroy the iniquity that says that others know more than I do.

I break, shatter, cut off, dissolve, and destroy the iniquity that says others are more important than I am.

✠ I break, shatter, cut off, dissolve, and destroy the curse that says I am not good at anything.

✠ I break, shatter, cut off, dissolve, and destroy the curse that says I will not speak or laugh in public.

✠ I break, shatter, cut off, dissolve, and destroy the curse that says that no one cares about me.

✠ I break, shatter, cut off, dissolve, and destroy the curse that says I cannot be taught anything.

Notes:

1. *En flyktning krysser sitt spor* (1933, English translation published in the USA in 1936).

2. *The Pulpit Commentary: Titus,* ed.,H. D. M. Spence-Jones (Bellingham, WA: Logos Research Systems, Inc., 2004), notation for Titus 1:12.

The Blood and Heart Prayer

PAUL L. COX

During the early days of offering generational deliverance through our ministry, I noticed a similar pattern in many prayer sessions. As I asked the Lord to lead individuals to an event in their generational lines that may have empowered the issue being dealt with, the person would see a blood or human sacrifice. This happened so often that I realized there was something significant about blood and human sacrifices that we did not comprehend. While the Old Testament teaches the use of blood sacrifices in fulfilling the law, it strongly prohibits human sacrifices and never permits sacrifices to other gods and goddesses. What is the significance of these sacrifices; why is Scripture so clearly against them, and why do they have power to affect families for generations? I pondered these questions for quite a while.

The first breakthrough to finding an answer came on a ministry trip to Austin, Texas. A prophet who was a member of the team told me I needed to read *The Blood Covenant*, a book taken from a lecture series by H. Clay Trumbull in 1885 and released again in 1998 by Impact Christian Books.[1] The Lord gave me a new understanding of the blood covenant through reading Dr. Trumbull's material.

A few years later the Lord gave me even more amazing insights about the blood covenant in a most interesting way when a friend of our family invited a man who does live blood analysis[2] to check the health of the blood of our family members. He set up his equipment, including a microscope, video camera, and television screen. I watched as he took a drop of blood from a person, put it on a slide, placed it under the microscope, and projected it onto the screen. With interest, I listened and observed as he explained what he saw in the blood of each person.

Then it was my turn, and I was amazed as I saw my blood appear on the screen! He made some favorable comments about how young my blood looked, but then he said, "Oh, What is this?" That certainly got my attention! My response was somewhere between mild interest and panic as I prepared myself for what might come next. When the drop of blood on the screen started moving very rapidly, I asked what was happening. "You are still connected to your blood," was the response of the technician. When I saw the drop of blood swirling on the slide I felt a spiritual line between the place on my finger where the blood had been drawn and the drop of blood on the slide. Sure enough, I was still connected to my blood.

Sometime later, as I was telling this story to a church in Tulsa, Oklahoma, I felt my finger and realized that I was still connected with that same drop of blood. At that point I cut the connection, and a light went on in my brain. Of course! When we receive Jesus Christ as our personal savior, his blood is appropriated to us, and a blood connection is formed between Jesus and us. Blood is important because "life is in the blood!" Therefore, any connection through any other blood is an ungodly connection. Only his perfect death on the cross and the shedding of his innocent blood can give life and establish the blood covenant (connection) necessary to secure our salvation.

Look at these Scriptures:

The cup of blessing which we bless, is it not the communion of the blood of Christ? (1 Corinthians 10:16a)

The *New American Standard Bible* translates the word *communion* as *sharing.* At the moment of salvation, we share in his blood.

To the pilgrims of the Dispersion in Pontus, Galatia, Cappadocia, Asia, and Bithynia, elect according to the foreknowledge of God the Father, in sanctification of the Spirit, for obedience and sprinkling of the blood of Jesus Christ. (1 Peter 1:1–2)

But Christ came as High Priest of the good things to come, with the greater and more perfect tabernacle not made with hands, that is, not of this creation. Not with the blood of goats and calves, but with His own blood He entered the Most Holy Place once for all, having obtained eternal redemption. For if the blood of bulls and goats and the ashes of a heifer, sprinkling the unclean, sanctifies for the purifying of the flesh, how much more shall the blood of Christ, who through the eternal Spirit offered Himself without spot to God, cleanse your conscience from dead works to serve the living God? And for this reason He is the Mediator of the new covenant, by means of death, for the redemption of the transgressions under the first covenant, that those who are called may receive the promise of the eternal inheritance. (Hebrews 9:11–15)

Much more then, having now been justified by His blood, we shall be saved from wrath through Him. For if when we were enemies we were reconciled to God through the death of His Son, much more, having been reconciled, we shall be saved by His life. (Romans 5:9–10)

Jesus' blood is shed for the remission of our sins and to establish our covenant (connection) with him. When his blood is sprinkled on us, the blood connection is formed.

Our culture doesn't understand the blood covenant. Even though I'd studied the blood covenant in seminary and knew the Scriptures about it, I didn't begin to "get it" until reading H. Clay Trumbull's book. His history about the blood covenant is so significant and sheds so much light on its importance that I will quote several passages in their entirety. Trumbull writes,

From the beginning, and everywhere, blood seems to have been looked upon as pre-eminently the representative of life: as, indeed, in a peculiar sense, life itself. The transference of blood from one organism to another has been counted the transference of life, with all that life includes. The inter-commingling of blood by its inter-transference has been understood as equivalent to an inter-commingling of natures. Two natures thus inter-commingled, by the inter-commingling of blood, have been considered as forming, thenceforward, one blood, one life, one nature, one soul—in two organisms. The inter-commingling of natures by the inter-commingling of blood[3] has been deemed possible between man and a lower organism; and between man and a higher organism,—even between man and Deity[4] actually or by symbol; as well as between man and his immediate fellow.

The mode of inter-transference of blood, with all that this carries, has been deemed practicable, alike by way of the lips and by way of the opened and interflowing veins. It has been also represented by blood bathing, by blood anointing, and by blood sprinkling; or, again, by the inter-drinking of wine—which was formerly commingled with blood itself in the drinking. And the yielding of . . . the blood of a chosen and a suitable substitute . . . has [often] . . . represented . . . the yielding of one's life by the yielding of one's blood. Similarly the blood, or the nature, of divinities, has been represented, vicariously, in divine covenanting, by the blood of a devoted and an accepted substitute. Inter-communion between the parties in a blood-covenant has been a recognized privilege, in conjunction with any and every observance of the rite of blood covenanting. And the body of the divinely accepted offering, the blood of which is a means of divine-human inter-union, has been counted a very part of the divinity; and to partake of that body as food has been deemed equivalent to being nourished by the very divinity himself."[5]

Trumbull also discusses the friendship bonds formed through blood covenants in many cultures. In lecture 1, section 2, discussing the history of blood covenants among the Semitic tribes of the Middle East, he says,

Blood Covenanting,[6] a form of mutual covenanting, by which two people enter into the closest, the most enduring, and the most sacred of compacts, as friends and brothers, or as more than brothers, through the inter-commingling of their blood, by means of its mutual tasting, or of its inter-transfusion."[7] [This] has been recognized as the closest, the holiest, and the most indissoluble[8], compact conceivable. Such a covenant clearly involves an absolute surrender of one's separate self, and an irrevocable merging of one's individual nature into the dual, or the multiplied, personality included in the compact. Man's highest and noblest outreaching of soul have, therefore, been for such a union with the divine nature as is typified in this human covenant of blood.[9]

Across many cultures, Trumbull found similar beliefs linking blood, life and friendship.

> The root idea of this rite of blood-friendship seems to include the belief, that the blood is the life of a living being; not merely that the blood is *essential* to life, but that, in a peculiar sense, it *is* life; that it actually vivifies by its presence; and that by its passing from one organism to another it carries and imparts life. The inter-commingling of the blood of two organisms is, therefore, according to this view, equivalent to the inter-commingling of the lives, of the personalities, of the natures, thus brought together; so that there is, thereby and thenceforward, one life in the two bodies, a common life between the two friends."[10]

Trumbull also notes that the symbols of the blood covenant are identical across cultures and over time, noting that, " the armlet, the bracelet, and the ring, . . . [are] the tokens of a mutual unending covenant."[11]

In his discussion of *Suggestions and Perversions of the Rite* (lecture 2), Trumbull examines the connections between blood rites and communion or union with God. Historically, the offering of one's blood was often done in the context of worshiping of other gods.[12]

According to Trumbull,

> Man longed for oneness of life with God. Oneness of life could come only through oneness of blood. To secure such oneness of life, man would give of his own blood, or of that substitute blood which could best represent himself. Counting himself in oneness of life with God, through the covenant of blood, man has sought for nourishment and growth through partaking of that food which in a sense was life . . . because it was the food of God, and because it was the food which stood for God. In misdirected pursuance of this thought, men have given the blood of a consecrated human victim to bring themselves into union with God; and then they have eaten of the flesh of that victim which had supplied the blood, which made them one with God.[13]

There was a common belief that the divinities were fed and nourished by the blood of sacrifices, while the worshipers were brought into communion and union with the divinities through this offering. This view seems to have prevailed among the Greeks and Romans; even many Christian fathers accepted its truth as applicable to the demons.[14]

As early as 2697 BC, offering the firstborn to a god was considered a means of gaining favor.[15]

Connections between life and blood are ancient and pervasive; they continue to live in popular culture. Even the pervasive eighteenth-century superstition of the vampire, "that transfused blood is revivification," expresses the universally held beliefs of earliest civilizations.[16]

Trumbull, indicates that the earliest records of ancient Egyptians not only link blood with life, but also see the heart as the "symbol and sustance of life."[17] The heart[18] was "counted as the blood source and the blood center of the body."[19] It was therefore the heart that was to be dedicated to the gods. The Mayans would take a "bleeding and quivering heart," presenting it to the sun, and then would place it into a bowl, prepared for its reception.

> An assistant priest sucked the blood from the gash in the chest, through a hollow cane; the end of which he elevated towards the sun, and then discharged its contents into a plume-bordered cup held by the captor of the prisoner just slain. This cup was carried around to all the idols in the temples and chapels, before whom another blood-filled tube was held up, as if to give them a taste of the contents.[20]

The heart as a living organ, as the blood source and blood fountain, has been recognized as the representative of its owner's highest personality and as the diffuser of the issues of his life and nature.

At times a curse was pronounced at the making of the blood covenant. An African oath quoted by Trumbull, is:

> If either of you break this brotherhood now established between you, may the lion devour him, the serpent poison him, bitterness be in his food, his friends desert him, his gun burst in his hands and wound him, and everything that is bad do wrong to him until death.[21]

God called Abraham to leave a culture where children were sacrificed to the gods. He established his covenant with Abraham through substitutionary sacrifice, and because of Abraham's faith, God made Abraham the father of a nation of people who were commanded never to eat the life-blood of other creatures or sacrifice their own children.

Again and again God emphasized the differences between Israel and the surrounding nations. It was important for the Israelites to know that blood covenanting was secured by symbolic sacrifices and not through the ingesting of blood. Psalm 50:16 (NIV) says, "What right have you to recite my laws or take my covenant on your lips?"[22]

The word of God is clear that one is not to eat blood.[23]

The word of God also prohibits the cutting of the body over the dead.[24] This was for the purpose of mourning the dead, but may have also been part of a seasonal rite within the Canaanite fertility cult designed to revitalize the god Baal on whom the fertility of the land was believed to depend.[25]

So how does this apply to our lives? It has long been the purpose of the enemy to pervert the eternal redemptive plan of God by manufacturing his own sacrificial system. Jesus, our great High Priest, by offering himself, accomplished the cleansing from sin that was needed. He revealed the perversity of unsanctioned sacrifies; he ended the necessity of the repeated shedding of blood and sacrifices that were called for on behalf of the people; he made union with God possible. "For by one offering He has perfected forever those who are being sanctified."[26] Because of God's spiritual laws, participation in the enemy's counterfeit systems puts a person into demonic bondage, and the blood covenants made with the demonic create curses that pass down through the generational lines. These iniquities must be canceled so that there can be complete freedom in Christ.

The Prayer: The Blood and Heart

✠ Father, I acknowledge you and your power. I praise you. I ask you, Father, to remove all evil in my family line from before the beginning of time to the present. I repent for all the sins of my ancestors and I totally renounce:

- All blood covenants and oaths

- All communions with demons

- All blood sacrifices

- All eating of flesh or blood

- All blood rites and rituals

- All offerings of the heart
- All union with demons through blood rites
- All eating of organs
- All ungodly shedding of blood
- All cutting of the dead and self
- All blood covenant curses
- All sacrifices to Molech
- All bloodletting or commingling of blood
- All sacrifices of children
- All drinking or tasting of blood
- All belief in vampires
- All blood bathing
- All false weddings
- All blood anointing
- All ungodly dedications
- All blood sprinkling
- All bitterness and unforgiveness
- All yielding of blood for a substitute
- All hard, calloused, and blind hearts
- All mixing of wine and blood
- All murder and innocent bloodshed

✖ I renounce all evil done in my family line.

✖ I renounce all sacrifices to and the worship of other gods.

✖ I repent of and I renounce all idol worship.

� I renounce all ungodly armlets, bracelets, charms, rings, earrings, or other tokens.

� In the name of Jesus Christ I ask you, Father, to cleanse my family line and to break all curses, covenants, and oaths from before the beginning of time to the present.

� Lord, please break all curses from my family line associated with heart and blood disorders. I apply the blood of Jesus over all the iniquity. All evil, I command you to leave, from before the beginning of time to the present, to my children, to my children's children, to a thousand generations.[27]

Notes:

1. H. Clay Trumbull, *The Blood Covenant* (Kirkwood, MO: Impact Christian Books, 1998). Used with permission.

2. It seems to me that live blood analysis can be a helpful diagnostic tool in the hands of a skilled microscopist. Although I have learned from it, I am not wholly endorsing the procedure because unfortunately, like many diagnostic tools, it can be misinterpreted by unskilled technicians and also misused to sell unneeded supplements.

3. "The clasping of hands in token of covenant is . . . [from] the custom of joining pierced hands in the covenant of blood friendship." Trumbull, 340.

4. 2 Peter 1:4.

5. Trumbull, 202–203.

6. The word for covenant in the Hebrew, *bereeth*, has the apparent meaning of a thing "cut" as apart from, or as in addition to, its primary meaning of a thing eaten. See John 6:53–58.

7. Trumbull, 4.

8. Trumbull, *The Blood Covenant*, 313. Rev. R. M. Luther, missionary in Burma, 1800's. "I never heard of the blood-covenant being broken. I do not remember to have inquired particularly on this point, because the way in which the blood covenant was spoken of, always implied that its rupture was an unheard of thing."

9. Trumbull, 202–204.

10. Trumbull, 38

11. Trumbull, 65.

12. Trumbull, 90–91.

Notes (continued):

13. Trumbull,184.

14. Ibid.

15. Trumbull,150.

16. Trumbull, 114.

17. Trumbull, 99.

18. In more than nine hundred instances in the English Bible, the Hebrew or the Greek word heart, as a physical organ, is applied to man's personality; as if it were, in a sense, synonymous with his life, his self, his soul, his nature.

19. See endnote 8 (above).

20. Trumbull, *The Blood Covenant*, 106.

21. Trumbull, 20.

22. *See also* Exodus 24:1–11 and Leviticus 17:3–14.

23. Leviticus 17:1–12.

24. Leviticus 19:28; Deuteronomy 14:1.

25. Peter Craigie, *The Book of Deuteronomy* (Grand Rapids, MI: Eerdmans, 1976).

26. Hebrews 10:14.

27. Leviticus 17:11; Proverbs 4:23, 14:10, 28:14; Joel 3:21; Psalms 31:24, 73:26. Prayer written by Richard Sicheneder.

Renunciation of Curses:
Deuteronomy 28:15–68

PAUL L. COX

In 1989, when I first started doing deliverances, the word *curse* frequently came up in dealing with evil issues in people's lives. Following those early deliverances, we began looking at generational curses and asking the Lord to cancel their affects in people's lives. Then, from what the Lord had been teaching us, I started teaching a seminar called *Tipping the Scales, Blessings and Curses.* This seminar was recorded and released. In 2008, after some intensive research, I discovered that what I had been teaching about the biblical view of curses was basically wrong. Needless to say, I was chagrined to find out that I had been releasing incorrect information.

In my defense, I have noticed that many do not understand the actual biblical meaning of the word *curse.* The English word *curse* has broad connotations ranging from a simple synonym for misfortune to a condition of unrelieved hopelessness brought on by supernatural forces, magical or divine. Therefore, when we read the translated Old Testament and see the English word *curse,* we assume that we understand the meaning of that word. However, in reality, the four Hebrew words that are translated as *curse* have many more than four different meanings.

My serendipity about the word curse began when I noticed that many books about the nature of curses listed as a primary source an article in the Journal of Biblical Literature entitled, *The Problem of "Curse" in the Hebrew Bible.*[1] This doctoral dissertation by H. C. Brichto includes a multi-language study of the word *curse* and clearly delineates the precise meaning of each of the four Hebrew words translated as *curse* in the Old Testament.

Brichto makes it clear that the starting point for our understanding of the word *curse* must be the exact definition of the word. The historical meaning of the word *curse*, by definition, is an imprecation. An imprecation is an exact formula or series of words by which a curse is invoked. Therefore, to say that some evil took place in the family line that *cursed* or brought a *curse* on subsequent generations would be to misuse the word *curse*. The word *curse* is a formulized set of words uttered against someone else. So, what are these Hebrew words?

According to Brichto, four Hebrew words are translated into the English as curse: *alah, arur, qualet,* and *qabab.* Only *qabab* means imprecation. Here is his explanation of the other words:

1. *Alah*—The number one meaning is "oath." An oath is a promise with the understanding that a penalty will take place (curse) if there is a false assertion or failing of one to keep his word.[2] Although other scholars have translated *alah* as an imprecation, Brichto's argument for the definition of *alah* is convincing.

2. *Arur*—The Authorized Version translates this word as "curse" sixty-two times, and as "bitterly" once; forms include to curse, cursed be he, to be cursed, cursed; to curse, lay under a curse, put a curse on, to be made a curse, be cursed.[3] The word is best rendered "banned." Its basic sense is best rendered "spell." When applied to the earth or rain, it is a spell which bars fertility to men. When applied to men or animals, it bars them from the benefits of fertility or association with their fellow creatures. The power of the curse is derived from deity or an agency endowed by the god of the society with unusual powers.

3. *Qualet*—translated as "curse" thirty-nine times, "swifter" five times, "light thing" five times, "vile" four times, "lighter" four times, "despise" three times, "abated" twice, "ease" twice, "light" twice, "lighten" twice, "slightly" twice, and is translated miscellaneously twelve times. The word actually means to be slight, be swift, be trifling, be of little account, be light, be abated (of water), to be swift, to be trifling, to be of little account, to be swift, show oneself swift, to appear trifling, be too trifling, be insignificant, to be lightly esteemed, to make despicable, to curse, to be cursed, to make light,

lighten, to treat with contempt, bring contempt or dishonor, to shake, to whet, to shake oneself, to be moved to and fro.[4] *Qualet* is best translated "abuse" or "to treat harshly or injuriously." It is a general term for punishment, misfortune, disaster, or harm.[5]

4. *Qabab, qabab*—A primitive root; eight occurrences; translates as "curse" seven times, and "at all" once. It means to curse, utter a curse against.

With this understanding we can now carefully examine the passage in Deuteronomy 28:15–68. The Hebrew word translated as curse in the *New King James Version* in Deuteronomy 28:15 is *qualet*.

> But it shall come to pass, if you do not obey the voice of the LORD *your God, to observe carefully all His commandments and His statutes which I command you today, that all these curses will come upon you and overtake you.*

Rather than translating *qualet* as *curse*, a more accurate translation for qualet is misfortune, disaster, or harm. In other words, the evil that would come down the family line could result in generational misfortune, disaster, or harm.

Deuteronomy 28:20 uses another Hebrew word, *arur*.

> *The LORD will send on you cursing, confusion, and rebuke in all that you set your hand to do, until you are destroyed and until you perish quickly, because of the wickedness of your doings in which you have forsaken Me.*

In this passage the Lord is saying that because of your sin, he will "ban" you from enjoying the benefits of his blessings.

An accurate reading of the Deuteronomy passage is that evil in a generational line will be passed down as an *iniquity* rather than as a curse. The Old Testament word for iniquity is the Hebrew word *avah* meaning *to bend or twist*. The sin in a family line starts a twisting in that line, and that twisting is carried down through the line until it is broken by the power of the blood of Jesus Christ.

What happens when this generational iniquity is broken? The good news is that breaking this generational evil through the power of the blood of Jesus Christ releases the generational blessings given to the family line. The word *bless* is a translation of the Hebrew word *bārak* which means "to endue with power for success, prosperity, fecundity, longevity."[6] The generational iniquity covers up the blessings which are available for thousands of generations.[7]

Now is the time to renounce all the generational evil and to ask the Lord to release the generational blessings given to your line.

The Prayer: Renunciation of Curses Deuteronomy 28:15–68

In the name of Jesus—

✠ I break off all evil that has come against me from generational iniquity committed in the city and from all curses in the country.

✠ I break all generational iniquity that has come against my provision for a healthy life.

✠ I break off all generational iniquity that has come against my creativity, my ability to produce and reproduce, my need for food and shelter, the work of my hands, and the capital I have invested.

✠ I break off all generational iniquity that has come against me and against my family in the areas of travel and transportation.

✠ I repent for any evil we have done in our family line in forsaking the Lord Jesus Christ.

✠ I renounce all generational iniquity that has resulted in confusion; I renounce all generational iniquity that has resulted in rebuke; and I renounce all generational iniquity that has brought destruction and sudden ruin. Father, will you remove all confusion, rebuke, destruction, and ruin that has touched my family line and the things we have put our hands to do.

I repent of all generational sin and iniquity that has resulted in my family line being plagued with diseases and that has brought destruction to my family line to prevent us from taking the land the Lord wants us to have.

I renounce all generational iniquity that has brought wasting disease, fever and inflammation, scorching heat and drought, and blight and mildew to plague us until we perish.

I renounce all generational iniquity that has resulted in the sky above us being bronze and the ground beneath us being iron, so that God does not hear our prayers and our work becomes fruitless toil.

I renounce all generational iniquity that has resulted in the rain upon our country turning into dust and powder. I renounce all generational iniquity that has resulted in the rain coming down from the skies until we are destroyed.

I renounce all generational iniquity that has resulted in defeat before our enemies. I renounce all generational iniquity that has allowed our enemies to come against us from one direction and caused us to flee in seven directions. I renounce all generational iniquity that has caused my family line to become a thing of horror to all the kingdoms of the earth.

I renounce all generational iniquity that would cause our carcasses to become food for all the birds of the air and the beasts of the earth with no one to frighten them away.

I renounce all generational iniquity that resulted in boils like those of Egypt and in tumors, diseases, festering sores, and the itch, from which we cannot be cured.

I renounce the all generational iniquity that has resulted in the affliction of madness, blindness, and confusion of mind.

I renounce all generational iniquity that has allowed, at midday, the groping about like a blind man in the dark. I renounce all generational iniquity that has resulted in being unsuccessful in everything we do, day after day being oppressed and robbed, with no one to rescue us.

✠ I renounce all generational iniquity that has resulted in times when the woman we were pledged to be married to was taken and ravished by another. I renounce all generational iniquity that resulted in building a house without being able to live in it. I renounce all generational iniquity that has resulted in planting a vineyard but not enjoying its fruit.

✠ I renounce all generational iniquity that resulted in our oxen being slaughtered before our eyes and not being able to eat any of it. I renounce all generational iniquity that resulted in our donkeys being forcibly taken from us without being returned. I renounce all generational iniquity that resulted in our sheep being given to our enemies with no one to rescue them.

✠ I renounce all generational iniquity that has resulted in our sons and daughters being given to another nation and the wearing out of our eyes watching for them day after day, powerless to lift a hand.

✠ I renounce all generational iniquity that resulted in people whom we do not know eating what our land produces.

✠ I renounce all generational iniquity that resulted in our ancestors having nothing but cruel oppression all of their days.

✠ I renounce all generational iniquity that caused many seeds to produce little harvest because locusts devoured the crop.

✠ I renounce all generational iniquity that caused my ancestors to plant vineyards and cultivate them but not to drink the wine or gather the grapes because worms ate them. I renounce all generational iniquity that resulted in my ancestors not benefiting from their labor.

✠ I renounce all generational iniquity that resulted in the alien who lived among us rising above us higher and higher, and resulted in our sinking lower and lower.

✠ I renounce all generational iniquity that resulted in others lending to me, and my being unable to lend to them; I renounce all generational iniquity that made others the head, and me the tail.

✠ I renounce all generational iniquity in my family line that resulted in others coming upon me to pursue me and overtake me until I was destroyed, because I did not obey the Lord my God and observe the commands and decrees he gave me.

✠ I renounce all generational iniquity that came upon me because my ancestors did not serve the Lord their God joyfully and gladly in the time of prosperity, and as a consequence, they had to serve the enemies the Lord sent against them in hunger and thirst, in nakedness and dire poverty,

✠ I renounce all generational iniquity that resulted in an iron yoke being put on my ancestors' necks until they were destroyed.

✠ I renounce all generational iniquity that came against my ancestors and me causing fearful plagues, harsh and prolonged disasters, and severe and lingering illnesses.

✠ I renounce all generational iniquity that came against my ancestors and me causing all the clinging diseases of Egypt.

✠ I renounce all generational iniquity that came against my ancestors and me to destroy us, and all generational iniquity that brought any kind of sickness and disaster that was not recorded by Moses in the Book of the Law.

✠ I renounce all generational iniquity that caused our family not to be as numerous as the stars in the sky but caused us to be few in number, because we did not obey the Lord our God.

✠ I renounce all generational iniquity that came upon my ancestors and has come upon me to ruin and destroy us and to uproot us from the land that we were to possess.

✠ I renounce all generational iniquity that came upon my ancestors and me so that we would be scattered among all nations, from one end of the earth to the other.

✠ I renounce all generational iniquity that came upon my ancestors and me so that we would find no resting place for the soles of our feet.

✠ I renounce all generational iniquity that came upon my ancestors and me so that we would have an anxious mind, eyes weary with longing, and a despairing heart.

✠ I renounce all generational iniquity that came upon my ancestors and me so that we would live in constant suspense, filled with dread both night and day, never sure of our lives.

✠ I renounce all generational iniquity that resulted in saying in the morning, "If only it were evening!" and in the evening, "If only it were morning!"—because of the terror that would fill our hearts and the sights that our eyes would see.

Notes:

1. Herbert Chanan Brichto, *The Problem of "Curse" in the Hebrew Bible*. Society of Biblical Literature Monograph Series 13 (Philadelphia, PA: Society of Biblical Literature and Exegesis, 1963).

2. Genesis 24:40–41, 26:28; Deuteronomy 29:12; Ezekiel 17:13; Proverbs 29:24.

3. Genesis 3:14, 4:11, 27:29; Deuteronomy 27:15–26; Joshua 6:26; 1 Samuel 14:24; Jeremiah 20:14–16; Joshua 9:22; Numbers 22:6–12; Malachi 2:2, 3:9–11.

4. Genesis 8:21; Leviticus 19:14; Isaiah 65:20; Nehemiah 13:25; Psalms 37:22, 109:28; Proverbs 30:10; Job 3:1.

5. Deuteronomy 11:26–29; 27:12–13; 28:15; 30:1; 30:19. In Proverbs 26:1–2 the word translated as *curse* really has the meaning of disgrace rather than curse.

6. R. Laird Harris, Gleason L. Archer, Jr., and Bruce K. Waltke, *Theological Wordbook of the Old Testament*, electronic edition (Chicago: Moody Press, 1999, 1980), 285.

7. Exodus 20:6.

CHAPTER TWELVE

Renunciation of Generational Druidism

PAUL L. COX

Druids functioned as the priests and judges in the Celtic culture; they were suppressed by the Romans during the first century AD and seem to have disappeared from Europe by the second century AD. Druids may have continued in the British Isles, particularly in Ireland where they are mentioned in eighth-century mythology. Most of what we know about the Druids is from archeological evidence or from Roman writers. The Druids did not seem to have written down what they believed or practiced and most of what they did in training was done in secret.[1]

The word *Druid* seems to be derived from the words "oak," "firm or solid," "magic", and "wisdom." Pliny the Elder, author in the first century AD, writes of a Druid ceremony which took place among oak trees.

> The druids—that is what they call their magicians—hold nothing more sacred than the mistletoe and a tree on which it is growing, provided it is Valonia Oak. . . . Mistletoe is rare and when found it is gathered with great ceremony, and particularly on the sixth day of the moon. . . . Hailing the moon in a native word that means 'healing all things;' they prepare a ritual sacrifice and banquet beneath a tree and bring up two white bulls whose horns are bound for the first time on this occasion. A priest arrayed in white vestments climbs the tree and, with a golden sickle, cuts down the mistletoe, which is caught in a white cloak. Then finally they kill the victims, praying to a god to render his gift propitious to those on whom he has bestowed

it. They believe that mistletoe given in drink will impart fertility to any animal that is barren and that it is an antidote to all poisons.[2]

There is evidence that the Druids practiced human sacrifices. Julius Caesar writes in his *Gallic Wars* describing the Druidic practice of human sacrificing.

[The Gauls] believe, in effect, that unless a man's life is paid for by another man's, the majesty of the immortal gods might not be appeased. They use figures of immense size, whose limbs, woven out of twigs; they fill with living men and set on fire, and the men perish in a sheet of flame. They believe that the execution of those who have been caught in the act of theft or robbery is more pleasing to the immortal gods; but when the supply of such fails, they resort to the execution even of the innocent.[3]

Diodorus Siculus, a Greek historian in the years before the time of Christ, also writes about the Druidic practice of human sacrifices.

These men predict the future by observing the flight and calls of birds and by the sacrifice of holy animals: all orders of society are in their power . . . and in very important matters, they prepare a human victim, plunging a dagger into his chest; by observing the way his limbs convulse as he falls and the gushing of his blood, they are able to read the future.[4]

The Druids believed in the immortality of the soul and reincarnation, believing the soul of a dead person is passed on to another body. They were polytheistic. They practiced augury,[5] soothsaying, sorcery, magic, casting of spells, foretelling the future,[6] divination, and magic. Of particular interest was their use of wells. They would often throw money into a well[7] or offer sacrifices by tossing people into wells.

Here are some definitions of words in the prayer:

- *The Carnutes* were a Celtic people group living in central Gaul between the Seine and Loire Rivers. A yearly general assembly of Druids was held in their territory.

- *Dis* is the god of the underworld and also a Roman god.

- *Epona* was a protector of horses, donkeys, and mules. She was also a goddess of fertility. She was said to be the leader of the soul in the afterlife. Epona was also worshipped in Rome.

- *Baco* was a Celtic god and was known as a boar god.

- *Cernunnos* was a horned god associated with horned animals, especially the stag and ram-horned snake. He was related to the god of the underworld.

The Prayer: Renunciation of Generational Druidism

✠ I renounce any and all participation by my ancestors in druidic worship, sacrifices, or rituals.

✠ I renounce any human sacrifice made by my ancestors. I renounce human sacrifice by burning, drowning in wells, or suffocating in cauldrons, or by slitting of throats over a cauldron to catch the blood.

✠ I renounce the Druid animal gods, especially Baco the Boar, Cernunnos the stag-antlered man, and Epona and her horse.

✠ I renounce the false god Dis, god of night.

✠ I renounce looking to the stars to tell the future or for assistance in decision making. I renounce all divination.

✠ I renounce the tossing of valuables into wells as a prayer or offering for any purpose.

✠ I renounce the annual meetings in the territory of the Carnutes.

✠ I renounce allegiance to the high priest of the Druids.

✠ I renounce the control of the peasant people by the Druidic orders. I renounce the slavery of the average person while Druids held power.

✠ I renounce any religious rites involving mistletoe, oak trees, or acorns, or the gathering of these items. I renounce any spirits of oak trees[8] or other plant life.

�֎ I renounce all placing of human skulls or bones into buildings for decorative or foundational purposes.

✖ I renounce the Druidic control of the government of the land.

✖ I command all spirits associated with the above to leave me now in the name of Jesus.

Notes:

1. *Wikipedia*, s.v. "Druid," http://.en.wikipedia.org/wiki/Druid.

2. Pliny. *Natural History*. XVI. Page 95.

3. Julius Caesar, *Gallic Wars* vi.14.3.

4. Diodorius Siculus v.28.6; Hippolytus *Philosophumena* i.25.

5. An augur interprets the will of the gods by studying the flight of the birds.

6. This was sometimes done by mathematical calculations.

7. Perhaps the root of throwing money into wells, wishing wells.

8. Dryads.

CHAPTER THIRTEEN

Breaking Ungodly Spiritual Ties

PAUL L. COX

I was given a unique opportunity. I had been invited to Colorado to pray for four generations of one family living on adjoining properties. The ministry time included individual and family ministry. At the end of the time, when all four generations were together in one room, I had a sudden impression to feel for ties between each person. I was amazed to discover that every member of that multigenerational family was connected at the belly button. I was discerning spiritual ties between each of them.

For several years, I had heard of the term *soul ties*. It is not used in the Bible, but to the best of my knowledge, it has been coined in the last century as a way of describing a reality in the spirit. Soul ties are actually spiritual connections between people. With my hand, I can feel them. Those with the gift of spiritual seeing have seen them. I have come to believe that these ties are, in fact, spiritual ties, connecting people to each other. These spiritual ties can link two people together through their bodies, souls, or spirits. I am thinking that perhaps a more accurate way of describing these ties would be the term "spiritual ties."

The strongest Biblical reference for these ties is found in 1 Samuel 18:1: "Now when he had finished speaking to Saul, the soul of Jonathan was knit to the soul[1] of David, and Jonathan loved him as his own soul." The Hebrew word for knit is *qashar* and means to bind, tie, or bind together.[2] Clearly here we have a soul tie, a spiritual connection of friendship, between David and Jonathan. It is also clear that this was considered to be a good connection.

Scriptures indicated other types of godly ties between people.

- Genesis 2:24: "Therefore a man shall leave his father and mother and be joined to his wife, and they shall become one flesh." Ephesians 5:30–31: "For we are members of His body, of His flesh and of His bones. For this reason, a man shall leave his father and mother and be joined to his wife, and the two shall become one flesh." Here we have spiritual ties between the physical, emotional, and spiritual aspects of a husband and wife. I can feel this tie between the sides of the husband and wife. In marriage man and woman become one.

- 1 Chronicles 12:17: "And David went out to meet them, and answered and said to them, 'If you have come peaceably to me to help me, my heart will be united with you; but if to betray me to my enemies, since there is no wrong in my hands, may the God of our fathers look and bring judgment.'" I can feel this tie between the hearts of those who are friends or those who are in agreement with others.

- Colossians 2:2: "That their hearts may be encouraged, being knit together in love, and attaining to all riches of the full assurance of understanding, to the knowledge of the mystery of God, both of the Father and of Christ." I can discern the connections between believers as seven lines connecting believer to believer from the head to the feet. One of these connections is at the heart.

- Acts 1:14: "These all continued with one accord in prayer and supplication, with the women and Mary the mother of Jesus, and with His brothers."

In Biblical Greek, *one accord* is translated *homothumadon*. *Homothumadon* is a compound of two words meaning "to rush along" and "in unison." The image is almost musical; a number of notes are sounded which, while different, harmonize in pitch and tone. As the instruments of a great orchestra move and blend under the direction of a concertmaster, so the Holy Spirit moves and blends together the lives of members of Christ's church.[3]

Every believer I have discerned has spiritual ties on their side connecting them to other believers. Whenever I have discerned these ties, I can feel seven spiritual lines, from the head to the feet, between believers. Others have seen these ties in colors like the colors of a rainbow.

Spiritual ties can serve many functions. They can tie two souls together in the spiritual realm. Spiritual ties between married couples draw them together like magnets, while soul ties between fornicators can draw a beaten and abused woman to a man whom, in the natural realm, she would hate and run from. Instead, she runs to him even though it's obvious he doesn't love her and treats her like dirt. In the demonic world, unholy spiritual ties can serve as bridges between two people connecting an otherwise innocent person to ungodliness. Spiritual ties can also allow one person to manipulate and control another person, sometimes without the other person's awareness.[4]

There can be many ungodly spiritual ties. There can be ungodly ties to inanimate objects, things like sex images, objects, or fetishes. The Bible is explicit about these ungodly ties. Hosea notes, "Ephraim is joined[5] to idols, let him alone."[6] Paul writes about ungodly sexual ties with others. In 1 Corinthians 6:16, he says, "Or do you not know that he who is joined to a harlot is one body with her? For 'the two,' He says, 'shall become one flesh.'" Moses recorded an ungodly spiritual tie in Genesis 34:1–3:

> *Now Dinah the daughter of Leah, whom she had borne to Jacob, went out to see the daughters of the land. And when Shechem the son of Hamor the Hivite, prince of the country, saw her, he took her and lay with her, and violated her. His soul was strongly attracted to Dinah the daughter of Jacob, and he loved the young woman and spoke kindly to the young woman.*

Here, the joining clearly resulted in an ungodly spiritual tie. These ties can cause spiritual confusion, emotional confusion, sexual addiction, compulsivity, and obsession.

These ungodly ties are not always sexual. Believers in Jesus can be unequally yoked with unbelievers. Second Corinthians 6:14 says, "Do not be unequally yoked together with unbelievers. For what fellowship has righteousness with lawlessness? And what communion has light with darkness?"

There can also be a joining together because of an oath. This spiritual tie could be godly or ungodly. According to Numbers 30:2, "If a man makes a vow to the Lord, or swears an oath to bind himself by some agreement, he shall not break his word; he shall do according to all that proceeds out of his mouth." *Bind* is the Hebrew word *acar* and means to tie, bind, imprison, to harness.[7]

The Lord has also taught us another interesting aspect about these ties. A homosexual couple had come to Aslan's Place for prayer because they wanted to end their relationship. As I prayed for them, I had a sense that both of them were holding on to a silver cord coming from the other. I could place my hand on each cord and follow it to the other person's hand. The silver cord is mentioned in Ecclesiastes 12:6: "Remember your Creator before the silver cord is loosed."[8] As I talked with them, they admitted that they were trying to draw life from each other rather than drawing life from the Lord. In a real sense, they were making the other person their "god." It was clear they needed to release the other person's silver cord to the Lord and repent for using one another to satisfy their own needs.

Since then, we have seen married couples holding on to each other's cords, parents holding on to their children's cords, students holding on to a teacher's cords, clients holding on to their therapist's cords, and church members holding on to their leader's cords. It seems there is no end to the ungodly spiritual ties that can be formed.

The following prayer has been written to break all ungodly ties between you and others. Perhaps the Lord will inform you of other connections that need to be broken.[9]

The Prayer: Breaking Ungodly Spiritual Ties

Father, I renounce all ungodly spiritual ties with:

- My husband [or wife], my children, friends, mother, father, grandparents, brothers, sisters, uncles, aunts, and sexual partners.

- I renounce all ungodly spiritual ties with anyone who has had homosexual relationships, with sexual abusers, with pornography, with any person who has engaged in an inappropriate touch, with emotional abusers, physical abusers, with anyone I've had a romantic relationship with and with any object of fantasy.

� I renounce all ungodly spiritual ties with pastors, leaders, other Christians, ungodly prophecies, past churches, denominations, false doctrines, ungodly ministries, employers, fellow workers, ungodly intellectuals, teachers, classmates, entertainers, heroes, musicians, ungodly music, political figures, and gangs.

✕ I renounce all ungodly spiritual ties with the dead, inanimate objects, trinkets, charms, idols, jewelry, any material object, false gods, saints, psychics, fortune tellers, occult leaders, mediums, astrologers, spiritualists, New Age individuals, martial arts, gurus, mantras, chanting, yoga, fraternities, secret societies, and sororities.

✕ I renounce all ungodly ties with pets, animals, food, books, law enforcement groups, people I have made blood pacts with, military personnel, doctors, nurses, lawyers, acupuncturists, and healers; with buildings, land areas, anyone who cursed me because of an accident, anyone who was angry, dishonest people, and foolish people.

Notes:

1. Inner being of a person.
2. James Strong, *Enhanced Strong's Lexicon 2.0* (Woodside Bible Fellowship, 1995).
3. James Strong, *Enhanced Strong's Lexicon 2.0* (Woodside Bible Fellowship, 1995).
4. http://www.greatbiblestudy.com/soulties.php
5. Hebrew word *chabar*—to unite, join, bind together, be joined, be coupled.
6. Hosea 4:17.
7. James Strong, *Enhanced Strong's Lexicon 2.0* (Woodside Bible Fellowship, 1995).
8. Hebrew word *chebel*—cord rope from the word chabal meaning to bind. James Strong, *Enhanced Strong's Lexicon 2.0* (Woodside Bible Fellowship, 1995).
9. You can find more information about spiritual ties on the internet: http://www.porn-free.org/soul-ties.htm; http://www.gotquestions.org; http://www.b4prayer.org/index11.html; http://www.greatbiblestudy.come/soulties.php.

Replacing Ungodly Elders

PAUL L. COX

It started with a thought. Several years ago while I was ministering with Ian, a teenage boy, I had the strange impression that evil beings were sitting in a semicircle in front of the man we were praying for. When I placed my hand in the first position, I felt a short evil being, about three feet high. As I moved farther away from the man, I sensed another being of similar size. As I moved in a semicircle around the person, I concluded that there were twelve of these beings. *What or who were they? They seemed different than anything I had ever discerned before.* I knew they were evil, but I was not sure they were demonic. I asked Ian what he was seeing and he started describing wrinkled old men sitting on small chairs or thrones. I then heard the word *elders.*

Once again, my discernment came up against what I had assumed as true. Scripture clearly speaks of the twenty-four elders around the throne of God in heaven. *Is it possible that there are other levels of elders?* Often we argue about what Scripture says by assuming that the Bible declares everything that could ever be true. That is not the case. All words in the Word of God are true. However, many truths are not in the Bible. For example, 1 + 1 = 2 is not in the Bible, but it is true. I call this an argument from silence. Many have told me that because the Bible only mentions the twenty-four elders around the throne, there could not be any others. Scripture does not say there "are not" any other elders. It simply states that there are twenty-four around the throne.

After the discovery of the twelve elders seated in front of the person, I started wondering if there might possibly be twenty-four elders around each of us. I explored behind the person we were praying for, but could discern no more spiritual elders.

Some months later, during a forum at Aslan's Place, we started seeking the Lord about this and the response was, "This information is too dangerous for you to receive now." That was very mystifying for me, but it was enough to know that we should not proceed. Several months later, after I had taught on elders and wondered more than once why we only sensed twelve on earth when we know there were twenty-four in heaven, Mimi Lowe from Canada started prophesying that the key was the "wheel within a wheel."[1] I immediately knew the answer. The man we were praying for was sitting on a horizontal spiritual wheel. The twelve ungodly elders were sitting on this wheel in front on him. But the man was also sitting on a vertical wheel, like a ferris wheel, with twelve other ungodly eders. He was on a "wheel within a wheel."

So far I only know the qualities that were discerned for the original twelve ungodly elders. These qualities are:

- Ungodly stewardship and self-exaltation

- Hoarding spirit

- Pride

- Disempowerment

- Resistance to forward movement: "God's will is that I move slowly."

- Looking away from God

- False vision in leadership: "I am the sole interpreter of what God wants."

- Corrupt intentions in sabotaging oneself and others

- Rigidity; not working with others and denying others access to their gifts: "The answer is always NO."

- Stagnation; holding on to the things of the past; traditionalism

- Passivity; anything goes

- Intimidation and manipulation

It appears that these two wheels are constantly moving so that two different elders on each wheel come into agreement at the ear of the person. These ungodly elders then whisper lies into the person's ear. There seem to be twenty-four ungodly elders around each person and another set around marriages. I have also discerned twenty-four elders over churches, over organizations, over cities, over states, and over countries.

As I have been teaching on the elders, many have asked, "What do elders do?" My response has been, "Elders do what elders do." Although, hopefully, the response is amusing, I believe it is also accurate. Spiritual elders seem to do what physical elders do. Righteous elders operate in dispensing wisdom, guidance, counsel, guiding finances, and so forth. The ungodly elders would do the opposite.

The book of Revelation outlines the ministry of the twenty-four elders around the throne of God. I believe all levels of righteous elders are involved in similar spiritual ministry. The twenty-four elders around the throne are the highest governing body under the headship of the Trinity. The following is a list of what the righteous elders do and their characteristics:

- Worship God[2]

- Lay their crowns before God[3]

- Communicate with human beings[4]

- Hold the prayers of the saints in bowls[5]

- Move forward in time[6]

- Sit before the throne of God

- Are mentioned with the living creatures[7]

- Sing a new song[8]

Revelation leads to inspiration! After I had received all this revelation about the ungodly elders, I wondered, "Now what?" At first, we simply asked the Lord to unseat the ungodly elders and seat the righteous elders.

That worked. The ungodly elders simply moved away and the righteous elders were seated on righteous thrones.

After this, while in Hawaii ministering to a small group of pastors, I felt the presence of the ungodly elders and hesitantly spoke about them. A lively discussion followed, but there was agreement that we should pray and ask the Lord to remove the ungodly elders around the people and around the church in which we were meeting. The feedback was amazing. Two pastors reported back to me that the attitudes of their people toward them had positively shifted after praying that prayer.

Something else has happened since the first discovery of ungodly elders. At times the Lord has revealed ungodly elders over a state, city, or country. This has not happened often, but when the revelation has come, the Lord has always instructed me and a small group of believers to ask him to unseat the ungodly elders over regions. I do not feel released to reveal where this has taken place, but I can say that the results of these prayers have been significant. It is as if the Lord has collected all the prayers of the saints in those particular geographic areas and acted suddenly to bring a new level of freedom to the area. I should also add that this is never to be done without clear direction from the Lord. I remember so clearly the early words we had about the ungodly elders, "This is too dangerous for you to know now." This is a sobering thought to me. This is a new level of warfare that must be led by the Lord.

The Lord led a ministry school to write the prayer *Replacing Ungodly Elders.* Since then, literally hundreds of people have prayed this prayer. There is still more revelation to come about these ungodly and godly elders. Let us know what the Lord is teaching you.

The Prayer: Replacing Ungodly Elders

I repent for myself and for those in my family line who only took care of themselves and did not lovingly shepherd the flock of the Lord. I repent for those who ate well and clothed themselves well but did not take care of the flock.

✠ I repent for myself and for those in my family line who did not strengthen the weak or heal the sick, did not bind up the injured, did not bring back the strays or search for the lost and ruled harshly and brutally.

✠ I repent for myself and for those in my family line who caused the sheep to be scattered over all the mountains and on every high hill and over the whole earth and made them vulnerable to wild animals because there was no shepherd. I specifically repent for those who allowed wolves in sheep's clothing to enter and devour the flock.

✠ I repent for myself and for those in my family line who cared more for themselves rather than for the flock of the Lord and who enriched themselves at the expense of the flock.

✠ I repent for myself and for those in my family line who refused or laid down or fled from any calling of God on our lives.

✠ I repent for myself and for those in my family line who brought disunity, disorder, disharmony, and wounding to the flock.

✠ I repent for myself and for those in my family line who through evil practices polluted the flock.

✠ I repent for myself and for those who accepted or taught the doctrine of demons.

✠ I repent for myself and for those in my family who agreed with unrighteous religious authorities.

✠ Lord, I choose to be a leader who is patient and kind. I choose not to be envious. I choose not to boast or to be proud. I will not be rude or self-seeking. I will not be easily angered or keep a record of wrongs. I will not delight in evil but will rejoice in truth. I will always protect, always trust, always hope, and always persevere.

Lord, please unseat all ungodly elders.

Lord, please now invite and seat all the righteous elders assigned to me.[9]

Notes:

1. Ecclesiastes 12:6.
2. Revelation 4:10–11, 14.
3. Revelation 4:10.
4. Revelation 7:13.
5. Revelation 5:8.
6. Revelation 11:17–18.
7. Revelation 5:8.
8. Revelation 5:9.
9. Ezekiel 34; 1 Corinthians 13:1–13; Jude 1:4–25.

Prayer to Heal ADD

PAUL L. COX

The Apostle Paul writes in the first chapter of the book of Colossians about the profound and complete supremacy of Christ over all situations.[1] I believe that this insight into the nature of Jesus Christ speaks volumes of truth regarding the approach that should be followed when developing a treatment plan for attention deficit disorder (ADD).

When children begin to have academic difficulties in school, usually psychological testing, special academic remediation, and medication become the core aspects of the treatment plan. Unfortunately often prayer for the brain oten becomes an afterthought rather than the primary treatment. In reality it may be wise to consider an approach in which prayer becomes the focal point of the treatment model for attention deficit disorder.

It is not that academic and medical models have nothing to offer, it is rather that we must first seek Jesus to heal the brain. This prayer was written as a beginning effort to bring the supremacy of Jesus into the treatment model. The prayer can be read over a child at night when he is sleeping or, if the child is older, it can be read by parent and child together, daily, until changes begin to happen in the brain that influence school performance.

At the risk of causing controversy in the fields of psychology and education, I must promote my personal conviction that attention deficit disorder has its roots primarily in the spiritual realm rather than in the medical or educational realms. The healing power purchased through the cross of Calvary is available today and will make the difference in returning the brain to the form and function created by Father God.

When you read through the text of this prayer, you will notice that one area of emphasis is removing negative words that have been spoken about the brain. These negative words might have come from teachers, relatives, or doctors who unknowingly limit brain healing by speaking words of discouragement about the potential to succeed in the learning environment.

I believe the most damaging negative thoughts are those that learning disabled individuals think about themselves when they see themselves as defective or incompetent. The worst negative words are those that learning-disabled individuals speak about themselves.

Another focus of this prayer is to command the key components of the brain to heal. Words such as *axons, dendrites, synapses,* and so forth, are all medical terms for brain function. It is valuable to pray with precision asking Jesus to specifically put his touch on the various parts of our brains.

Be of good cheer; people who have ADD can lead productive and exciting lives, and Jesus can change learning habits and brain function. Thinking otherwise would be a lie and simply play into the hands of the enemy in destroying the birthright Jesus has placed in each and every one of us.

The Prayer: For Healing ADD

�incross Lord Jesus, I thank you that your healing power, purchased through the cross of Calvary is available for me today.

✚ I declare that you created my brain for the purpose of bringing glory to your name. I do not want my brain to be conformed to the patterns of this world instead I ask for your transforming power to enter all areas of my brain so that you might give me the ability to process academic and spiritual wisdom from your Holy Spirit.

✚ I declare that I believe that you created my innermost being and that my brain is fearfully and wonderfully made by your hand.

✠ Lord, I repent of all the times I have not regarded my brain and my learning abilities as gifts from you. I ask you to forgive me for the negative thoughts and words that I have spoken against my own brain and learning abilities.

✠ I repent of trying to solve my learning problems through my own efforts rather than turning to you first to receive your love, grace, and healing touch.

✠ I choose to forgive parents, teachers, and friends who have not believed in my mental abilities or who have made learning more difficult for me. In the name of Jesus, I now free them from unreasonable expectations I may have placed upon them.

✠ Lord, I ask you to remove all generational sin from my family line that may have played a part in my present learning struggles. As a member of my family line I repent for all those who, although they knew you, did not use their brains to glorify you, but engaged in futile and foolish thinking.

✠ Lord, I repent for those in my family line who used their brains to misuse the spiritual gifts that you had provided for them.

✠ In the name of Jesus, I command the neurons in my brain to function properly. I command in Jesus name that the damaged dendrites in my brain be healed. All axons and synapses will respond to the healing touch of Jesus Christ and function the way they were created to work.

✠ In Jesus name, I command my right and left brain to function normally and in complete balance, and I command that all my academic and creative abilities will flow like a river.

✠ In Jesus name, I command that the electrical and chemical frequencies in every cell of my brain come into harmony and balance.

✠ In Jesus name, I command my Wernicke's area (speech) and Broca's area (understanding of language) to function normally.

In the name of Jesus I declare that all lack of impulse control and lack of attention to task be healed.

In the name of Jesus, I declare that I have a new academic and occupational future. I break, shatter, dissolve, and destroy the lie that says my brain will always remain the same.

In the name of Jesus, I declare that I will not have a spirit of fear about learning new things. I accept your gift of the Spirit of power, love, and self-discipline into my brain.

Lord, I now ask you to give me the Spirit of wisdom and revelation that I might succeed in school and that I might know you better.[2,3]

Notes:

1. Colossians 1:16–17.
2. Prayer written by Jeffrey Barsch, EdD.
3. Ephesians 1:17–18.

Releasing the Fullness
of the Holy Spirit

PAUL L. COX

Seminary did not prepare me for the amazing revelation the Lord would give me from the Word of God. Of course, I had been taught about the finer points of theology and all about higher and lower criticism. I was exposed to endless debates about the sources and dating for each book of the Bible. I was informed about the nature of literary techniques and how much of the Bible was written in symbolic terms, utilizing metaphors, synonyms, and hyperbole, but I was not prepared for being taught by the master teacher, the Holy Spirit.

We were in Pennsylvania in June 2005, and the Holy Spirit had drawn us to Zechariah 4:1–6 and 4:11–14.

> Now the angel who talked with me came back and wakened me, as a man who is wakened out of his sleep. And he said to me, "What do you see?" So I said, "I am looking, and there is a lampstand of solid gold with a bowl on top of it, and on the stand seven lamps with seven pipes to the seven lamps. Two olive trees are by it, one at the right of the bowl and the other at its left." So I answered and spoke to the angel who talked with me, saying, "What are these, my lord?" Then the angel who talked with me answered and said to me, "Do you not know what these are?" And I said, "No, my lord." So he answered and said to me: "This is the word of the LORD to Zerubbabel: 'Not by might nor by power, but by My Spirit,' says the LORD of hosts.

> *Then I answered and said to him, "What are these two olive trees—at the right of the lampstand and at its left?" And I further answered and said to him, "What are these two olive branches that drip into the receptacles of the two gold pipes from which the golden oil drains?" Then he answered me and said, "Do you not know what these are?" And I said, "No, my lord." So he said, "These are the two anointed ones, who stand beside the Lord of the whole earth."*

After I read this Scripture, I had the impression that there might be a tree on either side of a person, just like in the Zechariah text. As I felt to the right and left side of a person, I was able to discern a power.[1] I asked the seers present, "What do you see?" When they said that they were seeing what looked like an olive tree, their insight confirmed my impression. I then placed my hand in front of the person and could discern a lampstand, like a menorah, with seven branches. On top of the lampstand, resting on top of the person's head, I could discern a bowl. We had received the beginning of new revelation and the Lord was waiting to launch us into a new understand about the spiritual world.

As I pondered the olive trees, the Lord impressed on me that these trees were the *trees of life*. I was mystified by that thought. *Wasn't there only one tree of life?* I turned to the text in Revelation 22:1–2:

> *And he showed me a pure river of water of life, clear as crystal, proceeding from the throne of God and of the Lamb. In the middle of its street, and on either side of the river, was the tree of life, which bore twelve fruits, each tree yielding its fruit every month. The leaves of the tree were for the healing of the nations.*

I was stunned. The text says "on either side of the river was the tree of life." I looked up the original Greek text and found no article *the* in front of *tree of life*. What the text actually said was "tree on either side of the river." Perhaps there are two trees. If so, is it also possible that the two trees of life are the two olive trees mentioned in Revelation 22? It is also noteworthy that in Genesis 2:9 no article designates how many *trees of life* were present in the Garden of Eden.

On top of the lampstand is the golden bowl. The golden bowl is mentioned in Ecclesiastes 12 and Revelation 5.

Remember your Creator before the silver cord is loosed, or the golden bowl is broken, or the pitcher shattered at the fountain, or the wheel broken at the well.[2] (Ecclesiastes 12:6)

Now when He had taken the scroll, the four living creatures and the twenty-four elders fell down before the Lamb, each having a harp, and golden bowls full of incense, which are the prayers of the saints. (Revelation 5:8)

The two olive trees extend two branches over the bowl into two pipes. From the bowl seven spouts provide oil for the seven lamps.

These bowls are filled with the prayers of the saints. As I felt the outside of the bowl on the head of the person between the olive trees, I could discern an elder holding the bowl. I wondered, "What does the inside of the bowl feel like?" I put my hand in the center of the bowl and immediately felt evil. *What was this?* Somehow the bowl, which should have been filled with the pure oil of the Holy Spirit, was contaminated.

The central idea of the oil is found by looking at Zechariah 4:6, "This is the word of the LORD to Zerubbabel: 'Not by might nor by power, but by My Spirit,' says the LORD of hosts.'" The olive oil represents the Holy Spirit and his power. Now I had gained some understanding. Somehow, because of generational sin, an ungodly spirit, a counterfeit of the Holy Spirit had gained a right to influence the person before me, thus contaminating the contents of the bowl. When I first discerned this contamination I received the Scripture Ezekiel 8:10: "So I went in and saw, and there—every sort of creeping thing, abominable beasts, and all the idols of the house of Israel, portrayed all around on the walls." Somehow the bowl was filled with all this evil, and this contamination seemed to be initiated by an ungodly holy spirit. *Who was this ungodly holy spirit?* I believe it was the *queen of heaven.*

The Queen of Heaven

Paul L. Cox and Richard Sicheneder

The queen of heaven is mentioned in Jeremiah 7:18 and 44:15–19:

The children gather wood, the fathers kindle the fire, and the women knead dough, to make cakes for the queen of heaven; and they pour out drink offerings to other gods, that they may provoke Me to anger.

Then all the men who knew that their wives had burned incense to other gods, with all the women who stood by, a great multitude, and all the people who dwelt in the land of Egypt, in Pathros, answered Jeremiah, saying: "As for the word that you have spoken to us in the name of the LORD, we will not listen to you! But we will certainly do whatever has gone out of our own mouth, to burn incense to the queen of heaven and pour out drink offerings to her, as we have done, we and our fathers, our kings and our princes, in the cities of Judah and in the streets of Jerusalem. For then we had plenty of food, were well-off, and saw no trouble. But since we stopped burning incense to the queen of heaven and pouring out drink offerings to her, we have lacked everything and have been consumed by the sword and by famine." The women also said, "And when we burned incense to the queen of heaven and poured out drink offerings to her, did we make cakes for her, to worship her, and pour out drink offerings to her without our husbands' permission?

The queen of heaven was Astarte, the goddess of Venus. She was called Ashtoreth by the Phoenicians and other Canaanites and Ishtar in the Akkadian pantheon. She was said to be the sister or consort of Baal. She was associated with the moon and symbolized the generative powers of nature.[3] Two aspects of her character were prominent: eroticism and belligerence.[4] She was associated with Tammuz. Worship of the queen of heaven included making cakes, possibly in the shape of figures or crescent moons.[5]

109

There seems to be a direct tie between the term *queen of heaven* and the word *harlot*. The Hebrew word *zonah* is translated harlot. It means a woman consecrated or devoted to prostitution. In Genesis 38:21 the term prostitute, *kedeshah*, is connected to the worship of Asherah or Astarte. With this connection between the queen of heaven, prostitution, and harlotry, we can enlarge our biblical understanding about the character of the queen of heaven.

Because of the multitude of harlotries of the seductive harlot, the mistress of sorceries, who sells nations through her harlotries, and families through her sorceries. (Nahum 3:4)

So he carried me away in the Spirit into the wilderness. And I saw a woman sitting on a scarlet beast which was full of names of blasphemy, having seven heads and ten horns. The woman was arrayed in purple and scarlet, and adorned with gold and precious stones and pearls, having in her hand a golden cup full of abominations and the filthiness of her fornication. And on her forehead a name was written: MYSTERY, BABYLON THE GREAT, THE MOTHER OF HARLOTS AND OF THE ABOMINATIONS OF THE EARTH. I saw the woman, drunk with the blood of the saints and with the blood of the martyrs of Jesus. And when I saw her, I marveled with great amazement. (Revelation 17:3–6)

The spirit of the queen of heaven has many characteristics:

• Worshipers of it say that it brings provision and safety, and it causes people to trust it, become dependent upon it, and loyal to it.[6]

• The harlot allures, enslaves, and deceives all peoples and nations. She does it by her prostitution, magic, sorceries, and witchcraft. She promotes ungodly sex, drugs, drunkenness, and idolatry.[7]

• The harlot brings a curse of death, mourning, and famine. She leads men to the grave and is responsible for the blood of the saints.[8] She has a connection to alcohol; remember they call liquor "spirits." These spirits lead to sexual sin.[9]

- She is connected to us through her drugs or sorceries.[10] The word *sorcery* in the New Testament is *pharmakeia* from which we derive our English word *pharmacy.*

- Pornography and its origins are tied to the harlot spirit.[11]

- She never repents because of her pride, and she leads others into immorality by compromise.[12]

It was now time to construct a prayer to repent for and renounce all the evil in a family line that inhibited the working of the Holy Spirit. Revelation came and the Lord gave us the following prayer.

The Prayer: Releasing the Fullness of the Holy Spirit

In the name of the Lord Jesus Christ and by the power of his blood I choose to remember my Creator before the golden bowl[13] is broken. I renounce and repent for all those in my family line who did not acknowledge the Creator.

I repent for myself and those in my generational line who committed the seven sins in Proverbs 6:17–19:

A proud look, a lying tongue, hands that shed innocent blood, a heart that devises wicked plans, feet that are swift in running to evil, a false witness who speaks lies, and one who sows discord among brethern.

I repent for myself and all those in my family line who have entered into rebellion, defiance, apostasy, and who have entered into unholy covenants, divination, and legalism.

I renounce and repent for all ungodly agreements with leadership and of all recognition and acknowledgement of unholy elders in word, thought, or deed for myself and my generational line.

✖ I repent for myself and my ancestors who prayed against the will of God and spoke false prophecies.

✖ I repent for alignment with any counterfeit holy spirit.

✖ I repent for all allegiance to the ungodly world system; I break all connections to the queen of heaven in my life and my generational line; I choose to come out of the ungodly world system.

✖ I repent for any apostasy and abomination which honored the queen of heaven, including human blood sacrifice on God's holy altar which is on God's holy mountain.

✖ I repent for myself and for those in my generational line who chose to draw life from the queen of heaven. Lord, I ask that any attachment between myself and the queen of heaven be severed and burned. Lord would you remove all evil I received from the queen of heaven and cleanse me and reconnect me to you so that I might draw life only from you?

✖ Lord, would you close all ungodly portals connected with the queen of heaven?

✖ I choose to empty the golden bowl of any ungodly contents and I ask you, Lord Jesus, to sanctify and make the bowl holy.

✖ Lord Jesus, I ask that you deal with the queen of heaven according to your Word.

✖ Lord, would you fill the golden bowl with everything you have for me?

✖ I come into agreement with all that you have for me through the finished work of the cross.

Notes:

1. *See* chapter 4, "Prayer to Dismantle the Powers."
2. This would all happen at death.

3. Stelman Smith and Judson Cornwall, *The Exhaustive Dictionary of Bible Names* (North Brunswick, NJ: Bridge-Logos, 1998).

4. Paul J. Achtemeier, *Harper's Bible Dictionary* (San Francisco: Harper & Society of Biblical Literature, 1985).

5. D. R. W. Wood, *New Bible Dictionary* (Downers Grove, IL: Inter Varsity Press, 1996).

6. Jeremiah 44:15–19.

7. Nahum 3:4; Revelation 17–18.

8. Proverbs 2:16–18; 5; 7:4–5; 9:18; 22:14; 23:26; Ecclesiastes 7:26.

9. Proverbs 23:22–35.

10. Revelation 18:23.

11. The Greek word *pornographos* (pornography) literally means "writing about harlots" or "the writing of harlots."

12. 2 Timothy 3:1–6.

13. Ecclesiastes 12:6.

St. Patrick's Breastplate

NIGEL REID

In March 2005 I attended the second week of a ministry school at Aslan's Place in Hisperia, California. It was led by Paul Cox and his team. During the early part of the week Paul started to share some of his experiences in Hawaii and some of the significant revelation he had received in those islands. I had previously visited Honolulu with Paul and had been part of his team there.

I felt the Lord begin to stir my spirit as Paul spoke, and over the following days a deepening sense of connection between these islands and my own homeland of Ireland began to germinate. On the Thursday of that week, as we continued to pursue the revelation we were receiving, a friend of Paul's spoke on the phone of a connection across the globe between Ireland and Hawaii through an axis of Washington, DC. That day was the 17th of March, St. Patrick's Day, and at that time, unknown to us, the Irish Taoiseach (prime minister) was in the White House in Washington, DC, presenting the traditional bowl of shamrocks to the president of the United States. Through mutual friends, the relationships between leaders in Hawaii and Ireland were growing.

As the ministry school continued, I was reminded of the unique place this Christian man, Patrick, holds in the hearts of people all over the world. He is the patron saint of Ireland, and with the Irish diaspora his fame has reached the uttermost parts of the earth. There are churches dedicated to St. Patrick everywhere. During the remainder of that school we began to create a prayer, and I was reminded that Patrick himself confronted the pagan deities of Ireland 1600 years before and out of his own experiences developed the prayer now known as St. Patrick's Breastplate.

Patrick's story is well known, through a combination of traditional Irish storytelling and some of his own written work. Originally captured in Britain by Irish sea raiders, he was transported to Ireland as a slave and herded swine in the north of the island. Through a dream, an escape plan was revealed to him, and he did indeed escape to return home to his family in Britain. There he pursued his Christian faith. Although he writes of travelling through Gaul and Italy during the years that are missing from his history, it is most probable that he returned to Britain where he served as a deacon and was ordained as a priest before returning to Ireland.[1]

In his *Confessio* he describes his call to Ireland and even names the spiritual being who delivers the message!

> On another occasion a few years later, I was in Britain with my relatives who had welcomed me as if I were their son and earnestly begged me that I should never leave them, especially in view of all the hardships I had endured. It was there one night I saw the vision of a man called Victor, who appeared to have come from Ireland with an unlimited number of letters. He gave me one of them and I read the opening words which were: "The voice of the Irish." As I read the beginning of the letter I seemed at the same moment to hear the voice of those who were by the wood of Voclut which is near the Western Sea. They shouted with one voice: "We ask you boy, come and walk once more amongst us." I was cut to the very heart and could read no more, and so I woke up. Thank God, after many years the Lord answered their cry.[2]

Patrick returned to Ireland in AD 431 and began his work of evangelism. He was not the first Christian missionary to the island and there is evidence of earlier mission trips, but undoubtedly, Patrick was the most effective of these missionaries.

The Ireland Patrick returned to was steeped in pagan religion, often very violent with both human and animal sacrifices. The country was divided into *tuatha*, governed by local kings, who in turn showed an allegiance to a high king over the whole island. Legend and story tell how Patrick used this culture to spread the message of the gospel. At a local level he engaged with the king or tribal leaders. One story tells of Patrick praying over the dead children of a local chieftain and seeing them resurrected. Another of the more famous stories tells of Patrick confronting the high king and his pagan priests on the Hill of Tara, where the tribes had gathered for the annual celebration and sacrifice with fire.

Patrick was an evangelist who used local culture to spread the gospel with signs and wonders and, at the same time, confronted the pagan strongholds in the nation.

His *Confessio* describe the difficulties he encountered with his fellow clergy, those who originally commissioned him as a minister.

> I was put to the test by a number of my seniors who came to cast up my sins at me in order to discredit my hard work as bishop of this mission.[3]

During this time of trouble he describes a vision:

> I was confronted by the document that dishounoured me and simultaneously I heard God's voice saying to me "We have seen with disapproval the face of the chosen one deprived of his good name" He did not say "you have disapproved" but "we have disapproved" as if to include himself. As he says: He who touches you, touches the apple of my eye. Thanks be to God who supported me in everything.[4]

Patrick encountered opposition from both the pagan rulers in the nation and senior figures within his own sending church. In this context we return to the prayer originally crafted by St. Patrick and begin to understand how each phrase was honed in the face of extreme opposition to his mission to the Irish. In the prayer, we can hear an echo of Paul's exhortation in Ephesians 6 to put on the armor of God and stand.

The original prayer is found in the ninth-century *Book of Armagh* alongside Patrick's *Confessio*.[5]

The Prayer: Saint Patrick's Breastplate[6]

I bind unto myself today
The strong Name of the Trinity,
By invocation of the same
The Three in One and One in Three.

I bind this today to me forever
By power of faith, Christ's incarnation;
His baptism in Jordan river,
His death on Cross for my salvation;
His bursting from the spicèd tomb,
His riding up the heavenly way,
His coming at the day of doom
I bind unto myself today.
I bind unto myself the power
Of the great love of cherubim;
The sweet "Well done" in judgment hour,
The service of the seraphim,
Confessors' faith, Apostles' word,
The Patriarchs' prayers, the prophets' scrolls,
All good deeds done unto the Lord
And purity of virgin souls.
I bind unto myself today
The virtues of the star lit heaven,
The glorious sun's life giving ray,
The whiteness of the moon at even,
The flashing of the lightning free,
The whirling wind's tempestuous shocks,
The stable earth, the deep salt sea
Around the old eternal rocks.
I bind unto myself today
The power of God to hold and lead,
His eye to watch, His might to stay,
His ear to hearken to my need.
The wisdom of my God to teach,
His hand to guide, His shield to ward;
The word of God to give me speech,
His heavenly host to be my guard.
Against the demon snares of sin,
The vice that gives temptation force,
The natural lusts that war within,
The hostile men that mar my course;
Or few or many, far or nigh,

117

In every place and in all hours,
Against their fierce hostility
I bind to me these holy powers.
Against all Satan's spells and wiles,
Against false words of heresy,
Against the knowledge that defiles,
Against the heart's idolatry,
Against the wizard's evil craft,
Against the death wound and the burning,
The choking wave, the poisoned shaft,
Protect me, Christ, till Thy returning.
Christ be with me, Christ within me,
Christ behind me, Christ before me,
Christ beside me, Christ to win me,
Christ to comfort and restore me.
Christ beneath me, Christ above me,
Christ in quiet, Christ in danger,
Christ in hearts of all that love me,
Christ in mouth of friend and stranger.
I bind unto myself the Name,
The strong Name of the Trinity,
By invocation of the same,
The Three in One and One in Three.
By Whom all nature hath creation,
Eternal Father, Spirit, Word:
Praise to the Lord of my salvation,
Salvation is of Christ the Lord.

Notes:

1. Philip Freeman, *St. Patrick of Ireland* (Simon & Schuster, 2004), 63–64.

2. Saint Patrick, *Confessio*, http://www.cin.org/patrick.html.

3. Ibid.

4. Ibid.

5. Nigel Reid is Senior Pastor at Mountain View Community Church, Bray, County Wicklow, Ireland.

6. Cecil F. Alexander, 1889. http://nethymnal.org/htm/s/t/stpatric.htm.

Releasing God-Given
Spheres of Authority

PAUL L. COX

Now what? The left side of my back had started burning, and I didn't know if I was discerning something new or if I should go to the doctor. I often don't know, and the burning sensation on my back made me wonder. At times it was so painful that I was beginning to become concerned. It was unique, how the awareness of heat was like a straight line going down my back. Finally, at a ministry school, I said to the group that I needed to find out what was going on with my back. I stood in the middle of the room and asked what they saw spiritually. Confirmation came. I had a rod on the left side of my back.

What did that mean? I started checking to see if others also had a rod on their back. It was amazing! Yes, everyone had a rod. If a person was right handed, the rod was on the left side of their back. If a person was left handed, the rod would be on the right side. If the person was ambidextrous, the rod was in the middle of the back. We had begun another journey into the supernatural!

Frequently, the journey to a new prayer begins with a simple revelation of a physical sensation followed by marvelous insights into Scripture. The Lord had much to say to us about the rod. When Moses encountered the Lord in the burning bush, the Lord asked, "What is that in your hand?" Moses' response was, "A rod." Several Hebrew words can be translated as *rod*. In Exodus 4:2, the word *matteh* is translated as *rod* in the *New King James Version* but as *staff* in the *New International Version*. There is a distinction between a rod and a staff. The word *rod* literally means to stretch out, extend, spread out, pitch, turn, pervert, incline, bend, and bow.[1] As Moses stretched out the rod in his hand, miracles took place and battles were won.[2] Moses' rod in verse 2 becomes the "rod of God" in Exodus 4:20. In Exodus 17:8–16, as Moses holds up his rod, the Israelites are victorious against the followers of Amalek. Following the victory of Israel, "Moses built an altar and named it The LORD is My Banner" (NASB). The word for *banner* is *nes* and can be translated as a pole or a signal pole. Perhaps this is another use of the "rod." Here the "pole" is a symbol of deliverance and mighty salvation that caused God's people to be victorious over their enemies.[3] In Numbers 20:8, the *New American Standard Bible* joins the *New King James* in translating the word *matteh* into the English word *rod*.

This was all very interesting but unsatisfying. What more did we need to understand about the rod? Casually a student at the school shared that the Lord had recently given her a passage. She shared with us 2 Corinthians 10:8–18:

> *For even if I should boast somewhat more about our authority, which the Lord gave us for edification and not for your destruction, I shall not be ashamed— lest I seem to terrify you by letters. "For his letters," they say, "are weighty and powerful, but his bodily presence is weak, and his speech contemptible." Let such a person consider this, that what we are in word by letters when we are absent, such we will also be in deed when we are present. For we dare not class ourselves or compare ourselves with those who commend themselves. But they, measuring themselves by themselves, and comparing themselves among themselves, are not wise. We, however, will not boast beyond measure, but within the limits of the sphere which God appointed us—a sphere which especially includes you. For we are not overextending ourselves (as though our authority did not extend to you), for it was to you that we came with the gospel of Christ; not boasting of things beyond measure, that is, in other men's labors, but having hope, that as your faith is increased, we shall be greatly enlarged by you in our sphere, to preach the gospel in the regions beyond you, and not to boast in another man's sphere of accomplishment. But "he who glories, let him glory in the LORD." For not he who commends himself is approved, but whom the Lord commends.*

I was not sure how this passage was tied to the discussion about a rod, so I researched the Greek words in the original text. I was astonished with what I found. The English word *sphere* is a translation of the Greek word *kanon*, and it means a rod. It denotes a definitely limited or fixed space within the limits of which one's sphere of activity or one's power of influence is confined. Now I was beginning to understand!

We have a rod on our back. It is not just a symbol. It is real in the spiritual world. Somehow, we use this rod or authority in our warfare; we also use it when we are used by the Lord to do signs, wonders, and miracles. In the spiritual world, others can see the boundaries of our sphere of influence. I believe this sphere is a definitively marked spiritual area that is linked to the rod on our back.

There was more to learn. Several people in the group who have traveled to heaven had seen the elders holding rods. Often, they have seen elders vote by pounding their rods on the floor. I had wondered about this, so I felt the "spiritual" surface of the rod and found that I could discern an elder holding onto the rod. There are actually times when the rod seems to move from a person's back to his front. At all times, it seems that a spiritual elder holds onto the rod.

During this same ministry school, we began discussing the passage from 2 Corinthians 10. In this Scripture, the apostle Paul compares his authority, which has been established by God, to the outward pretense of those who are boastfully trying to establish their own authority. Paul is certain of his authority and his sphere of authority. He understands that others' authority may cross over into his sphere of authority, but he is not insecure about what he has been called to do.

After this discussion, it seemed clear to everyone in the school that we needed to repent, both for ourselves and those in our generational lines. We saw that we might have been guilty of moving out of our own spheres of authority into the spheres of others, or that we might not have exercised the authority God intended us to use within our own spheres of authority. The result of this revelation is the prayer: *Releasing God-Given Spheres of Authority.*

The Prayer: Releasing God-given Spheres of Authority

✠ I am a bondservant of Jesus Christ who will operate only in my God-given spheres of authority under the authority of Jesus Christ.

✠ I repent for not being obedient and for not yielding to and operating in the sphere of authority in which you, Lord, want me to operate.[4]

✠ I repent for limiting the sphere of authority in which you, Lord, want me to operate.

✠ I repent for being jealous of others' spheres of authority.

✠ I repent for being jealous and not partnering when spheres of authority overlap in the body of Christ.

✠ I repent for not helping and serving others to succeed in their ministries.

✠ I repent for not valuing others' spheres of authority.

✠ I repent for operating in self-proclaimed spheres of authority in which the Lord did not want me operate.

✠ I repent for not trusting you, Lord, to be the Head over other spheres of authority.

✠ I repent for not believing or trusting that you, Lord, can work through another person.

✠ I repent for not acknowledging that there is a level of revelation that can only come through unity.

✠ I repent for yielding to the fear of man and not operating in my sphere of authority.

✠ I repent for allowing others to exploit my sphere of authority, and I repent for exploiting others'.

✠ I repent for not recognizing and valuing the other parts of the body of Christ.

✠ I repent as a leader for any time I did not release people into their God-given spheres of authority.

✠ I repent for not waiting on God's timing to place me in my sphere of authority.

✠ I repent for speaking curses and death over other people's spheres of authority and making bitter root judgments against them.

✠ I repent for operating in suspicion and judgment rather than in the gift of discernment.

✠ I repent for not following the biblical guidelines for confrontation and correction in love while dealing with others within my sphere of authority.[5]

✠ I repent for not casting down every thought that exalts itself against you, Lord, and for exalting myself and my giftings above the knowledge of you, God.

✠ I repent for self-exaltation, esteeming myself over esteeming you, Lord.

✠ I repent for operating in pride and false humility instead of true humility.

✠ I repent for bumping out others and not embracing them.

✠ I repent for rejecting the new and unusual revelations of you, God.

Declarations – Proclamations[6]

✠ I declare that I will glorify your name by finishing the work you, Lord, gave me to do in my sphere of authority.[7]

✠ I declare that in my sphere of authority, I will have love, joy, peace, patience, kindness, humility, mercy, meekness, goodness, faithfulness, gentleness, and self- control.

✠ I declare that I will live a life worthy of the calling I have received.[8] I declare that I will always be humble and gentle.

✠ I declare that I will be patient, making allowances for my own and others' faults.

✠ I declare that I will operate in the grace of God and his power and not in my own strength and understanding.

✠ I declare that I will be united with others in the Holy Spirit and bound together with others in peace.

✠ I declare the truth that Jesus Christ has blessed me with every spiritual blessing in the heavenly places in Christ.[9]

✠ I declare the work Christ has begun in me will be completed.[10]

✠ I declare that I will be like-minded with Christ.[11]

✠ I declare that I will intentionally guard against division.

✠ I declare that I will be united in purpose, and stand in one spirit and one mind with my brothers and sisters in the Lord.[12]

✠ I declare to the heavens that as far as it is up to me, I will walk in peace and unity with all men.

✠ I declare that I embrace the spirit of wisdom and revelation in the knowledge of him so that the eyes of my understanding may be enlightened, that I may know the hope of his calling and what are the riches of the glory of his inheritance in the saints.[13]

✠ I declare that I will not reject the unusual and the new revelation of God.

✠ I declare that I will embrace others and not try to bump them out.

✠ I declare that I will yield my will to the will of God.[14]

✠ I declare that I desire to have open heavens and visions of God.[15]

✠ I declare that I will walk in the spirit and not in the flesh.[16]

Notes:

1. James Strong, *Enhanced Strong's Lexicon 2.0* (Woodside Bible Fellowship, 1995).

2. Exodus 14:16.

3. Bruce K. Waltke, Robert Laird Harris, and Gleason Leonard Archer, *Theological Wordbook of the Old Testament,* electronic edition (Chicago: Moody Press, 1999).

4. 2 Corinthians 10:13.

5. Matthew 13.

6. Galatians 5:22; 2 Corinthians 10:12–18.

7. John 17:4.

8. Ephesians 4:1–3.

9. Ephesians 1:3.

10. Philippians 1:6.

11. Philippians 2:2–3.

12. 1 Corinthians 1:10; Philippians 1:27.

13. Ephesians 1:17–18.

14. Luke 22:42.

15. Ezekiel 1:1.

16. Galatians 5:16, 25.

Prayer for Chronic
Physical, Mental, and Spiritual Disorders

PAUL L. COX

The ministry school had started like any other. I was in Sugar Hill, Georgia, with over fifty people who had assembled to see what the Lord would do. The group included two medical doctors and several others who were familiar with medical issues. We had no idea what the Lord was about to do!

One lady had asked for prayer for a personal complex set of medical issues including sugar diabetes, breathing problems, and fibromyalgia. I remembered that I had previously discerned a spiritual spider on a person with sugar diabetes. I approached the woman and placed my hand over the top portion of her pancreas. As I suspected, I could feel a spiritual spider with its fangs inserted into the tissue. We agreed to pray against the spider. Others began to raise their hands for prayer and we found ourselves ministering to one another for healing. The journey had begun!

Almost immediately, the students then started bombarding me with questions: Why is a spider in that particular place in the body? Why does the spider have fangs? What does this have to do with diabetes? The Lord had given me the answer to these questions several years ago. The key text is Isaiah 59:4–5:

No one calls for justice, nor does any plead for truth. They trust in empty words and speak lies; they conceive evil and bring forth iniquity. They hatch vipers' eggs and weave the spider's web; he who eats of their eggs dies, and from that which is crushed a viper breaks out.

After reviewing these verses, the group came to the consensus that keys are implanted in Isaiah 59 for aspects of physical, emotional, and spiritual healing. The framework for a new prayer had begun. It would take several hours of receiving and testing additional revelation and coming into unity before it was finished.

Isaiah 59 has to do with the negative words of our mouths. The writer begins by declaring that the Lord has the ability to save and to hear our prayers. The problem is that we, as his people, do not know how to control our mouths. These sins are generational. The Hebrew word *iniquity* in Isaiah 59:2-4[1] is rendered as *twisted*, and it indicates a twisting in the generational line. The Hebrew clearly indicates that *iniquity* is not merely a current difficulty, it refers to something that has happened repeatedly in the past. "Your lips have spoken lies; your tongue has muttered perversity."[2] The issue is a lying tongue. The Hebrew word *perversity* is best translated as lie, deception, falsehood, and deceit.[3] These muttered *perversities* or negative evaluations of others have no basis in fact. The words have no support from truth.[4] There is also a passive agreement in one's failure to call for justice and to plead for the truth.[5] These verbal acts are so violent that the spoken assaults "shed" innocent blood.[6] Individuals are literally destroyed by these false statements.

The sins of an individual appear to combine together with the sins of others and empower the deterioration of society. Injustice and falsehood collaborate in a downward spiral that works itself out in further injustice and unrighteousness.[7]

What are the results? A hybrid spiritual spider is released. This spider hatches viper[8] eggs. The snakes that are released from these eggs lead to death—premature death. Evil words released from a person's mouth have a cascading effect that leads not only to the destruction of their own lives but also to destroying the lives of others. Before death, physical, mental,[9] and spiritual consequences can unravel a healthy life into one of disorder, pain, and suffering. The roots of all of this can be generational. This evil permeates society. Deception is provoked to such an extent that those who are convicted of their sin and want to turn toward righteousness, become victims to the verbal attacks of others.[10]

It is not necessary to simply base our biblical conclusions about the consequences of oral falsehood on the Old Testament. The New Testament also speaks of the dangers of not controlling our tongues. James 3:5–18 indicates that the dire result of an uncontrolled tongue is a defiled[11] body.[12] James then says an amazing thing! "The tongue is an unruly[13] evil, full of deadly poison." Since the tongue is full of poison (from the Latin word *potion* or *drink*), its words necessarily have an effect upon the physical body: an evil tongue is a poison to the body. When I examined the word *poison* in the Greek, I was stunned. The word literally means venom as "venom of an asp." The tie to Isaiah 59 is complete. The evil words of our mouths are not an innocent release of sounds. Literally, we damage ourselves and others by our words. Instead of enjoying and savoring the delicacies of "hateful" words, we will suffer from disease, mental illness, spiritual disorder, and finally death. Lying words that hide bitter jealousy and selfish ambition can open us up to "every evil thing."[14]

In 2008, I was invited to do prayer ministry and training at a Roman Catholic church in Ottawa, Canada. This was the first time I had ministered in a Catholic environment, and I was wondering how I would adjust to the theological differences. Before I went, I kept hearing, "What are you for, not what are you against?" I pondered these words, but it was not until I arrived in Ottawa that I realized their significance. While attending a Sunday night introductory dinner, the Lord clearly spoke to me. *This priest is your brother.* I realized that I must focus on what we were "for." Mutually, we wanted to see the Lord bring freedom and healing to his church.

The Lord wants unity in his church. I fully understand that unity does not mean "compromise" but working together for the sake of the Kingdom of God. This also means that we do not talk "against" each other. Our words have power, and we must be careful not to give the enemy any ground. Such ground surrendered to the enemy entitles the enemy to cause physical, mental, and spiritual destruction. Gossip, envy,[15] and jealousy have no place in the body of Christ! Malicious and discontented words corrupt unity and lead to a fragmented church. Psalm 133 is clear. When brothers dwell together in unity, the anointing flows! This anointing is like the "dew of [Mount] Hermon."[16] While in Jerusalem I experienced this dew. Early in the morning, as we were leaving for the airport in Tel Aviv, I saw water running down the streets. Inquiring of our tour guide, I found out that this was the dew that falls nightly on the City of God. What a thought! When we dwell in unity, the anointing of the Lord falls in such abundance that it flows like streams. It is like water flowing on the streets of Mt. Zion!

I have a couple of favorite statements. One is, "Nothing is as simple as it seems," and the other is, "Nothing is everything." These phrases have an important meaning to me. I am very cautious not to convey the idea that if one prays a certain prayer then some type of healing will automatically take place. Life is far too complex for this naïve concept. However, I want to be equally cautious to never limit God, to never exclude the possibility of healing, or to ever suggest in any way that some type of healing will not occur. I praise God that throughout the years, we have seen the Lord heal many times. This is what happened in Sugar Hill, Georgia.

After working on the prayer for many agonizing hours, we prayed it together as a group. The woman who had initiated the whole process by asking for prayer for sugar diabetes reported later that her sugar levels had significantly improved, her breathing was easier, and she was in less pain. Another also rejoiced in improvement with diabetes. Since then, we have had many wonderful testimonies from those God has healed through this prayer, but others have seen no improvement—"Nothing is as simple as it seems."

So what are we doing in this prayer? First, we want to take ground from the enemy by asking God to remove iniquity. We ask him specifically to remove the iniquity in our family line, that has been empowered by the evils associated with our tongues. Second, we want to be repositioned, on ground that gives no right to the enemy to plunder us—by doing this we will no longer be a prey of the enemy. Third, we want to declare our commitment to keep the ground taken: we will no longer be a prey of the enemy. Personally, I am tired of being plundered. How do we stop the robbery? We must, through the Lord's direction, do all we can to move ourselves into a position of being invulnerable to the enemy's attack. This is where Abraham found himself in Genesis 15. After Abraham saw the Lord passing through the cut sacrifices, the "vultures" came, but Abraham drove them away. Why was he able to defeat them? I believe it was because the enemy found no ground for an attack. This is what I want. I want to be in such a position that the enemy has no ground for an attack. Finally, to keep the new and higher ground, we declare that we will now constantly guard our tongues and not speak against others.

In this prayer, I renounce and repent for the iniquity that entered my past generations through our spoken words and for my personal sins of agreement with it. I ask that the generational blessings in my line come

129

down to me because there is now no ground for the enemy to withhold them. I receive the truth that the enemy's attack (vultures) can be driven away.

The Prayer: Release from Chronic Physical, Mental, and Spiritual Disorders

Lord, for myself and my generational line, I repent and renounce coming into agreement with gossip, slander, critical judgment, envy, strife, holding offenses, accusation, and jealousy.

Lord, I ask you to forgive me and my generational line for all agreement with gossip, slander, critical judgment, envy, strife, holding offenses, accusation, and jealousy.

Lord, I repent for myself and those in my generational line who came against you by lying, denying you, speaking accusations against you, conceiving and uttering falsehoods from the heart, speaking oppression and revolt, and entering into witchcraft.

Lord, I ask you to break the generational curse and agreement when accusations came into the generational line. Lord, I break and renounce assignments and agreements with any lying spirit and the generational curse resulting from that. I ask your forgiveness Lord, and I repent on behalf of myself and my forefathers. I ask you to break the generational curse and loose a blessing. I choose to bring my spirit, soul, and body into agreement with the Spirit of Truth.

Lord, please make null and void and cancel any reinforcement of curses and their assignments in their allotted times. Lord, please disconnect me from all ungodly heavenly places. Lord, please now seat me in your heavenly places.

Lord, I repent and ask forgiveness for operating in an independent spirit when I came into agreement with gossip, slander, and accusation and walked away from you and the body of Christ, causing disunity and isolation in the body of Christ. Today, I choose by your mercy to be reconciled and to be restored into the unity of your body.

✠ Lord, I repent for coming into agreement with slander that has been spoken against me and for receiving the offenses and not blessing my enemy.

✠ Lord, I ask that I not conceive trouble. Please destroy the viper and spider eggs that have been placed into me: slander, hatred, self-rejection, and gossip. May no adders or spiders be allowed to come forth from this generation forward.

✠ Lord, please remove all cobwebs of false clothing and nesting places that may be covering my body. Lord, please also remove the cobwebs of false identity from my body and soul and remove all deception that clouds my perception of my true identity. And where my past generations and I have allowed the enemy to weave within me a web of false identity, coming into agreement with this illness as who I am, forgive me for gaining my identity from diseases and not from you. Release me, for you wove me in my mother's womb, and I agree that I am fearfully and wonderfully made. Lord, give me your revelation of my true identity in Christ, which I now receive.

✠ Lord, please completely restore my ability to receive all that I need from you including healing, revelation, and restoration of my spirit, soul, and body.

✠ Lord, I forgive the body of Christ for reacting in judgment and rejection against those who are being wounded by witchcraft and curses that are being empowered and reinforced over time. Lord, forgive me for making bitter root judgments against those who have harmed me in any way. I forgive the body of Christ for not accepting, understanding, and protecting me.

✠ Lord, I choose to forgive those who have rejected me and who in doing so have further empowered the curses already against me.

✠ Lord, forgive me and my generational line for not having the strength to resist the enemy's assault on my mind day and night and therefore accepting the feeling of helplessness in stopping this demonic flow. Lord, please renew my mind so that I can have your mind and know that I can take every thought captive to the Lord Jesus Christ. I know that you are my sure defense and that I am safe in the shelter of your wings.

✠ Lord, I ask you to raise up a standard based upon Ephesians 4:31 and remove all effects of bitterness, rage, anger, brawling, and slander along with every form of malice. Lord, break off all generational curses, the reinforcement of curses in their allotted times in all heavenly places, and all spiritual, mental, and physical retribution. Lord, please protect those who repent and turn from their generational sin, witchcraft, and idolatry.

✠ Lord, please realign me with your purpose and heal the receptors of the cells that make up my being so my divine calling and birthright will be fulfilled.

✠ I receive the promise that I am no longer a prey of the enemy. You are my Good Shepherd. You feed me, and I receive your covenant of peace that I may dwell safely. I choose to be a blessing around your holy hill and receive the showers of blessings you promise in season that there would be fruitfulness and increase in my life. I know that the bands of the yoke are broken, and I am delivered from the hands and words of those who have made me a prey. I know that I belong to you, and you are with me. I embrace my restoration within the body of Christ and the restoration of receptor sites of my own body.

✠ Lord, thank you for considering my cause and my affliction and delivering me and my generations—past, present, and future, for I do not forget your law.

✠ Lord, thank you for pleading my cause through the generations and reviving me and my family line according to your Word. Because I trust you, Lord, I am like Mt. Zion which cannot be moved but abides forever. So I thank you, Lord, for delivering me and my family generations—past, present, and future. Thank you for redeeming me and reviving me and my family line throughout the generations according to your Word. For as the mountains surround Jerusalem, so you, Lord, surround me and my family generations— past, present, and future from this time forth and forever.

✠ Thank you Lord that the scepter of wickedness shall not rest on the land allotted to the righteous because the entirety of your Word is truth, and every one of your righteous judgments endures forever. Lord, thank you for restoring the scepter of righteousness.

✠ Lord, please forgive me and my generational line for closing the doors of your anointing and blessing. Lord, please now bless me and open the doors of your anointing and blessing and release the generational blessings, gifts, callings, and goodness that my generational line did not receive.

Notes:

1. *avah*/aw·vaw/.

2. Isaiah 59:3.

3. *sheqer.*

4. Bruce K. Waltke, Robert Laird Harris, Gleason Leonard Archer, *Theological Wordbook of the Old Testament*, electronic edition (Chicago: Moody Press, 1999), 2461a.

5. Isaiah 59:4.

6. Isaiah 59:7.

7. Isaiah 59:12–14.

8. *Enhanced Strongs Lexicon* – adder: *tsepha`* /tseh·fah or tsiphnaloniy tsif·o·**nee**. poisonous serpent. A viper, snake, or adder.

9. Isaiah 59:8–10: There is no peace thus indicating mental anguish. "We are like dead men" also denotes mental and physical anguish.

10. Isaiah 59:15. Prey here has the idea of being plundered.

11. *Merriam-Webster's 11th Collegiate Dictionary*: Defile—to corrupt the purity or perfection of.

12. James 3:6.

13. κατάστατος *(akatastatos)* not controlled, unstable, inconstant.

14. James 3:14–16.

15. Envy actually means that I want to take what others have and make it my own.

16. Psalm 133:3.

Prayer to Release
Financial Freedom

PAUL L. COX

At the Advanced Discernment Training and Exploration School near Perth Australia in June 2006, Linda Cessano had a vision of a man holding a stack of money. In the dream Linda asked me to discern the lines coming from the money. I could feel lines connecting the money to the person's heart and mind. I also felt lines coming off of the money and connecting to banks, institutions, other people, and Freemasonry groups. Linda then asked the Lord to what the money should be connected. His response was very clear. All money is to be connected to him, the Lord of Creation.

The context of formulating this prayer was personally interesting! My great–grandmother once lived in Perth; her parents had been sent to Australia from England as Gypsy Jewish criminals. They were one family among some one hundred sixty–two thousand men and women sent to Australia between 1787 and 1868. More than likely they were in debt and were banished as debtors. The times then were very difficult in Australia. The country was filled with poverty and hopelessness. The prison population was typically slaves who were ruled over by prison guards, who were also poor. The soil in Perth is very sandy and does not lend itself to food production. The supply of food was so dreadful that some women prostituted themselves for food. Malnutrition was so prevalent that the average size of men was shorter there than in their English homeland.[1] It was in Perth that the Lord spoke to us about leading us into financial freedom. Redemption of the land of Australia, my family line, and the generational lines of others was at hand.

The discovery phase of a prayer is sometimes very tedious. After the initial word, vision, or dream, the discussions begin. As believers work together as one to hear the Spirit of God and to follow his leading, it's the unity of those in the school that brings forth the prayer. The whole process can take over a week, and the final construction of the prayer itself may take up to eight hours. Several times during the process, the Lord sends angels or other spiritual beings with messages to guide us in the process. Two messages were received by intercessors during that week. Dale Shannon had this word:

[Dale sees us all in a heavenly place with the twenty–four elders.]

All I have given to you belongs to me. Release your treasures. I see him cutting connections from our hearts to our treasures. There will be a release of treasures to you when you release the treasures to me. Destroy the connections and the lines to the treasures. Then, there'll be a rain of treasures coming down from heaven to you. That is why you have not received all your promises and your blessings, because your heart is connected to the treasures. So, cut the lines off your heart and mind to release the treasures that are yours in heaven. It is deeper than you thought. It is deeper than you thought. So, search your hearts and minds for your treasures and release your treasures to the Lord. Do not hold on to anything. Everything belongs to the Lord.

[Dale saw a canopy holding back blessings and gifts. They are restrained in the second heaven and God will release them. There will be a transference of wealth.]

Mimi Lowe received this word:

Harlotry! Harlotry! Prostitution of the heart! What have you sold your heart to? Sever the ungodly connections between your heart and what you value the most. What do you value the most? Money? Possessions? Position? These are all idolatries of the heart. Disconnect the money from Freemasonry, secret societies, secret agendas, covert operations, ungodly funding of churches, ungodly funding of institutions, building altars with money, and funding of prostitutes. Repent for not feeding the poor and not taking care of the widow and the orphan. Do not see money with physical eyes, but see with spiritual eyes. Money is God's resource, not yours. It is not dollars and cents. All money belongs to God; it comes from God and it goes back to God. Release it! Release it! Release it! And God will release it to you. But you must release it first, then God will release it to you. Where is your heart? Where is your heart?

It has been my experience that the Lord speaks in many different ways. Often what seem to be irrelevant dreams line up with angelic messages and experiences to form a warp on which the tapestry of a prayer can be woven. After the school on the way back home to Southern California, Dale Shannon had this dream that reinforced what had been written in Perth.

I had a dream early in the morning on the seventeenth when you were flying home. It's strange, but I think I should share it. I was observing a situation. A man (short, weak looking, with blond hair) had two daughters and wasn't treating them very well. They were probably in their twenties, and he was using them to earn money. They were living in a small cabin and would do what he told them. They were to sell their long beautiful brunette hair and their little cabin to an evil–looking couple. I was sad and angry that no one would protect and provide for these girls, and they had to sell their hair.

In the next scene, I was telling you, Paul, that there was significance to your returning [to the States] on Father's Day, knowing you are a spiritual father to many. You replied, "There's something to that." My spirit was very stirred about fatherlessness on Father's Day, and I was crying out to God in the dream about it.

The girls could represent ministries that are selling their wisdom and glory for money or financial gain. I was upset about the fatherlessness of so many and the problems it's brought to us.

Linda's original vision indicated that a key problem with finances could be financial ties with Freemasonry. I shared with the group that several years ago a relative approached me about financial issues. As I prayed with her, it became clear that she had Freemasonry in her background (her father is a thirty–third–degree mason). In praying for people with financial difficulties and family ties to Freemasonry I've observed a pattern. It seems that as long as the family line was tied to Freemasonry, the enemy could make sure that finances were not a problem. However, when a family member decided to live a dedicated Christian life, their finances came under a curse. That curse was passed down the family line.

The possibility that a family's finances might be cursed because of an event tied to Freemasonry became part of the discussion about financial freedom. (Of course, a multitude of other factors are also coupled with Freemasonry that might affect finances. It is essential to allow the Holy Spirit to guide each person and family in their own search to find out all the information needed to gain total freedom in the arena of finances.)

By the last hours of the school, we were finally ready to write the prayer. As we shared again the original vision by Linda Cessano and reviewed the many other words we had received, the Lord began moving in our midst. He brought to our remembrance Scripture after Scripture that spoke of the relationship we are to have with money. The Lord then led us to construct a prayer of renunciation for the way, we and our generational lines have thought of and handled money. This prayer has been sent around the world and many have reported breakthroughs in their finances after praying it. It is our prayer that the Lord will use this prayer to reestablish a godly connection between you and your past, current, and potential finances.

Following this prayer is a previously written prayer on breaking the curse of poverty in the family line.

The Prayer: Release Us Into Financial Freedom

⛭ I repent that I have not treated and valued the Kingdom of Heaven as I should and that I have exchanged the value of the Kingdom of Heaven for the desires of my heart in the form of an earthly kingdom. Lord, I repent for worrying about life, food, and clothing. I repent for laying up treasures on earth where moths and rust destroy and where thieves break in and steal.[2] I repent for robbing you, Lord, and not freely and cheerfully giving my offerings to you out of a heart of love.

⛭ Lord I repent for loving money, for serving mammon,[3] for greed, and for covetousness.

⛭ I repent of the belief that money is the answer to everything in my life. I repent of expecting money to be my answer and my friend. I repent for forsaking you as my life source and for focusing my eyes on the pursuit of wealth to my own harm and the harm of others. I repent for choosing to serve mammon in preference to you and thereby filling my life with darkness. On behalf of my ancestors and myself, I renounce every agreement made with mammon by using money in ungodly ways and for ungodly purposes. I repent for being double-minded with money and unstable in all of my ways. I choose to hate mammon and to love you, Lord, with my whole heart. I choose to place my treasure where my heart is, in the Kingdom of Heaven, for you to use as you choose.

⌗ I repent for making money my defender, security, and protection.

⌗ I repent for believing that chants, spells, fate, superstition, and luck will provide the money I need.

⌗ I repent for myself and my family line for using diverse weights and measures and not paying employees their due.

⌗ I repent for making money, not you, Lord, the center of the universe.

⌗ I repent for pride, gaining wealth by dishonest means, and vain striving for silver and gold. I repent for myself and my family line for not exercising my responsibility to pay money that was owed to governmental agencies. I repent for defrauding, cheating, lying, and stealing from the government. I also repent for a begrudging and bitter attitude in paying my taxes. I repent for not recognizing your anointing on government to provide for the basic necessities of our corporate life. I repent for criticizing, complaining, and cursing my government for not providing enough for the people.

⌗ I repent for myself and my generational line for seeking, accepting, treasuring, profiting from, and spending blood money. I also repent for adding blood money to my children's inheritance. On behalf of my ancestors, I choose to forgive those financial institutions that have foreclosed on mortgages and stolen property which rightfully belonged to me and my descendants as an inheritance.

✠ I repent across my generational line for abandoning and sacrificing family and relationships, land, culture, and even faith in God to seek gold and earthly treasures. I choose to seek after the ultimate treasure of my Lord Jesus Christ with all my heart.

✠ I repent on behalf of myself and my ancestors for believing in a poverty mind-set and for being stingy with the body of Christ. I declare that Jesus came to give us abundant life. Father, in your mercy, please free me and my future generations of the consequences of this. I repent and confess the lie that godliness implies poverty, lacking in basic necessities, living in poverty, always being in need, and that the children will never procure their education. I choose to believe and accept that God will supply all of my needs, that there will be an inheritance for a thousand generations, that my descendants will not have to beg for food, and that all my needs will be met.

✠ I repent for being disconnected from the River of Life of God's endless supply. I choose to be connected to the River of Life where God will grant me the ability to acquire wealth for his Kingdom. I repent for spending money on that which does not satisfy and for not coming to God's living waters to drink.

✠ I repent for myself and my generational line for hardening my heart and shutting my hand against my poorer brothers in their need. I repent for not feeding the poor or taking care of the widows and orphans. I repent of holding back my possessions and services to get higher prices from those in need. I declare that I will open my hand and heart to the poor, sharing my resources as you lead, so no one will lack, your power will not be hindered, and your grace will remain. I repent for not bringing unity in the body of Christ. I choose to not hold back from the needy. Jesus, would you break the curses and evil that have come against me and my generational line for demanding unfair prices from the needy? Lord, please release your blessings and grace on my selling and trading, especially to those in need.

✠ I repent for myself and my family line for not receiving the inheritance that you had for us and I choose now to receive the inheritance, abundance, and gifts that you have for us. I ask that they will come in such abundance that we will be able to leave an inheritance for our children and grandchildren.

✠ Lord, I ask you to disconnect my ancestors, me, and my descendants from money that was tied to Freemasonry, secret societies, secret agendas, covert operations, ungodly funding of churches and institutions, and for money tied to the building of ungodly altars and funding prostitutes.

✠ Lord, break off the curse of sowing much and bringing in little, of eating and not having enough, and of earning wages only to put them into a bag with holes.

✠ Lord, I ask you to destroy the connectors and cleanse the ley lines attached to earthly treasures.

✠ Lord, connect me to you alone. I choose not to hold on to anything but you. I give everything I have to you.

✠ I repent for myself and my family line for the belief that the gifts of the Holy Spirit could be purchased or sold. I break the curse that the money in my generational line and in my life will perish with me. I repent for my wickedness and my generational wickedness and ask that my heart will be restored into a right relationship with you.

✠ Lord, I repent for making my giving an obligation to you and not a free act of my love. Lord remove the canopy of law and the canopy and yoke of obligation from me. Lord, allow me to live in your grace and your provision.

✠ I ask you, Holy Spirit, to be the One who directs me in what to give. Lord, make my giving come from an attitude of gratitude and love. I choose to seek and follow your guidance in my giving.

✠ Lord, I repent for not trusting you and not trusting you to provide.

✠ On behalf of my ancestors and myself and for future generations, I choose to forgive those who have swindled me, especially banks, financial institutions, and government agencies; I forgive those who have charged me and my ancestors usurious interest, and who have tried to keep us in poverty and have disinherited our children.

✠ I declare that I will be content in you and in my wages in whatever financial state I am in.

✠ Lord, thank you for giving me the creativity to produce wealth in seed. Holy Spirit, teach me what to sow, what to reap, and what to harvest for your purpose.

✠ I declare that I will eat of the bread of life and delight in your abundance.

✠ I declare that I am one of many members of the body of Christ in whom are all the hidden treasures of wisdom and knowledge.

✠ Lord, please release into me the blessing and joy of giving freely in accordance with your will for my life.

✠ Lord, help me to see money with spiritual eyes, knowing it is your resource and belongs to you. Lord, please release the treasures that the enemy has stolen from me and my family line.

✠ I declare what your Word says: You will go before us and make the crooked places straight; I will break in pieces the gates of bronze and cut the bars of iron. You will give us the treasures of darkness and hidden riches of secret places. You are the One who gives power to get wealth that you may establish your covenant which you swore to our fathers, as it is this day. The blessing of the Lord makes one rich, and you add no sorrow with it. The generous soul will be made rich, and he who waters will also be watered himself. Thank you for enabling me to leave an inheritance to my children's children.

✠ Lord, please give me a circumcised heart, so you can release your treasure from heaven.[4]

Prayer to Break the Curse of Poverty

✠ Father, I come in the name of Jesus to repent for the sins and transgressions of my ancestors. I repent for all disobedience to your commands caused by turning away and listening to the enemy or to other people. Father, I receive the redemption from the curse by the blood of Jesus and ask you to break off all curses of poverty upon my family line and upon me. I declare that the blood of Jesus has broken every curse.

✠ Lord, I repent for anyone in my family line who offered sacrifices that were not favorable and right. I repent for any withholding of the first fruits and the best portions; I repent for all wrong motives and attitudes of heart. I repent for anger, resentment, and bloodshed of my brother. Lord, please forgive any bloodshed and bring peace to the blood that cries out.

✠ Lord, please break all Canaanite curses against me, as today I declare I am my brother's keeper! Lord, please restore the ground to me and please restore your promise of blessings and fruitfulness. Lord, please remove any marks on me and break the curse of wandering. Father, please allow my family to come into your presence again as a chosen covenant people.

✠ I repent for all my ancestors who denied justice to the poor, for all who held on to ill will, and for all who withheld forgiveness to a brother. I repent for shutting my ears to the poor, for exploitation of the poor, and for crushing them in court. I repent for all who did not forgive but held grudges and became bitter against those who unjustly exploited them or crushed them.

✠ Lord, please break all curses others have spoken against my ancestors or me because of the guilt of our sins and transgressions. Lord, please remove any curses that have put up walls of separation between you and me. Hear my prayers again and please open my eyes, ears, and heart.

✠ I repent for any generational dishonesty, even the smallest hidden, accepted, or self-justified dishonesty.

� I repent for any of my ancestors who would not forgive debts in the Lord's timing and who ignored the poor. I repent for all hard–heartedness, tightfistedness, and unforgiveness. Lord, please restore mercy and cheerful giving in my family line. Please bless me as you promised in your Word.

✚ Lord, I repent for generational idolatry, for disobedience, and for not following your commands. I repent for not serving you joyfully and gladly in my time of prosperity.

✚ Lord, please break all curses against us that send locusts and worms; Lord, please break all skies of bronze and ground of iron. Please release any captive sons or daughters and stop the destruction. Lord, please remove all iron yokes, all blindness, oppression, and spirits of robbery. Lord, please break the curses of hunger, nakedness, dire poverty, and slavery.

✚ Lord, I repent for any of my ancestors who were unfaithful, greedy, disobedient, thieves, or liars. I repent for breaking the covenant and covet–ing or keeping the things of the pagans and not totally destroying them as commanded.

✚ Lord, please break any curses that have come on my family for the evil they did, especially the curse of destruction by fire.

✚ I repent for all ancestors who were evil and tried to control and frustrate the poor. Lord, I repent for any in my family line who put up security or pledges for another. Lord, please forgive any unfulfilled debts. I break all ungodly covenants, oaths, and alliances. Lord, please remove all traps or snares from the words of my mouth. Please break all sluggish and slumbering spirits from me and restore wisdom and ambition.

✚ I repent for all my ancestors who unduly withheld from others and for all who trusted in riches rather than in God. I repent for all who ignored discipline and correction. I repent for all greed, bribes, and for idle talk and boasting. I repent for inaction, nonperformance, and not keeping my word.

Lord, please break all curses of injustice and shunning and please break any walls between me and others and between me and you. Please restore honor to our family.

Lord, I repent for myself and for all my ancestors for being liars, hasty, proud, arrogant, selfish, and lovers of the world and its pleasures. I repent for our lack of diligence, oppression of the needy, exploitation, and favoritism. I repent for all rejection of God and any cursing or blasphemy of God.

Lord, I repent for all my family's sluggishness, laziness, neglect, and lack of judgment; I repent for anyone in my family who charged exorbitant interest. I repent for any and all family concealed sins. I repent for spiritual pride in those who would not repent.

I repent for any ancestors who chased fantasies because they were stingy and greedy. I repent for all who did not fight injustice, were unfair, and closed their ears to the cries of the poor and needy.

Lord, please break all poverty curses off of me and change my heart.

Lord, I repent for myself and anyone in my family who followed deceptive words and relied on social or religious identity for salvation. I repent for injustice, for oppressing the aliens, the widows, and the fatherless. I repent for any idolatry, for all ungodly sacrifices and worship, all innocent bloodshed, and for stealing, adultery, perjury, and murder for myself and my family line. I repent for all our backsliding, rebellion, disobedience, pride, and spiritual pride. Lord, please break all connections and control that the queen of heaven has on my family and please restore in me wholeheartedness. Please make my heart pure, noble, faithful, and sensitive to you.

Lord, I repent for all generational idolatry and ask you to remove any spirit of prostitution in my heart. I repent for all corruption, guilt, sin, arrogance, and unfaithfulness. Lord, I repent for all illegitimacy in my line.

Lord, please set me free from the spiritual enemies of righteous finances: moths, rot, lions, sickness, and sores. Please restore your covenant as promised.

Lord, I repent for all my ancestors who were boastful and proud of their position, standing, and authority. I renounce all love of sin or iniquity. I repent for myself and for all in my family line who became comfortable, selfish hoarders and trusted in their wealth. I repent for all who sold their righteousness, for all who enslaved others, and for all who trampled the poor. I repent for all who were stingy and controlling of wealth.

Lord, please remove any curse that keeps me from enjoying the fruit of my labor. Please break off from me any poverty curses that have been passed on through my generational line, from Adam to me. Lord, please break off from me all curses "that there will never be enough." Lord, please restore to me a new purse without any holes. Please break off from me all curses of lack, shrinking, theft, loss, blight, mildew, and hail.

Lord, I repent for myself and for all those in my family line for being controlling and deceptive, and for putting ungodly burdens on others. I repent for trying to please man rather than God and for accepting praise, honor, worship, or ungodly authority and titles from men. I renounce all religious spirits, legalistic spirits, self-exaltation, and hypocrisy. I repent for myself and my generational line for not entering the door to heaven and for shutting it on others. I repent for being a blind guide, and I ask you, Lord, to break all ungodly oaths, covenants, pledges, dedications, and alliances. I repent for all ungodly and insincere sacrifices or for any sacrifice on an unholy altar. I repent for being unjust, merciless, unfaithful, greedy, and self-indulgent. I repent for harboring sin or wickedness. I repent for myself and my family line for rejecting, mocking, cursing, or killing the prophets and the messengers from God. I renounce any spiritual pride that rebels against repentance, and I apply the blood of Jesus to all the roots of iniquity. I repent for all my ancestors who would not believe or declare that Jesus was Lord.

Lord, please give me the mind of Christ in the matters of finance.

�҉ I repent for myself and my ancestors who committed adultery with the queen of Babylon and enjoyed or benefited from her luxuries. Lord, please break all ungodly ties and connections with the queen of Babylon. I repent for myself and for those my family line who did not come out of the queen of Babylon. Lord, please remove all consequences and plagues that were a result of any alliances with the queen of Babylon. Please remove all plagues of death, mourning, famine, and judgment fire.

�҉ Lord, please guide me by your Spirit and your Word in the godly use of wealth, and teach me to be a faithful servant.[5]

Notes:

1. For more information about the history of Australia read *The Fatal Shore: The Epic of Australia's Founding* by Robert Hughes. (New York: Random House, 1986).

2. Matthew 6:19-34.

3. Material wealth or possessions especially as having a debasing influence. Matthew 6:24: "You cannot serve God and mammon."

4. Genesis 8:22; Deuteronomy 8:18, 10:16, 15:7-8; Psalm 62:6; Proverbs 10:22, 11:25-26, 13:10-11, 13:22,8,11, 20:13; Ecclesiastes 5:10, 7:12, 10:19; Isaiah 45:1-3, 55:1-2; Haggai 1:5-6; Matthew 6:21, 13:44-66, 13:19-24, 22:19-22, 27:6; Luke 3:14, 12:22-23; Acts 4:32-35, 8:18-24; 1 Corinthians 12:12; 2 Corinthians 8-9; 1 Timothy 3:2-3, 6:10; Hebrews 13:5; Revelation 3:17-18.

5. Genesis 3:1-7, Genesis 12; Deuteronomy 2:13, Deuteronomy 28; 1 Samuel 15:22-25; Proverbs 3:5-6; Isaiah 11:1-2, 14:13-14; Luke 11:52; John 17:21; 1 Corinthians 10:23; Colossians 1:9, Colossians 2; James 3:1-12; 1 John 5:20.

CHAPTER TWENTY-ONE

Prayer to Establish Us as Living Stones

PAUL L. COX

Over the years I have learned that the discernment of revelation is progressive. Often, new revelation begins by simply feeling something I do not understand. As others feel the same thing, as words are received, and new understanding is gained, a foundation is established for additional discernment. Then, over the course of several months or years, God builds on that revelation. Such is the revelation about the "living stones."

It began in the dining room at Aslan's Place several years ago when I noticed that it was extremely cold. I went into other rooms and noticed that they were not as cold. An intercessor in the dining room also noticed the unusual cold. I decided to call my son, Brian and ask what he saw. He saw nothing, but as he listened to the Lord, he got the word *stoicheia*. We knew that other intercessors at Aslan's Place had recently heard the word *stoicheia* as a part of a ministry session or in a vision. What was the Lord trying to teach us?

The Greek word *stoicheia* is mentioned in four passages in the New Testament:

> But is under guardians and stewards until the time appointed by the father. Even so we, when we were children, were in bondage under the **elements [stoicheia]** of the world. (Galatians 4:2–3)

*But now after you have known God, or rather are known by God, how is it **that** you turn again to the weak and beggarly elements [stoicheia], to which you desire again to be in bondage?* (Galatians 4:9)

*Beware lest anyone cheat you through **philosophy** [stoicheia] and empty deceit, according to the tradition of men, according to the basic principles of the world, and not according to Christ.* (Colossians 2:8)

*Therefore, if you died with Christ from the basic **principles** [stoicheia] of the world, why, as though living in the world, do you subject yourselves to regulations?* (Colossians 2:20)

Stoicheia is defined as something orderly in arrangement, i.e. (by implication) a serial (basal, fundamental, initial), constituent (literally), proposition (figuratively): Basic elements "such as letters of alphabet or basic elements of the universe – earth, air, fire, and water."[1] *Stoicheion* is used in the plural to primarily signify any first things from which others in a series or a composite whole take their rise. The word denotes "an element, first principle" (from *stoichos*, a row, rank, series)."[2]

Clinton Arnold writes that the interpretation of *stoicheia* as personal spiritual entities is the most common view.[3] In other words *stoicheion* are living beings that are "base" elements of creation. So, what does that mean?

I wasn't even looking for the answer when it came. In September 2006 I was in Trenton, Ontario, Canada. I had just finished a conference at the Toronto Airport Christian Fellowship with Randy Clark. The night the conference ended, I stopped sleeping. After several nights of not sleeping, I became desperate to understand why. As I talked with others in the United States, they shared with me that they, too, were having great difficulty sleeping. *What was this all about?*

During those sleepless days and nights, Amybeth Brenner from New Jersey was desperately trying to reach me by phone. When we were finally able to talk, I was astounded by what she shared.

She was having trouble sleeping, too, and the Lord had kept impressing her to tell me about a dream she had a year before in July 2005.

It was nighttime and the moon was full. I could see the moon glimmering on the tops of the small waves. As I was walking along the shore a woman was standing on my right-hand side, and a man was standing to the left. My father looked at the woman, and I had the sense that he wanted me to marry her. I looked at my father and said that if you like her so much, you be with her. I left angry.

Moving away from that scene, I noticed swirling water, like tide, rushing against the coast. As I walked along the rocks on the shore, a white arm reached out from underneath the rocks and paralyzed me. I heard the music "Mary Jane's Last Dance" playing.

I noticed that I was stuck on one tentacle of a white opaque octopus. The octopus looked like the Chinese man from *Karate Kid*; he talked to me and said he wanted to dance with me. He thought that I would choose him after the music for the "Last Dance" stopped playing. I was looking for a way to escape.

As Amybeth sought the Lord about the dream, she realized that this octopus was tied to powerlessness in her life. She saw that the octopus was on the back of her neck and its arms slipped into a connector at the base of her head and were wrapped around her brain. Somehow these arms affected internal emotional conflicts.

As we were talking on the phone, I felt the octopus behind me. I discerned it immediately. It was a *stoicheia*, an elemental spirit. Previously, the Lord had taught me that a spiritual spring comes out of the back of the neck.[4] It seemed that this elemental spirit was somehow drawing power out of people as it floated in this spiritual spring. The result of this "life-sucking" power was sleeplessness and powerlessness. It also seemed that this evil was somehow affecting the normal electromagnetic fields of the physical bodies it attached itself to. It was almost as if this were an ungodly "electrolysis system."

It was time for action. I asked the Lord to remove the octopus. Immediately, I felt a shift! In place of the octopus, I felt a righteous elemental spirit. An intercessor in the room with me looked at the righteous elemental spirit; he said it had the appearance of a cube. A surge of power and an anointing like a shock wave descended on me. That night I slept for the first time in almost a week! We had discovered a new truth, but what did it all mean? Further revelation would be coming.

At the school in Trenton, Ontario, Canada, the Lord sent many angels with messages about these elemental spirits. Intercessor after intercessor began speaking:

> In the centre of the room, I see one section of a Rubik's cube measuring 20 by 20 feet. The smaller, individual cubes are roughly 16 by 16 by 16 inches. The large section is rotating counter clockwise on an axis in the center of the room. As it rotates, the cubes are spinning on another axis [plane] moving counterclockwise to the first axis.

> On the face of each side of these cubes are colors, all different.

> On another plane I see the equations of the periodic table.

Some of the seers are seeing keys; they've seen them before and heard about them in earlier prophetic words.[5] The keys are on the remaining planes; we understand that they are the keys to realigning the cubes so that the periodic table can be called back into order. It is as if everything is out of alignment, and it needs to be unlocked to restore order, to bring back every plane into alignment with the center of it all.

> On the surface of the cubes there are colors—blue, red, yellow. The elements of the periodic table are on the side opposite the face. There is a correct order for the table. There is a key for this. In the center is light.

> Here is one of the keys. It has to do with light having all of the colors [sic]. They need to be realigned, so we can reflect his light.

> I will give you the keys to realignment. I will download the mysteries of the Kingdom to release on earth through my church. I will release my power, and my love, and my revelation. I will reveal my power, and my love, and my revelation to my church. My revelation will supersede the newest discoveries in quantum physics. I am about to open the gates of the Kingdom of Heaven to my church in a way she has not seen before.

> Prepare yourselves before me, for I have much to give you so that the world may know my love. So I can bring my people into the fullness of my life. It is life abundant. It will be complete, whole, and perfect. You will enter my rest in this life and release my love to a world that does not know it and bring it into my love and life.

We received much revelation at the school in Trenton, but the picture was still incomplete. It would take an extraordinary prayer session at Aslan's Place to increase my understanding.

It all began when a woman returned to Aslan's Place for ministry. The first ministry time with her had been extremely difficult and exhausting. The level of demonization was severe, and we did not understand the root cause of the attack against her. *Where were we to go from this point?*

While praying with her, I had the sudden impression of layers of evil surrounding her. With my hand, I discerned vertical layers of evil radiating from the center of her head away from her body. I also discerned horizontal layers down the front of her and more layers in a circumference around her. I immediately knew there was some type of inter dimensional chessboard around her and in front of her. I was actually feeling layers of different sets of eight by eight (sixty-four) cubes. I discerned that these squares or cubes on the chessboard felt like elemental spirits and that the cubes were alternately evil and righteous. More revelation came as I realized that was a truth the Lord was trying to give me about the number eight. So what now?

Although I do not understand why, there is an important function of the number eight in elemental spirits. A chessboard is made up of sixty-four squares (dimensional cubes), which is eight by eight. Eight seems to be a key number in Creation. According to Gematria or alphabetics, the number of Jesus is 888. The sun cycles every eighth day so that a different part of the sun faces the earth. Every eighth musical note is similar to the first in a series of seven notes. Every eighth element on the periodic table is similar to the first in a series of seven elements. A supercomputer is run on a base eight system. There are sixty-four layers (eight times eight) in a woman's birth canal. The brain has eight sections. Eight is a very important number in alchemy. Among the Pythagoreans, the number eight was esteemed as the first cube, being formed by the continued multiplication of two by two by two, and it signified friendship, prudence, counsel, and justice. As the cube or reduplication of the first even number, eight was made to refer to the primitive law of nature, which supposes all men to be equal. There are sixty-four elements in the ground that vibrate with the earth's atmosphere. These sixty-four elements are found in the blood of human beings.[6] Sixty-four is key in the DNA makeup. In 1953,

James Watson and Francis Crick developed the three-dimensional model of the genetic code (for which they received the Nobel Prize in 1962). They found that genetic material is a biochemical code that created a double helix formation. This double helix is like a spiral staircase. The horizontal steps of the ladder carry the unique genetic material. The rungs on the helix ladder spell out the DNA code. Four different nucleotide bases (A, T, G, or C) are found on the rungs of this ladder. Since the nucleotide's code is for twenty amino acids, a sequence of at least three bases is required. A double sequence would only provide 4 times 4 (sixteen possibilities) which is not enough. A triple sequence provides 4 times 4 times 4 (or sixty-four possibilities), which is more than enough. Therefore, there are sixty-four unique codes in DNA.[7]

Not knowing what to do in the ministry to the woman with this chessboard of eight by eight cubes around her, I asked the Lord for direction. I had a strong sense that these elemental spirits were neutral; they were either contaminated by evil or not contaminated by it. So, I asked the Lord to clean off the evil on the contaminated elemental spirits. I was not prepared for what happened next. Suddenly, the lady we were praying for remembered something new, something that she had no previous recall of! With this prayer, the Lord had opened something important to us. Since that time, many others who have prayed this prayer have experienced key memories that had been completely lost from consciousness.

Learning about the living stones continued. I was startled by the next level of revelation! It seemed to be true. The elemental spirits that are a cube in a cube in a cube (like the Rubik's cube) are actually the elements of the periodic table. This makes perfect sense. If you remember the definition of stoicheia, it establishes that these elements are beings and that these beings are the basic building blocks of Creation. Now it made sense! The building blocks of Creation, the elements of the periodic table are living entities, and they make up the basic building blocks of all matter. Could it be? If this was true, then perhaps the Lord was giving us a new key to healing. If the basic building blocks of Creation can be cleaned up, then perhaps a new level of healing and freedom will be made manifest.

We had received many pieces of discernment revelation about living stones, but they didn't coalesce into a prayer until October 2006. Over seventy of us had gathered to see what the Lord would say to us in the largest advanced school in the history of Aslan's Place. It was at this school that the Lord gave us the Prayer to Establish Us as Living Stones.

Since then, the Lord has given us more and more revelation. Often, in prayer sessions, the Lord reveals elements from the periodic table that are contaminated and need to be cleansed by his power. As we follow his direction, we have seen many healed. He continues to tell us that there is more revelation about this to come.

In June 2007, we returned to Trenton, Ontario, Canada, and the Lord initiated some of that additional revelation about these elemental spirits. Often during a school, angels (the word *angel* means *messenger*) show up and a message is received by an intercessor. Mimi Lowe of Toronto, Canada, received this word.

> We are elemental spirits. We are cubes within a cube. We are the cube within a cube within a cube and in the center is a life force. It is that light that has been contaminated. Do not forget the color elemental within the cube within the cube within the cube. In the center of all this are colors, which are keys. That is where you get your primary colors. There is an equation that is yet to be discovered.

Persis Tiner of Los Angeles, California, received this word:

> Light, Alignment, Movement, Power, Authority. Keep digging. There is a key. There's more. There's a key, there's more.

Two months after the Lord gave us the Prayer to Establish Us as Living Stones, I was with Patricia King and several other prophetic people in Mariposa, Arizona. I was shocked when Stacy Campbell gave the following word. What a confirmation it was of what the Lord had been speaking to us!

> And when John the Baptist said, "Behold the Lamb of God," all the structures—they broke down. They came down—falling down— it literally fell down. First in his body, then in the natural in AD 70. Everything they knew came down. Because we're living stones. Living stones! Living stones! The life is not in the form. The life is in the stone. The DNA is in the brick. God is building his church and the final revelation of the church in heaven is not even the bride, it's a city, a city made of stones. The church as you now know it—it will never be the same! And this is the key—the life is in the bricks. Living stones. They're alive! They're alive! They're alive! They're alive

and they contain his Spirit! So the key is not to discern the form, but the key is to discern the brick.

The Prayer: Establish Us as Living Stones

✠ Father, in the name of Jesus, I come before your throne. I repent for being so stuck and focused on the past that I have been unable to see your calling for me.

✠ I repent for not rightly discerning your presence.

✠ I repent for not acknowledging your presence when you have acknowledged mine.

✠ I repent for asking you for things that you have already done and are doing.

✠ Lord, I repent for not using my keys to unlock the mysteries of the Kingdom of Heaven.

✠ Father, I repent for looking to man for wisdom, knowledge, understanding, and counsel and for looking into my flesh for might, strength, and ability. Forgive me for being arrogant and disrespectful, and for not honoring your Spirit even as it comes forth through others. As you forgive me, I ask you, Lord, to restore the reverential and obedient fear of the mighty God.[8]

✠ Lord, I want to repent for myself and for anyone in my past generations who spoke harshly against your body and the brethren. Lord, I repent for coming into agreement with anybody who spoke against the body of Christ. Lord, I choose now to bless your entire body and to speak health and wholeness to those things I don't understand of your body.

✠ Jesus, I repent for agreement with the spirit of slavery, for choosing to be subject to the law, and for not choosing to be free as a son and daughter.

154

I choose to birth forth the promises of God and his inheritance in me. I declare that this is the set time of the Lord, and I will be realigned with the New Jerusalem.

✠ Lord, I repent for grasping onto the world instead of you. Lord, I repent for getting caught up in generational addictions rather than in your generational blessings. I ask you for your forgiveness and your redemption for the rest of my days.

✠ Father, I repent for myself and my generational line for often being people pleasers rather than God pleasers. I declare for me and my household, that today, right now, we are stepping over the line to serve you. From this day forth, I am and I will continue to be a God pleaser rather than a man pleaser.

✠ Lord, I ask you to forgive me for not trusting you. Lord, I ask you to untangle my feet. I ask you to forgive me for not being able to jump over the fences of offenses. I ask that you will continue to show us our inheritance so that we can receive all that you have already given.

✠ I choose to repent for and to forgive all of those in my family line who were involved in Satanism and corporate mind control in efforts to pervert and abort God's plans and promises.

✠ Father, I forgive all offenses of those who have traumatized me and my past generations. I thank you for cleansing all pathways and ungodly heavenly places so that I can be seated with Christ in heavenly places.

✠ I thank you for redeeming me from my past. The past is not my identity. I leave the past at your feet and choose to pursue the calling and inheritance you have for me.

✠ I choose now to take the key of faith to unlock my inheritance so that I may step forward into my birthright, my calling, and my anointing. I choose to be a restorer of all things.

✠ I want to have faith like Abraham who searched diligently for the city whose builder and maker is God. Help me fix my eyes on your purpose, your will, and your plan for me.[9]

✠ I thank you that you have made me your son.

✠ Lord, would you disconnect me from the things of the earth and remove the sin and the snares that so easily entangle[10] and hinder me from running the race marked before me.

✠ Father, I ask you to establish your glory on me and be my rear guard.[11] Lord, please establish your plumb line between my inner man and your throne.

✠ Lord, I remember your body that was broken for me and your blood that was shed for me. I accept the sacrifice that you gave for me on the cross.

✠ Lord, please remove all contamination on the elemental spirits.[12] I recognize that this contamination has come from the human traditions and the basic principles of the world rather than from Christ.[13]

✠ Lord, please realign my spirit, soul, and body to your plumb line.[14]

✠ Lord, as you created Adam from the dust of the earth and breathed into him your breath of life, so breathe on the elements of my life.

✠ I choose to die to myself and die to the world and to lay down my life as a living sacrifice.[15]

✠ I declare that my heart will be encouraged and knit together in love with other believers and that my heart will attain all wealth that comes from the full assurance of understanding that results in the true knowledge of God's mystery, which is Christ himself.[16]

✠ I declare that I am a living stone and will operate in unity with the body of Christ.

Notes:

1. James Strong, *The Exhaustive Concordance of the Bible: Showing Every Word of the Text of the Common English Version of the Canonical Books, and Every Occurrence of Each Word in Regular Order*, electronic ed. (Ontario: Woodside Bible Fellowship, 1996).

2. W. E. Vine, Merrill F. Unger and William White, Jr., *Vine's Complete Expository Dictionary of Old and New Testament Words* (Nashville: Thomas Nelson, 1996).

3. Clinton E. Arnold, *Powers of Darkness*. (Downers Grove, IL: InterVarsity Press, 1992).

4. Ecclesiastes 12:6.

5. The prophetic word often comes as unfolding information so that future revelation is needed to understand past words.

6. http://www.bibliotecapleyades.net/scalar_tech/esp_scalartech04.htm.

7. *Wikipedia.* s.v. "DNA," http://en.wikipedia.org/wiki/DNA.

8. Isaiah 11:2.

9. Hebrews 11:10.

10. Hebrews 12:1.

11. Isaiah 58:8.

12. Galatians 4:3–5, 9; Colossians 2:8, 20.

13. Colossians 2:2.

14. Zechariah 4:10; Amos 7:8.

15. Romans 12:1–2.

16. Colossians 2:2.

CHAPTER TWENTY-TWO

Prayer to Release
Intimacy with the Lord

PAUL L. COX

In the "Prayer to Establish Us as Living Stones", I quoted Scriptures from Galatians and Colossians about elemental spirits. In Galatians, the Apostle Paul ties his discussion of the elemental spirits with bondage to the law, the religious thinking of man in the pharisaic traditions. In Colossians, where the word *stoicheia* or elemental spirits is often translated philosophy, here again Paul links these elemental spirits with human thinking, what he calls the deceitful traditions of men.

The thought may have occurred to you: What do elemental spirits have to do with philosophy and empty thinking? Is there a connection between these living "elemental spirits" and Greek thought?

Because Greek philosophers (including Plato) taught that *stoicheia* were the first four components of the world, Paul would have linked these elemental spirits to Greek philosophy, but the connection goes deeper. To understand this, we must look at Greek thinking. In Western culture, we assume that science and mathematics are based on logical thought. This is not necessarily correct. The Greeks had a totally different view of reality.

And, ironically, concrete, logical Western science, including physics, is rooted in the first period of Greek philosophy in the sixth century BC, in a culture where science, philosophy, and religion were not separated. The aim of Greek philosophy was to discover the essential nature or real construction of things, which they called *physis*. The word *physis* is derived from this Greek word and originally meant seeing the essential nature of all things. The Greeks believed that matter was alive; they saw no distinction between animate and inanimate, spirit and matter. In fact, they did not even have a word for matter, since they saw all forms of existence as manifestations of the *physis*, endowed with life and spirituality. Thales declared all things to be full of gods. Science and mathematics were studied so that would understand be full of gods.[1] Science and mathematics were studied so that one would understand the spiritual world. The Greeks were very influenced by their belief in shamanism and the ability of the shaman to connect with the spiritual world. W. K. C. Guthrie in his *Orpheus and Greek Religion* discusses the shamanic beliefs about how they could travel and receive information and influence. Guthrie wrote that Orpheus was the founder of mystery religions and "the first to reveal to men the meanings of the initiation rites."[2] Orphic teaching pervaded the Greek thinking; it influenced Greek philosophers and was used to train the cult of Dionysus.

Pythagoras, a mathematician and geometer who lived from about 570 BC to 500 BC, was also a religious figure and a mystic. He appeared to be greatly influenced by Orphic cult religion. His mystical religious practice was not separate from his practice of material science. He was the first Western philosopher to teach that mathematics, or numbers, is the key to the universe. This laid the foundation for science as we know it today.

The mystical aspects of Pythagoras's teachings included reincarnation, vegetarianism (because human souls may be reincarnated into animals), asceticism, meditation, and ritual practices designed to facilitate the experience of revelation and union with the divine.

Because in the early Greek world a philosopher was also a scientist, philosophers always had something to say about the nature of "being" and the origin of the material world. For many of the Greek philosophers, the material world was "alive," endowed with an inner life and sentience of its own.

The last of the great pre-Socratic teachers was Empedocles of Acragas. A "believer in the orphic mysteries as well as a scientific thinker," Empedocles is the originator of the theory of the four elements: earth, water, air, and fire. This concept continues to be a widely held view in Western esoteric thought. Elemental spirits can be translated as the basic elements of the universe such as earth, water, air and fire. According to E. R. Dodds, these philosophers[3] were shamans and magicians who, through philosophical magic, wanted to find immortality and a connection with the divine through ritual, initiations, or techniques of inner journeying. All this was to be done in a rational system.[4]

Therefore, when the Apostle Paul writes of a connection between the elemental spirits, philosophy, and empty thinking, he clearly understands the Greek way of thinking. He comprehends that the Greeks really do see living beings, the elemental spirits, as being foundational to science, mathematics, and philosophy.

This kind of thinking did not begin with the Greeks. Its source is further back in antiquity. All ungodly thought began at the foot of the tree of the knowledge of good and evil where man turned away from the tree of life, the real source of the knowledge of God. It began when man directed his attention to the tree of the knowledge of good and evil and first tried to apprehend the nature of the universe through the natural mind. At that point in time, man attempted to understand the natural world through his own thinking, discounting any involvement by the Almighty God. For the first time, man discounted God in the equation of existence.

The Greek mind-set has not only permeated our Western thought in science, mathematics, and the arts, but it has also permeated our Christian belief system. Our religious practices and some interpretations of Scripture are based on this thinking. The following prayer is a repentance of this wrong kind of thinking and a request to the Lord to align us again with his thinking and ways.

The Prayer: Release Intimacy with the Lord

✠ Lord, I repent for and renounce the sin of transgressing your will and command by partaking of the tree of the knowledge of good and evil.

✠ I repent for disobedience to your known will, which stopped me from being fruitful, filling the earth and subduing it, and having dominion as you intended. I repent for surrendering the authority you gave to me.

✠ I repent for the lust of my eyes, the lust of my flesh, and the boastful pride of life. I repent for the desire to make myself wise and for taking the fruit of the tree of knowledge of good and evil.

✠ I renounce and repent for allowing my senses to be perverted by the deception of the enemy. Lord, I repent for surrendering my senses by seeing, hearing, tasting, touching, and smelling the fruit from the tree of the knowledge of good and evil.

✠ I repent for believing that you were withholding good from me. I repent for believing the enemy's lie about your character. I repent for not trusting in your love and forgiveness by not submitting to you.

✠ I repent for fear and for separating myself from you by hiding and covering up my transgressions against you.

✠ I repent for feasting on human knowledge rather than on your life.

✠ I repent for a rebellious spirit against your command not to eat of the fruit of the tree of the knowledge of good and evil.

✠ I repent for listening to another voice and not trusting the voice of the Lord.

✠ I repent for trading God's truth for a lie.

✠ I repent for taking and accepting any seed of doubt from the enemy and I ask you, Lord, to crush any seeds of doubt, to destroy any growth from them, and to now replace all doubt with the implanted Word of God.

✠ I repent for seeking to be like you, God, and for trying to steal your glory.

✠ I repent for and renounce abdicating responsibility and blaming others, hiding, and covering up my sin.

✠ I repent for rejecting my inheritance as a son of God.

✠ I repent for listening to the voice of the enemy and for embracing the wisdom of man, and for believing, agreeing with, and embracing the enemy's lies.

✠ I repent for the sin of independence from God in seeking for wisdom apart from God.

✠ I repent for the sin of covetousness.

✠ I repent for the sin of independence from God in my responsibilities in relationships.

✠ I repent for the sin of independence from God in my responsibility as a caretaker of Creation.

✠ I repent for choosing independence from God in the exaltation of my own knowledge, wisdom, and understanding above and apart from the life of God.

✠ I repent for myself and all those in my family line who allowed Satan to cheat us through philosophy and empty deceit and allowed Satan to capture or influence our thinking according to the traditions of men and the basic principles of the world.

✠ I repent for acting like an expert in the law and taking away the key of the knowledge of God and shutting out the Kingdom of Heaven from men.

✠ I repent for not entering into the Kingdom of Heaven and for hindering others from entering into the Kingdom of Heaven.

✠ I renounce the sin of boasting great things and of allowing my tongue to curse and not bless. I repent for gossip, backbiting, malice, slander, lies, and all evil speaking. I repent for judging others. I repent for using my tongue to set on fire the course of nature.

✠ I repent for trying to walk in the world and in the Kingdom of God at the same time.

I repent for allowing others to defraud me of the prize of my full calling and inheritance in Christ. Lord, I repent for not holding fast to you as the head of your body, the church.

I repent for agreeing with the doctrines of men in legalism and asceticism and not walking in the fullness of life.

I repent for myself and all those in my family line who chose to serve other gods and broke all covenants with you.

Father, I ask for the sevenfold Spirit of the Lord. I ask for the release of the Spirit of Wisdom, the Spirit of Understanding, the Spirit of Counsel, the Spirit of Strength, the Spirit of Knowledge, the Spirit of the Fear of the Lord, and the Spirit of the Lord.

Lord, I declare that you are the way. You are the life. You are the brilliance of the light that shines and pierces through the darkness. You are the door and the center of all. You are the key.[5]

I declare, in the name of Jesus, that I will rise up and take my place. I declare my authority in Christ. I declare that no one can come against me. I will fight and prevail. I declare I am the head and not the tail.[6]

I declare that the enemy is crushed beneath my heel, and I am seated with Christ at the right hand of the Father.[7]

Grant me according to the riches of your glory to be strengthened with might through your Spirit in my inner man.[8]

I take my place and authority, the place and authority that you have given me in Christ, and I choose this day to stand firm and be strong so that no one can come against me.[9]

Lord, in all my relationships, please restore male and female partnership according to your perfect design.

Lord, please cleanse my senses from all defilement and enhance them for the glory of God.

✠ Lord, please restore my relationship with you; make it like Adam's relationship was in the Garden before the Fall so that I can enter into the intimacy with you that you have always intended for me.

✠ I declare that in you dwells the fullness of the Deity, and in you I have been made complete. You are the Head over all rule and authority.[10]

✠ Lord please restore the wisdom of the fear of the Lord.[11]

✠ I declare that I will hear you above all other voices.[12]

✠ I declare that I will acknowledge you in all my ways.

✠ Lord please remove from me all curses in Deuteronomy 28; Lord remove your anger against the land. Lord please heal the land.

✠ I declare that the secret things belong to you, Lord, my God, and that you will reveal what you want to reveal to me and to my sons and daughters forever.[13]

✠ I choose to be circumcised, buried with Jesus in baptism, and raised with him through faith in the working of God, who raised him from the dead. Lord, I choose to be encouraged; I choose for my heart to be knit together with others, in Christ through love, attaining full assurance and understanding in the knowledge and mystery of God and of the Father and of Christ, in whom are hidden all the treasures of wisdom and knowledge. I choose to make every effort to keep the unity of the Spirit through the bond of peace.[14]

✠ I declare that I will know you, Jesus, as the Son of God who has come to give me understanding so that I may know you. I declare that you are true and that I am in you.

✠ I ask that you bring me into oneness with you and with the Father, even as you are one in the Father.

Notes:

1. Franz Capra, "Mystical Eastern Philosophies Connection with the Scientific Knowledge of Physics," http://www.unique-design.net/library/god/psyche/capra.html.

2. W. K. C. Guthrie, *Orpheus and Greek Religion* (Princeon, NJ: Princeton University Press, 1993). Courtesy of Amazon.com.

3. *Wikipedia*. s.v. "Empedocles," http://en.wikipedia.org/wiki/Empedocles.

4. Hannah M. G. Shapero, "Ancient Greek Mysticism", http://www.eocto.org /article/103

5. 2 Corinthians 4:6.

6. Deuteronomy 28:13.

7. Romans 16:20.

8. 2 Corinthians 4:16.

9. Philippians 4:19.

10. Colossians 2:9–10.

11. Psalm 111:10.

12. John 10:27.

13. Deuteronomy 29:29.

14. Colossians 2:2.

The Wheel of Influence

PAUL L. COX AND PATTI VELOTTA

Several years ago during a ministry session, the Lord revealed a spiritual wheel around each person. The text he gave me was from a passage that speaks of what happens at death. Ecclesiastes 12:6 reads as follows:

> Remember your Creator before the silver cord is loosed, or the golden bowl is broken, or the pitcher shattered at the fountain, or the wheel broken at the well.

What is this wheel?

As I stood next to a person, I discerned that he was sitting on a spiritual wheel. Those who could see in the spirit described a wooden wheel with a metal rim and spokes like a wagon wheel. One person saw the Lord Jesus as the center of the wheel. After discerning wheels around numerous people, the idea came that the wheel was a sphere of influence which the Lord has assigned to each person. It was amazing to me that several times, after I asked those present what they saw in the spirit, and without knowing what others had seen and described before them, they described the same wooden wheels with wooden spokes rotating parallel to the ground around the person. Recently many have seen another wheel, a wheel with within a wheel, that rotates vertically to the ground.

It appears that the Lord assigns to us a certain degree of influence to extend in a certain area around us. We have noticed that when a husband and wife stand next to each other, their influence is much greater than if they stand alone. Further, if several Christians stand together in unity, their influence that is, the wheel, is even greater, sometimes covering hundreds of miles.

Webster's dictionary clarifies the word *influence*. *Influence* is "an emanation of spiritual or moral force" or "the act or power of producing an effect without apparent exertion of force or direct exercise of command." There is an influence that the Lord wants us to have. Unfortunately, because of generational issues or lifetime restrictions placed on us, we do not always operate in our God-given area of influence. In other words, we have been restrained by others from fulfilling our God-given purpose. One example of this is the way restrictions placed upon women have denied and/or limited the influence God wants for them.

Can a Woman Have Influence in Ministry?

PATTI VELOTTA

Jesus is coming back for a bride without spot or wrinkle. Among the things to be healed before his return is the gender issue in the church. The true root of the "women's issue" is shared disobedience to God. By disobedience, men and women together have opened the door to satanic attack, and men and women have both borne the consequences. Evidence of the attack is seen in the mind-sets, choices, and actions of both genders.

Deception about the role of women in ministry and disobedience to God's intent are embedded in the misinterpretation of Scripture. Women may hide behind the misinterpretation because of their own reluctance to lead—denying their own gifts and calling. In addition to denying themselves, women also deny the leadership and calling of other women. This failure to agree with Jesus' intent for women is often rooted in ideas of natural or human preference, or plain old jealousy. On the other hand, men, motivated by tradition, historical superiority, or fear of women, have kept women out of leadership roles.

In the beginning, God created Adam[1] in his own image; he created them, male and female. Then God blessed them and gave them two jobs to do: first, they were to be fruitful and multiply, to fill the earth; and second, they were to subdue it. They were to have dominion over fish, birds, and every other living thing that moves on the earth. He did not tell them to have dominion over each other. In a closer look at their creation, the Bible explains that Adam was placed in the Garden of Eden where he cultivated and kept it. But God said, "It is not good for the man to be alone; I will make a helper suitable for him." The Hebrew word translated helper, *ezer*, is a word commonly used in the Old Testament as "superior strength," such as "God is my helper." The Hebrew word translated as suitable, *kenegdwo*, means "fit for" or "business partner" or "equal." God then created all the living creatures out of the earth and Adam named them, demonstrating his rule over them. None of these were found to be the partner God wanted for Adam. So God put Adam into a deep sleep and removed from his side the material to fashion his equal. This intimate and unique creation of woman is very different from that of the living creatures. Woman came out of man, therefore she is his equal. Paul says, "However, in the Lord, neither is woman independent of man, nor is man independent of woman. For as the woman originates from the man, so also the man has his birth through the woman; and all things originate from God."[2]

However, the man and the woman together disobeyed God's command and ate from the tree of the knowledge of good and evil. The "very good" of God was fractured. Dominion of the earth was transferred to Satan. The loving working relationship between male and female became a war. She did it! God describes the future: there will be hatred between Satan and the woman, but her seed will defeat Satan. The woman will have pain in childbearing, and the man will work by the sweat of his brow in the now-cursed ground. The relationship between male and female will be a constant battle for dominion over each other. In Genesis 3:16, the Hebrew word translated as desire, *tshuqah*, means "longing or appetite". This word occurs only three times in the Old Testament. Many have interpreted the meaning as sexual desire from its use in Song of Solomon. The reasoning goes that women will be ruled by men because women will so want sexual fulfillment that they will let men rule them. However, the important clues to the meaning of this word can be found in Genesis 4:7. There the word desire describes the fight that sin is putting up for control of Cain. The desire is not for sex but for control and domination. Competition, not complementary cooperation, becomes the norm between men and women in this fallen world. And in this broken state, men will rule over women.[3] In the first act following God's prophecy of how things will be (as opposed to how he planned them), Adam takes possession of his wife and names her.

The enmity between Satan and the woman has played out in nearly every culture. Women, the weaker sex, are generally weaker in strength, but not in endurance, intelligence, pain tolerance in childbearing, or in spirituality. This physical weakness has left women vulnerable to domination and limitation. Men have owned, resisted, and silenced women; women have manipulated, controlled, and dominated men. The miserable result is seen in both unredeemed marriage and ministry.

Jesus Christ came to overcome the work of the devil! Once again, by the Holy Spirit, the sexes can submit to one another. Once again a wife can be a helper suitable for her husband, and a husband can lay down his life for his wife. In Jesus, we are free to discover that there is neither Jew nor Greek, slave nor free man, neither male nor female, for we are all one in Christ Jesus. "As each one has received a special gift, employ it in serving one another as good stewards of the manifold grace of God."[4]

So why, in Christian circles, are women, despite their gifts and abilities, routinely relegated by themselves or others to secondary or supporting roles? Often the answer comes in quoting the apostle Paul. "But I do not allow a woman to teach or exercise authority over a man, but to remain quiet."[5] If Paul is laying down a timeless law prohibiting women from having authority or teaching men in the church, why does he commend the many women leaders in the church of Rome who are doing just that? Romans 16 is a chapter of honor and gratefulness from Paul to his colaborers in Rome, and one-third of them are women. In Romans 16:1–2, Phoebe, who is described as a servant, *diakonos*, meaning "deacon or minister," probably pastored in Cenchrea. She is also described as a helper, *prostatis*, meaning "succorer" or, in verb form, *proistemi*, meaning "set over many," including Paul himself! She is responsible not only for delivering but also for probably teaching the contents of Paul's letter to the Roman church; she undertook a dangerous journey and was given a prestigious assignment, one worthy of the Romans' honor and help. Prisca, in Romans 16:3–5a, who was a fellow worker with Paul, was unconventionally mentioned first before her husband, Aquila, to indicate her prominence and leadership in the ministry. Her teaching of doctrine to Apollos qualifies her as a teacher, and her church in their home qualifies her as a pastor. In verse 7, the name Junia is given. Junia is a common Roman female name that has been marginalized in favor of an unknown Greek male name, Junias.

Early commentators[6] assumed that Junia was a woman. It was not until Aegidus of Rome[7] that Junia was referred to as a man. Junia is a female apostle who, along with her male colleague, Andronicus, is outstanding among the apostles. They were Paul's counterparts in Rome.[8] "As an apostle sent by God to witness to the resurrection of Jesus, Paul would lay the foundation for a church. Certainly authoritative preaching would have to be part of such an understanding. Junia and Andronicus, apparently laid the foundation for the churches in Rome: Paul writes of them, 'they came before me in Christ.'"[9]

Phoebe, Prisca, Junia, Stephana, Tryphaena, and Tryphosa are all leaders commended by Paul for their work in the church. Therefore, his prohibition expressed in 1 Timothy 2:12 seems to have a temporary and specific meaning. Could it be that the women in Ephesus at that time were uneducated in the Word of the Lord and had to learn before they were permitted to teach or exercise authority over a man? The tense of the verb *to permit* can be translated "I do not now permit." In fact, the only imperative in 1 Timothy 2 is: "A woman must quietly receive instruction with entire submissiveness."[10] This is a description of rabbinic learning. Paul's encouragement of women in leadership roles is consistent. In 1 Timothy, he is commanding women to learn so that they can take appropriate positions in the ministry of the gospel. The principle behind the passage is not a question of gender, but one of education.

The same lack of learning appears to be the root of the problem in 1 Corinthians 14:34, "Let your women keep silent in the churches, for they are not permitted to speak." This passage has been cited to limit the pulpit to men, but if Paul meant that women should not have a significant contribution or even speak in the church, why did he give guidelines for women to pray and prophesy a few chapters earlier in 1 Corinthians 11:5–6,10,13,15? If 1 Corinthians 14:34 is an absolute prohibition, women should not be allowed to sing or play the organ, let alone share, preach, or teach. Since women in the Jewish culture were prohibited from religious training, perhaps the restriction arose because they had many questions and were rudely interrupting the preaching of the Word. The word for *speak* is the present infinitive which can be translated "continually speaking up" and implies disruptive, annoying, and shameful speech. This made for another disorderly situation in the Corinthian church that Paul needed to straighten out. His command was for the women to ask their own husbands at home because it was improper for them to continually interrupt the service. As for praying or prophesying in church, it is available to both women and men equally.

God gifts and calls whom he will without regard to gender. The Bible reports many women in leadership in both Testaments. Some of my favorites are: Deborah, the judge and prophetess; Huldah the prophetess, who alone gave witness to the Word of God; Esther, the Hebrew queen of Persia and Media who saved her nation; Jephthah's daughter, who died for God, her father, and her nation; Miriam, a prophetess; the wife of Isaiah, a prophetess; Mary, the mother of Jesus; Mary, the disciple of Jesus; Lydia, the first convert in Europe, perhaps pastor of a church in her home; Hannah, a prophetess and the obedient mother of Samuel; the daughters of Zelophehad, who knew and trusted God for justice; Jael, who killed the enemy of Israel; Sarah, Rebekah, and Rachel, three mothers in Israel; Rahab, whose belief saved her family; Ruth, the faithful, who is in the line of the Messiah; the Queen of Sheba, a wise student and believer; Anna, a prophetess intercessor; Phillip's four daughters, prophetesses. The history of the Christian church also records women who held leadership positions, many of whom have given their lives for the glory of God.

Christ also loved the church and gave Himself up for her, that He might sanctify and cleanse her with the washing of water by the word, that He might present her to Himself a glorious church, not having spot or wrinkle or any such thing, but that she should be holy and without blemish. (Ephesians 5:25–27)

Before Jesus' return, we need true understanding of the Word, cleansed garments. Men and women must return to their original assignment and work together according to his pleasure.

The Prayer

PAUL L. COX

Recently at our Advanced Discernment School in Trenton, Ontario, Canada, the Lord began speaking to us about his desire that we be released into the fullness of the spiritual influence that he has designed for us. The following prayer was the result of our time together.

May the Lord use this prayer to release you into the fullest calling that is on your life.

The Prayer: Release Me into My God-Given Influence

✠ I choose to forgive those who have come against my spiritual authority and influence. I forgive those who declared that I was not operating in the Spirit because they wanted to restrict me to a dimension of their understanding in the natural realm. I forgive them for coming against the influence that you chose for me to have.

✠ I choose to forgive those who have suppressed women and children and limited their potential for growth. I forgive those who have silenced women and children and placed barriers over women and children that have hindered them from coming into their birthright. Lord, forgive me and my ancestors for suppressing, limiting, silencing, and hindering women and children from their birthright.

✠ I repent for myself and for those in my generational line who have limited authority to those who express themselves logically and have shut out those who express themselves emotionally, intuitively, and through their spiritual giftings.

✠ I ask now, Jesus, that you bring my wheel of influence into proper balance, put the spokes back into place, repair the rim, and repair all the dings and damage. Lord, please remove all influence of ungodly elders.

✠ Lord please put the hub in the right place and center it in Jesus Christ. I am choosing to be in the center of Jesus' will and only have the influence that Jesus wants me to have. Lord, please remove any evil attack against the wheel, and align the wheel to your Kingdom purposes.

✠ Lord, please place the anointing that you want me to have on the hub.

⌘ Lord, please destroy any birds, especially ravens, that would seek to attack this wheel and the influence you want me to have.

⌘ Lord, please bring the speed of the wheel back into balance.

⌘ Lord please bring the wheel back into right alignment within the dimensions and within time. I demand that Kronos get off my wheel. Lord, please release your power on this wheel.

⌘ Lord, may the wheel only operate under your power, not mine or the enemy's. I draw strength only from you. I choose to have my influence totally guided by you and affected by you. If, Lord, in any way, the wheel is out of control or other people are trying to control my wheel, Lord, please break that off. I declare again that my godly influence will only be affected by you. I demand all man-fearing spirits to leave, all codependency to leave, all manipulation to leave and all control to leave.

Notes:

1. Humankind.
2. 1 Corinthians 11:11–12 (NASB).
3. Genesis 3:16.
4. 1 Peter 4:10 (NASB).
5. 1 Timothy 2:12 (NASB).
6. Origen, Chrysostom, Jerome.
7. AD 1245–1316.
8. Romans 16:7.
9. Aida Besancon Spencer, *Beyond the Curse: Women Called to Ministry* (Peabody, MA: Hendrickson Publishers, 1989), 102.
10. 1 Timothy 2:11 (NASB).

Prayer of
Restoration and Regeneration

PAUL L. COX

Generational prayer is never dull! A session seems to be typical—
then the Lord surprises us! That happened several years ago while I was
ministering with a team in Orefield, Pennsylvania.

A woman who had been diagnosed with dissociative identity disorder
had come for ministry—once again. Often, after praying for someone
several times, I realize that I have nothing offer. *What were we going to do?*
Where would the Lord take us? I was staggered by what the Lord showed
me.

While praying for her, I suddenly sensed an ungodly tabernacle. *How*
was this possible? What right did the enemy have to construct an ungodly
tabernacle? I shared with the team and as we prayed, we realized that
she was inside this ungodly tabernacle; not only that, some of her parts
were trapped in the ungodly ark of the covenant in an ungodly holy of
holies. As I started speaking out loud, one of her altars looked at me in
surprise and said, "How did you know this? Who told you about this? No
one knows about this!" Ignoring the questioning, we pursued the Lord to
see what right the enemy had to do this. The Lord took us back to the Old
Testament.

First Samuel 4–6 relates the account of the Israelites taking the ark
of the covenant out of the Holy of Holies and into battle against the
Philistines. What is not clear is how Eli allowed his sons to remove the
ark. Only the high priest had the right to go into the Holy of Holies, and

then only one day a year! The battle did not go well for Israel. The armies of Israel were defeated and the ark was stolen. It was then taken to the city of Ashdod and placed in the pagan temple of Dagon. We know the story! The next day the Philistines came to the temple and found that the statue of Dagon had fallen on its face in front of the temple. The idol was put back in place, but the next morning the idol was found fallen once again, but this time its head and the palms of its hands were broken off. The ark was then moved to Gath. As I pondered this event, I felt I had a new understanding about what may have happened when the ark was in Ashdod.

When we think of idolatry in our modern world, we forget that the ancient concept of idolatry involved much more than a simple bowing down to idols. Early civilizations actually offered human sacrifices, sometimes hundreds of sacrifices a year. Their ungodly worship also included all types of sexual perversion, including temple prostitution. With this understanding, I began to realize what had happened when the sons of Eli took the ark. When the ark was captured by the Philistines, in essence, the priests of the Lord gave the ark of the covenant to the enemies of God. If indeed this actually did happen and I think it did, then one consequence of this disobedience would have been for Lucifer to gain the legal right to construct an ungodly "spiritual" ark and tabernacle in the second heaven. I believe it is also quite possible that human sacrifices and even temple prostitution might have taken place on the ark. If so, a complete defilement of the ark would have taken place.

But, is there any evidence that the Philistines even tampered with the ark? Yes! Remember that the ark was to contain three items: Aaron's rod that budded, the two tablets of the testimony of God, and the pot of manna.[3] However, when Solomon dedicated the temple of the Lord, the only contents of the ark of the covenant were the tablets.[4]

Then the priests brought in the ark of the covenant of the LORD to its place, into the inner sanctuary of the temple, to the Most Holy Place, under the wings of the cherubim. For the cherubim spread their wings over the place of the ark, and the cherubim overshadowed the ark and its poles. The poles extended so that the ends of the poles of the ark could be seen from the holy place, in front of the inner sanctuary; but they could not be seen from outside. And they are there to this day. Nothing was in the ark except the two tablets

which Moses put there at Horeb, when the LORD made a covenant
with the children of Israel, when they had come out of Egypt.
(2 Chronicles 5:7–10)

So what happened to Aaron's rod and the pot of manna? Could they have been removed during the ark's captivity?[5] It is likely.

If indeed this happened, the corruption of the ark and of the tabernacle could have untold spiritual implications. Since we are to dwell in the true tabernacle of God, the enemy would seek to counterfeit the intentions of God by in some way trapping people, or even parts (altars) of people, in an ungodly ark and tabernacle. This is exactly what we found as we prayed for the lady in Orefield. As she prayed and repented for what her ancestors had done, she asked the Lord to remove her parts from the ungodly ark. A new level of freedom came to her.

But, you might ask "What do the actions of the sons of Eli have to do with me?" After all, that was several centuries ago! Notice from the biblical account that not just the sons of Eli were culpable. The entire army of Israel entered into agreement with them by taking the ark of the covenant into battle. Now this is the amazing fact. It is more than likely that either the sons of Eli or at least one of those warriors was an ancestor of yours! How is that possible? An astounding article by a reporter, Matt Crenson, explains how.

Study Traces Humanity's Roots to Single Individual

MATT CRENSON[6†]

Whoever it was probably lived a few thousand years ago, somewhere in East Asia—Taiwan, Malaysia and Siberia all are likely locations. He—or she—did nothing more remarkable than be born, live, have children and die.

Yet this unknown person was the ancestor of every person now living on Earth—the last person in history whose family tree branches out to touch all 6.5 billion people on the planet today.

That means everybody on Earth descends from somebody who was around as recently as the reign of Tutankhamen, maybe even

† Used with permission of The Associated Press Copyright © 2010. All rights reserved.

during the Golden Age of ancient Greece. There's even a chance that our last shared ancestor lived at the time of Christ.

"It's a mathematical certainty that that person existed." said Steve Olson, whose 2002 book, *Mapping Human History,* traces the history of the species since its origins in Africa more than one hundred thousand years ago.

It is human nature to wonder about our ancestors—who they were, where they lived, what they were like. People trace their genealogy, collect antiques and visit historical sites hoping to capture just a glimpse of those who came before, to locate themselves in the sweep of history and position themselves in the web of human existence.

But few people realize just how intricately that web connects them not just to people living on the planet today, but to everyone who ever lived.

With the help of a statistician, a computer scientist, and a supercomputer, Olson has calculated just how interconnected the human family tree is. You would have to go back in time only two thousand to five thousand years —and probably on the low side of that range—to find somebody who could count every person alive today as a descendant.

Furthermore, Olson and his colleagues have found that if you go back a little farther—about five thousand to seven thousand years ago—everybody living today has exactly the same set of ancestors. In other words, every person who was alive at that time is either an ancestor to all six billion people living today, or their line died out and they have no remaining descendants.

That revelation is "especially startling," statistician Jotun Hein of England's Oxford University wrote in a commentary on the research published by the journal *Nature.*

"Had you entered any village on Earth in around three thousand BC, the first person you would have met would probably be your ancestor." Hein marveled.

It also means that all of us have ancestors of every color and creed. Every Palestinian suicide bomber has Jews in his past. Every

Sunni Muslim in Iraq is descended from at least one Shiite. And every Klansman's family has African roots.

How can this be?

It's simple math. Every person has two parents, four grandparents, and eight great-grandparents. Keep doubling back through generations—sixteen, thirty-two, sixty-four, one hundred twenty-eight—and within a few hundred years you have thousands of ancestors.

Exponential Growth

It's nothing more than exponential growth combined with the facts of life. By the fifteenth century you've got a million ancestors. By the thirteenth you've got a billion. Sometime around the ninth century—just forty generations ago—the number tops a trillion.

But wait. How could anybody—much less everybody—alive today have had a trillion ancestors living during the ninth century?

The answer is, they didn't. Imagine there was a man living twelve hundred years ago whose daughter was your mother's thirty-sixth great-grandmother, and whose son was your father's thirty-sixth great-grandfather. That would put him on two branches on your family tree, one on your mother's side and one on your father's.

In fact, most of the people who lived twelve hundred years ago appear not twice, but thousands of time on our family trees, because there were only 200 million people on Earth back then. Simple division —a trillion divided by 200 million—shows that on average, each person back then would appear five thousand times on the family tree of every single individual living today.

But things are never average. Many of the people who were alive in the year eight hundred never had children; they don't appear on anybody's family tree. Meanwhile, more prolific members of society would show up many more than five thousand times on a lot of people's trees.

Keep going back in time, and there are fewer and fewer people available to put on more and more branches of the 6.5 billion family trees of people living today. It is mathematically inevitable that at some point, there will be a person who appears at least once on everybody's tree.

But don't stop there; keep going back. As the number of potential ancestors dwindles and the number of branches explodes, there comes a time when every single person on Earth is an ancestor to all of us, except the ones who never had children or whose lines eventually died out.

And it wasn't all that long ago. When you walk through an exhibit of Ancient Egyptian art from the time of the pyramids, everything there was very likely created by one of your ancestors —every statue, every hieroglyph, every gold necklace. If there is a mummy lying in the center of the room, that person was almost certainly your ancestor, too.

Migration Issues Crucial

It means when Muslims, Jews, or Christians claim to be children of Abraham, they are all bound to be right.

"No matter the languages we speak or the color of our skin, we share ancestors who planted rice on the banks of the Yangtze, who first domesticated horses on the steppes of the Ukraine, who hunted giant sloths in the forests of North and South America, and who labored to build the Great Pyramid of Khufu," Olson and his colleagues wrote in the journal *Nature*.

How can they be so sure?

Seven years ago one of Olson's colleagues, a Yale University statistician named Joseph Chang, started thinking about how to estimate when the last common ancestor of everybody on Earth today lived. In a paper published by the journal "Advances in Applied Probability," Chang showed that there is a mathematical relationship between the size of a population and the number of generations back to a common ancestor.

A few years later Chang was contacted by Olson, who had started thinking about the world's interrelatedness while writing his book. They started corresponding by e-mail and soon included in their deliberations Douglas Rohde, a Massachusetts Institute of Technology neuroscientist and computer expert who now works for Google.

Rohde created a computer program that put an initial population on a map of the world at some date in the past, ranging from seven thousand to twenty thousand years ago. Then the program allowed those initial inhabitants to go about their business. He allowed them to expand in number according to accepted estimates of past population growth.

The model also had to allow for migration based on what historians, anthropologists, and archaeologists know about how frequently past populations moved, both within and between continents. Rohde, Chang, and Olson chose a range of migration rates, from a low level where almost nobody left their native home to a much higher one where up to twenty percent of the population reproduced in a town other than the one where they were born, and one person in four hundred moved to a foreign country.

Allowing very little migration, Rohde's stimulation produced a date of about 5,000 BC for humanity's most recent common ancestor. Assuming a higher, but still realistic, migration rate produced a shockingly recent date of around AD 1.

Some people even suspect that the most recent common ancestor could have lived later than that.

The impact of what the Israelites did many centuries ago could have easily had an impact on you! Perhaps it is time to take back what was lost in that event so long ago.

Prayer of Restoration and Regeneration

✠ I renounce and repent for myself and for all those in my family generational line and also as a current member of the body of Christ for:

- Not interceding for justice.

- Rebellion, treachery, falsehood, muttering wicked things, disunity, mockery, and not valuing truth.

- Those who cursed or crushed the children of God who were weaker, injured, or immature. I bless them and pray that they will come into the full knowledge of Christ.

- All participation that I have had in causing the shredding of the body of Christ.

- Resisting the Kingdom of the Lord; driving out the priests of the Lord, the sons of Aaron, and the Levites; and making our own people priests as other lands do.

- Removing the ark of the covenant from its rightful place, subjecting it to defilement, and birthing the name Ichabod, "The Glory has departed."

- Those who stole the manna and Aaron's rod out of the ark of God, thus cursing our provision and our authority.

- Giving the enemy legal access to the ark and its contents and causing the defilement of the ark.

- All my sins against the sanctuary, the sin of abomination that leads to desolation.

- Defiling my body as the temple of the Holy Spirit.

- Ungodly worship and for despising and disdaining godly worship.

- Attempting to connect God's worship with ungodly worship.

- Worshipping heavenly bodies and any forms of ungodly light.

- Any generational worship of any counterfeit deity that established itself against the true priestly order of Melchizedek.

- Profaning the covenant of our fathers by breaking faith with one another.

- Teaching false doctrine that does not agree with the sound instruction of our Lord Jesus Christ and with godly teaching. I repent for an unhealthy interest in controversy and for quarrels about words that result in envy, strife, malicious talk, evil suspicion, and constant friction.

- Ungodly sacrifices and sexual perversion that defiled the holy places of the Lord.

- All unholy alliances that mingle the seed of God with the seed of Satan.

- Cooperating with the perversion of our DNA and all genetic and spiritual components of DNA, including the cellular and sub-cellular levels.

- Believing I have the right to create life, alter life, or destroy life.

- The sin of passivity and for not standing or speaking out against the sin of trying to create life, manipulate life, or destroy life.

- Sacrificing our children and unborn children on the fires of Molech and for all shedding of innocent blood.

- Exchanging your true divine light for the counterfeit light of Satan.

- Not being in my position or sphere of influence as a watchman over the Creation of God and therefore relinquishing my position of stewardship of the Creation by not subduing it in accord with Godly principles.

- Speaking against the Most High, oppressing his saints, and trying to change the set times and the laws.

Lord, would you reconnect us to you, our Head and true Source, and cut any ungodly connections that would cause any ungodly electrical impulses? Lord, would you balance all electromagnetic fields that would deceive, defile, corrupt, and contaminate our spirits, souls, and bodies?

✠ Would you please disconnect me from all ungodly heavenly places?

✠ Please complete our regeneration.

✠ Would you cleanse and reconnect the DNA of our bloodlines and of the body of Christ and weld the fragments together with the fire and glory of God?

✠ Would you give me discernment of my memories in my brain and in my cells? Please allow me to know if they are true or false, if they are past or present, ancestral or my own. Please give me your wisdom and direction to know what to do with your answer.

✠ I declare that as all believers are called into the priesthood of the Lord, I bear the iniquity of the sins against the sanctuary.

✠ Oh Lord, the great and awesome God who keeps his covenant of love with all who love him and obey his commands, we have sinned and done wrong. We have committed iniquity. We have done wickedly and rebelled and even by departing from your precepts and judgments. Neither have we heeded your servants, the prophets, who spoke in your name, to our kings and to our princes, to our fathers and all of the people of the land.

✠ I declare that you are the head and establisher of the true priestly line of Melchizedek.

✠ I declare that you are the one who establishes us as living stones who are being built into a spiritual house, a holy priesthood, to offer spiritual sacrifices acceptable to you Father, through Jesus Christ.

✠ I declare that I am part of a chosen people, a royal priesthood, a holy nation, a people belonging to God, and that we will reign on earth with you.[7]

✠ Now therefore, O God, hear the prayer of your servants and our supplications, and for the Lord's sake cause your face to shine on your sanctuary, which is desolate. O Lord God, incline your ear and hear; open your eyes and see our desolations and the city which is called by your name; for we do not present our supplications before you because of our righteous deeds but because of your great mercies. O Lord, hear! O Lord, forgive! O Lord, listen and act! Do not delay for your own sake, O God, for your city and your people are called by your name.[8]

Notes:

1. 1 Samuel 4.

2. 1 Samuel 5.

3. Deuteronomy 31:26; Exodus 16:33; Numbers 17:10.

4. 1 Kings 8:9.

5. View supported by *Zondervan NIV Study Bible,* gen. ed. Kenneth L. Barker (Grand Rapids, MI: Zondervan, 2002), 627, note on 2 Chronicles 5:10.

6. Matt Crenson, "Roots of Human Family Tree are Shallow," *The Associated Press,* July 1, 2006. Used with permission of The Associated Press Copyright © 2010. All rights reserved.

7. 1 Peter 2:9.

8. Isaiah 59; Numbers 18; 2 Chronicles 13:8–9; Revelation 1:5–6; Daniel 9; 1 Samuel 4–5; 1 Corinthians 6:18–20; Hebrews 5:8; Malachi 2:10; 1 Timothy 6:3–5; Genesis 1:28; Psalm 41:1; 1 Peter 2:5, 9; Daniel 7:25.

CHAPTER TWENTY-FIVE

Prayer to Release
Evangelistic Healing

PAUL L. COX

My back had been itching for days! *Was this a new kind of discernment or did I need to go to the doctor?* I did not know. All I knew was that my back was itching.

I was in Dallas, Texas, in January 2006, leading an Advanced Discernment Training and Exploration School, when I had finally taken the itching for as long as I could. I told the school that my back had been itching. Others immediately reported that their backs had been itching too. *So, what was this all about?* I asked the seers what they were observing and they saw what looked like a bramble bush on my back. We began a search through the Word of God, trying to understand what connection a bramble bush might have to issues in our lives and our generational lines. We included all references to bramble bushes, thorns, thistles, and nettles in our search. This is what we found:

Both thorns and thistles it shall bring forth for you, and you shall eat the herb of the field. (Genesis 3:18)

But now they mock at me, men younger than I, whose fathers I disdained to put with the dogs of my flock. (Job 30:1)

Among the bushes they brayed, under the nettles they nestled. (Job 30:7)

I went by the field of the lazy man, and by the vineyard of the man devoid of understanding; and there it was, all overgrown with thorns; its surface was covered with nettles; its stone wall was broken down. When I saw it, I considered it well; I looked on it and received instruction. (Proverbs 24:30–32)

For they are impudent and stubborn children. I am sending you to them, and you shall say to them, "Thus says the LORD GOD." As for them, whether they hear or whether they refuse—for they are a rebellious house—yet they will know that a prophet has been among them. And you, son of man, do not be afraid of them nor be afraid of their words, though briers and thorns are with you and you dwell among scorpions; do not be afraid of their words or dismayed by their looks, though they are a rebellious house. (Ezekiel 2:4–6)

Now when they told Jotham, he went and stood on top of Mount Gerizim, and lifted his voice and cried out. And he said to them: "Listen to me, you men of Shechem, that God may listen to you! The trees once went forth to anoint a king over them. And they said to the olive tree, 'Reign over us!' But the olive tree said to them, 'Should I cease giving my oil, with which they honor God and men, and go to sway over trees?' Then the trees said to the fig tree, 'You come and reign over us!' But the fig tree said to them, 'Should I cease my sweetness and my good fruit, and go to sway over trees?' Then the trees said to the vine, 'You come and reign over us!' But the vine said to them, 'Should I cease my new wine, which cheers both God and men, and go to sway over trees?' Then all the trees said to the bramble, 'You come and reign over us!' And the bramble said to the trees, 'If in truth you anoint me as king over you, then come and take shelter in my shade; but if not, let fire come out of the bramble and devour the cedars of Lebanon!'" (Judges 9:7–15)

You will know them by their fruits. Do men gather grapes from thornbushes or figs from thistles? Even so, every good tree bears good fruit, but a bad tree bears bad fruit. A good tree cannot bear bad fruit, nor can a bad tree bear good fruit. (Matthew 7:16–18)

We began to tie some thoughts together as we read the verses and waited upon the Lord. It seemed clear that if brambles and thorns prohibited physical reproduction in the land, then spiritual brambles and thorns would inhibit spiritual reproduction. *Was there a connection here between us and physical land?* In the past, we had observed connections between us and land. Romans 8:22 says that because of humanity's sin, all Creation groans. "For we know that the whole creation groans and labors with birth pangs together until now." The resolution of this groaning will come with the revealing of the sons of God.[1] When that revealing takes place, the land will be redeemed—"set free from its bondage to decay" (Romans 5:21, NIV). This suggests not only an increase of physical production on the land but also of spiritual reproduction.

How does this spiritual reproduction begin? It is through evangelism. When all restrictions are removed from evangelism, spiritual reproduction will take place naturally. Even as physical reproduction on the land takes place easily and naturally, spiritual reproduction will also take place naturally and easily when restrictions to reproduction are removed.

The way all of this happens is in rest. When we rest in the Triune God, then he works with power through us. Evangelism is effortless when we rely on him to do the ministry through us.

Come to me, all you who are weary and burdened, and I will give you rest. Take my yoke upon you and learn from me, for I am gentle and humble in heart, and you will find rest for your souls. (Matthew 11:28–29, NIV)

For if Joshua had given them rest, then He would not afterward have spoken of another day. There remains therefore a rest for the people of God. (Hebrews 4:8–9)

As the Lord revealed these truths to us, we asked him to remove the bramble bushes from our backs. I was not prepared for what happened next. As the bramble bushes came off, several saw what looked like wings[2] on our backs! Now I have been stretched before, but this was way beyond my comfort zone! As I placed my hands on these wings, I could indeed feel them. I also noticed that I could discern healing in the wings. I then remembered Malachi 4:2, "But to you who fear My name the Sun of

Righteousness shall arise with healing in His wings; and you shall go out and grow fat like stall-fed calves." We do not know if there is a connection between the spiritual being, Sun of Righteousness, and the wings upon our backs, but I do feel confident that there is something about healing and evangelism with these wings.

Perhaps the Lord is leading us to discover a new way of doing evangelism. Allow the Lord to use the following prayer to reposition you and to bring you into a place of rest, a place where his power will flow through you to accomplish his will.

Prayer to Release Evangelistic Healing

❄ Heavenly Father, I lift up the land. I lift up myself as a keeper and tiller of the land. I lift up myself as an employee and an employer. Forgive me, Father, forgive me for not giving the land a Sabbath rest. Forgive me for not giving myself a Sabbath rest. Forgive me for not giving our employees a Sabbath rest. Forgive me because in disobeying your commands to rest, I have rejected your holy principles and ordinances. I have turned away and gone my own way. I have done what is right in my own eyes. Forgive me for unrighteousness and turn me so that I will be turned back to you. Lord, break off all consequences on me and upon the land from any curses related to not taking a Sabbath rest and not giving the land rest.

❄ Heavenly Father, forgive me for not entering into the rest of God. Forgive me for not allowing my giftings and calling to enter into your rest. Forgive me for not allowing your healing gifts, as you originally planned for them to be expressed through me, to enter into your rest. I acknowledge that you give these healing gifts so that the work of evangelism will function in your rest. I acknowledge your ways as greater than my ways. Forgive me for not choosing your ways and your rest, for you have given the healing gifts so that the work of evangelism might be effortless, so that it might be accomplished not by my might, not by my power, but by your Spirit. I regret that rather than receiving your way, I have leaned on my own understanding. I have chosen to formulize and institutionalize both healing and evangelism. I am guilty of deciding that evangelism and healing be done according to man's methods. Forgive me, Father. Allow the Spirit of repentance to come upon me so that I might weep and wail and cry out for the unrest of my land, for the unrest of myself, for the unrest of my brothers and sisters, for the unrest of ministers of the Gospel, so that your plan and your purposes, which were derailed by my unrighteousness, might be reinstated into the place of prominence in your world.

✠ Father, remove from me anything that absorbs your Spirit and everything that insulates me from your Spirit. I renounce any elemental spirits.[4] that absorb or block the workings of your Holy Spirit both to and through me. Remove any and all contamination from the elemental spirits and return them to neutrality.

✠ Father, I humbly repent for and renounce turning evangelism and healing into methods and formulas, and I repent for not allowing your power to flow through me according to your will. Forgive me, Mighty God. I ask that you be placed in the highest place, for you are the Lord, my God. You and you alone can accomplish true evangelism and healing. I desire that you bring these forth so that your holy, worthy, wonderful name be glorified.

✠ Father, I ask to be open to fully receive your grace and your rest. Father, in Jesus' name, give me an ability to no longer work in the flesh or to lean on the arm of the flesh. Thank you.

✠ Father, I repent for and renounce any way in which I or my generations past have manifested an ungodly gift of healing or have relied on or called upon any powers for healing other than your own. I repent for and renounce any rejection of your authentic healing gifts by me or by anyone in my family line—including all my ancestors. Lord please remove from me and my family line all curses and iniquity against the gift of healing. Remove from us all thorns and nettles.

✠ Father I receive your callings and giftings, even those I have previously refused, for the gifts and callings from you, God, are without repentance. I accept that it is not necessary to rely on my own methods. I do not need to know how to make this work. I need only say yes to your gifts and your callings.

✠ I agree with the Word which states: "But those who wait on the Lord shall renew their strength; they shall mount up with wings like eagles, they shall run and not be weary, they shall walk and not faint."[5]

✠ Lord, I want to soar like eagles, catch the heat vents, fly, and have an eagle's eye to see afar. I want to know where to go after food and provision. I thank you that I can run and not be weary.

✠ Lord, I declare this to be the time of running and renewing strength. I want to disciple the next generation so that they will fly higher than I can fly. I will not shut them down in the way I was shut down. I will disciple them in your power and might. They will move into the unusual, the far beyond, and that which was unusual for me will be normal for them.

✠ Help me to make every effort to walk into your rest. Father, on the seventh day you rested. You ask me to rest. You ask me to separate myself one day a week from all that is profane—to come apart and be holy, to focus on you and gather together with those who are holy. You are my God who makes a distinction between the holy and the profane, between the sacred and the vile, between the clean and the unclean.[6]

✠ When I enter the world, as I must, O Lord, separate and mark the holy from the profane. You pardon my transgressions, great and slight. You multiply my seed as the sand. I call upon you to fill all my needs.

✠ Cause me to enter into your rest, that your name may be glorified. Turn back my enemies so that your name will not be mocked. Let none say, "Where is the God who created you?" Arouse in me your love to save a people who live in your rest.

✠ Bring forth your healing gifts; bring forth your life to raise the dead. Bring forth evangelism that your glory may cover the earth. Cause your Kingdom to come and your will to be done. And in all these matters cause me to move in the might of your rest.

✠ I declare the truth of your Word:

For as the heavens are higher than the earth, so are My ways higher than your ways, and My thoughts than your thoughts. For as the rain comes down, and the snow from heaven, and do not return there, but water the earth, and make it bring forth and bud, that it may give seed to the sower and bread to the eater, so shall My word be that goes forth from My mouth; it shall not return to Me void, but it shall accomplish what I please, and it shall prosper in the thing for which I sent it. For you shall go out with joy, and be led out with peace; the mountains and the hills shall break forth into singing before you, and all the trees of the field shall clap their hands. Instead of the thorn shall come up the cypress tree, and instead of the brier shall come up the myrtle tree; and it shall be to the LORD for a name, for an everlasting sign that shall not be cut off. (Isaiah 55:9–13)

�֍ Heavenly Father, I love you. Lord Jesus, I love you. Holy Spirit of the living God, I love you. Yahweh, I must have you at the center of everything. I ask you to take the sum of my humanity and spread it around your throne.

✖ I ask you now to take all that is pleasing to you and to build me up— with you as the center and with me within your confines. I ask you to take all that remains and do what you want with it. Take it as far as the East is from the West, for I only want what pleases you.

✖ Lord Jesus, I renounce and repent for all those in my family line, all the way back to Adam and Eve, who, because of their sin, released thorns and thistles into the ground placing a curse on reproduction— the reproduction of the land, the reproduction of business, spiritual reproduction, and human reproduction.

✖ As a parent, I renounce and repent for myself and my family line for provoking my children to anger and not blessing them to walk in sonship. I now release them to walk in godly inheritance, authority, and as sons properly placed within a redeemed family tree. As a son, I renounce and repent for myself and my generational line for not honoring my parents. I ask for your realignment of our redeemed family tree. I receive the parental blessing and move forward in freedom.

For myself and my family line,

✠ I repent for and renounce those who focus on the moon, fear the moon, and worship the moon rather than the Son of God. Lord, please break all curses related to moon worship.

✠ Lord I repent for those who denied the gift of healing, spoke against the gift, and cursed the gift of healing. Please break all curses that came against me. Lord, please destroy the ungodly reflection of the sun of righteousness with healing in her wings—that ungodly reflection, that imposter, who is like a bramble bush, and who brings the counterfeit healing gift. Please the one that brings sickness and disease—the anti-healing one.

✠ Lord, please heal the damage done to my back. Please break all the curses on reproduction that have come against me. Lord, disconnect me and my family from all fertility cults and sacrifices that have brought curses, barrenness, and thorns into our lives and upon our land.

✠ Father, I repent for and renounce choosing to drink the water of affliction rather than drinking from the River of Life. Father, I repent for and renounce silencing the seed, shutting the truth within my bowels, allowing the moons of unrighteousness to overshadow the righteousness within me.

✠ Lord, for myself and my family line, I repent for and renounce any who have spilled their seed on the ground or caused the seed of others to be spilled upon the ground. Lord I repent for and renounce blocking the seed of evangelism.

✠ Father, forgive me and my family line for covering your light and not bringing it forth for all to see. Forgive me for hiding your light under a bushel. Cause your light to shine through me that others might see you and come to know you.

✠ Lord, please burn up the bramble bush—that ungodly misrepresentation of the evangelism and healing you desire to bring forth. On behalf of myself and my family line, I repent for and renounce hiding my light under a bush. I repent for and renounce those in my generations who hid their lights in any way. We submit to Jesus, the burning bush, the all-consuming fire. Lord, will you burn away the things that entangle, and release me to fly in the fullness of my inheritance?

✠ Lord, please turn the wilderness and wasteland into streams in the desert and the parched land into a pool. I receive the healing of the land and of my body. Lord, please open the blind eyes, unstop the deaf ears, heal the lame, and release the mute to shout for joy.[7]

✠ I want to be like trees planted by the rivers of water that bring forth the fruit of the season.[8]

✠ Moreover the light of the moon will be as the light of the sun, and the light of the sun will be sevenfold, as the light of seven days, in the day that the Lord binds up the bruise of his people and heals the stroke of their wound.[9]

✠ I repent for and renounce the Rahab spirit—that "do nothing" spirit.

✠ I renounce and repent, on behalf of myself and my generational line, for all ungodly plantings, for not being grounded and rooted in love, and for receiving nourishment and strength from the land and not from you. I renounce and repent for receiving and relying on the ungodly fruit that was produced from this ungodly planting. On behalf of myself and my generational line, I renounce and repent for all ungodly dependence on the land. I renounce and repent for all worship of the land. I break all ungodly ties for me and my generational line with the land.

✠ Father, I renounce and repent for trying to reap fruit from thorns and from bramble bushes. Cause me to see and discern the trees from which I pick fruit. I want only fruit from your hand—from what and from whom you have ordained for me—not from any imposters. I acknowledge that good fruit comes only from good trees. Thorns and bramble bushes yield only bad fruit and desolation.

✠ Reach deep, clean out, and wash the cisterns of our hearts and lives.

✠ Father, I renounce and repent for all false gifts of healing. I repent and renounce for myself and for anyone in my generations who declared that healing was not of God but came from my enemy. I repent for and renounce any false healing gifts or the misuse of any healing gifts both for myself and for my ancestors. I renounce and repent for turning away from or discrediting the healing gifts.

✠ Lord, please break the curse off of the land. Please heal the land. Please break the curse off of the gift of healing. Please break the curse off of me. Please appropriate your blood over the land and over me and over the healing gifts in these specific matters.

✠ I now accept and receive your healing, your healing gifts, callings, and mantles. Help me not to look to myself to make the gifts work. Grant me faith that you will do all that needs to be done. You alone are God.

✠ I ask that all healing and healing giftings and mantles from you come forth in your order to move evangelism forward. Even as the Sun of Righteousness, with healing in his wings, flies or moves by means of wings, so sweep evangelism forward through healing. Let it take wing and fly—even according to your will. Glorify your name. Cover the earth with your glory.[10]

Notes:

1. Romans 8:19.

2. These are not angel wings! Humans are not angels and we don't become angels when we die.

3. The Hebrew article is actually feminine.

4. See chapter 21, Prayer to Establish Us as Living Stones.

5. Isaiah 40:31.

6. Leviticus 10:10; Ezekiel 22:26; 44:23.

7. Isaiah 35.

8. Psalm 1:3.

9. Isaiah 30:26.

10. Isaiah 41:18ff; 2 Peter 2:21; Matthew 5:14–15; Psalm 129:1–4; Genesis 3; Hebrews 12:11; Romans 8:18–23; Psalm 124:7; Psalm 91:3; Malachi 4:1–3; Mark 5:25–27; Judges 9:1–15; Luke 6:43–45; 2 Chronicles 7:14; Proverbs 24:30–34.

Breaking Ties to Incubus and Succubus Spirits

ANNEMIE-JOY MUNNIK

Incubi is a spirit being that comes to have intimate relationships with women while they are asleep, while *succubae* is a spirit being that comes to have relationships with men in their sleep. These night-time experiences are sometimes called encounters with spirit husbands and spirit wives. In West Africa they call these dream visitors "night husbands and night wives."

When a nightmare-dream is sexual in content, the word *incubus* is often used interchangeably with the *Mare* or *mara* demon. *Mara* is "an Anglo-Saxon and Old Norse term for a demon that sat on sleepers' chests, causing them to have bad dreams.";[1] in fact, the Latin word for nightmare is *incubo* (to lie upon). Night spells are charms or enchantments used by witches and warlocks at night. The incubus can assume a male or a female shape; sometimes they appear as full-grown adults.

Many times incubus and succubus spirits operate within a person's life because of generational curses passed down through the family line. Ancestors may have gone to a witch or warlock for love witchcraft. Witches and warlocks conjure up and then sell or give people their potions; they perform rituals, offer up invocations, use baths, washes, charms, and psychic prayers. What they don't tell the person who is looking for love is that they are unloosing a demon, in the form of lust, upon the very life of that person, and not only upon that person, but upon each successive generation until it is broken from that family line by repentance and prayer.

According to many church leaders, an incubus is an angel who fell because of lust. According to Hebrew legends, the *incubi* (plural) are lewd demon children of Lilith who seek sexual intercourse with men and women and can assume either sex to have sex with humans. They are also referred to as *follet*,[2] *alp*,[3] *duende*,[4] and *folletto*.[5]

As mentioned above, the demon Mare works with the incubus and succubus demons. This demon is alleged to cause dreams of sexual content coupled with those evil spirits. It causes bad dreams or nightmares. It also manifests during the night by sitting on a person's chest and causing feelings of suffocation and choking. It causes a feeling of being paralyzed and like a weight, crushes the breath out of a person.

Theses spirits can enter through many doors:

• They can be passed down from one generation to the next. Generational sexual healing and deliverance needs to take place if there are family patterns of adultery, incest, pornography, sexual addiction, or homosexuality.

• They can come from spells, charms, and other forms of witchcraft.

• They can come in through rape, adultery, fornication, homosexuality, or any kind of ungodly sexual contact with other men, women, or animals.

Those who experience sexual encounters in their dreams may meet with numerous frustrations if they attempt to marry; if they do marry, they are likely to have difficulty in their marriages. Many unhappy and broken homes are the result of the evil manipulations of these jealous spirits. The final evil effect of the presence of a spirit husband or spirit wife is difficulty in having children. These spirits introduce different diseases of the reproductive system into the woman, making it difficult or impossible for her to conceive. Often there is no physical reason why she cannot conceive children.

These demons can lodge themselves deep within the sexual organs, on the tongue, and on the hands and fingers of the physical body of the individual they inhabit. Incubus and succubus also lodge themselves within the soulish realm of the person. These spirits have the ability to somehow reduce and control the will of the individual they inhabit.

Here is an account from one who was set free.

We were playing and his arms were strong when he picked me up and threw me in the air. And then it happened . . .

I was three years old when the sexual abuse started and it continued for nine years. At the age of twelve, I realized that this was not normal and that I could say no. As far back as I can remember the sexual night dreams were my companions. Like the abuse, I thought it was just a normal part of life. Today I know the dreams were not normal.

In 2003, a friend and I started a ministry that works with young people from informal settlement areas in South Africa and further abroad in Africa.

As we built relationships with these young people, they started taking us into their confidence and told us about the sexual dreams they were having at night. Some of them could see these spirits going from bed to bed, and they could hear them running on the roofs from house to house. Some people believe that if you raise your bed by having it stand on tins or bricks, these spirits, called *Thokholosh*, are not able to reach them. In Africa these phenomena are nothing new or strange. They are often perceived as a normal part of life.

In 2007, the Lord impressed upon my spirit to write a prayer about these issues.

To be open and honest about what was happening to me was part of the answer and healing I found. In my case, the open door for these things to have happened was generational. Jesus came to set the captives free![6]

There is an answer to this, there is a way out! I want to encourage you to stand up and say no to this kind of abuse. We are allowed to.

The Prayer: Breaking Ties to Incubus and Succubus Spirits

Father, in the name of Jesus, I repent on behalf of myself and those in my family line who had sexual relations with evil spirits, familiar spirits, with incubus/succubus spirits, and the demon Mare. I renounce and break any covenants or dedications to the Nephilim,[7] Baal, or Belial.

✠ I repent for anyone in my family line who has had any connections, ties, pacts, or allegiances to the harlot spirit and the queen of heaven.[8] I repent for all who participated in any fertility rites or rituals, and who sacrificed, worshipped, danced before, or gave offerings to any gods or goddesses.

✠ Lord, I repent for myself and all those in my family line who had night or spirit husbands or night or spirit wives. Lord, forgive us for rejecting you as our husband and forgive us for our unfaithfulness toward you. Forgive us for finding comfort from these spirits and for looking to them to fulfill our desires and needs. I choose to rely upon you and to trust in you for everything I need. Please restore my joy and faithfulness to Jesus Christ, the Bridegroom.

✠ Lord, I repent of every contact, personal and generational, with all night husbands and night wives and I and renounce all night husbands and night wives that have been assigned to function specifically within my family. I repent of the blood covenants that opened the door to this family night husband and night wife. I cut every soul tie with this family spirit. I repent of the deception adopted by my ancestors that polygamy is acceptable and for any deception that was one of the ways in which the door was opened to incubus and succubus and mara.

✠ I repent for those in my family line who were involved in astral travel, dark practices such as the occult, and New Age practices. I repent for any involvement with witches, sorcerers, magistellus, or familiar spirits. I renounce all night spells, charms, enchantments, or allurements used by witches and warlocks at night. I renounce any secret knowledge or any positions, possessions, or powers that have come from darkness. Please close all ungodly pathways, gateways, portals, cracks, or seams into ungodly realms or the underworld. Remove all defilement and tainting, and as your child, please restore my godly dreams from heavenly places.

✠ I repent for myself or any of my ancestors who have visited sangomas,[9] witches, or warlocks for their "love witchcraft." I repent of buying, accepting, and using their love potions. I repent of rituals performed, invocations offered up, and any using of baths, washes, charms, and psychic prayers. I repent of having my body rubbed with ungodly ceremonial liquids, or allowing ungodly ceremonial or commercial liquids to be poured over my body.

✠ I repent for the breaking up of marriages and covenants, for divorces and the destroyed relationships that resulted from having relations with these spirits. I ask that you would break off from me and my family line all false love, lust, hatred, impotency, frigidity, sickness, and diseases that have been caused by these spirits.

✠ I repent on behalf of myself and my family line for all fornication, adultery, incest, orgies, sodomy, homosexuality, and sexual addiction. I repent for all pornography, rape, abuse, ungodly masturbation, lust, and fantasy lust, and any ungodly sexual contact with other people, any bestiality, and all sexual perversion and sex for money.

✠ I repent on behalf of myself and my family line for shedding innocent blood through abortion and human sacrifices. I repent of murder, pride, greed, rage, hate, jealousy, pretense, falseness, cursing, and lying.

✠ Father, on behalf of myself and my family line I repent of having been involved in acts that showed worship and obedience to Satan and his demons through having sexual relations outside of marriage. Lord, forgive us for not following your commands.

✠ In the name of Jesus I renounce all ungodly soul ties with every person I have been sexually involved with, physically or spiritually. Father, I ask you to break these soul ties from my spirit, my mind, and my body. Break in Jesus' Name! I now apply the blood of Jesus Christ over all ungodly ties.

✠ Father, I repent for allowing these evil spirits to reduce and control my will. I now choose to put my spirit, will, emotions, mind, and body under the lordship of Jesus Christ.[10]

✠ Now in the name of Jesus Christ I renounce and demand the demons Incubus, Succubus, Incubi, Succubi, Eldonna, and Mare to come out of my body and my physical and spiritual conscious, subconscious, and unconscious mind.

✠ I break off these spirits from my tongue, hands, fingers, breasts, sexual organs, or any part of my body.

✠ I will no longer serve these demon spirits. I renounce Satan and all his works. I stand in the authority that I have as a believer, and in the name of Jesus, I cast out any spirits that have been residing in my body.

✠ I command all confusion to leave, and I call back all parts that have been scattered or fragmented.

✠ Father, I ask you to forgive me, to wash me and cleanse me, and I ask you to restore my innocence. Please increase my love for you and give me the ability to be truly faithful and intimate with you.[11]

Notes:

1. D. L. Ashliman, "Night-Mares" http://www.pitt.edu/~dash/nightmare.html.
2. French.
3. German.
4. Spanish.
5. Italian.
6. Isaiah 61:1.
7. Genesis 6:1–6.
8. Nahum 3:5; Revelation 17:1–5.
9. South African witch doctors.
10. Romans 13:14.
11. Prayer written by Annemie-Joy Munnik.

Divine Intervention and Releasing Your Birthright

PAUL L. COX

The essence of every prayer discussed in this book is repentance for generational iniquity. The reason for each prayer is the need for repentance; the purpose of every prayer is to release ourselves and others into our birthright. The Prayer for Divine Intervention and Releasing Your Birthright is a prayer that was specifically given by the Lord to claim back all the treasures that have been lost in the family line by generational sin. The following article, which Kelsey Budd allowed me to use here, discusses some of the issues surrounding generational iniquity.

What's All This "Generational" Stuff?

KELSEY BUDD

You shall not bow down to them nor serve them [idols]; for I, the LORD your God, am a jealous God, visiting the iniquity of the fathers upon the children to the third and fourth generations of those who hate Me, but showing mercy to thousands, to those who love Me and keep My commandments. (Exodus 20:5–6)

We believe the issue of generational iniquity is best illustrated in the familiar story of Cain. Let's review. Cain and his brother Abel brought a sacrifice to the Lord; Abel's sacrifice was found worthy in God's eyes, while Cain's was not. This story marks an important distinction between sin, rebellion, and iniquity. When Cain became angry, sad, and dejected, the Lord said to Cain, "Sin crouches at your door; its desire is for you, but you must master it." In response to this, Cain did three things. First, and perhaps most profoundly, he departed from the presence of the Lord. Next, he convinced his brother to come out to the field, where he killed him. Finally, when the Lord asked him where his brother was, Cain replied, "Am I my brother's keeper?" And after this answer, the Lord cursed Cain.[1]

We may define sin simply as separation from God, and Cain's departing from the presence of the Lord illustrates this. The Old Testament law required sin offerings for unintentional and, at times, unavoidable acts like coming in contact with a dead animal carcass or a dead body. Separation from God does not necessarily involve any malicious intent. It occurs from actions as simple as taking our eyes off God and going astray. Rebellion, on the other hand, occurs when we knowingly do something that God has commanded us and charged us not to do, when we "do it anyway."

For generational issues, however, iniquity becomes our primary concern, and Cain's answer to God demonstrates iniquity. The Lord asks Cain, "Where is your brother?" and Cain does not say, "Lord, I have sinned greatly, for I have committed murder upon my own brother." He does not even respond rebelliously, "Listen, I know it's against the rules, but I killed Abel, so could we just get this punishment thing over with, Lord?" Instead, he replies, "Am I my brother's keeper?" Cain gives an answer that distorts the truth; he neither chooses to confess the truth with contrition, nor acknowledge the truth without remorse (like the second response example). Instead, his response is crafted to cover his sin and rebellion, and he tries to evade the consequences altogether.

Thus, we may define iniquity as a twisted response to God. The Hebrew word *avown* is translated here as iniquity. This word comes from the root word *avah*, which Strong's translates as "do amiss, bow down, make crooked, pervert."[2] God curses Cain for his actions, and Cain replies, "My punishment is too great!" The word translated as *punishment* is actually *avown*; Cain is quite literally saying, "My crookedness is too great." *Crookedness* may refer to either his own crooked ways, the punishment that comes with crooked ways, or both. Thus, it is quite literally this crookedness, this twisting of Cain's sin, that is visited upon his descendants, not only in the sense of the curse, the punishment, but also in the sense of Cain's distorted response.

Let's get some perspective. The Father sent his Son, Jesus, to atone once and for all for our sins on the cross. He bore the weight of all our sins, and he became a curse for us, so that we might have freedom. He has conquered sin once and for all. He alone could bear it. The victory is his. If we can become as Paul described, so that "it is no longer I who lives, but Christ lives in me,"[3] then we can carry his victory in us. We believe the Father "visit[s] the iniquity of the fathers upon the children"[4] not because he has a heart to burden us, but to confront us with this twisting of the truth and give us the opportunity to rise to the challenge and overcome it, not through our own righteousness, but through the righteous sacrifice of the one who lives in us, Jesus. We believe this occurs so that we, the sons, may face this wrong response, perceive it as sin, and take the opportunity to "master it" that our fathers squandered. Revelation 3:5 says the following:

He who overcomes shall be clothed in white garments, and I will not blot out his name from the Book of Life; but I will confess his name before My Father and before His angels.

The reward is promised to be great for those who persevere and learn to overcome. That's so Old Testament! Yes. That is exactly where it is.

Consider this question: What is a *testament*? The *American Heritage Dictionary* defines it this way: "*Testament* serves as tangible proof of evidence." It comes from the Latin word *testis*, which can be translated roughly to mean *witness*. Who or what does the Old Testament give evidence of? Who or what is it a witness to? You may be rolling your eyes, because, of course, it is Jesus to whom the Old Testament gives witness. But don't shrug this aside; it's the reason we still carry around all those pages in our Bibles. The Testament may be old, but the Jesus it testifies about is still the same. He does not change. If doubt still lingers about the relevance of the Old Testament, consider Luke 16:31, where Jesus gives us some stunning words in his parable about the rich man and the beggar, Lazarus. "But he said to him, 'If they do not hear Moses and the prophets, neither will they be persuaded though one rise from the dead.'" Those are probably not particularly comforting words.

Those who find themselves echoing the objection about generational iniquity being confined to the Old Testament probably consider Galatians 5:3–4, which says: "And I testify again to every man who becomes circumcised that he is a debtor to keep the whole law. You have become estranged from Christ, you who attempt to be justified by law; you have fallen from grace."

Much of the Old Testament, in other words, the law, describes God's commands to the Israelites. Paul exhorts us here not to try and work out our salvation through the law. But even in the Old Testament, when the people's attitude is wrong, God expresses contempt for and rejects the songs, offerings, and festivals that were in keeping with the law. The Lord almost killed Balaam for his wrong attitude and spiritual insensitivity, even though he was following the command of the Lord.

The law was created to give witness to God, to his holiness. It was created to guard us from sin before we put faith in Jesus. It was also created to produce conviction in us, which, in turn would reveal to us our inability to achieve right standing with God through our own efforts. For that, we need a savior. Jesus lived his life in perfect submission to the law so that we would not place our faith in the law, but in the one who fulfilled it. Again, he said, "I did not come to destroy [the law] but to fulfill [it]."[5] Through him, we can live in harmony as Paul describes in Ephesians 2:20: "having been built on the foundation of the apostles and prophets, Jesus Christ Himself being the chief cornerstone."

God can change and has changed his commands in keeping with his time or season. Acts 11 describes how he repealed the commands to only eat the flesh of certain animals as a way of letting Peter know that it was not unclean to take the message of repentance and faith in Jesus to the Gentiles. In the same chapter, Paul fervently urges his Jewish brethren to move beyond the Jewish legalism about circumcision and to accept uncircumcised Gentiles who were filled with the Holy Spirit.

Let's reexamine Exodus 20:5. This verse, describing generational iniquity, has no command. It's not the law. It is not even an impersonal, categorical description of how God's legal system works, such as, "The wages of sin are death." Exodus 20:5–6 describes God. Read it again:

You shall not bow down to them nor serve them. For I, the LORD your God, am a jealous God, visiting the iniquity of the fathers upon the children to the third and fourth generations of those who hate Me, but showing mercy to thousands, to those who love Me and keep My commandments.

This describes not the law, but a characteristic of God's ways and his justice. The Lord loves righteousness right now, today, just as much as he did in the days of Adam. He never despises those with a contrite heart and a broken spirit.[6] And although he sent Jesus to be a friend to sinners and to release us from bondage, he still hates sin. What he tells us to do may vary with the context, but his character does not change.

Lest there be any confusion about the subject of generational sin in our "new covenant times," consider the words of the Lord in Luke 11:47–50.

Woe to you! For you build the tombs of the prophets, and your fathers killed them. In fact, you bear witness that you approve the deeds of your fathers; for they indeed killed them, and you build their tombs . . . that the blood of all the prophets which was shed from the foundation of the world may be required of this generation.

Clearly, Jesus is explicitly saying that since these men inherited the sins of their fathers, they could be held accountable for them because they sanctioned their generational sins, identified with them, and repeated them. The Pharisees chose to honor the prophets in much the same way that they honored Jesus; they honored him with their mouths, but their hearts were far from him. The word *hypocrisy* comes from the word for "actor," or "play-acting."[7] The honor of the Pharisees was an act. They performed this act so that they would be seen honoring Jesus and the prophets. They were courting the favor of the people and seeking to be esteemed by those who loved Jesus and the prophets. They loved the honor of men, and they loved for men to bow down to them in public. Deep generational iniquity was being passed down from their fathers. They maintained the same attitude as their fathers. On the outside they behaved as if they were respectful, but inside, they despised the prophets. Jesus called them on this by saying they were simply coating their sin and covering it with a thick layer of whitewash.

So, we know that iniquity can be passed down through the generations; thus the term, "generational iniquity." We have a very vague idea of what generational iniquity looks like. We can conceive a seemingly infinite number of scenarios that might indicate the presence of generational iniquity. Generally, though, we look for patterns of destruction and devouring that occur pervasively and repeatedly throughout a family. After identifying that pattern, we do something that we call, "identificational repentance," that simply means:

- We perceive, through the Spirit, the presence of the twistedness, the iniquity.

- We identify with those in our family line who fell into this sin (as in Daniel 9).

- We confess it as sin.

- We place that sin in the hands of Jesus on the cross.

- We turn away from it and turn back to God (repent).

We also ask the Lord to remove the curses and consequences that resulted from that iniquity. In other words, the process is the same process of repentance described repeatedly by the prophets and, for that matter, by Jesus. The only wrinkle unique to identificational repentance is that we intentionally choose to identify with those in our family line, rather than being like the Pharisee who said, "Thank you, God, that you didn't make me like that sinner." God expresses his heart for this repentance clearly in Leviticus 26:40–42.

> But if they confess their iniquity and the iniquity of their fathers, with their unfaithfulness in which they were unfaithful to Me, and that they also have walked contrary to Me . . . I will remember My covenant with Jacob, and My covenant with Isaac, and My covenant with Abraham I will remember; I will remember the land.

In this way, we can "work out [our] own salvation with fear and trembling."[8]

We must be careful, however, as we walk through this process, to rely on the guidance of the Holy Spirit. We cannot conquer iniquity through our own power or might, but only by God's Holy Spirit,[9] who is released to us through our faith in Jesus. I implore you to understand this. It is the primary and the most important caveat of all. Do what you must to get this imprinted. Picture a drill sergeant, and imagine the sound of thunder booming through these words as you reread them. I warn you, I caution you, I beg you to rely on the Holy Spirit. In identificational repentance, identify with those who committed the sin and repent for their sin.

I emphasize this again because we cannot manipulate God. He is indeed *Jehovah Rapha*, the God who heals. He is the liberator we seek. But we cannot force his hand by our actions, our formulas, our procedures, or our protocols; we can never push him into acting in a particular manner. He forgives because he wants to, because he is our Father, and he loves us so much that he sent Jesus to bear all the weight that we cannot. He does not act because we found the secret formula to force his hand or because of our own merits, but he acts on our behalf because of who he is.[10]

The Prayer: For Divine Intervention and Release into Your Birthright

For myself and my family line, I repent for and renounce:

- Forgetting you, Lord, and exalting myself as lord of my life
- Misusing godly supplies and money
- Worshiping your gifts instead of you, God, the Giver of the gifts
- Not guarding my heart with all diligence towards you, Lord
- Not reading and acting upon the Word of God
- Not spending time with you
- Not sowing with an attitude of righteousness and therefore not reaping the fruit of unfailing love
- Not breaking up my unplowed ground which has resulted in hardheartedness
- Not extending and receiving mercy for myself and others
- Plowing wickedness and reaping injustice
- Eating the fruit of lies and deception
- Trusting in my own ways and my own strength

For myself and my family line, I repent for and renounce wearing a crown of pride.

I choose to exchange the crown of pride for your crown of glory and a diadem of beauty.

For myself and my family line, I repent for and renounce being apathetic and passive towards our governmental inheritance and not being partakers and stewards of prayer concerning the government and the battle at the gate. I choose now to be a gatekeeper and a watchman of prayer concerning the government of my home, neighborhood, city, county, state, country, and the world. I have a longing for justice and righteousness. I receive your wisdom for strategies that will bring victory to your Kingdom on earth.

For myself and my family line, I repent for and renounce not seizing the opportunity to pray and speak into the realm of influence into which you placed us. I now choose to be obedient and redeem the time. Will you now bring me out of man's time and into your *kairos* time, into the present moment of your presence and will, and will you establish your authority in me on earth as it is in heaven?

For myself and my family line, I repent for the priests, prophets, and leaders who have erred in vision and stumbled in judgment and were partakers in generational addictions. I repent for and renounce those teachers who did not teach godly precepts and did not develop line upon line, but gave milk instead of true discernment. I repent for not receiving with an open heart the godly precepts of the Lord and for closing the door to the blessings. I renounce and repent for hard-heartedness and for allowing my heart to become dull.

For myself and my family line, I repent for and renounce putting up walls that keep us from hearing and receiving your Word. I ask you to remove the walls that keep me from hearing and receiving your godly precepts. I ask you, Lord, to break off the curse of hearing but not understanding, and of seeing but not perceiving.[11]

For myself and my family line, I repent for and renounce not hearing your call to enter into your rest. I repent for myself and all those in my generational line who strived in an attempt to minister to the flock. I repent for the leaders in my family line who did not offer living water but offered human wisdom and knowledge as the answer for spiritual matters. I repent for leaders in my family line who chose to bear the sin of the people rather than allow Christ to be the sacrifice.

✠ For myself and my family line, I repent for those who were in positions of spiritual leadership and did not shepherd or feed the sheep but fleeced them. I repent for myself and those in my generational line who ruled by force and hardhearted harshness, who did not strengthen the diseased and the weak, who did not heal the sick, who did not bandage the hurt, and who did not bring back the lost who had gone astray. I repent for receiving and holding offense against unholy shepherds. Lord, I ask you to restore the scattered sheep. I ask that you return godly shepherds' hearts to this generational line. Lord please break off all the consequences that came as a result of being weak, exhausted, and poor leaders who caused your sheep to be led astray.

✠ For myself and my family line, I repent and renounce all attempts to satisfy our spiritual thirst by going to broken cisterns and drawing from poisoned wells instead of the fountain of living water and for using human methods to accomplish the purposes of the Spirit.

✠ For myself and all in my family line, I repent for forsaking you, the Lord of Hosts, through weakness and backsliding. I did not consider or realize what an evil and bitter thing it is to forsake you, Lord. I realize now that I did not fear you, Lord.

✠ For myself and my family line, I repent for and renounce being unwise, impatient, and going here and there to increase knowledge instead of seeking you first.

✠ Please fill me with your Holy Spirit so I can move in your love; illuminate me with your revelation. Please release me as a leader to walk in the fullness of your wisdom and to shine like the stars of heaven, leading many to righteousness.

✠ For myself and my family line, I renounce and repent for calling you, "Lord" but not obeying your words. I repent for not healing the sick, casting out demons, and raising the dead as you commanded your followers to do. I invite you to do these works through me by your Spirit. I choose to obey your commands.

✠ For myself and my family line, I repent for and renounce building on a refuge of lies and deceptions and striking agreements with the god of death to avoid the grave and the coming destruction. Please annul this covenant with death and break this curse off me. I choose to build on you, Lord Jesus, the true foundation, the Living Stone in whom I will never be shaken.

✠ For myself and my family line, I renounce and repent for being intoxicated with the world instead of being filled with the Holy Spirit.

✠ For myself and my family line, I repent for and renounce not following your command to submit to the Father and to one another.

✠ For myself and my family line, I repent for and renounce not abiding in your light and partaking in unfruitful works of darkness. Lord, please free me to awaken and to arise to do your will.

✠ For myself and my family line, I repent for and renounce all hidden sins and ask you to reveal them in the light of your presence. Help me discern my error and the error of my generational line. Cleanse me from hidden faults; uncover any lies which hide my sin and any deceptions I have concealed from myself and others.

✠ Lord, help me to confess my faults to others and to pray for others so that I may be healed and so that you may present me faultless before the presence of your glory.

✠ For myself and my family line, I repent for and renounce disobeying you and not keeping your commandments. Lord, please remove all the consequences that have come upon me and my generational line: sickness, depression, despair, oppression, mental illness, loss, debt, lack, famine, slavery, fear, barrenness, fruitlessness, and failed marriages.

✖ Lord, I choose to obey you. Holy Spirit, please help me to obey the Father. Please command all of your blessings to come and overtake me and my generational line: fruitfulness, fertility, divine health, increase in the storehouses of finances and goods, harvests, blessings in all my ways, rain to the land in the right seasons, godly rulership and authority, a sevenfold victory over my enemies, and establishment as a part of your holy people.

✖ For myself and my family line, I repent for and renounce all selfishness, self-centeredness, self-protection and decisions not to love myself and others. I choose now to live in all the fullness of love which will lead me to my birthright ordained by Jesus Christ. Lord, please disconnect me from the tree of the knowledge of good and evil and connect me to the tree of life so that your love will flow through me and touch others.

✖ I confess that in Christ, I am free from the spirit of slavery and I am adopted as your son. I agree with you that I am your child and your heir according to your promise. I pray for your divine intervention in my life. I also ask you to reveal your glory in me, so that I can take my place as a son of God and so that I will rule over Creation according to your original call.

✖ Lord, please break the seal of the revelation of Daniel in my life and release me into the fullness of my birthright.

✖ Lord, I choose to turn toward you. I ask that you remove from my face the veil that separates me from you. Lord, please remove all ungodly devices and religious spirits and disconnect me from all ungodly heavenly places that keep me from your glory. I ask you to reveal your glory in me. I receive freedom from your Holy Spirit and ask you to transform me into your likeness with ever-increasing glory.

I declare I will:

- Remember all the blessings and faithfulness of you, God, with a thankful heart

- Be a good steward of everything you give me as you direct me

- Keep my eyes on your face and not on your hands

- Seek you

- Guard my heart with all diligence by being careful to protect my eye gate, ear gate, and heart gate

- Extend mercy to myself and others and receive mercy for myself

- Sow righteousness and reap justice and the fruit of unfailing love

- Eat of the fruit of the Tree of Life, which is Jesus Christ

- Trust in your Word, your ways, and your strength

- Be an overcomer through your grace and take back dominion over the land and over all Creation

I declare I will enter into your glory. I declare I will no longer allow my sin to separate me from your glory. I declare I want to come and sup with you, Lord. I declare I want you to disclose your face to me. I declare I will no longer hide from you. I declare this is the time to move into your realms of glory. I declare this is a new time, a new period, and a new season. I declare that this is the time of a directional shift into your birthright for me.[12]

Notes:

1. Genesis 4:1–16.

2. James Strong, *Strong's Exhaustive Concordance of the Bible*, (McLean, VA: McDonald Publishing), 86.

3. Galatians 2:20.

4. Exodus 34:7.

5. Matthew 5:17.

6. Psalm 51:17.

7. Michael Agnes, ed., *Webster's New World Dictionary and Thesaurus*, (Wiley Publishing, 2002).

8. Philippians 2:12.

9. Zechariah 4:6.

10. *See* Key Word Index for praying for specific generational issues.

11. Matthew 13:13; Mark 4:12; Luke 8:10.

12. Psalms 19:12; 90:8; Deuteronomy 8; 28; Isaiah 25:7–8; 28; Jeremiah 2:13, 19; Ezekiel 34:1–5; Daniel 12:3–4; Hosea 10:12–13; Matthew 13:14–16; 27:45–52; Luke 6:46; Romans 8; 2 Corinthians 3; Ephesians 5; James 5:16; Jude 1:24. Prayer constructed by the Advanced Discernment and Exploration School, Hesperia, CA, August 16, 2007.

Releasing the Favorable
Year of the Lord

PAUL L. COX

Singapore is an amazing city with wonderful people. After four trips to this city/country, I am still awed by the kindness and graciousness of the people. If you have not experienced Singaporean hospitality, you have not experienced true hospitality!

Singapore was the setting for the formulation of the Prayer to Release Supernatural Favor and to Proclaim the Favorable Year of the Lord. It was an appropriate context for the prayer. In the heart of the city is the largest fountain in the world. The Suntec City Mall Fountain of Wealth is said by feng shui masters and Chinese geomancers,[1] to be well-positioned to bring good fortune to those who touch its waters. It would seem that the Chinese culture is all about good fortune and good luck. Every effort is made to maximize the possibility of this good luck through any means possible, except by relying on the Lord.

The beginning of this good luck is the transition into the New Year. The Chinese New Year celebration is unlike any New Year's celebration Westerners are familiar with. The European model of the New Year is to "wish" someone a good year in the future, the Chinese idea is to insure good fortune and prosperity for the New Year.

The Chinese New Year celebration is a way to bring luck into the lives of the Chinese. This good luck is accomplished by performing certain rituals in the belief that this will insure that the coming year will be prosperous.[2] Every effort is made to regulate what you eat, wear, and say during that day. If you are successful, then good fortune will give you prosperity, good grades, children, health, and employment during the coming year. The following is a list of some of the superstitious beliefs about this New Year's Day:

- Get new dollar bills from the bank. Insert the new dollar bills into a red envelope, called a *lee see,* or lucky money envelope. This will pass good luck to the next generation.

- Pay respect to ancestors and household gods. Acknowledge the presence of ancestors because they are responsible for the fortunes of future generations.

- Decorate your home with symbols of good fortune. Here are some suggestions: bright red means happiness; gold/orange means wealth and happiness.

- Eat fruits: oranges and tangerines symbolize good health and long life; tangerines with leaves symbolize long-lasting relationships, fruitfulness, and multiplication as in having children; persimmons represent happiness and wealth.

- Respect signs and omens. For example, if flowers bloom on New Year's Day, know that it will bring a prosperous year.

- Eat *jai,* a food that represents good fortune. *Jai* is comprised of ginkgo nuts, black moss, dried bean curd, bamboo shoots, vermicelli, and scallions.

- Eat fish and chicken, which represent prosperity. Always present the fish and chicken whole. Do not cut them in pieces. The head, tail, and feet (for chicken) must be present to symbolize completeness.

- Eat noodles; they represent longevity.

- Greet others with "gung hey fat choy," which means "wishing you prosperity and wealth."

- Wear brand new clothes, preferably red one. Children should wear new clothes and new shoes.

- Don't wash your hair.

- Don't sweep the floor.

- Don't say the number "four" (a Chinese homonym[3] for *death*) or mention death.

- Don't borrow or lend money.

- Consult with those who know the Chinese zodiac to learn what kind of a year you will have, and get their prescriptions of feng shui principles to remedy any difficulties.

Also prominent in the Chinese pursuit of good fortune is the superstitious belief in the power of numbers. For example, a zero can represent nothingness, completion, and god. The number three is believed to bring good luck and success. The number nine is tied to longevity. The number six, *liù*, is considered to be a very auspicious number because it is a homonym of the word for "flowing" or "smooth." This is why the biblical ominous number 666 does not bother Chinese people. Number sequences made of different numbers may have positive or negative connotations. For example, 168, *yāo liù bā*, can be translated as "want smooth prosperity," or "road to prosperity." Five hundred eighteen can be read as, "I will prosper." The most fortunate number in Mandarin, the Chinese official language, is eight, which means "prosperity," "fortune," or "wealth." This is why starting the Beijing Olympics on 8/8/08 was significant for the Chinese. The most unlucky number in the Chinese culture is the number four because it is closely tied to the pronunciation of the word death.

Feng Shui[4]

A "new" phenomenon affecting the United States is actually part of an ancient Chinese philosophy of nature. *Feng shui* is now such an influence that many real estate agents take courses to understand it, so they can sell houses more readily. Businesses and hotels use the design to attract customers.

Feng shui[5] (pronounced "fung schwee" and meaning literally "wind-water") is part of an ancient Chinese philosophy of nature. Feng shui is often identified as a form of geomancy, divination by geographic features, but it is mainly concerned with understanding the relationships between nature and ourselves so that we might live in harmony within our environment.

Feng shui is related to the very sensible notion that living with rather than against nature benefits both humans and our environment. It is also related to the equally sensible notion that our lives are deeply affected by our physical and emotional environs. If we surround ourselves with symbols of death, contempt, and indifference toward life and nature, with noise and various forms of ugliness, we will corrupt ourselves in the process. If we surround ourselves with beauty, gentleness, kindness, sympathy, music, and various expressions of the sweetness of life, we ennoble ourselves as well as our environment.

Alleged masters of feng shui, those who understand the five elements and the two energies such as *chi*[6] and *sha*,[7] are supposed to be able to detect metaphysical energies and give directions for their optimal flow. Feng shui has become a kind of architectural acupuncture: wizards and magi insert themselves into buildings or landscapes and use their metaphysical sensors to detect the flow of good and bad "energy." These masters for hire declare where bathrooms should go, which way doorways should face, where mirrors should hang, which room needs green plants and which one needs red flowers, which direction the head of the bed should face, etc. They decide these things on the basis of their feel for the flow of *chi*, electromagnetic fields, or whatever other form of energy the client will worry about.

In short, feng shui has become an aspect of interior decorating in the Western world, and alleged masters of feng shui now hire themselves out for hefty sums to tell people such as Donald Trump which way his doors and other things should hang. Feng shui has also become another New Age "energy" scam with arrays of metaphysical products from paper cutouts of half moons and planets, to octagonal mirrors and wooden flutes; of course these products are all offered for sale to help you improve your health, maximize your potential, and guarantee fulfillment of some fortune-cookie philosophy.

Feng shui literally means "wind and water," and its origins date back more than four thousand years. It is based on a Chinese interpretation of the natural world and the study of heavenly bodies to determine the

216

passage of time. It has its origins in Taoism. Over the centuries, the interpretation of feng shui grew more complex and became removed from its original purpose. The single factor setting feng shui apart from other philosophical systems is that it has the capacity for change built into it. Withstanding the test of time, feng shui has remained a philosophy that can be used in any culture and alongside any belief system.

In the book *Feng Shui Secrets Revealed*, we are told how feng shui can help us. This is an example of what feng shui promises:

• Learn how to avoid "bad energy" that manifests woes such as cash flow problems and relationship troubles.

• Discover the ten things that can create prosperity and the eight things that can put you in the poor house.

• Learn the unbelievable six things that can enhance relationships and the surprising six things that can disrupt them.

• Learn how to organize your space so that *chi* (good energy) is allowed to freely flow through your life.

• Learn how to design houses and workplaces that harmonize with the environment instead of clashing with it.

• Learn steps you can take to diagnose your space to see if there are problems and try to improve the overall "vibe" of your environment.

• Discover the five things that can increase your talent and wisdom.

• Learn the amazing five things that can increase your chances of conception.

• Learn how to achieve a balance of *yin* and *yang* elements.

• Understand the cycles of the five elements to determine how to arrange your living quarters.

• Learn the secrets on how to arrange your room to enhance your love life.

• Learn how to arrange your room to increase your prosperity.

- Learn how to arrange your house to improve your health.

- Learn how to identify destructive placements in your home that might be causing havoc in your life with your reputation, your love life, your finances, or your health, etc.

- Learn the secret six feng shui cures!

What should be a Christian response to feng shui? What are some biblical concepts that relate to feng shui?

- The Lord calls us to take dominion over our world (Genesis 1:26–28), and he is the Lord over all (Philippians 2:9–11).

- Jesus is the way, the truth, and the life (John 14:6).

- We are to seek him for wisdom (Colossians 1:9; James 1:5) and guidance (John 16:13), and not seek feng shui masters, books, templates, etc.

- God is clear regarding idols: "Have no other gods before Me." (Exodus 20:1–17).

- Seeking others for wisdom instead of God opens us up to ungodly influences (Colossians 2:2–4).

- Feng shui has origins in Taoism and includes other New Age, occult, and witchcraft influences (Acts 19:18–20).

Tai Chi

Tai chi[8] is a form of Chinese martial art which is characterized by slow motion routines that people practice every morning in parks across China and other parts of the world. There are different styles of tai chi based on the traditions and practices of the Chinese families that developed various techniques. It is primarily practiced for its health benefits, especially dealing with tension and stress.

These health benefits are founded in Taoism and are viewed by many as an essential part of Taoist practice. In China, the spiritual and physical realms are traditionally not seen as separate: thus, in Taoism, the cultivation and exercise of the body is often viewed as an essential part of the religious and spiritual development of the individual.

There are two basic types of martial arts: "hard," for example, *karate* and *kung fu*, which use a degree of tension in the muscles, and the "soft" style, including *tai chi*, in which the musculature maintains deep relaxation or softness. Tai chi is noted for exhibiting soft, slow flowing movements, which are executed with precision. In emphasizing relaxation, tai chi is essentially a form of meditation.

As a form of meditation, tai chi is said to have certain psychological as well as physical benefits. Its intent is to help one understand oneself and therefore to help deal with others more effectively, primarily, through learning the control of self. At the foundation of this philosophy is the fundamental Taoist principle of *yin* and *yang*. It is believed that these two principles are opposites, with one merging into the other, thereby creating the natural balance of self and world. Tai chi is meant to enable one to bring the principles back into their natural harmony. According to Taoism and tai chi, the ultimate effect of this harmony is one's physical and spiritual well-being.

Although the history of tai chi is difficult to trace, its roots go back to the practice of yoga in India two thousand years before Christ. In the thirteenth century AD, a Taoist monk in China developed what has come to be known as tai chi. The principles of yielding, softness, centeredness, slowness, balance, suppleness, and rootedness are all elements of Taoist philosophy that tai chi has drawn upon in its understanding of movement, both in relation to health and also in its martial applications. Today, although most styles of tai chi are not forms of Taoist practice, they all owe their origins to this Chinese religious tradition and have maintained a tenuous link to the more spiritual or religious facets found in Taoist training. Therefore, if a Christian believer practices tai chi or yoga, he is tapping into the spiritual roots of Taoism.[9]

The question must then be asked, Why is there a problem with all of these superstitions and practices? The answer is, People are looking to the wrong source! Proverbs 3:5–6 is clear: "Trust in the Lord with all your heart, and lean not on your own understanding; in all your ways acknowledge Him, and He shall direct your paths." Whenever we look to a way of obtaining prosperity, favor, and health that is not from the Lord, then we place ourselves in a position to be attacked by the enemy. The Lord is the only source of what is good and beneficial in life.

The Prayer: Release Supernatural Favor and Proclaim the Favorable Year of the Lord[10]

✠ Father God, I repent for myself and for those in my generational line for seeking fortune, wealth, health, and prosperity using all evil forces and powers like feng shui, fortune telling, palmistry, face reading, divination, astrology, numerology, Ouija boards, I Ching, the Chinese almanac, tarot cards, and all superstitious practices.

✠ I repent for myself and for those in my generational line for seeking false destinies, magical healings, and good fortune.

✠ I repent for myself and for those in my generational line for financing the worship of idols and the building of temples. I repent for all false burning of candles, oil lamps, joss sticks,[11] paper money, paper material assets, and incense.

✠ I repent for myself and for those in my generational line for the practice of false spiritual cleansing and purification using flowers and water blessed by ungodly beings.

✠ I repent for myself and for those in my generational line for the worship of all false gods and any allegiance with demons. I repent for all attempts to communicate with false idols for the purpose of prosperity, fertility, longevity, health, protection, and destiny.

✠ I repent for myself and those in my generational line for consulting mediums, witch doctors, shamans, bomohs, and false healers.

✠ I repent for myself and my generational line for dedicating families, possessions, land, and ourselves to other gods and idols of the land and water.

✠ I repent for myself and for those in my generational line who received names for their children from leaders of false religions. I repent for myself and my generational line for dedicating and associating our names to the dragon and other ungodly deities.

�incross I repent for myself and for those in my generational line for marrying and communicating with the dead.[12]

✝ I repent for myself and for those in my generational line for worshipping the gods and goddesses of the sun, moon, heavens, and stars.

✝ I repent for myself and for those in my generational line who relied on the cycles of the moon for all ungodly festivals and religious activities.

✝ I repent for myself and for those in my generational line who denied and spoke against your Word and offered burnt sacrifices and flowers to the queen of heaven.[13]

✝ I repent for myself and for those in my generational line for discrediting you because we relied on our own prosperity, strength, and abilities, and we assumed we lacked nothing.[14]

✝ I repent for myself and for those in my generational line for temple prostitution, sexual immorality, bestiality, licentiousness, and its associated vices.

✝ I repent for myself and for those in my generational line for the worship and manipulation of the five elements—metals, wood, water, fire, and earth.

✝ I repent for myself and for those in my generational line for practicing other forms of religion in conjunction with the Christian faith.

✝ I repent for myself and for those in my generational line for all ancestral worship and all belief in reincarnation.

✝ I repent for myself and for those in my generational line for all practice and worship of Buddhism, Hinduism, Taoism, Confucianism, Islam, and Shintoism.

✠ I repent for myself and for those in my generational line for trading our birthright for ungodly gains.

✠ I repent for myself and for those in my generational line for forsaking you Lord and your holy mountain and setting a sacrificial table for fortune and filling cups with mixed wine for destiny.[15] Lord, please remove the curse of the sword and slaughter.[16]

✠ I repent for myself and for those in my generational line for any misuse and manipulation of the prophetic gifts for self-gain and for following the ways of Balaam.

✠ I repent for myself and for those in my generational line for all participation in the martial arts, tai chi, meditation, yoga, and qigong.

✠ I repent for myself and for those in my generational line for bowing to and honoring our ancestors and bowing to and honoring all who called themselves masters or gurus, exalting themselves above you, God, rather than honoring and bowing to you, Lord.

✠ I repent for myself and for those in my generational line for all worship of animals according to Chinese zodiac signs and for trying to take on the spirit, personality, and characteristics of animals.

✠ I repent for myself and for those in my generational line for binding our children to animals and gods.

✠ I repent for myself and for those in my generational line for receiving impartations of skills of power from an ungodly source.

✠ I repent for myself and for those in my generational line for ungodly animal expressions of the body.

✠ I repent for myself and for those in my generational line who tied their coins and paper money to the signs of the zodiac and thus caused their funds to become defiled.

✠ I repent for myself and for those in my generational line for all ungodly medical practices based on the zodiac and the spiritual realm.

✠ I repent for myself and for those in my generational line who, even though we knew God's invisible attributes and divine power, did not honor him and give thanks to him. On behalf of my generation line, I repent for exchanging the truth of God for a lie and for worshipping and serving the creature rather than the Creator. I repent that I became futile in my speculations and my foolish heart was darkened. I repent that instead of being wise, I became a fool. I repent for exchanging the glory of the incorruptible God for images in the form of corruptible men, birds, crawling creatures, and animals, and I repent for all in my generational line who worshipped them.[17]

✠ I repent for myself and for those in my generational line for all ungodly use of colors, sounds, objects, symbols, numbers, and fragrances to attract supernatural and ungodly powers for prosperity and control over people for prosperity and control over nature and people.

✠ I repent for myself and for those in my generational line for all ungodly chanting, dancing, prayer wheels, and trances.

✠ I repent for myself and for those in my generational line for believing we could have eternal life by means other than Jesus Christ.

✠ I repent for myself and for those in my generational line for putting our birthright under the ungodly oaths and covenants in friendships, family relationships, and relationships with authority and with our country.

✠ I repent for myself and for those in my generational line for all compromises in the house of the Lord, for perverting the Word of the Lord and manipulating the people in the house of the Lord in order to build a personal kingdom rather than the Kingdom of God.

✠ I repent for myself and for those in my generational line who manipulated and controlled people in order to build with bricks and mortar rather than allowing Christ to build his church with living stones.

�ібⴎ I repent for myself and for those in my generational line who were leaders and boasted that they did work when it was really the work of others and of the Lord.[18]

✖ I repent for myself and for those in my generational line for choosing to listen to the voice of the enemy and calling it the words of God.

✖ I repent for myself and for those in my generational line for worshipping water spirits and for calling upon them to make a way in the water to go through.

✖ I repent for myself and for those in my generational line for all forms of fire worship, including sacrifices by fire and fire walking.

✖ I repent for myself and for those in my generational line for the ungodly association of wealth with water and the ungodly use and acquisition of wealth.

✖ I repent for myself and for those in my generational line for ungodly mixing of God's Creation in the physical and spiritual realms.[19]

✖ I repent for myself and for those in my generational line who based decisions on man's honor rather than on the Word of God.

✖ I repent for myself and for those in my generational line for all abortions and rejection of fetuses and babies, especially female babies.

✖ I repent for myself and for those in my generational line for exalting evil.

✖ I repent for myself and for those in my generational line for not thinking about you, Lord, or noticing what you were doing. I repent for calling evil good and good evil, darkness light and light darkness, and bitter sweet and sweet bitter, and mocking you, the Holy One of Israel, by saying "Hurry up and do something quickly. Show us what you can do. We want to see what you have planned." I repent for dragging my sins behind me and tying myself with cords of falsehood. I repent for taking bribes to pervert justice and letting the wicked go free and for punishing the innocent.[20]

✠ I repent for myself and for those in my generational line for all ungodly blood covenants and oaths, ungodly blood sacrifices, all drinking of blood, and blood anointings made to achieve fame, prosperity, and success.

✠ I repent for myself and for those in my generational line for rejecting and despising your law and work.

✠ I repent for myself and for those in my generational line for idolizing church and ministry leadership rather than you, Jesus Christ, as the Builder and Cornerstone of my faith.

✠ I repent for myself and for all those in my generational line who supported religious leaders who hindered and criticized the true, free, and lavish worship of you, Jesus.[21]

✠ I repent for myself and for those in my generational line who, as religious leaders, were stumbling blocks and shut out the Kingdom of Heaven to others.[22]

✠ I repent for myself and for those in my generational line for all attitudes of pride and rebellion against God's righteous authorities, and for calling what is holy, profane.

✠ I repent for myself and for those in my generational line who did not seek your heart, Lord, for our family, church, and nation. I repent for not seeking after your Kingdom will.[23]

✠ I repent for myself, religious leaders, and my generational line for the spirit of anti-Semitism and the ignorance of your purposes for the nation of Israel. I choose to bless and pray for the peace of Jerusalem, according to your Word.

✠ I declare that my leaders will lead God's people into true and intimate worship of the living God.

✠ I declare that the Lord knows me by name, and I have grace in his sight.[24]

✠ I declare that the Lord Jesus Christ is the only true leader of my church and ministry.

✠ I declare that I only have purpose in you, Jesus Christ, and I will walk in your purposes.

✠ I declare that you, Jesus, are the Alpha and Omega, the Beginning and the End, the First and the Last. I choose to obey your commandments. I declare that I will have the right to the tree of life and enter through the gates into the city of God.[25]

✠ I declare that I shall no longer be called forsaken, nor shall my land be called desolate. From henceforth I shall be called Hephzibah[26] and Beulah.[27]

✠ I declare that I will always give thanks for all the saints who are increasing more and more in love and the power of faith.[28]

✠ I declare that I will look to the Lord God Almighty and be radiant, and my face will never be covered in shame.[29]

✠ I declare that I will overcome by the Spirit of God, and the name I receive is the name connected to the Lord my God. Lord, give me my new name written on the white stone.[30]

✠ I declare that my desire is to buy your gold, refined in fire, the true wealth of the Kingdom of God.

✠ I declare that you, God, will call me by name, and I will follow your voice and your direction for my life. I will not follow the voice of the stranger, but I will follow the Good Shepherd of my life.[31]

✠ I declare I will pray for the saints and my leaders to preach the gospel in regions beyond my nation, and I will continue to grow in godly activity and allow you, Lord, to produce your fruit in me.[32]

✠ I declare my allegiance and submission to the lordship of Jesus Christ of Nazareth, the root and offspring of David, the Bright and Morning Star.[33]

✠ I declare that I will be a fool for your sake knowing that this is your wisdom.

✠ I declare that although I am weak, in you, Christ Jesus, I am strong.[34]

✠ I declare I will cry out for wisdom and understanding. I will look for wisdom and understanding as if they were silver or hidden treasure. I will look to you, Lord, for wisdom.

✠ I declare that from your mouth comes wisdom and understanding.

✠ I declare that I am now in you, Christ Jesus, and I am a new creation. The old has passed away and the new has come.[35]

✠ I declare that my will shall come into alignment with your will for my life.

✠ I declare that you, Lord, have saved your best wine for the last and that you will manifest your glory.[36] As for me and for my family, we will believe in you, and we will fear and serve you, Lord, in sincerity and truth.[37]

✠ I declare that I, and the children that you, Lord, have given me, have names that reveal the plans that you, Lord Almighty, have for your use.[38]

✠ I declare that I will only accept the true prophetic, which is like a lamp shining in a dark place and like the rising of the morning star and the beginning of a new day.

✠ I declare that you, the Lord God Almighty, have redeemed and restored salvation to your Creation and established your throne in the heavens. Your sovereignty rules over all the earth and all it contains.[39]

✠ Lord Jesus, I honor you and exalt you as you reign over my nation. I ask you this day to establish your plumb line of righteousness and holiness over my nation.

✠ Lord, shepherd your people, the flock of your heritage, with your staff. Who is like you, God, pardoning iniquity and passing over the transgressions of the remnant of your heritage? Lord, you do not retain your anger forever because you delight in mercy. I pray that you will again have compassion on me and will subdue my iniquities. I pray you will cast all my sins into the depths of the sea. Lord, please give truth and mercy to all nations. Please extend mercy, which you have sworn to my fathers from the days of old.[40]

Notes:

1. Divination by means of figures or lines or geographic features.

2. http://www.familyculture.com/holidays/chinese_new_year.htm.

3. One of two or more words spelled and pronounced alike but different in meaning, as the noun *quail* and the verb *quail.*

4. This section was written by Mary Upham.

5. Robert Todd Carroll. *Skeptics Dictionary*, http://www.SkepDic.com.

6. Universal life force.

7. Hard energy, the opposite of *chi.*

8. Tai Chi section written by Mary Upham.

9. *Wikipedia.* Sources: *Tai Chi and Taoism, Tai Chi Chuan* by J. Purcell, Taoist Lineage from International Taoist Tai Chi Society, Tai Chi Chuan, http://en.wikipedia .org/wiki/Tai_chi_chuan.

10. Prayer constructed at the Advanced Discernment Training and Exploration School – Singapore, January 2008.

11. *Joss sticks* are a type of incense used in many East Asian countries, traditionally burned before a Chinese religious image, idol, or shrine. They can also be burned in front of a door or open window as an offering to heaven or devas.

12. In Chinese tradition, a *ghost marriage*, also referred to as *spirit marriage*, is a marriage in which one or both parties are deceased. Other forms of ghost marriage are practiced worldwide, from Sudan, to India, to post-WWI France (see Levirate marriage, ghost marriage, posthumous marriage). The origins of Chinese ghost marriage are largely unknown, and reports of it being practiced today can still be found.

13. Jeremiah 44:17.

14. Jeremiah 44:18; Revelation 3:17.

15. *Destiny* means good fortune, luck.

16. Isaiah 65:11.

17. Romans 1:20–23.

18. 2 Corinthians 10:15.

19. Leviticus 19:19.

20. Isaiah 5:11–25.

21. Mark 14:3–6.

22. Matthew 23:13.

23. Matthew 6:33.

24. Exodus 33:12.

25. Revelation 22:13–14.

26. My delight is in her.

27. Isaiah 62:4. *Beulah* means married.

28. 2 Thessalonians 1:3–4

29. Psalm 34:5.

30. Revelation 2:17.

31. John 10:3–5.

32. 2 Corinthians 10:15–16.

33. Revelation 22:6–16.

34. 2 Corinthians 4:10.

35. 2 Corinthians 5:17.

36. John 2:10–11.

37. Joshua 24:14–15.

38. Isaiah 8:18.

39. Psalms 24:1; 85:4; 103:19.

40. Micah 7:14–20.

Rescinding the Evils of Buddhism

PAUL L. COX

Not too long ago, we were invited to India. After much prayer and several words, we sensed that the Lord was leading us there. Several of our intercessors were in agreement, but a couple of these prayer warriors were very concerned. One had a vision of me in India with a white elephant next to me. The elephant was wearing what looked like prayer beads. I was ignoring the white elephant, and this greatly concerned the intercessor. At the time, we had no clue what the vision meant. After prayerful consideration, we decided that it was not the right time to go to India.

Some time later, I was ministering to a lady from Hong Kong, and we received a word from the Lord that, all tradition of celibacy aside, she was descended from Rahula, Buddha's son, so Buddha himself was in her generational line. I started reading about Buddha and found the tradition that Buddha's mother believed that he was conceived by a white elephant. This white elephant is often portrayed wearing prayer beads. I was astounded as this was exactly what the intercessor had seen.

In thinking about my trip to India, I had been very focused on researching Hinduism and the hundreds of gods associated with that religion. I had been in conversation with Sarah Victor, who eventually constructed a prayer of renunciation of Hinduism. I never considered studying about Buddha, but now, because of the vision and the word of the Lord during ministry time, I started doing research on Buddha and was amazed at my findings!

Buddhism is one of the most insidious of all belief systems in the world. Most non-Christian religions worship other gods, but Buddhism believes that humans, in and of themselves, are, or can become gods.

This is one of the two great lies of Lucifer at the fall of mankind. The first was, "You will not die," and the second, "You shall be like God." These two lies are the basis of the whole New Age movement.

Seeing this, I realized why the intercessor was troubled when I ignored the white elephant in the vision. I had been focusing on Hinduism and ignoring the dangerous beliefs of Buddhism and the evil associated with that religion. It was time to do even more research.

I found that Buddha was born in 563 BC. It was like a lightning bolt hit me. Buddha was born just after the Babylonian captivity in 586 BC. Daniel lived during that captivity (It is believed that the book of Daniel was completed around 530 BC,) and during that captivity Daniel had received the seventy-week vision, which finally made the plan of the coming of the Messiah "publicly" clear. *Is it possible that Lucifer, at that time, began to understand what God was up to, and in reaction he initiated a plan to establish a religion focused on the great lie that "humans" are gods?* If so, the timing was strategic—for the plan would be well in place by the coming of the Messiah.

I continued my research and found a curriculum for Buddhist initiates. At the end of this school, the Buddhist teacher leads the initiates to make a series of proclamations. I was astounded by what I read. The initiates not only declared that they were a "god," but also took on the very names of God listed in Scripture.

With all this information in hand, I was now prepared to pray effectively for the woman with Buddhism in her generational line. When I led her to renounce all the declarations of divinity and the ungodly appropriation of God's names made by her Buddhist ancestors, the results were profound. Even though she had been through several prayer sessions, a dramatic change took place in her life!

New revelations came to me. I remembered that it was believed that the gypsies had been taken from India to Persia around AD 900. After a period of time, they moved west from Persia into Europe and from there into all parts of the world. It is very possible that many, if not all of them, were Buddhists. If so, this means that Buddhism could be in many, if not most, of our family lines. I know this is true of me! I have just recently learned that I am a descendant of gypsy Jews.

An extensive and detailed renunciation prayer has grown out of my research. Since the details of many Buddhist practices are unknown to non-Buddhists, I explain the prayer in footnotes following. However, understanding is not needed for this renunciation to be effective. It is my prayer that it will lead you into greater freedom in the Lord.

The Prayer: Rescinding the Evils of Buddhism[1]

✠ In the name of Jesus Christ, I repent for myself and for those in my generation line who asked for the ascension[2] process to start. I repent for those for calling forth their soul to fully descend into their consciousness and four-body system.[3]

✠ I repent for myself and for anyone in my family line who proclaimed and declared that they were the great "I Am."

✠ I repent for myself and for those in my family line who spoke the sound *om*,[4] as if it were a sacred sound.

✠ I repent for myself and my family line for calling forth our so-called glorified "light body"[5] to descend into our consciousness and four-body system.

✠ I repent for myself and for my family line, for calling forth the "ascension flame"[6] to descend and enter into our consciousness and entire four-body system.

✠ I repent for myself and for my family line for calling forth the full activation of our "alpha and omega" chakras.[7]

✠ I repent for myself and my family line for calling forth the Amrita,[8] fire letters, sacred geometries,[9] and key codes from *The Keys of Enoch*[10] to become fully activated.

✠ I repent for myself and for my family line for calling forth the full activation and creation of the potential twelve strands of DNA within our physical vehicle.

✠ I repent for myself and for my family line for calling forth the full activation of our pituitary gland to create the life hormone and to stop producing the death hormone.

✠ I repent for myself and for my family line for calling forth the activation of our monadic[11] divine blueprints in our conscious, subconscious, and superconscious minds and four-body systems.

✠ I repent for myself and for my family line for calling forth and trying to fully activate the kundalini[12] energy to guide our monad and mighty "I Am" presence.

✠ I repent for myself and for my family line for calling forth the matchstick-sized spark of "cosmic fire" from the presence of "god himself" to illuminate and transform our entire beings into the light of god.

✠ I repent for myself and for my family line for calling forth the full axiatonal[13] alignment as described in *The Keys of Enoch* to perfectly align all our meridian[14] flows within their consciousness and four-body system.

✠ I repent for myself and for anyone in my family line who called forth and fully claimed our physical immortality and the complete cessation of the aging and death process.

✠ I repent for myself and my family line for claiming we were now "youthing"[15] and becoming younger every day.

✠ I repent for myself and my family line for calling forth the full opening of our third eye and all our psychic and channeling abilities, to use them for the glory and service of a false most high god and their brothers and sisters in the false christ on earth.

✠ I repent for myself and for my family line for calling forth perfect radiant health to manifest within our physical, emotional, mental, etheric,[16] and spiritual bodies.

✠ I repent for myself and my family line for asking and commanding that our bodies now manifest the health and perfection of the false christ.

✠ I repent for myself and my family line for calling forth our sixteenth chakra[17] to descend and move our chakras down our chakra column until the sixteenth chakra resides in our seventh, or crown chakra.

✠ I repent for myself and for my family line for calling forth our fifteenth chakra to descend, enter into our sixth, or third-eye chakra.

✠ I repent for myself and for my family line for calling forth our fourteenth chakra to descend and enter our throat chakra.

✠ I repent for myself and for my family line for calling forth our thirteenth chakra to descend and enter and reside in our heart chakra.

✠ I repent for myself and for my family line for calling forth our twelfth chakra to descend and enter and reside in our solar plexus chakra.

✠ I repent for myself and for my family line for calling forth our eleventh chakra to descend and enter and reside in our second chakra.

✠ I repent for myself and for my family line for calling forth our tenth chakra to descend and enter and reside in our first chakra.

✠ I repent for myself and for my family line for calling forth the rest of their chakras, nine through one, to descend down their legs and into the earth in a corresponding fashion. I break all ungodly ties with the earth that were made because of that evil.

✠ I repent for myself and for my family line for calling forth the complete stabilization of our new fifth-dimensional[18] chakra grid system within our consciousness and four-body system.

✠ I repent for myself and for my family line for calling forth our chakra column to light up like a Christmas tree with our first chakra becoming like a large ball of pearl-white light.[19]

✠ I repent for myself and for my family line for calling forth our second chakra to become like a large ball of pink-orange light.

✠ I repent for myself and for my family line for calling forth our third chakra to become a glowing ball of golden light.

✠ I repent for myself and for my family line for calling forth our heart chakra to light up with a pale violet-pink light.

✠ I repent for myself and for my family line for calling forth our fifth chakra to light up with a deep blue-violet light.

✠ I repent for myself and for my family line for calling forth our third-eye chakra to light up with a large ball of golden-white light.

✠ I repent for myself and for my family line for calling forth our crown chakra to light up with a violet-white light.

✠ I repent for myself and for my family line for declaring that our entire chakra columns have now been ignited with the fifth-dimensional ascension frequency.

✠ I repent for myself and for my family line for calling forth with all our hearts, souls, minds, and might the collective help of the eleven[20] other soul extensions[21] in our ascension process.

✠ I repent for myself and for my family line for calling forth the combined collective help of the one hundred forty-three[22] other soul extensions of our monadic[23] group in their ascension process.

✠ I repent for myself and for my family line for calling forth the complete descension and integration into our being of the rain cloud of knowable things.[24]

I repent for myself and for my family line for calling forth the trinity of Isis, Osiris, and Horus, and all pyramid energies that were aligned with the "source" to descend into our consciousnesses and four-body systems and to become fully activated.[25]

I repent for myself and for my family line for calling forth the "ascended master Serapis Bey"[26] and his ascension temple energies from Luxor to descend and become fully activated within our consciousnesses and four-body system.

I repent for myself and for my family line for calling forth our ascension column of light to surround our entire beings.

I repent for myself and for my family line for calling forth the complete balancing of our karmas[27] from all our past and future lives.

I repent for myself and for my family line for calling forth the raising of our vibration frequencies within our physical, astral, mental, etheric, and spiritual bodies to the fifth-dimensional frequencies.

I repent for myself and for my family line for calling forth the light of a thousand suns to descend into our beings and raise our vibration frequencies one thousandfold.

I repent for myself and for my family line for calling forth the sacred sound of *om* to descend and reverberate through our consciousnesses and four-body systems.

I repent for myself and my family line for calling forth a complete and full baptism of the ungodly holy spirit.

I repent for myself and for my family line for calling forth the perfect attunement and completion of our dharma,[28] purposes, and missions in our lifetime service of the ungodly plan.

I repent for myself and for my family line for calling forth the ability to descend into our "christ overself" bodies.

✠ I repent for myself and for my family line for calling forth our fifth-dimensional ascended selves. I repent for believing that we had already ascended within the understanding of simultaneous time, to now meld our consciousnesses with our unified fields and auras.

✠ I repent for myself and for my family line for calling forth any spiritual teacher to descend through our crown chakras and meld his or her ascended consciousness and light into our consciousnesses and four-body systems.

✠ I repent for myself and for my family line for calling forth the great "god flame" to descend and integrate and blend its greater flame within our lesser flames on earth.

✠ I repent for myself and for my family line for calling forth the monad, the mighty ungodly "I am presence and spirit" to fully descend into the consciousnesses and four-body systems and transform them into light. I repent for those who said they were the "ascended master."

✠ I repent for myself and for my family line for declaring:

- Be still and know I am god!

- I am the resurrection and the life!

- I am the mighty "I am presence" on earth forever more.

- I am the "ascended master."

- I am god living in this body.

- The mighty "I am" presence is now my real self.

- I am the "ascension in the light."

- I am the "truth, the way, and the light."

- I am the "open door which no man can shut."

- I am the "divine perfection made manifest now."

- I am the revelation of God.

- I am the light that lights every man that comes into the world.

- I am the cosmic flame of cosmic victory.

- I am the ascended being I wish to be now.

- I am the raised vibration of my full christ and "I am" potential.

- I am the *om* made manifest in the world.

- I am a full member of the "great white brotherhood and spiritual hierarchy."

- I am the realized manifestation of the eternal self.

- I am the embodiment of divine love in action.

- I live within all beings and all beings live within me.

- I am now one with the monadic plane of consciousness on earth.

- I am now living in my glorified body of light on earth.

⚜ I repent for myself and my family line for affirming our ability to transform our four bodies into light and travel anywhere in god's infinite universe.

⚜ I repent for myself and my family line for calling forth Helios, the "solar logos," to send forth into our consciousnesses through our crown chakras, the sixty-four "keys of Enoch"[29] in all five sacred languages, so they would be fully integrated into our beings on earth.

⚜ I repent for myself and my family line for affirming our identities as the "eternal self," "the christ," "the Buddha," "the ātman", [30] the monad, and the "I am presence" on earth in service of humankind.

⚜ I repent for myself and for my family line for affirming that we could remain on earth indefinitely without aging.

⚜ I repent for myself and for my family line for seeing every person, animal, and plant as the embodiment of the "eternal self."

⚜ I repent for myself and for my family line for believing we were the perfect integration of the monad, soul, and personality on earth.

I repent for myself and for my family line for declaring that salvation has come because of what we have done.

I repent for myself and for my family line for saying we were united with the "creator" because of our own efforts.

I repent for myself and for my family line for saying we were the "light of the world" because of our own efforts.

I repent for myself and for my family line for saying they we were fully ascended beings who had chosen to remain on earth to be of service to all sentient beings.[31]

I forgive anyone who has made any of these proclamations over me or any member of my family and break all ungodly power released by these proclamations over us, sending all that is ungodly to the feet of the true Son of God, Jesus of Nazareth.

Notes:

1. *Please Note:* All the footnotes are quotes from those who are Buddhists and believe in what they are saying. The footnotes ARE NOT affirmations of these beliefs but are explanations.
2. On an individual level, ascension is the process of changing one's consciousness from one reality, based on one set of beliefs, to another. On a group or planetary level, ascension is the collective expansion of a state of consciousness—a set of beliefs—to the point where that consciousness creates a new reality—a new state of being or dimension. Ascension is used to describe the very real possibility that you can, within your lifetime, transform your dense 3rd dimensional physical form into a lighter, more invisible 5th dimensional form.
3. Physical, mental, spiritual, emotional
4. Buddhists place *om* at the beginning of their *Vidya-Sadaksari* or mystical formulary in six syllables. As a seed syllable, it is also considered holy in esoteric Buddhism. With Buddhism's evolution and breaking away from Vedic/Hindu tradition, *om* and other symbology/cosmology/philosophies are shared with the Hindu tradition.

Notes (continued):

5. Buddhists believe that the lightbody is the eternal part of a human that never dies, the higher self, which is not dependent on one's body or mind to exist. It is what carries one from incarnation to incarnation, descending in the process of birth to activate our body minds with intelligence and our karmic histories.

6. There is a belief that there are three main ascension flames, which are the "threefold flame" which exists in the altar of each person's heart: threefold flame of love, wisdom, and power. The belief is that power is the god flame, love is the christ flame, and wisdom is the holy spirit flame.

7. The alpha/omega chakras, located 8 inches above and 8 inches below the spine respectively, form between them the waves of metatron of electric, magnetic, and gravitational function. They act as anchors—the alpha connects the lower bodies with its upper-dimensional counterparts, and the omega anchors the lower bodies across their holographic grid of incarnations.

8. Amrita, under its Tibetan name of Dutsi, also features in Tibetan Buddhist mythology, where it is linked to the killing of the monster Rahu by Vairapani. Blood dripped onto the surface of this earth, causing all kinds of medicinal plants to grow. Dutsi also refers to a herbal medicine made during ceremonies involving many high lamas in Tibetan Buddhism, known as Drubchens. It usually takes the form of small, dark brown grains that are taken with water or dissolved in very weak solutions of alcohol.

9. Sacred geometry may be understood as a worldview of pattern recognition, a complex system of hallowed attribution and signification that may subsume religious and cultural values to the fundamental structures and relationships of such complexes as space, time, and form. According to this discipline, the basic patterns of existence are perceived as sacred: for by contemplating and communing with them one is thereby contemplating the mysterium magnum, the patterning relationships of the great design. By studying the nature of these patterns, forms and relationships, and their manifold intra- and interconnectivity, one may gain insight into the scientific, philosophical, psychological, aesthetic, and mystical continuum, that is, the laws and lore of the universe.

10. *The Keys of Enoch* is a textbook that states the issues of the future in spiritual and scientific prose. *The Keys* examine the puzzles of life and give a spiritual explanation as to why we exist in this reality. In essence it provides both the scenario of an

ongoing past/present/future cosmology and a blueprint for a new direction in humankind's evolution into a higher state of consciousness.

11. Monadic is a singular metaphysical entity from which material properties are said to derive.

12. Kundalini according to various teachings is a type of "corporeal energy." Kundalini in Sanskrit literally means either "coiled up" or "coiling like a snake." There are a number of English renderings of the term, such as 'serpent power.' Kundalini is envisioned as a serpent coiled at the base of the spine.

13. The book *The Keys of Enoch* speaks of a fifth circulatory system, which is fifth-dimensional in nature and works through axiatonal arrangement. It is said to allow the higher self and the brotherhood of light to balance abnormalities in the body, re-generate tissue and organs, and evolve the current system of continuous cell division.

14. Energy meridians are the internal energy pathways throughout the physical body which energetically connect a person's organs and their many subsystems (e.g., cir-culatory, endocrine, nervous, digestive, etc.). These energy meridians and specific points on these meridians are used in healing modalities such as acupuncture and acupressure.

15. Not aging.

16. The etheric body, ether-body, aether body, or vital body is one of the subtle bodies in esoteric philosophies, in some religious teachings, and in New Age thought. It is understood as a sort of life force body or aura that constitutes the "blueprint" of the physical body and which sustains the physical body.

17. The word comes from the Sanskrit *cakra* meaning "wheel, circle," and sometimes also referring to the "wheel of life."

The highest crown chakra is said to be the chakra of consciousness, the master chakra that controls all the others. Its role would be very similar to that of the pituitary gland, which secretes hormones to control the rest of the endocrine system and also connects to the central nervous system via the hypothalamus. The thalamus is thought to have a key role in the physical basis of consciousness.

The Ajna chakra, or third eye, is linked to the pineal gland. Ajna is the chakra of time and awareness and of light. The pineal gland is a light sensitive gland, that produces the hormone melatonin, which regulates the instincts of going to sleep and awakening. It also produces trace amounts of the psychedelic chemical dimethyltryptamine.

The throat chakra, Vishuddha, is said to be related to communication and growth, growth being a form of expression. This chakra is paralleled to the thyroid, a gland that is also in the throat, and which produces thyroid hormone, responsible for growth and maturation.

Notes (continued):

The heart chakra, Anahata, is related to love, equilibrium, and well-being. It is related to the thymus, located in the chest. This organ is part of the immune system as well as being part of the endocrine system. It produces T cells responsible for fighting off disease and is adversely affected by stress.

The solar plexus chakra, Manipura, is related to energy, assimilation, and digestion, and is said to correspond to the roles played by the pancreas and the outer adrenal glands, the adrenal cortex. These play a valuable role in digestion, the conversion of food matter into energy for the body.

The sacral chakra, Swadhisthanna, is located in the groin, and is related to emotion, sexuality, and creativity. This chakra is said to correspond to the testes or the ovaries, producers of the various sex hormones involved in the reproductive cycle, which can cause dramatic mood swings.

The base or root chakra, Muludhara, is related to security, survival, and also to basic human potentiality. It is said the kundalini lies coiled here, ready to uncoil and bring man to his highest spiritual potential in the crown chakra. This center is located in the region between the genitals and the anus. Although no endocrine organ is placed here, it is said to relate to the inner adrenal glands, the adrenal medulla, responsible for the fight and flight response when survival is under threat. In this region is located a muscle that controls ejaculation in the sexual act.

18. The fifth-dimensional consciousness is a way of living in the world that perceives and understands the physical universe both within and beyond the limitations of linear time and is also fired by compassion and the sense of being one with all. While it accepts the right of each to determine his or her own destiny, it also sees how we are all interdependent in terms of natural resources and in terms of the deep empathic mind link between beings.

19. Notice how the colors and following are very similar to the rainbow spectrum of light.

20. Possibly the eleven ungodly elders.

21. There is a belief of an "I Am" presence, a unit of energy, a part of the source him/ herself. Here is a quote from an internet source. "There is no such think as a young 'I Am' Presences or old 'I Am' Presences. They just are. Some humans may judge and say, 'This is a young soul; this is an old soul.' There is no such thing. All were created at the same time, at the same outpouring from the Source, at the same moment of this

round of creation. So your 'I Am' Presence is you, your Higher Self. Don't confuse this with your soul. Many would think that the soul is the Higher Self. This is not correct. It is erroneous thinking and dis-information. The soul is something very different. Each 'I Am' Presence has the capability of expanding itself into twelve souls. It makes some human beings feel somewhat shaky, because they thought that they were individual, the only one. On an 'I Am' Presence level you are individual, you are the only one, but the 'I Am' Presence has the capability of expressing itself through twelve souls, and these twelve souls also have the capability of each creating another twelve souls, or soul extensions. So there could be 144 of you."

22. Possible antithesis of Psalm 143 and also could be compared with the number 144.

23. Monad was a term used by the ancient philosopher Epicurus to describe the smallest units of matter, much like Democritus's notion of an atom.

24. The "rain cloud of knowable things" is that impending, overshadowing, and revelatory storehouse of energy, which is the immediate cause of all events on earth and which indicates the emergence of that which is new and better and progressively right. The events and happenings thus precipitated demonstrate the moving onward of the human consciousness into greater light. These "knowable things" are the sources of all revelation and of all human cultural realizations and leading to what we call civilization. Their "condensation" (if I may use such a word) is brought about by the massed invocative appeal of the entire human family at any one period. This appeal has been, on the whole, projected unconsciously, but more and more it will be consciously voiced. Results, therefore, can be expected more rapidly and prove more effective. This rain cloud is formed through the joint action of the central spiritual sun, working through Shamballa, and humanity itself, working hitherto through appeal to the hierarchy, but increasingly making its own direct appeal.

25. Egyptian gods.

26. Serapis Bey is regarded in Theosophy as being one of the ascended masters, also called the *Masters of the Ancient Wisdom* or the Great White Brotherhood. He is regarded as the Master of the Fourth Ray. It is believed that Serapis Bey was incarnated as a high priest in one of the "Temples of the Sacred Fire" on Atlantis who migrated to Egypt at the time of the destruction of Atlantis. It is also believed that he was incarnated as the Egyptian Pharaoh Amenhotep III (who constructed the Temple of Luxor to the god Amon). Adherents of the Ascended Master Teachings believe that Serapis Bey became an Ascended Master about 400 BC. He has been identified by Theosophists with the god Serapis who was a Hellenistic/Egyptian god.

Notes (continued):

27. Karma in Indian philosophy is the influence of an individual's past actions on his future lives, or reincarnations. The doctrine of karma reflects the Hindu conviction that this life is but one in a chain of lives and that it is determined by man's actions in a previous life. This is accepted as a law of nature, not open to further discussion. Buddhism incorporated doctrines of karma as part of its Indian legacy. The Buddhists interpret it strictly in terms of ethical cause and effect.

28. In Buddhism, dharma is the doctrine, the universal truth common to all individuals at all times, proclaimed by the Buddha. Dharma, the Buddha, and the sangha (community of believers) make up the triratna, or "three jewels," to which Buddhists go for refuge. In Buddhist metaphysics, the term in the plural (dharmas) is used to describe the interrelated elements that make up the empirical world.

29. Note this is the same number on the chessboard and is tied to the DNA. *The Keys of Enoch* is a parapsychical "codebook" written in 1973 by Dr. J. J. Hurtak. It is a text of higher consciousness experience which explains how the human race is connected with a more advanced higher evolutionary structure of universal intelligence. This book is meant to prepare one for the paradigm shift that will affect all aspects of the social, psychological, and spiritual dimensions of life.

30. *Ātman* is Sanskrit; it literally means "self," but is sometimes translated as "soul" or "ego." In Buddhism, the misplaced or inappropriate belief in *ātman* is the prime consequence of ignorance, which is itself the cause of all misery.

31. According to Buddhism, a sentient being is one who is capable of experiencing suffering.

Prayer of Release
from Being a Sacrifice

PAUL L. COX

My journey as a leader began in high school when I was invited to lead a Sunday school class. While attending college, I was responsible for the data processing department of Signal Oil Company. After college, I served as a counselor at Green Oak Ranch Boys' Camp. During the following years, I was an eighth grade public school teacher for three years, a full-time youth worker for six years, a pastor for twenty years, and a schoolteacher in a child/adolescent psychiatric ward of a hospital for six months. For the past ten years, I have served with my wife as codirector of Aslan's Place.

In every leadership position, I noticed that some people were inclined to blame their sins and shortcomings on others, especially on their leaders. This became even more visible when I was a pastor. Over twenty years ago the Lord planted a seed in my mind for a manuscript first titled *Sacrifice the Pastor*. As a Baptist pastor, I had noticed a tendency for individuals who told me confidential issues to either turn against me or leave the church within a few months. I realized that in some way, I had become the sacrifice for their sins, instead of the Lord Jesus.

Now, over twenty years later, I see even more clearly that this practice is not limited to people and their pastors. Any compassionate Christian, who listens to the hurts of others, can be placed in a position to become a sacrifice. This happens to businessmen, therapists, schoolteachers, principals, small group leaders, and church staff professionals; it also happens between friends who listen with kind hearts.

Because of this, it might be helpful to clarify a term we often use in the church. It is the word *minister*. We have incorrectly defined a *minister* as anyone who has met the qualifications of a denomination and has been ordained. This is not the biblical definition of a minister. Ephesians 4:11–12 defines a minister as one who has been equipped by apostles, prophets, evangelists, pastors, and teachers to do the work of ministry. Therefore every follower of Jesus Christ is a minister. Any leader who is a Christian is a minister. For that reason, whenever I use the term minister, I am referring to all believers, with the focus on believers in leadership. Our ministry may be in a church, a religious organization, the marketplace, the educational arena, the government, the medical community, or at home. It does not matter. Wherever you are, you are a minister. Wherever you minister, you may find yourself counseling. Whenever you counsel, you may find yourself being set up to be a sacrifice.

We need to remember to keep our focus on Jesus: He is our only sacrifice. As we remember to place our sins on Jesus, we remain in unity so that the work of the Kingdom of God will progress here on earth.[1]

The Prayer: Release from Being a Sacrifice

Father forgive me and my generational line for placing our sins on others and chasing them away or making them scapegoats.

I repent for myself and my family line for wittingly or unwittingly receiving the sins of others or allowing myself to be the sacrifice or the scapegoat. Forgive me and cleanse me from all assigning or giving to others the sin that Jesus died for or from taking on myself and receiving any sin that Jesus died for.

I confess that I am no longer willing to be the sacrifice. I am no longer willing to be the scapegoat. I ask that all sins of others which have been placed upon me be removed. Break them off. I will not bear them. I refuse them.

�҉ Father, remove the consequences of this sin from me and from my generational line. I ask that the reaping of the consequences and all related curses be broken off of me from this time forward. I ask they be broken off my family line for all future generations. I ask they be removed from me and removed from my children based on your righteousness which you have imputed to me through the blood of Jesus. I ask that they also be removed from all of my grandchildren, all of my future grandchildren, and all future generations, from this time forward throughout eternity.

�҉ Father, right now in the name of Jesus, remove the scapegoat from me and my children and please remove every evil thing related to all ungodly sacrifices.

�҉ Lord, please replace these vacated areas with your Holy Spirit and with your blessings. Thank you for pouring your Spirit into me and into my descendants.

Notes:

1. Paul L. Cox, *Sacrifice the Leader* (Lake Mary, FL: Creation House, 2008).

Repentance for
Ungodly Intercession

PAUL L. COX

While I was ministering in Asheville, North Carolina, a woman complained about knee pain. As an intercessor prayed for her knee, it became apparent that this woman was drawing her identity from being an intercessor. She agreed that this was true and said that she felt much anxiety in praying for a wayward son. She felt like she needed to be in constant prayer and fasting for him, often for twenty-hours at a time.

During a prayer session with an intercessor from Aslan's Place, the Lord took her back to a time when she had been violated as a little girl. The four-year-old girl was hiding, afraid of men, and wasn't interested in meeting Jesus. Finally the four-year-old realized that Jesus was safe, and she could invite him into her place of hiding. As she did, Jesus came, healed her, and cleansed her.

A turning point came when the four-year-old and Jesus played together. When she was willing to let Jesus hold her doll, she realized that just as she could trust Jesus to care for her doll, she could also trust him to care for her son. She understood that the Lord loved her son even more than she did. She gave the Lord her son and the other burdens of prayer that she had been carrying.

We asked the Lord to break off all ungodly attachments to her knees that were associated with ungodly intercession based on striving and works. Her knee pain left as she came into his rest and trusted him with all her concerns. It was out of this experience that the Prayer to Repent for Ungodly Intercession was birthed.

On the surface, there seems to be nothing less dangerous than praying to the Lord. How could any prayer be wrong? As a Baptist pastor, I taught a lot about praying. We had prayer meetings and prayer seminars. I organized regional conferences on prayer. We encouraged and were encouraged to spend time in prayer. Our only problem with prayer was in believing that we may not have been praying enough! The concept that praying could go wrong was not even within the scope on my radar. I would have to learn the hard way! Many difficult lessons have been learned during the past few years.

In 1989, just before I began to learn about deliverance, the Lord brought Jackie Douglas-Thomas to our church. She told me that the Lord had called her to become an intercessor for me. I had no idea what she was talking about. She would fast and pray for me every week; sometimes she fasted two or three times a week. I had no idea how to respond to this type of praying. *Was I to do something?* Once, she came to me and said the Lord told her that my wife, Donna, was to stop working. Donna was making a very good salary then. My response was, "The Lord has not told me to have her stop working!" At that precise moment, the phone rang. I answered the phone, and Donna replied to my greeting by saying that she had just resigned her job because of the ungodly attitude and speech of her boss. All I could say was, "I guess this is God's will."

Over the years, I have been honored to have many wonderful intercessors invest in hours of prayer for me and Donna. Our lives have been richly blessed because of their sacrificial praying. However, this is not the whole story. I have also come under serious attack and suffered loss because of the ungodly nature of some intercessors with secret agendas behind their prayers. Motives and personal agendas can and do affect the results of prayers. This ungodly praying allows the enemy the right to interfere in the lives of those being prayed for. Although I do not completely understand how it happens, I can testify that when I come into agreement with these prayers, the effects are often devastating.

Some years ago, we had a woman who became very close to Donna and me. Her gifting was extraordinary, and she often prophesied over us. Frequently, she would speak of things that only Donna and I would know. Because of her supposed accuracy in these matters, we trusted her. As she would talk of these things, she spoke of seeing herself as part of the ministry given to Donna and me. Even though others around us warned us about her, we never completely felt as if we should be concerned. That was all to change. A series of events unfolded that caused us to have great apprehension about her motives. When a break in relationship took place, of course, she declared that we were the ones at fault. Donna and I held the matter closely, but the Lord was to reveal her heart. Within a couple of days, an intercessor, who had met the woman on a ministry trip and who knew nothing about what had happened, called and said that he had just seen a vision of a snake coming out of this woman's mouth; it hit Donna, my wallet, and my car. I knew instantly what this meant. Her words were trying to destroy my wife, my ministry, and my finances. I found out a day later that she had told five of my closest friends that I was in error because I had not employed her in the ministry, even though, at that time, Donna and I were not yet receiving a full-time salary ourselves.

What had happened? This woman wanted desperately to be a part of a thriving ministry. Her amazing gifting in prophetic intercession gave her the ability to actually "read" the prophetic call on our lives. She could see the wonderful things the Lord wanted to do with us. Because she wanted and needed to be a part of something like this, she would insert herself into the "call" on our lives. Her praying had become manipulative and controlling.

I would like to say that this never happened again; unfortunately, I can't. Many people have tried to get close to us because of their personal agendas. Whenever this happened, their prayers had a shocking effect upon us.

How do you guard yourself against ungodly intercession? I have learned the hard way that my first line of defense is my wife. If she has difficulty with anyone around me, then I must listen to her. Early in our ministry, the Lord said to me several times, "Listen first to your wife and then to your children." I put this into practice; since then I have added our children's spouses and now our grandchildren. Donna and I also have a very small group around us with whom we have a history of godly intercession. This team is key in limiting our victimization by others' self-centered prayers.

The following prayer is self-explanatory; it is well documented with Scripture. You will notice that we believe that the effects of ungodly intercession in family lines can be passed down through the generations into the present and can influence our lives and the lives of others around us. The goal of this prayer is to cleanse believers of generational contamination in intercession. Only as our hearts' intents are pure and we seek to pray to the Lord through the complete guidance of the Holy Spirit will our prayers further the Kingdom of God.

The Prayer: Repentance for Ungodly Intercession

✠ For myself and my generational line, I repent for and renounce all ungodly prayers ever uttered, including controlling witchcraft prayers and prayers birthed out of fear instead of faith. Lord, please remove all that evil from my life and from my DNA, and would you restore your presence and the power of your Holy Spirit to my life.

✠ Lord, please forgive me for misunderstanding the high calling and privilege of intercession.

✠ I repent for myself and those in my generational line who left their watch and station and did not wait on you. I choose now to be stationed on the rampart, to wait upon you and to hear what you will say to me. I will wait until I am corrected.[1] Lord, I choose to write down the vision, so future generations can run with it. I choose your timing so that the vision will not be delayed.[2]

✠ For both myself and my generational line, I repent for and renounce relying on our own understanding instead of yours, Lord. I repent for praying our will instead of your will. I renounce and repent for not relying on your living Word and for speaking death over my loved ones instead of the life which you so richly give.

✠ For myself and my generational line, I repent for seeking and praying our own will and desires and not yours. Lord, I repent for and renounce limiting you and all that is possible through you. I repent for and renounce not receiving your dreams and praying them into reality because they are so big. Would you release the gift of faith and expectancy in me, so that I will know with confidence that you are able to do more than I can think or imagine?[2] I choose to receive the dreams and desires that you have given me and to believe that all things are possible with you,[3] Lord.

� Lord, I repent for and renounce not acknowledging you, your power, and the time of your visitation; I repent for not knowing you and for not praying what is on your heart. Lord, I desire to know you and to pray what is on your heart and to receive your blessings.

✠ I repent for and renounce stepping out of my own realm of authority and fighting battles that you never told me to fight.

✠ For myself and my generational line, I repent for and renounce looking at my circumstances and praying from a soulish perspective and a worldly view. Lord, forgive me for being misled and for trusting in a system that has failed me because it was not based on truth or relationship with you. You paid the price of my sin in full.

✠ For myself and my generational line, I repent for and renounce praying prayers of doubt, unbelief, self-righteousness, pride, jealousy, envy, fear, hard-heartedness, strife, selfish ambition, judgment, and deception. Lord, please remove all bitter root judgments that I agreed with. Please remove all ungodly intercession based upon these sins. I ask for the angel, Breakthrough, to break, shatter, dissolve, and destroy all ungodly intercession, all ungodly prayers, all self-righteous prayers, all soulish prayers, and unsound mind prayers. I choose to walk in power, love, and a sound mind.

✠ I repent and renounce, for myself and my generational line, all jealousy, envy, and attempting to steal the giftings and callings of others. I repent for shutting the door on the children of God so that they would forfeit their callings. Lord, I admit that these things have interfered with my intimacy with you and my intercession for others. I choose to completely forgive those who have been jealous of me or tried to steal my giftings and callings or tried to shut the doors to my birthright or interfere with my intimacy with you and intercession for others. Lord, I now choose to freely give what you have given to me so that you may rebuke the thief in my life and in the lives of others. I choose to lay down my life so that you may raise it up again.

✠ For myself and my generational line, I repent for and renounce praying controlling, manipulative prayers out of a selfish motivation for the purpose of controlling others for selfish advantage.[4] Father, please remove and cancel the effects of all the soulish prayers, ungodly intercessions, prophecies, and declarations that have released curses against me, my family, and others. I forgive those who have knowingly or unknowingly brought curses upon my family by praying their will instead of yours.

✠ For myself and my generational line, I repent for those who rejected the identity of sonship with you and rejected the spirit of adoption and walked according to the futility of their minds. Lord, I receive the spirit of adoption, crying, "Abba, Father."[5] I choose to walk and pray by faith and not by sight.[6] I come into agreement with the truth that as your child I have direct access to you, and I can approach your throne by faith in the blood of Jesus.[7]

✠ For myself and my generational line, I repent for and renounce praying striving, compulsive prayers from a state of anxiousness and unrest instead of praying from a state of rest by being seated with you in heavenly places. Lord, I choose to have my eyes focused on the victory that you intend for me to have.[8,9]

✠ For myself and my generational line, I repent for and renounce taking on the yoke of religious, organizational, and man-made intercession instead of taking on your burden of intercession. I ask you to break off all ungodly yokes and false burdens of intercession from me and my family line. I break all agreements made to ungodly religious and governmental authorities.

✠ Lord, I ask you to break off of me and my family line the consequences of fatherlessness, abandonment, rejection, and the consequences of allowing a false spirit of Elijah to have power over my intercession and prayers.

✠ For myself and my generational line, I repent for and renounce withholding prayers and intercession that would release the sons and daughters of God.

✠ For myself and my generational line, I repent for and renounce all ungodly intercession directed to idols, gods, goddesses, objects, heavenly and earthly bodies, and the dead. Father, please break the consequences of ungodly intercession that hindered your answers to prayer from your throne.

✠ For myself and my generational line, I repent for and renounce all ungodly chanting, ritualistic, and repetitive prayers. Lord, would you remove the curses that were activated and the ungodly spiritual forces that were empowered by these unrighteous prayers? For myself and my generational line, I repent for and renounce trusting in man-made formulas. Lord, I repent for not surrendering to the Holy Spirit and not allowing him to make intercession through me according to his mind and the will of God.[10]

✠ Father, please remove from my heart, mind, and will all deception and wrongful motivations and intents that would cause me to pray misguided prayers.

✠ Father, please remove the brass heaven?[11] Father, please release an open heaven and pour out the bowls of the prayers of the saints according to your will.

✠ For myself and my ancestors, I repent for not honoring the godly priests and priestesses who have prayed your heart, Lord God. Please pour out the godly bowls of intercession prayed by the saints before me.

✠ Lord, I repent for not seeking your Kingdom first and for not trusting that you know and will fulfill my needs. I receive your promise that when I seek your Kingdom first, all these things will be added to me.[12]

✠ Lord, I repent for not asking from you as you have commanded me, so that I may receive from you and my joy may become full.[13]

Lord, I repent for not continuing to travail in prayer as Elijah did until your purposes have been joyously fulfilled, until heaven gives rain and the earth produces its fruit.[14] Lord, would you establish me as the trees planted by rivers of water which bring forth fruit in season, so that whatever I do will prosper?[15]

Lord, for both myself and my ancestors, I repent for and renounce praying faithless prayers and not having faith for you to heal the sick.[16] Lord, I desire to please you by praying in faith that all things are possible to those who believe. I believe you are good, and all good and perfect gifts come from you, the Father of lights.[17]

I repent for and renounce, for myself and my generational line, any agreement with the enemy's trickery or deceptive schemes that caused me to yield my God-given authority, thus affecting my prayers, decrees, proclamations, and myself. Thank you for bringing the revelation of truth, so I can repent and take back my authority.

For myself and my generational line, I repent for and renounce listening to or using flattery, which causes deception and ruin, and for misrepresenting God's truths in order to control others for my personal gain.[18]

Lord, I repent for and renounce, for myself and my ancestors, any coming to the altar of incense before being cleansed and confessing sins, faults, and offenses to one another.[19]

On behalf of myself and my ancestors, I repent for not seeking you daily and delighting to know your ways; I repent for doing as we pleased on the day of prayer and fasting. For myself and my ancestors, I repent for believing that the outward works of fasting and prayer would bring results when we inwardly held on to strife and dissension that resulted in cursing, hitting, and exploitation of your children. Lord, I choose the fast you have chosen—to loose the chains of injustice, to break the yokes of the oppressed, to feed the hungry, to provide for the homeless, and to clothe the naked.[20] I choose to do right, to seek justice, encourage the oppressed, defend the cause of the fatherless, and plead the case of the widow.[21]

✠ I repent for myself and for the women in my generational line who took it upon themselves to act as if they were the Holy Spirit to men. I repent for those women who did not allow men to be the spiritual leader in their marriage but tried to take on that position.[22]

✠ For myself and the men in my generational line, I repent for all inconsideration, for all dishonoring, and for not recognizing our wives as joint heirs by the grace of God. I choose to live in consideration of my spouse and honor her as a joint heir of God's grace.

✠ I repent for myself and the men in my family line who, because of fear and passivity, relinquished their responsibilities as leaders. I renounce and break all agreements with the spirits of Jezebel and Ahab in myself and my generational line.[23]

✠ I repent for myself and for those in my family line who did not know and/or care to know their responsibility for intercession.[24] For myself and my generational line, I repent for those who did not value intercession, said it was for others, and did not pray. Father, forgive me for prayerlessness.

✠ Lord, I ask forgiveness for not recognizing the creative arts as intercession. I repent for restricting dance, painting, music, and visual arts from worship and intercession to you. Lord, break the consequences off my family line of legalistic mocking, limiting, and restricting passionate worship and intercession through dance and the arts.

✠ I choose to forgive all those in the body of Christ who shut down and limited creativity in me as a worshipper and an intercessor. I choose to recognize and bless the creative arts in others as the word of God in the anointing of truth.[25]

✠ Lord, I choose to enter into your courts with praise and to worship you for who you are in Spirit and in truth.

✠ For myself and my generational line, I repent for and renounce being narrow-minded and not embracing all of you and your Kingdom. I repent for a narrow view of your Kingdom. I ask you to remove all the limitations that I have agreed with and replace them with your wisdom, your knowledge, your understanding, and the fullness of who you are.

✠ I repent for myself and my generational line for not praying for leaders and those in authority that you have placed over us.[26] For myself and my generational line, I repent for and renounce not submitting to governmental authority; I also repent for and renounce any praying against the president and other government officials; they have been appointed by God. I repent for using liberty as a cloak for cursing and speaking evil in my prayers against the established government. I repent for not honoring the leaders of my nation. I repent for not praying for and seeking the peace of the city, state, and nation where you have caused me to live.

✠ I repent for letting false prophets, diviners, and the news media deceive me and cause me to bring negative prayers to you. I repent for not seeking your divine insight. I renounce generational terrorism, treason, insurrection, and murder. Lord, please remove all judgments that I have brought against me, my family, and your people through unrighteous prayers.[27]

✠ Lord, please go before me as my King, please go before me with the breaker anointing so that I can pass through the gate, breach the womb, and break out and burst forth in multiplication and spread in all directions.[28]

✠ For myself and my generational line, I repent for and renounce believing lies, walking in discouragement, pain, suffering, disappointment, hopelessness, and allowing these circumstances to negatively affect my intercession.

✠ For myself and my generational line, I repent for and renounce praying prayers to look or sound righteous or spiritual in front of others rather than praying in the humility of true relationship and coming into your presence and communing with you, Lord.[29]

✠ For myself and my generational line, I repent for and renounce praying and bowing the knees to any man, angel, idol, or image rather than to you, Lord God. I repent for not relying on you to strengthen my feeble knees. I repent for confused, faithless, and complaining prayers during a time when you were chastening me. I acknowledge that your desire was to strengthen my feeble knees, but my attitude and prayers hindered me.

✠ From receiving your correction. Lord, forgive me for not exalting you in prayer as the Lord to whom every knee should bow.

✠ I repent for myself and my ancestors for prolonged kneeling, self-abasement, flagellation, and striving in prayer, and for going beyond the leading of your Holy Spirit so that we could boast of our prayers.[30] I repent for not strengthening the weak hands and feeble knees of others.[31]

✠ For myself and my generational line, I repent for and renounce praying out of a place of disunity with your body and praying out of a heart filled with selfish desires, envy, and jealousy. This has caused me to miss the mark. Forgive me for every time I have been pulled off course, either by the enemy or my own unyielding will. Forgive me for wanting to promote my own self-will rather than you. I repent for and renounce idolatry. I choose to set my face to know you and your heart of mercy and compassion, and I will pray your heart and not my own.

✠ Lord, release your sound as a war cry in me and others so that we may worship with one accord with your Spirit in such a way that will breach the walls, break through the bronze heaven, and pierce the canopy that holds back generational blessings.[32]

✠ Lord, on behalf of myself and my ancestors, I repent for and renounce everything that has allowed the enemy to steal my prayers. Lord, please remove all generational curses and evil assignments against intercession.

✠ Lord, please give me the breakthrough to plunder the enemy's camp and take back all righteous unanswered prayers for both myself and for anyone in my family line.

✠ Father, in Jesus' name I choose to empty myself of fleshly emotions and desires and ask you, Yahweh, to fill me with your mind, your heart, and your will.

✠ Lord, I ask you to forgive me and my generational line for not accurately perceiving who you are and for not approaching you in the true intercession that comes from worshipping you in the totality of who you are.

✠ I repent for and renounce, for myself and my generational line, coming into your presence with meaningless offerings; I repent for having evil assemblies; having unclean hands, unrepentant hearts, and pride; and for doing wrong.

✠ Lord, I ask that you would remove all ungodly powers, authorities, rulers, elders, and all ungodly spiritual devices that are a consequence of ungodly intercession.

✠ Lord, I ask that you break off of me all guilt and condemnation for not interceding correctly. I choose to forgive myself for this false guilt. Lord, I now receive your true intercession and any godly mantles of intercession you choose to give me.

✠ Lord, please remove all deception from me and my family. I repent for and renounce, for myself and for those in my generational line, all who squandered talents, gifts, resources, and money from the beginning of time to the present.

✠ I declare that I will not lean on my own understanding,[33] but in all my ways, I will acknowledge you in intercession.

✠ Lord, I declare that as I sit in the heavenly places with you, I will release your decrees and they will come into existence.[34]

✠ I declare Lord that I will allow you to teach me how to pray.

Notes:

1. Habakkuk 1:17–2:3.
2. Habakkuk 2:2–3.
3. Ephesians 3:20.

Notes (continued):

4. Matthew 19:26; Mark 9:23.

5. Isaiah 54:17.

6. Romans 8:15.

7. 2 Corinthians 5:7.

8. Hebrews 10:19.

9. Philippians 4:6.

10. Ephesians 2:6.

11. Romans 8:26–27.

12. Deuteronomy 28:23.

13. Matthew 6:31–34.

14. Matthew 7:9–11; John 16:24.

15. John 16:21; James 5:17–18.

16. Psalm 1:3.

17. James 5:14–15.

18. James 1:17.

19. Psalm 12:2; Proverbs 26:28; Romans 16:17–18.

20 Matthew 5:23–24; James 5:16.

21. Isaiah 58.

22. Isaiah 1:12–20.

23. 1 John 2:27; Genesis 3:16.

24. 1 Kings 21:7–15.

25. Genesis 3:12.

26. Psalm 150.

27. 1 Timothy 2:1–2.

28. 1 Peter 2:13–17; Romans 13:1–2; Jeremiah 29:7.

29. Micah 2:13.

30. Matthew 6:5–13; Proverbs 29:25.

31. Romans 11:4; Isaiah 45:23; Philippians 2:10; Hebrews 12:7–13; Ephesians 2:8–9.

32. Isaiah 35:3.

33. Deuteronomy 28:33; Joshua 6:20.

34. Proverbs 3:5.

35. Ephesians 2:6; Isaiah 48:6; 42:9.

Restoring Compassion
and the Fear of the Lord

PAUL L. COX

Come up higher!" The first time I remember hearing these words in a prophetic utterance was on August 17, 2004. As Mimi Lowe of Toronto, Canada stood in an angel, she received this message:

> Yes, the Establisher is here to establish what he wants to establish. He'll enlarge our spirits to receive all he has for us; higher and higher realms, beyond where we've never been, and dimensions not yet uncovered. You will come closer to the glory realm; get ready for lift-off because you are going up. Come on up. You are not high enough. Angels are waiting to receive you—come on, come on, come on.

Since that time, we have received these words many times. Often, the Lord said that we were not high enough. Sometimes he was very specific.

> Space travel, space travel, time travel, time travel, to take you into other dimensions, to take you higher, higher, higher, exploration, exploration, come and explore with us. You can soar, you can fly, come on up, come on up, fly with us, fly with us.

But why must we go higher? Since that first revelation about going higher, the Lord has sent many of his spiritual servants to speak to us about that. Over and over again, he has said, "Come up higher." And each time he has revealed more about higher places and what is accomplished by going there. The Lord wants us to go into new realms of revelation. He wants us to take back inheritances that were lost. He wants us to "rest" in him so that he can accomplish want he wants to accomplish. He wants us to receive new gifts, new hearts, and new minds. He wants to introduce us to new treasures, new anointings, and new places in the spirit. He desires that we receive new gems, new pearls and mantles of wisdom, new perspective, new manna, and new armor. He wants to reveal secrets of the Kingdom. He wants to take us to places of new levels of intimacy, new levels of protection, and new levels of healing, miracles, and wonders. These new places are places of the revelation of the sons of God and the mountain of the Lord. When we go with him to these new places, there is a deeper cleansing of the land and deeper generational healing. In these higher realms, we are able to dig deeper wells, find new doors of impartation, gain new authority, and develop new levels of freedom, new ideas, new plays, new songs, and new paintings.

I like what the Lord said one day!

You have not seen anything yet. Get out of the box. Expand, expand. I am a big God. What do you want? What do you want? This is the time to ask. You shall receive. Seek and you shall find. Knock and the door is open wide for you. Jump in. Jump in. The river is here. Jump in. Healing waters. Healing waters. The angel is stirring up the waters. Receive healing. Receive your healing. All who are lame and crippled, receive healing. The time is now. Harvest! Come on up and we will have fun in discovery, provision, revelation of the mysteries of God. It is fun!

The Lord was resonating with his word! Revelation 4:1 says:

After these things I looked, and behold, a door standing open in heaven. And the first voice which I heard was like a trumpet speaking with me, saying, "Come up here, and I will show you things which must take place after this."

During the August 2008 schools, the Lord was very specific. He said it was time to go higher still. In obedience we said, "Yes, Lord, we will go higher." I was not prepared for what would take place. Several youth had joined us for the Advanced Discernment Training and Exploration School. One of the youth said, "There is a spiritual chariot here, and Paul, you are to get on the chariot, and two of us will be the horses." I climbed unto the invisible chariot, and the power of God fell in the room in a way I had never experienced. All of a sudden the tangible fear of the Lord manifested in the room. We were overwhelmed with the holiness of God, and many of us literally trembled at his presence. He had revealed an aspect of himself that I had never experienced.

Dale Shannon prophetically spoke these words:

The battle is fierce. I am establishing my reign and my righteousness on this land. It will not be thwarted! I am taking each one of you higher to a new level. It is the heart of the matter. The Lord says, "I love you. My love is greater than you understand. I am surrounding your heart with a new covering, new protection, and a new shield. I'm putting a shield around your heart—around each of your hearts. The enemy has been pulling and tugging at each person's heart and trying to get you to not believe in my love, to not know my love—to doubt my love. But I'm asking you to come up higher, to walk the higher road and know that my love is greater than you understand, and nothing can separate you from my love. Cast away your questions, doubts, and unbelief. Even your anger, don't let it come between us.

The picture I see is a Ferris wheel going to the Lord's heart. Each time we go to a new heavenly realm, the Lord puts something new in the wheel, like oil, abundance, love, and forgiveness.

He says, "You must forgive others because I have forgiven you. This is my way—to come up higher. This is how you overcome—to walk in love, to walk in forgiveness and faith. I am extending my power, gifts, and authority. The rulers have given you new authority. You have wondered what it is all about. It's a new authority; you are walking in a new authority. You must know that, so that you don't go back to old ways. You have been called to subdue the earth, and you do have the authority now. You have the staff. You must know my heart. You must know my heart for the lost. Know my heart for the beaten. Know my heart for the oppressed. That is the fear of the Lord—to know my heart. Let me pierce your heart with compassion and mercy—not unsanctified mercy, but God-given mercy. I draw you near; like a magnet you are drawn to me. This is the fear of the Lord. I draw you. You are compelled to come to me. Yes, there is terror in my holiness. I give you grace to come near—to come higher, to know me, my ways, my heart, intimately."

He pulls us, yet we are afraid to come. It is so overwhelming. How can we approach God in our weakness and our flesh? How can we approach God? Only with contrite hearts, humbleness of mind, with hearts for the lost, and only through his grace. His love compels us to draw near, to not give up. A magnet draws us to him, by his love, his overwhelming love. He says, "Draw near, yet take your shoes off, for this is holy ground. Circumcise your heart."

Be ever mindful of the holiness of God. Do not approach him lightly. You must have the fear of the Lord.

He says, "I desire mercy over sacrifice. I desire justice for the poor, the weak and oppressed, but you have passed them by. Where is the fear of the Lord? You have been too busy to show compassion. Did you notice those suffering when you were in the store, or did you just pass them by? Look to me, I will show you who to stop for. I will show you who to go to. Ask, and I will show you. I will give you a discerning heart, so that you will know. I desire justice, I desire mercy, and I desire compassion. Ask me and I will fill your heart to overflowing for the weak, for the oppressed, for the lonely, for the downcast, for the rejected, for I was rejected. Rend your heart. Ask me and I will give you mercy and compassion to overflowing."

Persis Tiner then received this prophetic word:

Compassion. My people, who are filled with compassion, make my heart happy. If you only leave here this week with more compassion, you will have accomplished great things. I pass among you and put compassion in your heart. You will see and feel differently. You will see and feel differently. You will be a witness to people as you never have been before. Compassion, compassion, not judgment, not prejudice.

Word after word came. We had begun the day not knowing where the Lord was going to take us. We followed him as the Israelites followed the pillar of fire and the cloud of his presence. In obedience, we listened and followed. He was taking us to a higher place. He was instructing us in what he wanted us to do. This was nothing like pastoring a local congregation. While pastoring, I set the agenda. The Lord was telling us that in his true Church, he sets the agenda. He orders our steps. He instructs us and tells us what to do. When the fear of the Lord is present, then obedience is the only choice.

Jane Green received the next word. Through her the Lord said there would be another prayer. It would be a prayer about the fear of the Lord and compassion.

> Thrones are positions. You are kings and queens. It is not just position; it is protection. It begins with the fear of the Lord. It is the beginning of knowledge. For his delight is the fear of the Lord.[1] It is the canopy. The throne is the covering. I sense eagles with trumpets and eagles with trumpets. You are the trumpet for the fear of the Lord. Write the prayer for the fear of the Lord. It will change this nation and will change other nations. It will heal families. It will give you rest from all sides. Your new authority begins with the fear of the Lord. No eyes have seen or ears heard all that God has. There is new hope in your new position of fear before God. It is the revelation, your new position in relationship to the throne of God. It is his very essence, his very presence. It is his breath. He is going to breathe on you. He is going to breathe on you. It is the *ruach*, the breath of God. You will find out that the fear of the Lord is not what you think. There is joy in it. Declare it, trumpet it, run with it, and write it down. It is a new hope, a new beginning. Put your trust in the Lord, and he will do it.

What an unlikely combination of thoughts—compassion and the fear of the Lord! Yet, Scripture indicates that when we fear the Lord, then we will be obedient! *The New International Dictionary of New Testament Theology* clarifies the Old Testament word for fear, *phobos*:

> The Israelites can stand before God in fear and love. God is great, mighty and terrible. Nevertheless, he is gracious to man. Thus we can understand the frequent address to man which passes right on into the New Testament: "Fear Not." God's grace and favor do not abolish the solemnity of the address. It demands man's total obedience. It has to be proven in action, just as God's love is proved. Nevertheless, the motive of fear predominates. The fear of God is the first essential motive in the laws of the Pentateuch. It is the decisive religious factor in Old Testament.[2]

When a believer truly fears the Lord, then out of loving obedience compassion will flow. Unfortunately, compassion has not been a characteristic of many in our generational lines, and we have often fallen short of the compassion that the Lord desires for us to express. Lack of compassion has caused a hard-heartedness to come down through our family lines. It is time for us to repent of all that has blocked our true fear of the Lord and expressions of compassion, and again align ourselves to the revealed will of God.

The Prayer: Restoring Compassion and the Fear of the Lord

�ібₐ Lord, I repent for myself and for everyone in my family line who failed to have godly compassion toward others.

✴ I repent for myself and my family line for being impatient or angry with you, Lord, and for blaming you for our suffering and the suffering of our loved ones.

✴ For myself and for my family line, I renounce and repent for all false acts of compassion and all substitutionary acts of compassion.

✴ For myself and my for family line, I renounce and repent for condemning and judging instead of showing mercy and compassion.

✴ For myself and for my family line, I repent for all those who did not heed the voice of compassion from the Lord but silenced the cries of those who were ill, hurting, injured, or in pain.

✴ For myself and for my family line, I renounce and repent for mistaking compassion as weakness. I forgive those who have mistaken my compassion as weakness.

✴ For myself and for my family line, I renounce and repent for not showing compassion for others who were in pain. I forgive those who did not show compassion while I was suffering.

✴ For myself and for my family line, I renounce and repent for submitting to any ungodly authority which required us to suppress mercy and compassion.

✠ For myself and for my family line, I renounce and repent for not having the fear of the Lord and therefore ignoring your promptings to show mercy and compassion to the least[3] of your children because it would have been too inconvenient, uncomfortable, or costly to do so. Lord, would you forgive me for willingly disregarding your words and grieving your Holy Spirit? Lord, please forgive me for failing to show mercy and compassion to others as you have shown mercy and compassion to me.

✠ For myself and for my family line, I renounce and repent for not recognizing and acknowledging that you have blotted out our transgressions and the transgressions of others through your great compassion.[4]

✠ For myself and my family bloodline, I renounce and repent for rejecting those who were not healed after prayer. I renounce and repent for believing the lie that God does not care when the pain does not leave and others do not show mercy and compassion.

✠ For myself and for my family line, I renounce and repent for agreeing with being stuck in our own pain or understanding and for not expecting the Lord's compassionate acts of mercy for those who were suffering.

✠ For myself and for my family line, I renounce and repent for being impatient, judgmental, frustrated, and angry with those who were not healed and with those who don't seek to be healed but find their identity in their problems.

✠ For myself and for my family line, I renounce and repent for embracing self-righteousness and legalism, for denying the fear of the Lord, and for not acknowledging our need for compassion.

✠ For myself and for my family line, I renounce and repent for not showing mercy and compassion because we were convinced that the illness, disease, or affliction was a judgment sent from God, that it was for a person's own good, and that God was trying to teach them something.

✠ For myself and for my family line, I renounce and repent for embracing illnesses, diseases, and afflictions as God's will for our lives.

267

✠ For myself and for my family line, I repent for and renounce hardheartedness and passing by those in need. Lord, remove the heart of stone, and give me a heart of flesh so that I can feel what you feel and carry your heart.[5]

✠ For myself and my family line, I renounce and repent for loving our own comfort, selfish lives, and ease of living more than we loved offering compassion to others.

✠ For myself and my family line, I renounce and repent for believing that excellent health and abundant provision are signs of God's blessings and approval and that pain and suffering indicate God's withdrawal and disapproval.

✠ I renounce and repent for the idea that pain and suffering may be a person's own fault and that it might be a sign that they aren't even saved.

✠ For myself and for my family line, I renounce selfishness and repent for valuing money and the cost of caring more than the healing and comfort of those in need. Lord, please forgive me if I withheld charity because I did not trust in your timing and provision.

✠ For myself and for my family line, I renounce and repent for being fearful of allowing compassionate healing in the church because it would upset the status quo.

✠ For myself and my family line, I renounce and repent for withholding our own compassion and for stopping others from showing compassion—I repent for stopping emotional expressions of compassion, acts of compassion, and for blocking any demonstrations of empathy.

✠ For myself and my family line, I renounce and repent for not allowing ourselves to be vulnerable in compassionate acts because we believed that it would hurt our social standing in the church.

✠ I forgive all of those who seemed not to care and offered advice instead of prayer.

✠ I forgive all of those who, rather than showing mercy and compassion, offered to sell CDs, DVDs, nutritional supplements, and other products to me and my family while we were in need.

✠ I forgive all those who were selfish and stingy with resources, compassion, and mercy in my time of need.

✠ I ask forgiveness for condemning and accusing others for lack of faith because they remained sick. Lord, forgive me for coming into agreement with the accuser of the brethren.

✠ I choose to forgive those who have not listened to my soft-spoken voice as I have shared the compassionate heart of the Lord.

✠ I now reject the lie that Job's suffering was from God.

✠ I ask you, Lord, to tear down the walls that I have put up that keep me from experiencing the pain around me and from knowing your heart.

✠ For myself and for my family line, I renounce and repent for not believing and trusting that you, God, would bring us out of the wilderness times of our lives.

✠ For myself and for my family line, I renounce and repent for refusing, rejecting, burying, or compromising our identity as compassionate people of God who are agents of God's healing.

✠ For myself and for my family line, I renounce and repent for being unwilling to persevere in long-term compassion for the deeply wounded.[6]

✠ For myself and for my family line, I renounce and repent for caring more about schedules, programs, and decorum rather than stopping to help the ones in need.

✠ For myself and for my family line, I renounce and repent for carrying compassion burdens that were not from you, Lord, and for not giving back to you the prayer burdens you gave us. I repent for and renounce carrying false burdens and heavy yokes instead of your yoke which is light and easy.

✖ For myself and for my family line, I renounce and repent for enabling others in their sin, not setting godly boundaries as Jesus did, and for taking on the role of "savior" that only Jesus Christ can fulfill.

✖ For myself and for my family line, I renounce and repent for embracing the belief that "I must burn out" for the Lord in exercising compassion. I repent for not resting from times of ministry and seeking the Lord for rest and refreshment.

✖ For myself and for my family line, I renounce and repent for those who responded to compassion by taking on responsibility outside our spheres of authority.

✖ For myself and for those in my generational line, I renounce and repent for abusing those with the gift of mercy and compassion to the point of exhaustion.

✖ For myself and for my family line, I renounce and repent for seeing and hearing through our physical eyes and ears instead of the compassionate eyes and ears of Christ.

✖ For myself and for those in my generational line, I renounce and repent for despising true wisdom and instruction,[7] for hardening our hearts,[8] and for abandoning the fear of the Lord, which is the beginning of wisdom.[9]

✖ For myself and for my family line, I renounce and repent for not being motivated with the love of Christ and for believing that acts of mercy were a duty and an obligation to fulfill. I renounce and repent for teaching duty and law instead of compassion and the fear of the Lord.

✖ For myself and for my family line, I renounce and repent for ignoring the hurting and being too busy to show compassion.

✖ For myself and for my family line, I renounce and repent for not showing mercy, justice, and compassion for the poor, the weak, the oppressed, the downcast, and the rejected. I ask you, Lord, to show me whom to minister to and when. Lord, I ask you to pierce my heart with your love, compassion, grace, and mercy.

✠ For myself and my family line, I renounce and repent for giving tithes and offerings and fulfilling Christian obligations while lacking the fear of the Lord in the more important matters of holiness, character, righteousness, justice, mercy, and faithfulness.[10]

✠ For myself and my family line, I renounce and repent for not keeping the commandments, statues, or judgments you have commanded. Lord, I desire to fear your name and ask that you would prosper me as your servant and grant me mercy so that I can complete the work that you have prepared for me.[11]

✠ For myself and my family line, I renounce and repent for receiving the compassion of the Lord but not extending that compassion to others.

✠ I declare that the mercy and compassion of the Lord is with those who fear him and with their children's children.[12]

✠ For myself and my family line, I repent for those who did not choose to be taught the fear of the Lord. I choose to delight myself in the fear of the Lord and to gain understanding, so I may operate in true mercy and compassion.

✠ For myself and my family line, I renounce and repent for those who hated true knowledge,[13] coming from a fear of the Lord, but sought a false knowledge, wisdom, and understanding, coming from ungodly sources.

✠ For myself and my family line, I renounce and repent for those who did not fear the Lord and hate evil but instead practiced evil and were proud and arrogant and perverse in speech.[14]

✠ For myself and my family line, I renounce and repent for those who did not walk uprightly but despised the Lord by walking in devious ways,[15] and for those who did not shun evil but were foolish, hotheaded, and reckless.[16]

For myself and my family line, I renounce and repent for those who feared man instead of you, God, which led them into evil bondage.[17]

I choose to honor you, God, and to be like Daniel, who feared the Lord and did not obey an unrighteous law, trusting God with his very life.[18] I trust you to be my help and shield.[19]

I choose to be like Shadrach, Meshach, and Abednego, who feared the Lord over man's decree and would not worship a false god; they were willing to die in the fiery furnace yet trusted in God's ability to rescue them.[20]

I choose to fear you, Lord, to follow your precepts,[21] and to find great delight in your commands.[22]

I declare that the one who fears the Lord will not harden his heart towards those in need.[23]

I choose to be zealous for the fear of the Lord.[24]

I declare I will be God driven rather than need driven and be God-fearing rather than man fearing.

I declare that my delight is in the fear of the Lord, and therefore I trust the Lord to lead me in compassion.

I declare that I will have compassion on the members of the traditional church as they learn to walk in the true fear of the Lord, learn to recognize and accept the manifestation of the mercy and compassion of the Lord, and allow God to be God in his church.

I declare that I will approach you, Lord, with a contrite heart, a humble mind, and a heart for the lost.

I declare I will not live by the rules for being a Christian, but I will live in the fear of the Lord and his compassion.

✠ I declare that the fear of the Lord compels me to show compassion to others. I receive your grace to love others as you love them. I receive your showers of mercy to run the race set before me.

Notes:

1. Proverbs 1:7.
2. Colin Brown, ed, *The New International Dictionary of New Testament Theology* (Grand Rapids, MI: Zondervan, 1986), 622.
3. Matthew 25:40.
4. Isaiah 43:25.
5. Ezekiel 36:26.
6. James 5:11.
7. Proverbs 1:7.
8. Proverbs 28:14.
9. Psalm 111:10; Proverbs 1:7, Proverbs 9:10.
10. Matthew 23:23.
11. Nehemiah 1.
12. Psalm 103:17.
13. Proverbs 1:29.
14. Proverbs 8:13, NIV.
15. Proverbs 14:2, NIV.
16. Proverbs 14:16, NIV.
17. Proverbs 29:25. This prayer was constructed at the Hesperia Advanced Discernment School, August 2008.
18. Daniel 6:26.
19. Psalm 115:11.
20. Daniel 3:17–18.
21. Psalm 111:10, NIV.
22. Psalm 112:1.
23. Proverbs 28:14.
24. Proverbs 23:17.

Release into
Abundant Life

PAUL L. COX

It was a very short dream. As I woke up, I vividly remembered what I had seen. I was standing looking at someone. *Was it the Lord?* A voice said to me, "Your blood pressure is 197." I replied, "But I am not under stress." The voice responded, "It is about your thinking." I had absolutely no clarity about what that meant!

Over the next weeks, the memory of the dream often came back and I would ask those I was with, "Do you know what this dream means?" No satisfying answer came.

In October 2008 I made my third ministry trip to Australia. We were hosted by a church outside of Sydney and enjoyed a wonderful two weeks of schools. Sudden impressions started coming, and once again I was surprised by what happened!

Before the school, the Lord had taught me how to stand behind someone and feel their time line. Close to the person's back I could feel events early in their generational line; the further I stood from the person, the further back I was able to feel in their generational line. There was a point behind them where I could actually feel a marked change, and I realized that I was discerning the glory of the Lord and eternity. Since that time, many others have confirmed my experience by also feeling a strong anointing of the presence of the Lord at a specific point behind someone. New revelation was coming.

As I stood close to this point of eternity, I was able to discern the egg and sperm that formed the person. Then I could feel the zygote, the first split into two cells, and the second split into four cells. Just beyond the feeling of "eternity," I discerned a scroll, which seemed to be the person's written birthright. I could also feel many spiritual beings that were assigned to the person. Just after the second split, I was surprised at the evil that I felt. It seemed to be some type of gate. As I discerned the gate, I asked others to describe what they saw. There was confirmation that evil had been inserted into the person's life just after conception. As we sought the Lord about this, we felt him say that this was the entry place for generational evil from the family line.

Was I discerning "original sin?" Then I remembered my dream.

"It is about your thinking." *What thinking?* My blood pressure was 197. Was there a key here? Revelation came. I thought, "Look up Job 19:7."

If I cry out concerning wrong, I am not heard.
If I cry aloud, there is no justice.

Was this a clue? Then I thought, "Look up Psalm 19:7."

The law of the LORD is perfect, converting the soul;
The testimony of the LORD is sure, making wise the simple.

There it was! It is all about our thinking. *What is our perspective of God?* Generally, the world blames him for all the difficulties of life.[1] Supposedly, he is the source of all the evil in the world. We're programmed to ask, "Why doesn't he intervene in my life? He is all-powerful! Where is he when life goes bad? Why doesn't he help me in my need? Maybe he is doing all this against me because I deserve it. But what have I done to cause him to hate me so much?" So, on and on our thinking goes. We listen to others complain about God, and we agree with them. Our pain is immense and we must find someone to blame. "It must be God who is doing all this against me!" It is a mind-set established generations ago, in fact, a mind-set originating in the Garden of Eden. The root is not in the tree of life, but in the tree of the knowledge of good and evil. We have "bought into" the wrong mind-set! We have believed the lie that God is not good! Our presuppositions are all wrong. Our belief systems have been based on a lie! It is all about our thinking!

Job had suffered much! Agony overpowered him. His pain was immense. Who did he blame? Is God to be blamed for all the evil that has happened? No! It is my thinking that is all wrong. 2 Chronicles 5:13 gives us the correct starting place for our thinking. This is the prerequisite to all that we believe. "And when they lifted up their voice with the trumpets and cymbals and instruments of music, and praised the LORD, saying: 'For He is good, for His mercy endures forever.'" This is where I start! He is good! If that is true, then the blame must go elsewhere. This is where human thinking must be corrected. The enemy has deceived us into believing a lie about who God is. Our own perverted thinking, mind-sets, and belief systems have caused us to have an incorrect view of God.

During the last several years the Lord has repeatedly told us, "Go back to the origin." *What does that mean?* The origin is the Garden of Eden. It is the place where the incorrect thinking originated. The Fall was never the Lord's intent. We have chosen the wrong way, the incorrect path. We have taken a wrong turn and gone our own way. We must go back to the origin. *How?* The death of Jesus Christ on the cross has provided the only way. Through his blood shed on the cross, we have the provision through acceptance in that sacrifice to return to the ancient path. Thus says the Lord: "Stand in the ways and see, and ask for the old paths, where the good way is, and walk in it; then you will find rest for your souls." We must take back the land, our birthright, given away to the enemy. We must come against the strongholds in the land of our inheritance and take back what the enemy has stolen.

During the Sydney school, many words were received from the Lord that helped establish the foundation for this prayer. These words will be helpful in allowing you to understand the importance of this prayer.

> One friend spoke about Australia: "Right now, I feel very powerful angels all around you and us. One of them is saying: 'This trip is very different from the others, Paul. Look for the differences; there will be many. They are the keys to the new path, the path you are to walk on. I will show you the way. On this path, there is newness, more vision, more understanding, and deeper things. You will be outfitted for the warfare ahead. The battle rages, but you have the keys! We have been waiting for this time. We have been sent to help you find the path. Victorious victory! This is the time! Victory.'"

Another friend said: "Courage, courage my son, for the times and the seasons will begin to unfold as my glory rises up from the well. You must yet mine the wells and you must dig deep wells. In fact, all of you must have your wells dug. You must want the excavating work of the Spirit in your life, for at the bottom of the well there is a scroll and a path that goes deeper. Even as you would mine that well and beyond, there is another corridor and ancient path. My people have not walked this path before. You are traveling on holy ground. You must take the ground below you. Redeem the land."

Mimi: "Craft a prayer to set my people free. Craft a prayer to go through the grate, for the Lord is your head. The Lord goes before you. Change man's birthright for Australia. Establish God's birthright for this land, this people, for all future generations. The land was set to be desolate and forsaken. That is not my heart and not my will. Establish my will and my purpose for Australia. Call down the Kingdom for the will of God to be done."

Another woman said: "This is not a new plan. This plan has been on my heart since the foundation of the world. The passage of time has been moving toward this since the beginning of history. Carefully, I have placed each piece in place and I have built one thing upon another for nothing is by accident, and I have called my people to pray. The prayers of my faithful ones have laid the foundation. The ancient pathways are flowing with water. There are streams of living water following the ancient pathways. The river of God is flowing underground in the depths of the earth, waiting to bubble up bringing fresh life. The ancient pathways are pure. They carry pure water. Drink deeply of this water, the river of God that flows from my throne bringing life to everything it touches. Drink deeply from this well. Dig the wells to release the water."

A different friend said: "Put on your full armor. You need protective gear to dig your wells. I will take you to areas where you have never been before. You have gone up, and now you must go down, down to the depths where you were secretly made. Go back in time to conception, where you were intricately made and formed. Go there and retrieve. Retrieve what is yours, and I give you the secrets, the mysteries which are hidden in the depths. But you must be fully armed and armored because it is a dark place, but I will go with you."

Another friend said: "The fire must flow from the ancient pathways. Burn away to clear the chaff. The walls will crumble, and the way will be made new so that my people may walk on the words of life, so that they may see the glory of my sun as it rises above the land, so that they may take my hand and walk with me in the cool of day, in the rising of the sun and the coming of the moon. They will bow once again to me, and the ground will cry out, 'Holy, Holy, Holy am I.' All my ways are great. Who would question me on the designs of my creation? Who will tell me where to go and where to rest and where to rise and where to fall? For I am the Lord; my Word is forever, and I hold all things together. The very fabric of my thoughts I have fashioned together so that you might know me and know yourself, so that you might know love and walk without fear, and that you might break down the prison walls and life will flow from them. I have heard their cries and will answer them today. I am making a way and cutting down the tree. Step over it and come to me."

A woman said: "Dig up the ancient wells. The ancient wells were buried treasures of heaven. Remove the evil mind-sets over the ancient wells. The ancient wells were put in place and the ancient paths have been polluted and stopped up because I was rejected. The Word of God was rejected, so these ancient wells were stopped up. Go deep, deep, deep into the ancient wells, for that is where my glory wants to bubble up, rise up, and surface."

A couple said: "The mines are mine. Great wealth is coming. It is not man's wealth; it is his provision, his treasure. The wealth is in the people. Go low; go low; prostrate yourself before me. Seek. Seek my light, my path. Only the humble will enter, but the righteous shall live by faith. Open the eyes of your spirit. Seek me with all your heart."

Another friend: "Since time began, my heart has yearned for those who would seek me for these truths. My heart has yearned for the day that I might restore to my people the intimacy of my heart. I have wept for the obstacles that remain between my heart and my children, for I am indeed your Abba Father and I long to embrace you in a way you have never known and in a way you have never come. The ancient pathways will lead you to a secret place, a place of intimacy and joy and connection. My heart grieves for my children who, although they know me, have been kept back from me. Break through the grate by your words, by wisdom and declarations that come from the throne of God. I send my witnesses. I send my authority. I send my Son, for the words that I send forth from this day will change the pathways. It is time."

It is time to change our thinking!

The Prayer: Release into Abundant Life

✠ I repent for myself and for my generational line for blaming God for wronging us.

✠ For myself and for my generational line, I repent for blaming God for bringing us into shame by stripping us of our glory and removing the crowns from our heads.

✠ For myself and for my generational line, I repent for blaming God for surrounding us with his net, destroying us, and demolishing us on every side, thus destroying our hope.[2]

✠ I repent for myself and for my generational line for blaming God for being our enemy and blaming God for being furious with us, and for sending troops against us or sending troops to build up pathways to attack us and camp all around our bodies and dwelling places. I repent for myself and for my generational line for blaming God for blocking and walling up our way and plunging our path into darkness.

✠ I repent for myself and for all those in my generational line who had fearful and unbelieving hearts that caused us to depart from the way of holiness. I ask for the restoration of the ancient paths where gladness and joy overtake us. I embrace my birthright and choose to walk knowing the Lord.

✠ For myself and for all those in my generational line, I repent for using ungodly wisdom, for operating out of futile mind-sets, and for trying to work things out by ourselves. I choose, Lord, to work out of your knowledge, understanding, wisdom, and discernment. I choose to work with you, Lord, to change my ways so that I can walk in the ancient paths established before the Fall. I choose to walk in your healing and to allow your strength, which flows from your life giving water, to rise.[3]

✠ For myself and for all those in my generational line, I repent for using our God-given physical and spiritual senses in ungodly ways and for choosing to operate from our natural minds. Lord, please break off all the iniquity that flowed from those decisions to ignore your mind, heart, and will. Lord, please remove all iniquity from my God-given senses.

✠ I ask you, Lord, to restore my ability to use all of my senses to discern your mind, heart, and will.

✠ For myself and for all those in my generational line, I repent for blaming God for removing friends, family, and employees from us and for blaming God when people turned against us and despised and hated us to the point of death.

✠ For myself and for all those in my generational line, I repent for blaming God's hand for striking us and persecuting us.

✠ For myself and for all those in my generational line, I repent for wishing that our accusations against God and our suffering could be recorded forever in stone.

✠ Lord, for myself and for all those in my generational line, I repent for not looking for your path and your ways. I repent for not being willing to walk on your path and find rest for my soul.[4]

✠ For myself and for all those in my generational line, I repent for believing that God was withholding good from us and for believing that we could become like God, knowing good and evil.

✠ For myself and for all those in my generational line, I repent for rejecting the law of the Lord and the testimony of his Spirit, for departing from his wisdom and truth and entering the kingdom of our own souls.[5]

�֍ For myself and my family line, I renounce and repent for relying on the knowledge of the tree of the knowledge of good and evil. I repent for relying on our own thinking.

✖ For myself and for all those in my generational line, I renounce and repent for forsaking the Lord, the Fountain of Living Water, and for creating for ourselves broken cisterns that could hold no water.[6]

✖ On behalf of my ancestors and myself, I reject receiving the seed of Satan that was received in our minds with the fall of man, and I reject and repent of believing the lie that we could become like God.

✖ For my ancestors and myself, I renounce and repent for rejecting our birthright of being children of the Most High God and of relying upon him.

✖ On behalf of my ancestors and myself, I renounce and repent for receiving Satan's evil seed, for conceiving mischief and trouble, and for having wombs which prepared deception and birthed iniquity and evil intent into our generational line.[7]

✖ Lord, please remove and seal every access within my womb and the wombs of my ancestors that the enemy gained to take me into ungodly heavenly places.

✖ Lord, please remove and restore by the blood of Jesus any elemental part of me, including my inheritance and birthright, that is trapped in the second heaven or heavenly places. Lord, please close the ungodly doors to the second heaven.

✖ I repent for myself and for all those in my family line who relied upon the natural wisdom of man and rejected the Spirit of God.[8] I choose to rely on the precepts of truth and the Spirit of God to give me the mind of Christ to direct my mind on his righteous pathway.

✖ I reject the wisdom of man, and I repent for the pride in my family line that saw the wisdom of God as foolishness. I declare that I will be born of the Spirit and of water through Jesus Christ who calls me, justifies me, and glorifies me. I declare this truth of rebirth by the Spirit of God was established before the foundation of the earth and before the elemental spirits were created.

✠ I claim my spiritual birthright of being conceived in love,[9] of being given the Spirit of God who reveals wisdom to me,[10] and of being given spiritual eyes in my heart to see the riches of God's glorious inheritance.[11] I claim that I am being formed in the image of his glorious Son. I reject the seed of Satan and I reject my position as a child of the father of lies and murder.[12] I ask you, Abba Father, to close the ungodly eyes that were opened when the first man and woman ate fruit from the tree of the knowledge of good and evil.

✠ I renounce and reject any ungodly rights or authorities that were given to my soul to direct my mind along ungodly pathways.

✠ I agree with God's original plan for all spiritual wisdom about good and evil to originate from his throne and be revealed to the spirit of men by his Spirit. I receive the seed of the Holy Spirit into my spirit, and by his power I cry, Abba, Father. I give the Holy Spirit permission to direct my spirit and to lead my soul and body.

✠ Lord, on behalf of myself and my family line, I repent for questioning God's Word and therefore inviting the influence of Leviathan, the king of pride, into my life.[13]

✠ Lord, I choose to be directed by your commandments so that you might enlarge my heart.[14]

✠ I declare that my Redeemer lives and while I am yet alive, I will see God for myself with my own eyes.[15]

✠ I declare that my hope is in you, my Redeemer. I ask you now to restore the ancient pathways to me and shine your light on me so that I can see you with my eyes. I ask you to restore my stolen birthright, my glory, and my crown.

✠ Father, I thank you that before you formed me in my mother's womb, you had predetermined my birthright, the path of glory I should walk in.

✠ On behalf of myself and my generational line, I repent for and renounce rejecting the truth that you formed us in our inmost beings, and that before we came to be, you wrote in your book all the days preordained for us.

✠ Father, on behalf of myself and my generational line, I repent for and renounce rejecting the ancient paths that you chose for us to walk in.[16]

✠ Father, on behalf of myself and my generational line, I repent for and renounce listening to and aligning our thinking with the wicked. Lord, I reject them and their pursuit of bloodlust.[17]

✠ Father, I declare that I am fearfully and wonderfully made[18] and that you will lead me in the way everlasting.[19] I declare that all your works are wonderful.[20]

✠ Lord, I agree with your Word which says that the weapons of my warfare are not carnal but mighty through you to the pulling down of strongholds. I choose to cast down imaginations and every high thing that exalts itself against the knowledge of God, and I choose to bring into captivity every thought to the obedience of Christ.[21]

✠ Lord, please release the resurrection power of the Holy Spirit to restore me to the path of holiness. Lord, please cause your perfect love to run through my entire being, casting out all fear.[22] I ask you, Lord, to repair or replace any part of my brain or neural pathway required to establish your godly attachments with my Heavenly Father and my fellow man.

✠ Lord, please cause me to dwell in the secret place of the Most High. I declare my birthright is to walk with Abba Father in the garden, where I can hear his voice and enjoy intimate fellowship with him. I believe that Jesus Christ appropriated this intimacy for me when he yielded up his spirit on the cross and the veil in the Holy of Holies was ripped in two.[23]

Lord, I repent for my generational line because we tried to earn by works that which you had given freely by grace. Lord, please now usher me into that place of rest and perfect peace.[24]

Notes:

1. See two books by Gregory A. Boyd, *God at War* (Downers Grove, IL: InterVarsity, 1997) and *Is God to Blame?* (Downers Grove, IL: InterVarsity, 2003). [Thanks to Amazon.com.]

2. Job 19:6–26.

3. Isaiah 35.

4. Jeremiah 6:16.

5. Psalm 19:7.

6. Jeremiah 2:13.

7. Job 15:35.

8. 1 Corinthians 2:15.

9. Ephesians 1:4.

10. 1 Corinthians 2:10.

11. Ephesians 1:7–8.

12. John 8:44.

13. Job 41:34.

14. Psalm 119:32.

15. Job 19:25–26.

16. Jeremiah 18:15.

17. Proverbs 4:14.

18. Psalm 139:14.

19. Psalm 139:24.

20. Psalm 107:8.

21. 2 Corinthians 10:4–6.

22. 1 John 4:18.

23. Matthew 27:50–51; Mark 15:37–38; Luke 23:45–46.

24. Prayer written in Australia, October 2008.

Prayer to Retune
and Realign the Heart

PAUL L. COX

I had not been sleeping, again! It started gradually on the night of the winter solstice in 2008. By the end of January 2009 I was waking up in the middle of the night and could not go back to sleep. Weeks passed and my fatigue increased. Others were not sleeping either. We were consistently waking up around 1:30 a.m., unable to return to sleep. Then, we all shifted to waking up at 4:00 a.m., then 5:00 a.m., still unable to go back to sleep. I called intercessors and pleaded for the Lord to bring understanding about what was happening.

At the end of February 2009, we had an intern-training week at Aslan's Place in Hesperia, California. While praying for a man who was desperately seeking freedom in his life, the Lord revealed what seemed to be a spiritual stop sign in front of him. I was intrigued when I could not feel it as I moved away from him; it was clearly discernible directly in front of him. Moving my hand toward him, I asked if he felt as if he had been stopped in his forward movement; he immediately said, "Yes!" We prayed for him and asked the Lord to remove the stop sign. I felt we were finished until my daughter, Christy Lisle, reported seeing something evil in front of the man. I assured her that the stop sign was gone, but she was insistent! Humoring her, I put my hand close to his body and, indeed, I felt something like a pair of "spiritual" lungs. The Lord was leading me on another journey.

The next day we began to pursue what the Lord had shown us. When those with visual spiritual giftings looked at each of us, they began to see that what I had thought were lungs were, in reality, bat wings. As I felt the wings, I realized that these wings were tied to an ungodly spiritual ruler, who seemed to be blowing a trumpet, heralding an ungodly decree against each person's birthright. These ungodly decrees, rooted in idolatry, establish and maintain a stop sign in a person's life causing spiritual blindness and deafness. A trumpet was pointed toward the heart and neck of each individual. It seems that the decree is an inaudible vibration, beyond the range of human perception, with wavelengths that cause discord. The stop sign seems to magnify the vibrations coming from the ungodly ruler.

As we questioned the Lord about this vibration, he said that the vibration releases doubt, so that believers do not walk in faith. Fear is a consequence of this unbelief. It's the kind of fear Luke writes about, "Men's hearts failing them from fear and the expectation of those things which are coming on the earth, for the powers of the heavens will be shaken."[1]

This ungodly vibration also seems to disrupt the normal vibrations of DNA.[2] As I felt the direction of the vibration, I could discern it affecting the right lower ventricle of the heart. I was amazed to find out from a medical doctor later that the blood from that ventricle goes right to the lungs. There is a tie between the disruption of blood flow from that ventricle and sleep apnea. The Lord was connecting the dots!

The Lord then revealed that the generational root enabling the vibration was a lack of love which fostered disunity, especially disunity within a family. We asked the person we were praying for if there was a history of disunity in his family. He replied that it had been a major problem, both in his own life and in his generational line, especially brother against brother. Then the Lord gave us a Scripture, 1 John 4:7–16.

Beloved, let us love one another, for love is of God; and everyone who loves is born of God and knows God. He who does not love does not know God, for God is love. In this the love of God was manifested toward us, that God has sent His only begotten Son into the world, that we might live through Him. In this is love, not that we loved God, but that He loved us and sent His Son to be the propitiation for our sins. Beloved, if God so loved us, we also ought to love one

another. No one has seen God at any time. If we love one another,
God abides in us, and His love has been perfected in us. By this we
know that we abide in Him, and He in us, because He has given us
of His Spirit. And we have seen and testify that the Father has sent
the Son as Savior of the world. Whoever confesses that Jesus is the
Son of God, God abides in him, and he in God. And we have known
and believed the love that God has for us. God is love, and he who
abides in love abides in God, and God in him.

As we were talking to each other and hearing from the Lord, Ann
Smith from Collingwood, Canada, shared a dream she'd had some months
before. Ann suffers with an irregular heartbeat that seriously affects her
breathing. Here is Ann's dream:

> I was outside a house in Canada and was discerning something very
> evil. Paul Cox was there. I received a musical key At this point I
> became righteously angry. As Paul went into the house, I began to
> sing; I held one continuous note until all my breath had gone.

It seemed to me as if this musical key, this vibration, was somehow going
to be a solution to her healing.

A sudden realization occurred to me. Bats are awake at night! If there
are spiritual bats attached to us, then they would be active at night and
could disrupt sleep! Perhaps I had found the key to why I was not sleeping.

But, why could I not feel this bat in front on me? The Lord made it
clear. We are blinded to what is coming against us. 1 John 2:11 says, "But
he who hates his brother is in darkness and walks in darkness, and does
not know where he is going, because the darkness has blinded his eyes." It
all seemed so obvious now. Bats operate in darkness! A sonarlike vibration
allows them to navigate at nighttime. Isn't it interesting that we use the
term, "blind as a bat"?

I remembered that in Isaiah 34:14, the Hebrew word *Lilith* is translated
as "night creature" in the New King James Version. In tradition, Lilith is
said to be the daughter of Dracula and to manifest as a wolf or bat. Lilith
does not sleep at night! I have had a sense for a long time that this evil
spirit is tied to night terrors.

More insight came the following month. In March 2009, we held
two weeks of school in Hesperia, California. A couple of people who are

involved in the entertainment industry in Hollywood attended the school. As we discussed the revelation about the bat, many felt that the recent Batman movie, *The Dark Knight*, was helpful in understanding what the enemy was releasing on the earth through the media. We also realized that key words in Scripture applied to the movie and the prayer: night, fear, blindness, darkness, secret things, light, eye (as that which perceives darkness and light), and heart. At last "The Prayer to Retune and Realign the Heart" was ready to be written!

After the first intern training in January and getting revelation about the stop sign and the bat, my sleep gradually improved. After writing and praying the prayer during the school in March, my sleep improved greatly. On the very night of the spring equinox, my sleep pattern finally returned to normal. I had not slept well between the winter solstice (the point in the year when the sun is farthest from the celestial equator) until the spring equinox (the point in the year when the sun crosses the celestial equator and days and nights are almost equal in length). The Lord had revealed the plans of the enemy and once again, he had shown himself to be victorious!

The Prayer: Retune and Realign the Heart

✠ On behalf of myself and my generational line, I repent for and renounce viewing ungodly images, listening to ungodly sounds in the airwaves, and coming into agreement with ungodly sights and sounds. I repent for not taking every thought captive and meditating on things that are true, noble, just, pure, lovely, of good report, excellent and praiseworthy.[3]

✠ On behalf of myself and my generational line, I repent for and renounce satanic and demonic agreement with any demonic movie or media or the production of it. Lord, forgive me for rejoicing in the triumph of evil as portrayed in movies and books. I repent for reading any books and comic strips and for watching any films that exalted darkness or the bat in idolatry. I repent for idolizing and receiving the culture of and the artistic designs of bats and other creatures from the second heaven. Lord, please cut all ungodly ties between me and these dark images and movie characters.

� On behalf of myself and my generational line, I repent for and renounce worshipping bats. I renounce the belief that the worship of bats will avert disaster, bring abundance, and bring long life. I also repent for all generational vampirism.

✙ Lord, forgive me and my generational line for opening up the door to the spirit of death, sleep apnea, and night terrors. I repent for and renounce our giving access to Lilith, the spirit of night terrors, and I command in the name of Jesus that Lilith and the spirit of death leave my generational line. I repent for all generational witchcraft, lawlessness, and rebellion. Lord, please disconnect me from the night watches of the witches.

✙ On behalf of myself and my generational line, I repent for and renounce being irritated, angry, and jealous of family, the brethren in Christ, and those who have yet to embrace Christ's way. By the grace and enabling that you, Holy Spirit, have given me, I choose to respond with your Spirit of love and to dispense your living water. I declare that you will supply all my needs according to your riches in glory. I declare that the place you have chosen for me to occupy within your body is the best place for me. I will rejoice in the successes of others.

✙ On behalf of myself and my generational line, I repent of and renounce giving place to the devil and coming into agreement and aligning myself with his ways; I repent of and renounce embracing an ungodly vigilante spirit and trying to correct injustice by humanistic means. Lord, I repent for all perversion of justice by unrighteous enforcement of it. I acknowledge that you have said, "Vengeance is mine."[4] I declare that I will wait for your justice and for your restoration and recompense for every injustice to myself and my family line.

✙ On behalf of myself and my generational line, I repent of and renounce coming into agreement with ungodly spiritual rulers who have used lies and fear to stop me from walking in your ways. Lord, would you disconnect me from the consequences of believing these lies and fears? I declare that the end does not justify any means. I declare that true justice is found only in you, Lord. Your cross, Lord Jesus, provides the answer to all trauma and injustice.

✠ Heavenly Father, please tune me to your vibration, sound, frequency, and heartbeat, so that my heart beats in accord with yours. Let all the sounds that come out of my mouth be in harmony with your sound. Lord, would you replace the life-sucking fear the enemy has attached to me with peace, rest, and confidence in your eternal, unshakable love? Lord, please restore the righteous sound of all creation.

✠ On behalf of myself and my generational line, I repent for trying to control others and for not releasing them to you, Lord, to deal with. I repent for causing suspicion, disunity, fear, and darkness to come on them by my choices. I repent for operating in collusion with the spirit of Jezebel. I repent for not trusting in others' revelation by the Holy Spirit. I repent for misguided intercession motivated by fear, jealousy, insecurity, and envy.

✠ I repent for false discernment from a lack of love. I repent for harsh words that stir up anger, foolish words that are opposed to true wisdom, and for not using a wholesome tongue which is the tree of life.[5] I repent for speaking perverseness, distortion, and foolishness instead of wisdom.[6] I repent for and renounce, on behalf of myself and my family line, all negative speech and for harboring resentment in our hearts.

✠ Lord, on behalf of myself and my generational line, I ask your forgiveness for backbiting and reproaching our friends. I repent for not honoring those who have the fear of the Lord.[7] Lord, when our brothers may have sinned against us, I repent because we have taken action based on our suspicions and not checking our facts and not going to you before doing anything. When they have wronged us, I repent because we have not always gone to our brothers in love to show them their faults in private, but ignoring your command, we have taken action before giving them the opportunity to repent.[8] I repent for allowing religious and legalistic spirits to come against me and stop your designed purposes. I repent for not trusting you and my brothers.

✠ Lord, on behalf of myself and my generational line, I repent for and renounce criticizing, murmuring, complaining, speaking and listening to gossip and the lies of the enemy. I repent for listening to the ungodly whispering of humans and demonic beings, allowing the whispering to cause division. Lord, would you drive out the murmuring, complaining, critical, and whispering spirits?[9]

✠ Lord, I forgive all those who have spoken evil against me and my family, and I release them to you. I ask that you break all ungodly ties and connections between me and those coming against me. Lord, I forgive those who have offended me, and I choose to not hold on to or harbor offense. I ask you to give me an unoffendable and childlike heart.

✠ Lord, on behalf of myself and my generational line, I repent for accepting the enemy's lies and not being a lover of the truth.[10] I repent for not listening to the discernment of others. I repent for not humbling myself to listen to what others are saying and for not being willing to submit to others. I acknowledge that a lot of times I was trying to help, but I was in deception and did not use discernment. I ask for a release from deception so that I can intercede appropriately. I repent for not loving in the way that you, God, love.

✠ I renounce and repent for giving my body over to darkness and to lust, for being fascinated with darkness, and for worrying and not trusting in you, Lord. I repent for and renounce reacting to violence out of fear and suspicion.

✠ For myself and my ancestors, I renounce and repent for hatred, strife, bitterness, unforgiveness, jealousy, envy, division, doubt, and unbelief.

✠ For myself and my ancestors, I repent for and renounce the pride of life, the lust of the eyes, and lust of the flesh, which has empowered hardness in my heart and has produced fear, doubt, and unbelief.

✠ For myself and my ancestors, I renounce and repent for turning a deaf ear to the poor.[11] Lord, I choose to surrender to your will to honor the widows and orphans.

✠ For myself and my ancestors, I renounce and repent for not ministering with a pure heart of love. I repent for giving and receiving soulish revelation.[12] Lord, I submit to and delight in your Spirit of the fear of the Lord, and I ask you to convict and correct me before I speak. I ask that you would release the gift of discernment and your Spirit of counsel, might, wisdom, understanding, and knowledge upon me, so that I will know both the words and the timing of when and if I should speak.

✠ Lord, I choose to surrender to your will, and I declare that I will come into absolute surrender to your ultimate lordship of my whole being, surrendering my whole heart.

✠ For myself and my ancestors, I renounce and repent for being afraid of man and evil and for succumbing to the fear of man, which is a snare.[13]

✠ I renounce and repent, for myself and my ancestors, for listening to the enemy's sound; it is a false breastplate producing a false sense of security. Lord, I ask that you would remove the sound and sonar used by the enemy to send vibrations to track my path, identity, and inheritance. Lord, please remove the all sonar, sound, frequencies, and vibrations being sent to me or being emitted from me that would give the enemy insight into my birthright and place in the world.

✠ For myself and my ancestors, I renounce and repent for having a heart that has grown fat with spiritual plaque. I repent for hard-heartedness and for allowing my heart to grow dull, my ears to become hard of hearing, and my eyes to be become dim and blind. For myself and my family line, I repent for and renounce hardening our hearts to the voice of God. I repent for and renounce saying any words to suggest or declare that God doesn't hear, see, or care about our situations.

✠ On behalf of myself and any of my ancestors who sold our birthright, Lord, I repent for making agreements with the enemy and giving away our original birthright, the birthright you intended for us. I receive life back from you, Lord.

✠ For myself and my ancestors, I renounce and repent for spiritual adultery, for giving our hearts over to other lovers, and for not putting you first in our lives. Lord, remove all idolatry in my heart. I renounce and repent for everything and anything that I've placed in my heart above you, Lord Jesus.

✠ For myself and my ancestors, I renounce and repent for accepting false responsibility for others and usurping Christ's role as lord of their hearts. Lord, forgive me for accepting that responsibility of heart ownership that only belongs to you.

✠ I repent for exposing myself to any graven image or object that would affect my substance or being. Lord, would you cleanse my DNA from all transducers?[14]

✠ I repent for and renounce all our stagnation of spirit and all thinking in our hearts that the Lord will not do good or evil.[15]

✠ On behalf of myself and my family line, I repent for and renounce releasing ungodly sounds from the heart. Lord, remove the ungodly sounds, frequencies, and vibrations of the heart; cleanse my blood, and regenerate it by the water of the Holy Spirit.

✠ I repent for and renounce all words, prayers, and utterances that my ancestors and I have spoken that have given power and dominion to the prince of the air. Lord, please remove all sound, frequencies, and spoken words that have stopped and held back the children of God. Lord, please remove all cloaks of invisibility, shame, blame, disgrace, and reproach.

✠ Lord, I repent for finding my identity in who others say that I am rather than in who you say I am. Lord, remove all identity chips that the enemy has planted in me that I have come into agreement with regarding who I am. I repent for seeking man's approval over your approval and for trying to build my kingdom instead of your Kingdom. I repent for looking to myself and not keeping my eyes on you. Lord, I ask you to remove pride, selfishness, insecurity, rejection, and fear of rejection so that I can love you and your children wholeheartedly. Lord, break my heart with all that breaks your heart, remove my heart of stone, and give me your heart of flesh.

✠ Father, I repent for limiting you, for limiting all that you desire to do in my life and all that you desire to do through me. I repent for rejecting your dreams as being too grandiose. Lord, reawaken your visions and your dreams in me; reawaken all that you called me to partake in before the foundation of the earth. I choose to call into being that which is not and to partner with you in creation, declaring your purposes and will.

✠ Lord, you have tried my heart. You have visited me in the night. You have found no wickedness in me. I have avoided the ways of the violent. My feet have held fast to your paths. Lord, before you, I am a baby, an infant, trusting in your care. As a babe in arms, I praise you. Your works and your name are majestic above all the earth. Lord, you establish the universe by your word, and all creation is yours, yet you are mindful of man, having made him a little less than God, crowning him in Christ Jesus with glory and honor. Vindicate me, oh Lord, with your presence. Destroy your enemies in my life, oh God. Restore your dominion and victory.[16]

✠ I ask you to break off of me the consequences of negative words and curses that others and I have pronounced over my life. I break all agreements with negative thinking and the lies of the enemy, and I choose to walk in truth.

✠ Lord, I ask you to remove all ungodly spiritual rulers, authorities, and shields that have operated in my life. I ask that you release your godly spiritual rulers, authorities, and shields to operate in my life. I receive your breastplate of righteousness and your righteous spiritual rulers. Holy Spirit, I ask you to reveal to me your truth and remove all distorted vision and thinking.

Notes:

1. Luke 21:26.

2. Dr. David Whitehouse, "Sci/Tech: Listen to Your DNA," *BBC Online Network*, November 26, 1998, http://news.bbc.co.uk/1/hi/sci/tech/222591.stm.

3. Philippians 4:8.

4. Romans 12:19.

5. Proverbs 15:1–4.

6. James 3:9–12.

7. Psalm 15:1–4.

8. Matthew 18:15.

9. Proverbs 26:22, Proverbs 18:8; Job 28:21.

10. 2 Thessalonians 2:10–12.

11. Proverbs 21:13.

12. Proverbs 16:28.

13. Luke 13:29.

14. "A **transducer** is a device that converts one type of energy to another. The conversion can be to/from electrical, electro-mechanical, electromagnetic, photonic, or photovoltaic or any other form of energy." While the term *transducer* commonly implies use as a sensor/detector, any device which converts energy can be considered a transducer." (*Wikipedia*, s.v. "Transducer, http://en.wikipedia.org/wiki/Transducer.) It is used in two senses; the sensor, used to detect a parameter in one form and report it in another (usually an electrical or digital signal), and the audio loudspeaker, which converts electrical voltage variations representing music or speech into mechanical cone vibration and hence vibrates air molecules creating sound.

15. Zechariah 14:6; Zephaniah 1:12.

16. Psalm 139, Psalm 8.

God's Timing
and My Body Clock

LEWIS CRAMPTON

It was the first week in January, and I had flown over to Aslan's Place from London, England, for an internship week, not knowing what to expect but desiring God to move and set people free. The group of interns had been assigned to pray with a series of people, some with more spiritually complex problems than others; we would all be involved in the process of healing. On the second day we were ministering to a young man who was coming under attack from the enemy. The reason for the assault was not clear. We discerned issues with his generational line. During this session I saw what appeared to be a set of spiritual clockwork mechanisms covering his torso and heart. I thought it too strange, so since the session was flowing in a different direction, I set the vision aside and thought little more about it.

A day later, once again in intercession with Paul Cox and the interns, I started seeing these spiritual clockwork mechanisms on a young woman's the torso; once again part of the mechanism was over the heart. Some of pieces were of dull metal, like tarnished copper or bronze, and were partly damaged and dusty. In contrast to the duller, damaged pieces, I also saw golden cogs that appeared to be righteous. I mentioned them to Paul and told him I thought it might be a body clock. Revelation began to flow!

Paul started to question me as he felt led by the Lord. He asked if I could also see a clock face. I had not previously noticed one, but as I looked, right there, over the face of the girl, was an ungodly spiritual clock face. God spoke to me and said, "I want to disconnect the clock face from her spiritual being." I did not understand what this meant at all until I looked again. Then, in the spirit, I could see wires coming out of the back of the ungodly clock face and going into her eyes, nose, ears, and mouth and down to her hands. The revelation was expanding. God was doing a new work. Paul then discerned that a godly spiritual being called *Kairos*[1] had turned up with a message. I listened as the Lord spoke to me.

> This is about the land. [I then saw a time talisman[2] with what looked like a dream catcher.] We all have a spiritual clockwork on our bodies, it's something like a mechanical body clock! Some of the pieces are golden, others are like damaged copper. This time clock is connected with each person's time.[3] The clock needs to be put into proper rotations, good rotations. Remove the talisman from the land. Remove time control. Do you think you control time? Time is mine. No time bending, no time warping. You cannot warp through time. There needs to be a holy investment.

As the Lord spoke, I could see that the hands of the body clock on the young woman were moving faster than they had been. And—they were moving in different directions.

We started researching the body clock and found that it governs sleep patterns and self-awareness; it enables the brain to interpret language by recognizing the rhythms and timing of speech sounds.[4]

We then asked the Lord how this revelation was related to the woman we were praying for. He gave us more revelation and guided us in questioning her. We learned that she had been born prematurely and had been placed under a light for twenty-four hours a day. It seemed that this had affected her natural body clock and that the enemy had somehow been involved in it.

After the ministry session ended, the interns started discussing what we had learned. We decided to see if this ungodly body clock was on everybody; it turned out that it was. Some parts of each body clock were gold, but other parts were not. Not everyone had similar golden parts, but everyone did have a spiritual body clock.

The decision was then made to start crafting a prayer to ask to ask the Lord to adjust each person's body clock. It took weeks of praying, reading the Word, and receiving revelation from God to complete the prayer. When looking to the Bible for the basis of what we were discovering, many verses stood out as supportive and confirmatory.

One of these verses was Romans 5:6. It says, "For when we were still without strength, in due time Christ died for the ungodly." This *due time* is another Greek word for time identified as *kairos* time. *Kairos* time contrasts with another Greek word, *chronos* time. *Chronos* time is linear; it's where we get the word *chronological*. Chronos was a Greek god. *Kairos* time, however, is a due time, an appointed time; it is also a position that God calls us to fill. In the New Testament worldview, *kairos* time is primarily understood by its contrast with *chronos* time. Certain events can only take place in *kairos* time, that is, at their due or appointed time, their right time. *Chronos* time or chronological time was understood as a mechanical-clock time, not God's fullness of time, not his right time, or rather, not God's best for us.

Revelation 10:5–6 says:

> *The angel whom I saw standing on the sea and on the land raised up his hand to heaven and swore by Him who lives forever and ever, who created heaven and the things that are in it, the earth and the things that are in it, and the sea and the things that are in it, that there should be delay [chronos] no longer,*

The translation, *delay*, misses part of the meaning. The passage actually says, "that there should be *chronos time* no longer." As believers, we should, even now, be able to access, live, and be in *kairos* time, our appointed, right time. We've seen from Romans 5:6 that Christ came and died in *kairos* time. Therefore, as followers of Christ, our place and time should be that of Ephesians 2:5–6 because God has "made us alive together with Christ . . . and raised us up together, and made us sit together in the heavenly places in Christ Jesus."

Another example of the process God took me through in confirming what he was doing happened while I was at home in England. I was coming home from work on the bus when I started seeing hourglasses above the heads of people getting onto the bus. I contacted a friend of mine, a gifted seer, to confirm if I were seeing correctly or not. He told me that others had seen this at a school of ministry, but I had heard nothing about it. Through this, God not only showed me that he was in what was being revealed, but also that his revelation is both for our benefit and his glory.

Delta—Time for a Change

PAUL L. COX

I became a Christian at the age of six at the First Baptist Church of Honolulu, Hawaii, and grew up in Southern Baptist churches. At the end of my college education I started attending an American Baptist church. I was used to everything always being the same—every Sunday was identical to the one before; the only differences were new hymns and a new sermon. Do you remember those days? Every week it was the same thing, and you would wonder, "Is anything ever going to be different?" As a Baptist, I had preached that we are being changed from "glory to ever increasing glory," but, and if you were at all like me, you would wonder, "What does that mean?" I assumed that it meant exactly what it says, but I never knew it for sure. I had no evidence of this truth until God started doing new and interesting things in my life.

In the spring of 2007, my wife, Donna, and I went on a cruise. I love going on cruises because there is not as much demonic in the water as there is on land, so I can rest, and I can sleep, and I really like that. The night before we were to fly to Florida, I awoke in the middle of the night and heard the word "Delta." And I thought, "Airlines?" In the morning I remembered the word and was trying to figure it out, "Okay, what is *Delta?*" So I called my son and asked him, "Brian, what is Delta?" He replied, "Well, delta is a mathematical function that means change." I thought, "Okay, that's nice."

We got on the plane. I fly American Airlines and have logged over 1,700,000 miles now. Since I fly out of Ontario, California, anytime I fly anywhere east I usually have to go through Dallas International Airport (American's hub). I joke that when I go to heaven I will be going through Dallas. It seems that I am always going through Dallas. I have been through Dallas maybe a hundred-plus times. What happened on this trip to Dallas had never happened before.

On this trip, as we were landing in Dallas, the stewardess was making all of her announcements, "You need to go terminal A for . . . , terminal B for . . . , terminal C for . . . , and you need to go to terminal D for Delta." My wife looked at me and said, "They never said that before."

We landed, got off the plane, and walked to the end of the Jetway and into the terminal. A cart was there. The man driving the cart ignored over a hundred other people getting off the plane, looked at us and asked, "Do you want a ride?" I turned around and looked to see to whom he was talking. He repeated, "Do you want a ride?" I said, "Sure." Over a million miles and no one had ever done this before! So Donna and I got on the cart and he said into his two-way radio, "We have two VIPs with us." I was looking around to see who else was sitting on the cart, but it was only Donna and me. He continued, "Would you please have another cart ready for them after they go up the escalator and come down?" He dropped us off at the escalator and we went up, proceeded toward our destination, and then down the next escalator to where another cart waited. The driver spoke into his radio, "We have two VIPs with us," and he took us to the gate. I thought to myself, "I like this."

Landing at Fort Lauderdale in Florida, we checked into the Hilton Garden Inn. The next morning I had to do what all husbands have to do when they travel, which is to go to the store and get stuff that your wife has forgotten. I walked down to the lobby to the motel's little convenience store near the reception desk. The lady cashier said, "Well, my computer is not working; just go ahead and take it." In all of my life this had never happened. I was wondering, "What is *Delta*?" Something had changed!

That afternoon a tram took us to the cruise ship. I had preselected my cabin and was sure I knew where to find it on the ship so, keys in hand, we walked down the corridor, but it was farther than we expected. We kept on walking, all the way to the very end of the ship. I was thinking, "I don't think this is where my room is supposed to be." Opening the door, I looked into this room at the bow of the ship. The room was huge! On a cruise, I expect to walk into a room and out of it, but I do not expect to walk around in the room! Most cruise ship rooms are very small. Then we looked at the balcony: there were four chairs, a table, some lounges, and at the end of the balcony we could look out over the ocean. Friends who were traveling with us proceeded to their cabin. They soon came back and said, "What is it with you? We paid for the same cabin you paid for, but yours is huge." And I thought, "Delta."

When we came home from the cruise, I started thinking more and more about this Delta. It didn't take much research to find the mathematical definition of Delta: "Delta is equal to the acceleration integrated over time. It is a change in position. It is a change in time." Then I started thinking about time and remembered that a couple of years ago I woke up three or four times one night and looked at the clock. Each time I looked at the clock it was the same time. I was thinking, "This is really getting weird," when the Lord said to me, "You are stuck in time."

Next, I remembered reading *The Fabric of the Cosmos* by Brain Greene, a physicist from New York. Much of the book I do not understand, but as I read the book, I realized that I have done certain things that are described in the book. Although the book was complex, I felt it was important to read it all. On one occasion, I had been reading the book while flying and had stopped over in Dallas (once again) and was resting in the Admiral's Club. After getting on my next flight, I remembered that I had accidentally left the book in the Admiral's Club. I was really frustrated thinking, "I have invested all this time in *The Fabric of the Cosmos*, underlining it carefully, and now I have lost it! I had also noted all the experiences the Lord had given me that had been confirmed by the physicist. I was given permission to get off the plane to look for the book and went back to the Admiral's Club and asked, "Where is my book?" but no one had seen it.

I reboarded the plane and was sitting there, waiting for takeoff, when all of a sudden, a lady walked up to me and asked, "Are you Paul Cox and is this your book?" There are thousands of people and hundreds of planes in Dallas, so I looked at her in surprise and said, "Yes." She gave me the book and I thought, "God, you must really want me to have this book." Then she walked away, leaving me mystified, wondering how she ever found me.

In the book, the physicist-author, Brian Greene, says, "Time is not nothing but something and it flows."[5] Talking as a scientist, he believes it is possible to go back in time. If you are stuck at some point in time, as time keeps flowing on, you don't move with it. Now if your birthright is at a point in time that's ahead of the place where you are stuck, when the flow of time meets your birthright, you are not there, so you never meet your birthright. I believe that is why some prophetic words are never fulfilled—those who received them are stuck in time.

More bizarre experiences occurred. I was at home, working on the two books that the Lord had told me to finish—*Sacrifice the Leader* and *Heaven Trek*. For two or three days I had been spiritually warring and was really miserable—warring, warring, warring . . . writing, writing, writing . . . warring, warring, warring. It was really annoying. Suddenly my car alarm went off. It was parked in the driveway, and the garage door was open. When I walked into the garage, the power of God fell. The light switch in the garage turned on by itself, and the car alarm went off—the demonic was gone in an instant, and I was left wondering, "What was that all about?" I could feel the presence and power of God all over me. Delta!

A couple of weeks later my car was outside again. My daughter, Christy Lisle, who works for us, had purchased a bottle of acid for the swimming pool and left it in the trunk. When I opened the trunk I could smell the acid, so I took it out, put it in the garage, and left the trunk open to air out. I forgot about leaving the trunk hood up and went to bed.

Now, the Lord wakes me up at two specific times during the night. If I wake up at one specific time, I am to pray. If I wake up at another specific time, I know I am to fast for twenty-four hours. That night I woke up at the time to pray. The first thought in my mind was, "This is the time to pray," and the second thought was, "I left the car trunk open." So, in my underwear, I walked to the front door to go out and close the trunk—remember this is a specific time. Opening the door, I encountered a police officer standing on my porch who asked, "Why is your trunk open?"

Well, you know how it is when you wake up—I don't know about you, but I am rather disoriented—so I was rambling, trying to explain why my trunk was open. He just shook his head and went over and touched the car, setting off the car alarm. I thought, "I better get my keys to turn off the alarm," but it stopped on its own. The officer looked at me, shook his head as if wondering what I was doing, closed the trunk, got into his police car, and drove away. Then I heard the Lord say to me, "Your ministry is protected" (in dream interpretation, a car is a ministry). I was left asking, "What in the world is going on?" I called a friend the next day and he said, "I think that was an angel." And I said, "Well, did he steal a police car?" Really! Now what are the odds of this happening? Delta!

Some weeks later, in a motel room in Oregon, I'd taken off my trousers and put them over a couch before I went to bed. They had fallen to the floor and some change had fallen out of my pocket. Donna had picked up my trousers and put them back over the sofa, but she hadn't seen the coins. The next morning I looked down and saw five coins on the carpet, perfectly placed, like a five on a domino. As I was looking at the five coins, I was thinking, "How in the world did five coins fall on the floor perfectly like that?" I realized it was a sign and wonder—a third sign and wonder. Running late, I went to breakfast, but asked Donna to count the coins. There were five and they totaled forty cents. Five is the number of grace, eight means new beginnings, and forty indicates completion, so five times eight is equal to forty. I thought, "This is really getting bizarre," and I knew it had to do with Delta.

What does all of this mean? Here is the key; we need to get unstuck from time. The Greek word for the "right time" is *kairos*. We are told in Scripture that "at the right time," the *kairos*, Christ came to earth. *Kairos* is God's time. Ephesians 5:15–16 says, "See then that you walk circumspectly, not as fools but as wise, redeeming the time, because the days are evil." In Colossians 4:5 we read, "Walk in wisdom towards those who are outside, *[here is the same phrase]* redeeming the time." *Redeeming the time* means buying back the time. *Kairos* is also used in Acts 3:19, "Repent therefore and be converted, that your sins may be blotted out, so that times of refreshing may come from the presence of the Lord." If we are stuck in time, then we cannot be refreshed. Time is either *chronos* (ungodly, the Greek god of earthbound time) or *kairos* (godly time),[6] and most of us are in *chronos* time—we get trapped there.

How do we get stuck in time? I believe this can happen through some type of abuse or through disobedience. I remember a couple of recurring dreams indicating that I was stuck in time. I had these dreams over and over again. As an associate pastor at a Baptist church I became very interested in another staff position; I desired it, but it was not the Lord's will. I now believe that I was disobedient in desiring that position. As I began understanding the possibility that I might have gotten stuck in time, I confessed my disobedience and have never had that dream again. I had experienced Delta, a change in position.

The other recurring dream was set at the Baptist church where I had first experienced the power of God. Although many in the church were excited about the move of God, others were totally against what the Lord was doing. My family and I were severely criticized. Because we had suffered great abuse from this experience, I again realized that I could be stuck in time. I asked the Lord to remove the effects of abuse from me and have not had the dream since then. I had experienced a "change in time." Delta.

On one occasion, as I was telling a friend this about this new concept of being stuck in time, he said, "I just had a memory of being abused as a little boy." We dealt with the issue, and he was released from a "stuck" position in time and came into "current" time.

Before this revelation about Delta began, Dale Shannon, one of our intercessors, received this word.

> Tunnels of time, you can travel through the tunnels of time. There are sequences; one births another. He creates beings that create; expand your thinking. It is not what you think. There is more. Ask for the revelation. It is coming. It is possible to time travel, to go back and forth in time. You are stuck in a dimension of time. (We live in the third dimension. Length and width are two dimensions, height is the third dimension, and the fourth is time.) You are stuck in a dimension of time. You can go backward and forward. You are stuck in a dimension of time. Come out of the box of time. It is the enemy that caused you to get off the time. Do not miss the time of your visitation. You are to be stewards of time. Daniel sealed up the revelation. It is being unsealed. It is becoming unsealed in these last days. There are gears turning, wheels within wheels. It is important to align the gears.

I cannot remember when this happened first, but as I was praying generationally for someone, I realized the person was moving through time—because the clock was moving, so was the individual. By discerning with my hand behind the person, I could feel things in the person's time line, and by discerning evil, the ministry team could pray and ask the Lord to remove it from that point in the generational line.

A very prophetic lady said to me, "God said I am going to be the first of the revelation of the sons of God." Romans 8:19 reads, "For the earnest expectation of the creation eagerly awaits for the revealing of the sons of God." Now if you follow current prophetic teachings, you may have heard that now, in our day, there is a revelation of the sons of God. In other words, God is bringing us, as men and women, to rule over creation even as all creation is groaning because of sin. As this woman was saying this to me, I was thinking, "That is the most arrogant thing I have heard anybody say. How can you be the first of the revelation of the sons of God?" But I did not say this out loud. Then, as I was ministering to her, I started going back in time until all of a sudden I realized that I had gone all the way back to the glory realm. It was before the beginning of time, and I was in the glory and I could feel the celestial beings. I can't say that I understand all the details of it, but I knew that since she was revealed back then, she is the first; it doesn't matter who was revealed first in this century, she was revealed at the beginning of time. I had to repent. I had to repent to her. I thought, "Oh my goodness, you are the first because it has already been done—back there."

I continue to learn more about Delta as I teach the concept. Someone comes and asks, "Well do you know this?" And I say, "No, I don't." When I first started talking about Delta, I discovered that Delta is an actual spiritual being. People have described his appearance as triangles or tetrahedrons that are spinning.

Here is another way I've learned that Delta works. Delta is also Delta electricity. In the U.S. we have three-phase electricity: plus, minus, and ground. There is also Delta electricity; it is symbolized by the Delta sign, a triangle. The interesting thing about Delta electricity is that it is not grounded to the earth. On learning this, I had an amazing revelation! As Christians we are not grounded to the earth; we are seated with Christ in heavenly places. We are to be on the earth but not of the earth! Somehow Delta is involved in moving us into the heavenly realm.

In Oregon, a physicist had come to our *Heaven Trek* seminar. As I was speaking on the subject of Delta, he was getting more and more excited. Finally, he said to me, "I need to explain to you about Delta." (As if I could understand!) "You take an X-Y axis and then on the axis you have zeros [so 0, 0, 0, 0, 0], but then you have a 1 and the 1 goes into infinity and you have 0, 0, 0, 0, 0, again. That 1 is Delta." I said, "Okay." Then he said, "Let me make this practical," and I replied, "That would be helpful." He said, "As a non-Christian we are 0, 0, 0, 0, 0, 0, 0 but God wants to bring us to the 1, into infinity or eternity." And I thought, "Okay that works." He had established a mathematical association between Delta and the heavenly realm.

Then, at the break, a lady came up and said that she had to tell me about her dream because it was what he had just said. And I thought, "Now how is that possible because I don't understand what this is about?" And she said, "If you can understand the dream, then maybe it will help you understand what he said." I said, "Okay." She continued, "In my dream

I was going around, and around, and around (So what is that? A zero?). I'm going around and around and around a mountain. It is stormy, and it's rainy, and it is miserable, and I am not getting anywhere, and I know it is going to take seven weeks. Then someone (could it have been Delta?) opened a door in the mountain and said, 'You can come through here and go straight up; it will only take a week'" Up the mountain to Mt. Zion!

Before praying with the prophetic lady, and before any of these experiences with Delta, I had had a dream. Initially I thought the dream was about me, but often dreams about myself are given so that I can experience the emotions of the person I am going to pray for. In the dream I was in the Nevada desert on a train headed out into the desert, to nowhere, and I had to get back to a city on the border between California and Nevada. The city was called Delta. I was on the train, but I realized that I could not return to Delta because of a canyon on the right side of the train. No matter what I did, I could not cross the canyon to get back to Delta. At the first stop, I found myself at a beautiful hotel surrounded by beautiful scenery, but the train wasn't going back, so I was stuck. Although the hotel was beautiful, I was frustrated because I could not get back to Delta. As the train stopped at the hotel, I noticed that it was filled with baggage. I believe baggage represents past issues. The next stop was a trailer park in the desert, and there were many poverty-stricken people there. The scene was one of despair and misery. By now, I was much further out into the desert, literally at "nowhere." I thought, "How am I going to get back to Delta?"

The next night I woke up and heard the words, *XYZ axis*. In the morning I called a friend who is a knowledgeable about math. I told him about my dream and asked, "How do I get back to Delta and what does an *XYZ axis* have to do with all of this?" Somehow, I knew that the train was on the *Z axis* and needed to get to Delta, which was on the Y axis. He answered, "Paul, on an XYZ axis, the point where the three come together is called the origin and you have to go back to the origin to get to Delta." I replied, "This is so good—I don't understand any of this, but it is good." So that is what we prayed with the lady going around the mountain—we asked the Lord to take her back to the origin and set her free so she could get to Delta.

There is a story in Scripture about Saul. He was ordained by Samuel to be king. Saul was told to go to Gilgal and wait for seven days. He went to

Gilgal, but at the end of the seven days, the Philistine armies were coming, people were panicking, and King Saul was getting fearful. He felt as if he couldn't wait for Samuel any longer so he said, "I must make a sacrifice." As soon as he did it, Samuel showed up. This is the most terrifying story in all of Scripture to me. Saul missed fulfilling his calling because he was not obedient to the Word of the Lord. Samuel then told Saul, "Because you have done this and been disobedient you have lost your kingdom." Why? Because he did not wait for the right time. He was presumptuous and went ahead of God. That is scary isn't it? Even as a Baptist pastor, before I knew anything about the Delta, I knew I did not want to miss God's timing.

Now there is good news!

If you do miss God's timing, the good news is that, through the blood of Jesus Christ, you can repent and be covered, and he can move you into his *kairos* time. It is true that we all have generational issues that are causing us all types of problems. God wants to go back and clean them up. How does he do it? He changes our position in time.

While I was talking with my friend, he said to me, "I see that you are in the Lost and Found Room—in a heavenly place. Paul, you can go back into time and retrieve all that was good—everything that was lost and stolen from your generational line. You can bring it back into current time." That is what I did!! Since that time I have seen the Lord do absolutely amazing things in my life and in the life of Aslan's Place.

Why not ask the Lord now if you are stuck in time because of any issue of disobedience or abuse? Perhaps this is why you are not meeting your destiny. Why not ask the Lord to bring Delta and change you from *chronos* time to his *kairos* time? Ask him to release his call into your life and bring you to the point of his favor!

The Prayer: Restore God's Timing and Amend My Body Clock

Father, on behalf of myself and my family line, I renounce and repent for rejecting your timing and taking timing into our own hands. I repent for all those who used devices as a methods of time control including stop-watches, charms, amulets, talismans, clothing, or any other ungodly device.

✠ On behalf of myself and my family line, I renounce and repent for worshipping time instead of worshipping the God Most High who holds time in his hands.

✠ Lord, on behalf of myself and my generational line, I renounce and repent for all who attempted to control, bend, or warp time, for all who tried to control time for their own purposes, and for all who attempted to travel through time to change and manipulate their own lives or the lives of others.[7]

✠ Lord I ask that you will disconnect my family line from any ungodly clocks. Please disconnect me from the magnetic field of the land that seeks to control my body clock, and please disconnect me from any ungodly time. Please remove any ungodly connection to Greenwich.[8]

✠ Lord, I ask that you break any connection between me and any ungodly priest of time. Please break all soul ties between me and any false or ungodly fathers or mothers, grandfathers or grandmothers of time. Lord, please break any connection between me and any time lords. Lord, I renounce and repent on behalf of myself and those in my generational line for any agreements that were made with the grim reaper who we believed came when it was time to die.

✠ Lord, please remove any connection between the ungodly clock face and my physical and spiritual senses. Please break, shatter, cut off, and destroy the connectors between the ungodly clock face and my eyes, ears, mouth, nose, and hands. Please remove the ungodly pendulum so that I may be correctly balanced in your time.

✠ Lord please remove the ungodly clock face and replace it with your righteous clock face. Please cause the hands of the clock to move according to your time and bring my body clock back into your control and nobody else's. Please establish the correct time, so that confusion, lack of self-awareness, and loss of time will not occur.

✠ Lord, please stop the deceleration of my body clock and restore me to godly acceleration.

✠ Lord, I renounce and repent on behalf of myself and those in my generational line who spoke word curses to do with time against themselves and others. Lord, I repent for lies about time to myself and to others. I repent for believing or saying that we were 'living on borrowed time,' 'out of time,' or 'walking on the sands of time.' I repent of saying of myself and anyone else that our 'time is or was running out.' Lord, please remove from above my head the ungodly hourglass.

✠ I declare the truth that as a believer in Christ my time is not up and will never be up. I am seated in heavenly places[9] and will live for eternity. I choose to believe that whoever believes in you shall not die but have eternal life. I declare my eternal time line and nature in Christ who lives forever and ever.[10]

✠ Father, please restore eternity to my heart and readjust it to beat with your *kairos*. Lord, please make your timing my timing and your seasons my seasons. Lord, I ask that you give me a heart that is able to discern both time and judgment.[11]

✠ Lord, I declare the truth that you are the Alpha and Omega.[12] You are the one who places eternity in the hearts of man. You are the creator and controller of time. Lord, you are the one who has written all the days of my life in your book.[13] You knew them before even one came into being. You are the one who has seen the beginning and the end, and I now choose to place my time into your hands. I choose now to believe and trust that your timing in my life is better than my timing.

✠ Lord, I now ask that you apply your blood to the mechanisms, gears, and springs of my body so that they will work as you have ordained and planned them to work. Please now anoint with oil all the parts of my body clock. I choose now to step into your time for me and into your excellent glory.[14]

✠ Lord, please replace the ungodly clock parts with godly clock parts so that the body clock that you have given me will click and move, synchronized with you in glory from now onward.

✠ Lord, please unite my body clock to you and the body of Christ, so that we will be synchronized and not go ahead of one another or ahead of you. Please bring us collectively into right time.[15]

✠ Restore me now fully to correct time with a righteous body clock.[16]

Notes:

1. καιρός, the right time.

2. A talisman is an object supposed to give magical powers or supernatural protection to its bearer.

3. We understood the Lord was talking about our relationship to the dimension of time. This may be what we understand as *biorhythms*.

4. Individual patients tend to have time patterns when their seizures take place.

5. Brian Greene, *The Fabric of the Cosmos* (New York: Alfred A. Knopf, 2004) 127–142.

6. Although *Kairos* was a Greek god, according to the *Theological Dictionary of the New Testament*, this common Greek word for the opportune moment was used in the New Testament to means "The 'fateful and decisive point,' with strong, though not always explicit emphasis on that fact that it is ordained by God," 459. That is to say, *kairos* time is God's divinely appointed time, first in the life of Jesus and now in the life of believers. *Theological Dictionary of the New Testament*, ed. Gerhard Kittel, trans. Geoffrey Bromiley, (Grand Rapids, MI: Wm. B. Eerdmans, 1965), 459–461.

7. Daniel 7:25–26.

8. Ecclesiastes 9:11–12; Psalm 37:19.

9. Ephesians 2:6.

10. Revelation 10:6.

11. Ecclesiastes 8:5.

12. Revelation 22:11.

13. Psalm 139:16.

14. 2 Peter 1:17.

15. Ephesians 1:10.

16. Psalm 69:13; Galatians 4:4; Ephesians 1:10; 2:6; Revelation 10:6; 22:11; Daniel 7:25:26; Psalms 32:6; 37:19; 69:13; Ecclesiastes 9:11–12; 8:5; 2 Peter 1:17.

Renunciation of the Misogynistic Spirit

ALICE MILLS

My experience with the spirit of misogyny was a journey into the answer to certain questions that have profoundly affected my life. I found myself unexpectedly at a ministry training school at Aslan's Place one weekend while my teenage children were receiving ministry. Paul Cox began to describe the ties that one has to one's own blood, even after it has left the body. I mentioned to Paul that this is more poignant for women because of our menstrual cycles. We even refer to that time of the month as a curse. As we were praying to break those ties, my left shoulder became very hot. Normally, heat in deliverance comes and goes rather quickly, but this heat lingered. I asked Paul about it, and the other women in the training began to speak up. Their shoulders were also hot. We asked the Lord about it corporately, and one woman said that it was a woman-hating spirit. The left side of the body is associated with the feminine side, and so it seemed natural that my left shoulder would manifest. I wondered at the time if some of my own hormonal issues would be cleared up.

Two weeks later, I attended an event where Bill Johnson of Bethel in Redding, California, was speaking. After he finished speaking, I responded to his invitation to come to the front of the sanctuary. I went up for healing ministry for my hip, which has been painful since the birth of my first daughter twenty-two years ago. The ministry team prayed and nothing happened. Just before they prayed for me, they had prayed for a friend of mine, for a hip injury she had received in a car accident. The prayer minister asked her if she had forgiven the man who had caused the injury. She hadn't thought to do that, and after forgiving him, she received some relief. I realized then that my own hip injuries were, in part, because of gynecologists who were at best insensitive during the delivery of my daughter. I forgave those gynecologists, and my left hip went very hot and was healed. Since then, I have noticed healing in my hormones and cycles.

I have always considered modern gynecology a very mixed blessing. While the good news is that far fewer women die in childbirth, gynecology and obstetrics have a checkered history and, in some cases, have been a vehicle for violence against women. Suddenly, I began to realize the personal implications of the woman-hating, or *misogynistic*, spirit as well as the complications involved.

When Paul asked me to begin writing up a renunciation of the misogynistic spirit, my eyes opened up wider to the serious implications throughout history that misogyny has engendered. I watched a woman with the advanced stages of anorexia pass by me at the mall one day, and my left shoulder ached. I literally felt the woman-hating spirit devouring her.

Layoffs at my work involved only women in their fifties. As I began to search the Scriptures for examples of hatred of women, I realized some of the issues began in the Garden of Eden. Of course, with the blame game played in that scene where the Lord confronts Adam and Eve. Less obvious are the consequences of the blame cycle. Adam was faced with a choice. The choice was not merely about whether or not to eat the apple, but about what his relationship to Eve would look like if he did not eat the apple. His motivation is not completely clear, but it does seem clear that he did not want to lose Eve, even at the cost of his obedience. He blamed her for putting him in the position of having to choose—perhaps not recognizing that we all have to choose to some extent between our walk with the Lord and our relationships. This twist in relationship is at the core of the adversarial relationship between man and woman. Man desires woman and resents her for what it costs him.

Women themselves participate in misogyny. As I was praying for two women, my left shoulder began to ache. I asked if they had been discriminated against. This question did not resonate with either of them. My shoulder had been a little knotted that whole week as I had been processing my relationship with my own mother. The Lord had even told me to keep dealing with it. Everywhere I drove around town, I kept seeing construction signs that said Shoulder Work Ahead. Curious, I asked the two women if they were angry at their mothers. Even as I asked the question, my shoulder contracted. The answer was a resounding yes. After we went through a time of repentance and forgiveness for their mothers, my shoulder was released, and they felt heat in their shoulders.

God has been preparing me to write this prayer for some time. Two years ago, he kept me up all night to reveal how Jesus came to specifically free women. There are five women mentioned in Jesus' lineage: Rahab, Ruth, Tamar, Bathsheba, and Mary. Each represents a form of bondage that women wrestle with. Rahab, the prostitute who aided the Israelites, represents sexuality as commodity. Exchanging one's sexuality for economic survival, while not solely a female issue, is a bondage that affects women far more than men. Prostitution is often involuntary and involves an exploitation of women that Jesus responded to with mercy in the New Testament.

Ruth and her mother-in-law, Naomi, represent the lack of financial viability widowed women have sustained throughout history, as well as the lack of vision and loss of purpose widows often experience for their own lives. Naomi defines her life by her loss of the men in it. Without a husband, both Naomi and Ruth have little identity of their own. Ruth finds purpose in her care of Naomi. Fortunately, God had good plans for Ruth. Truly he is the comforter of widows.

Another widow, Tamar, represents the legal, financial, and emotional abuse that women often sustain within society. Her two husbands denied her inheritance and sexually humiliated her. Although she took matters into her own hands and God blessed her with the double inheritance of two sons, her experience within marriage is not an unusual one, even today, particularly within societies that deny women any legal rights.

Bathsheba represents the perilous relationship between sexuality and power. While the Bible does not explicitly reveal Bathsheba's response to King David's ardor, it begs the question of her appreciation of his position. Did she feel free to repulse his advances? Did she want to? Her continued relationship with David after the death of her husband suggests at least her tacit approval. The point is not about her role, but that women use sex to gain power while men use power to gain sex. Both directions reveal a hatred of women.

Lastly, Mary, the sixteen-year-old unwed mother, represents the shame that results from a misogynistic spirit. I have always found it very moving that God chose an illegitimate birth. It's clear that all pregnancies would be legitimate and never cause disgrace or bring censure from men if all women were cherished and honored as God intends, but the truth is, they are not. It is actually arguable that the majority of births in this world are illegitimate; Jesus began his trek under the same shadow that covers so many.

The issues surrounding the enemy's lengthy and vicious attack of women, through men's treatment of them as well as through the betrayal of women who agree with misogyny, are as vital today as they were in the Garden of Eden.

The Prayer: Renunciation of the Misogynistic Spirit[1]

✠ Heavenly Father, on behalf of myself and my generational line, I repent for and renounce all hatred and dishonor of women.

✠ For myself and my family line, I repent for and renounce engaging in forced marriages, prostitution, and the treating of women as objects to be bought and sold, without regard for their safety or calling, for the purpose of sexual exploitation or financial gain. I repent for all who used women, particularly older or unattractive women, as slave labor. Lord, please break off all the consequences on my family line for those who were treated as burdens and rejected as worthless because of their feminine gender.

✠ I repent for and renounce for myself and my family line for who considered women a little better than animals, without spirit or genuine intelligence. I repent for all who enforced female genital mutilation[2] to control and subdue women. I repent for all who believed the lie that women were created first and faulty.

✠ For myself and my family line, I repent for and renounce all who practiced droit du seigneur, a practice that enabled the owners of feudal estates to deflower virgins on their wedding night to other men. I repent for all who valued women based on proof, real or imagined, of their virginity. I repent for all who dehumanized women by romanticizing them as pure and untouchable, or demonized them by reducing them to only sexual roles. More specifically, I repent for all who were deceived by the manifestation of the misogynistic spirit known as the "Madonna/whore complex."

⬧ For myself and my family line, I repent for and renounce the generational hatred of the female gender that led to infanticide of girls in many cultures. I repent for all who murdered women.

⬧ For myself and my family line, I repent for and renounce getting hysterectomies without medical cause to solve emotional distresses in women.

⬧ For myself and my family line, I repent for and renounce all participation in dishonorable legal practices regarding women, including withholding from them the right to own property, to have custody of their own children, or to have a voice in their own lives.

⬧ For myself and my family line, I repent for and renounce all participation in legal violence against women. I repent for all who committed financial abuse against women, refusing to provide for them.

⬧ For myself and my family line, I repent for and renounce denying women access to education to subjugate them. I repent for all who have denied women access into various trades because of fear and greed, which denied them a way for providing for themselves. I repent for all who devalued the equal physical labor of a woman by seeing it as less than equal.

⬧ For myself and my family line, I repent for and renounce committing violence against women during the days when women peaceably demonstrated for the right to vote.

⬧ For myself and my family line, I repent for all who engaged in abortion, forced or voluntary, and renounce this act. I repent for all who participated in corrupt obstetrical practices, such as the outlawing of forceps, because of a belief that women were to suffer during childbirth.

✠ For myself and my family line, I repent for all who participated in modern gynecological practices that administered scopolamine, not to relieve pain, but to disorder a woman's mind so that she would not remember giving birth, and then removed the baby forcibly while the mother was trapped in restraints.[3]

✠ For myself and my family line, I repent for all who have participated in obstetrical practices that ignored the needs of the mother and gave preference to the doctor, practices such as giving unnecessary cesareans, episiotomies, and all other procedures that treat pregnancy as an illness.

✠ For myself and my family line, I repent for all who valued women solely on the basis of their ability to bear children, particularly male children. I particularly repent for all those who blamed their wives for the failure to produce children.

✠ For myself and my family line, I repent for and renounce all who have objectified women by valuing them solely on the basis of their beauty. I repent for all who have debased women by participating in pornography and prostitution.

✠ For myself and my family line, I repent for and renounce any rejection of women based on flaws in comparison with the beauty standard of the time. I repent for all who fixated on female beauty and missed the genuine beauty that God placed within woman.

✠ For myself and my family line, I repent for all who have twisted the original intent of the submission of women in marriage, dishonoring the knowledge that women are coheirs with Christ, and I renounce their error. I repent for all who have used their authority to humiliate, abuse, and control women.

✠ For myself and my family line, I repent on behalf of all of the mothers in my generational line who failed to bond with and support their children and passed on a distrust and hatred of women. I renounce this failure to love. I repent on behalf of the children in my generational line who held bitter root judgments against their mothers and sisters and opened a door to misogyny.

✖ For myself and my family line, I repent for all who have been deceived by the feminist mind-set, which views God, marriage, and motherhood as the primary avenues of violence against women, and I renounce this mind-set. I repent for all who rejected their roles as women. I repent for all who have dishonored women by this rejection.

✖ In the name of Jesus of Nazareth, I forgive everyone who has hurt me and my family by agreeing with and acting in a misogynist spirit.

✖ Father God, please cleanse all misogyny from my generational line and restore to the women in my family line the place you originally intended for them. I ask you to bless them with the knowledge of your love and a desire to claim their inheritance and an acceptance of their calling in you.

✖ I repent for and renounce my personal agreement with the woman-hating spirit. I now break every curse I have spoken over myself, including my body and its functions, in the name of Jesus. I repent for and renounce any spiritual rebellion or anger over the choice of my Heavenly Father to create me as woman. I accept my female gender and bless it, in the name of Jesus.

Notes:

1. Prayer by Professor Alice Mills. *Misogyny*—hatred of woman.

2. Female circumcision.

3. Majority of births in industrialized countries for seventy-five years.

Deliverance from
Transcendental Meditation

TERRY JOHNSON

In March of 1976, I began practicing *TM*, or the *Transcendental Meditation Program*, as taught by Maharishi Mahesh Yogi. A few years later I paid three thousand dollars to learn the Yoga Sutras and faithfully practiced the TM-Sidhi Program until November 1991, when God Almighty, out of his great love, power, and mercy, pulled me out of the occult through Benny Hinn's ministry.

As a young girl, I would fall asleep in church. Knowledge without an encounter with God is just plain old yucky "religion." My parents, at the time unsaved, gave me a Ouija board and a magic set for Christmas. I put them to good use. The demonic realm of the spirit began to open up to me.

In my early twenties, I attended an introductory lecture on TM. For years I was in a sexual relationship with the local TM leader, and for a short time my home was used for the center of this movement in my city. I had many friends who were TM teachers, and some of the leaders of this movement were guests in my home. My best girlfriend, Lori, a TM teacher, committed a successful, planned suicide by shooting herself in the head. She believed the lie of reincarnation, that she would get to come back in another body and could keep trying again until she became enlightened.

As a young lady I was in a stressful sales job. Some of the "benefits" the TM technique promised me were clearer thinking, better health, more energy, less stress, causing the weather to improve, reversing the aging process, increasing my intelligence and brainpower to full potential, reduction of crime in my city, and creating world peace.

At first I was hesitant to start TM because of my religious upbringing. Maharishi's appearance as a Hindu monk scared me. However, after having dinner with the local TM teacher and being given a flyer from a religious leader who taught TM at Notre Dame High School, I thought, "Surely this must be okay—if the these religious leaders are doing TM." Later, as my involvement with this cult increased, I attended several residence courses. Some were held at a Christian religious retreat house in California. The Christian leaders would cook our food, and I thought I was so holy. I did not have a clue at all about the evil I had opened myself to.

A few years later I wanted to advance and learn more powerful techniques like "yogic-flying." That's when I paid the three thousand dollars. Some will say this was just "bouncing around," but the Lord let me know that demonic power was lifting my body off the ground. Other advanced techniques that were taught by Maharishi, for a price, were invisibility, changing the weather, and walking through walls.

I was taught breathing exercises and yoga positions to practice daily; these opened my body up to even more demons. Many innocent people learn these techniques at their local YMCA or church. They do not have a clue to the evil doors that are being opened up and the demonic contamination infecting the gateways of their senses.

According to the official TM Web site, as of today over six million people have learned the basic foundational TM techniques, which now have a price tag of twenty-five hundred dollars. The price is a lot steeper than that. Personally, I became depressed, suicidal, and loaded up with many, many demons.

The TM movement boasts that over six hundred scientific research studies using TM have been conducted at more than two hundred universities including Harvard, UCLA, and Stanford. Today, according to the official TM Web site, if you are a veteran suffering with post-traumatic stress disorder, with authorization from your medical doctor, the Veterans Benefits Administration will pay the fee for you to start TM. People get involved in TM from across all belief systems. Although in 1977 the U.S. courts ruled in a lawsuit that TM is a religious movement, Hindu in nature, people are told that it is not a religion because they do not have to believe anything for the technique to work.

Maharishi and his TM and TM-Sidhi programs claim to be ushering in a new age of enlightenment and world peace. I believe this peace that Maharishi is promoting is the counterfeit false peace that we are warned about in the Bible and not the true peace that comes from Jesus, the Prince of Peace. It is also my opinion that this man and the movement he founded are really tools of Satan to influence people's mind-sets to accept a one-world religion, one-world government, and also the very Antichrist himself.

Millions of people have entered into this TM Movement with naïve and well-meaning intentions. Some just wanted to get rid of stress.

I have forgiven all those involved in my deception, including the leaders of this movement and even Maharishi himself.

Because of my experience with TM, I have a new understanding of Matthew 24:24. "For false christs and false prophets will rise and show great signs wonders to deceive, if possible, even the elect."

Only by the amazing grace of Jesus, the great love of Abba Father, and the power of the precious Holy Spirit was I set free. God used the ministry of Benny Hinn and his book *Good Morning Holy Spirit* for my initial encounter with the Holy Spirit and the start of much-needed deliverance prayer. God used Johanna Michaelsen's book, *The Beautiful Side of Evil*, to explain to me how I could be so deceived and blinded by the evil "Angel of Light."

My heart's desire is that many will have a powerful encounter with the one and only true God and be saved, healed, and completely set free by the Lord of lords, the King of kings, Jesus Christ.

The Prayer: Deliverance from Transcendental Meditation

I ask You, God, to forgive me, and I repent for and renounce any and all of my participation and involvement in the Transcendental Meditation/Sidhi Program, whether I knew or did not know what I was getting myself into.

I renounce and repent for the following evils:

- The giving of my time and money and talent toward this movement

- Being used as a spokesperson for this movement, encouraging and causing others to be snared into a movement designed to usher in the Age of Enlightenment, the Antichrist, his one-world religion, one-world government, and one-world monetary system

- Grieving the Holy Spirit

- Engaging in the Hindu religion false belief system

- Participating in the Puja ceremony and allowing myself to become involved in it, including bowing down to all gods invoked

- Calling countless times on my personal mantra, a Hindu deity, and for obtaining any blessings from this familiar spirit

- Being present and bowing down to all evil the TM teacher invoked, including

- the Hindu trinity, the Lord Narayana, Brahma—the false creator, and Vashista

- Agreeing with the TM teacher's request that the Hindu trinity enter my heart

- Worshiping Vashistha, Shakti, Parashar, Vyasa, Shukadeva, Gaudapada, Govinda[1] and his disciple, Shri Shankaracharya, Padma-Pada, Hasta-Malaka, Trotakacharya, and Vartika-kara, the teacher of Karma

- Believing the traditions of the masters, the wisdom and the ultimate evil authorities, the Shrutis,[2] the Smritis,[3] the Pranas,[4] Shankara,[5] Shakarya,[6] Badarayana, Brahmanada, and Indra

- Worshipping of Soma, Shiva, Kali, Ganesh, Lakashimi, and Krishna, Guru Dev, and Vendanta

I renounce and repent for all participation in the following techniques:

- Japa, the repeating of a mantra

- The checking procedure, hypnotism, and all of the reinforcement of evil planted, especially during the post-trance state of mind

- Any faith in karma and its laws of enforcement

- TM-Sidhi "age of enlightenment" techniques, described in Patanjali's Sutras according to the Dharan Tradition

- The nineteen sutras I practiced to develop supernormal abilities: friendliness, compassion, happiness, strength of an elephant, bronchial tube, inner light, sun, moon, polestar, trachea, navel, the distinction between intellect and transcendence, intuition, transcendence finest hearing, transcendence finest sight, transcendence finest taste, transcendence finest touch, transcendence finest smell, and the levitation/flying technique, the relationship of body and Akasha, and the lightness of cotton fiber

- The laws of Manu

- The practice of Soma Veda to gain supernatural powers from Indra

- The reading of the mandala

- Listening to Hindu monks chant

- Receiving the title "citizen of the age of enlightenment" and accepting the card with a crown on my head

- Yogic asanas, holding a certain body position that leaves the body open to demons

- *Pranayama*, breathing exercises designed to clear channel in my body for soma to enter

- Reading of the 9th and 10th mandalas, which resulted in inviting gods to feast on the soma in my stomach

- Any bond between me an the ancient Aryan cultures

- The watering of the Tree of Wisdom in the garden and its branches of knowledge

- The attunement of myself and my mind to any energy or wisdom from Satan

✠ I repent for opening my intellect to create divine unity between myself and Satan. I repent for believing and proclaiming that by practicing the techniques I learned from the TM and TM-Sidhi programs I would attain a gift of supreme knowledge, and that supreme knowledge would fulfill my life.

✠ I now ask you, Lord, to break all links, chains, bonds, and any connection between me and all TM teachers and the TM movement.

✠ I now ask God to breaks any lines connecting me to the generational lines of the ancient tradition and the masters of antiquity.

✠ I ask you, Lord, to heal my mind from being put on the field of the absolute.

✠ I ask you, Lord, to free me from the counterfeit harmony of my thoughts, speech, and action or my ego, intellect, mind, and senses.

✠ I ask you, Lord, to take from me any gifts, anointing, knowledge, and powers gained by my involvement in the TM-Sidhi program.

Notes:

1. Ruler of the yogis.

2. The divine revelators who expose divine revelation by impulses of the absolute to the seers; they bring the codes.

3. The codes of behavior.

4. The record keepers who keep all ancient records.

5. The emancipator of the world.

6. The redeemer hailed as Krishna.

Renunciation for Egypt

SARAH VICTOR

In November 2007, my family came under a series of attacks. I experienced the first one, a torn and wounded throat. This symptom sounded like the effect of a Freemasonry curse I'd read about. However, I had already renounced Freemasonry and its consequences, so I started seeking the Lord for insight and guidance on where the open door for the attack was.

The second attack was experienced by a family member who became the victim of domestic abuse. Several pastors prayed about this situation. Two of them gave us similar words. Both had to do with Egypt. The first was Isaiah 30:1–5.

> *"Woe to the rebellious children," says the LORD, "Who take counsel, but not of Me, and who devise plans, but not of My Spirit, that they may add sin to sin; who walk to go down to Egypt, and have not asked My advice, to strengthen themselves in the strength of Pharaoh, and to trust in the shadow of Egypt! Therefore the strength of Pharaoh shall be your shame, and trust in the shadow of Egypt shall be your humiliation. For his princes were at Zoan, and his ambassadors came to Hanes. They were all ashamed of a people who could not benefit them, or be help or benefit, but a shame and also a reproach."*

The second was Isaiah 31:1.

Woe to those who go down to Egypt for help, and rely on horses, who trust in chariots because they are many, and in horsemen because they are very strong, but who do not look to the Holy One of Israel, nor seek the LORD!

That year God had been taking our family on a journey of cleansing to remove ancient roots of idolatry and the occult, starting with the mystery religions of Babylon. Idolatry and the occult are thought to have started with the ancient mystery religion of Babylon in Nimrod's time and spread throughout the world, assuming different faces in Phoenicia, Pergamos, Greece, Egypt, Rome, China, and India. I realized that God wanted to go further back in time to remove the roots of the ancient mystery religion of Egypt from my family line.

I started researching Egyptian history and soon my attention turned to *The Egyptian Book of the Dead*.[1] As I read the first chapter, I started reversing the hymns of praise to the pagan gods aloud, renouncing and repenting of them and petitioning God to disconnect me from those pagan gods. As I started doing this, I discerned a lot of activity in the spiritual realms and felt lightness and joy as the deliverance started taking effect in me.

I wrote down my renunciations of the worship in this ancient occult prayer to make it easier for others who God leads to renounce these ancient Egyptian roots. I only used the first part of the book in the following renunciation prayer. You may continue the renunciation of the rest of the book, if the Lord so leads. I believe that this prayer may be the first in a series of tools that the Lord is releasing to set us free from the ancient mystery religions of Egypt and its current manifestations in our age.

The construction of such a renunciation prayer is based on the principle in 1 John 1:9. "If we confess our sins, He is faithful and just to forgive us our sins and to cleanse us from all unrighteousness."

Since we prayed this prayer, my family has not experienced such attacks.

Deliverance ministries have explored the links between the ancient mystery religion of Egypt and current deliverance issues for those seeking healing from Satanic ritual abuse (SRA) and Freemasonry.[2]

Masons themselves have explored and sought to establish the idea that Freemasonry may be one reincarnation of the ancient mystery religion of Egypt.[3,4] Masons have also explored similarities between Freemasonry and Hinduism, especially in rituals where energy is moved upward through the spinal column.[5]

All these religions, cults, and rituals have common aims—first to supposedly elevate man to the status of a god, sometimes using rituals known as ascensions, and second for the demonic to invade, take over, and to unite with the spirit of man to achieve control of our world. To this end, they devise rituals for men to illegally access ungodly heavenly dimensions or to allow the demonic to enter the human spirit.

Religions and cults that carry spiritual inheritance from mystery Egypt are believed to include Freemasonry, the Illuminati, SRA rituals, the Rosicrucian movement, Gnosticism, the Kabala, alchemy, Druidism, and the New Age Movement. Among the sacred texts of Ancient Egypt are the *Book of the Dead, Pyramid Texts, The Book of Thoth,* and the *Wisdom of Hermes Trismegistus.*

Among the most well-known deities is the unholy trinity of Osiris (supposedly of divine origin), his wife Isis, and their son Horus. This legend is the Egyptian face of Babylonian mystery religion[6] and parallels the legend of Nimrod, Semiramus (queen of heaven), and Tammuz. The legend recounts the killing and dismemberment of Osiris led by the evil Set, the brief resurrection of Osiris from the dead by his wife, Isis, and the subsequent birth of his posthumous son, Horus, by Isis. Osiris becomes the god of the underworld and Horus later kills Set.

Above all, the Egyptians were rulers and builders. They had an anointing for building and for transportation, whether on earth or in the heavens. They built great cities, colossi, temples, pyramids, obelisks, and boats. In the places where they erected buildings and monuments, portals were established to access the ungodly heavens.

These generational issues from ancient Egypt very possibily came into Great Britain and found their way into the traditional strongholds of Freemasonry.

The ancient Egyptians are also known for their fascination with death, resurrection, and the future life. They mummified their dead and built intricate tombs for them containing artifacts to help them in the afterlife.[7]

The *Book of the Dead* is a collection of hymns, spells, and instructions, commonly written on a papyrus scroll and placed in the tombs, to be the deceased's guide to entering the underworld, which many Christians believe are the ungodly heavenly places or dimensions.

Masons have referred to this book as "the open sesame" of symbolic Masonry.[8] David L. Carrico[9] has written in some detail noting many parallels between the references in the book to ancient Egyptian rituals and modern day Satanic ritual abuse (SRA). They note the similarities between the book's descriptions of self-inflicted torture and the programming of victims of SRA to self-destruct.

The influence of ancient Egypt was far reaching. Just as generational blessings can lie lost and forgotten within our family lines, ungodly Egyptian influences can hide and fester, unperceived, within our family histories. This chapter, based on my personal experience, takes a wide lens (shotgun) approach by first describing the myths, the places, and the gods referred to in Egyptian worship, and then, in the prayer, repenting for them. Readers can refer back to the following information for questions about the names in the prayer.

In keeping with the Egyptians' emphasis on dominion over regions, their deities have titles that designate them as rulers of various cities or realms. This gives us an idea of where their strongholds were established. Osiris is referred to as the ruler of the great cities of ancient Egypt— Abydos, Memphis, Busiris, Letopolis, as well as places in the ungodly heavens. These are the strongholds of the Osiris cult in Egypt.

The present day city of Busiris was also known as Tattu, or Tetu, in ancient Egypt. It has a pyramid complex which that is closed to the public and is thought to have a star gate.[10] The city of Letopolis was known as Sekhem in ancient Egypt. Memphis, known as the city of the white wall, was supposed to be the residence of Horus, who was supposed to be lord of Lower Egypt.

At one point, Nekhen, or Hierakonpolis, was the religious and political capital of Upper Egypt. It was the center of the cult of Horus. Khemenu, or Hermopolis, was the center of the cult of Thoth (the Greek god Hermes), the messenger false god of magic, healing, and wisdom, patron of scribes. Shas-hetep is the residence of Set who was supposed to be lord of Upper Egypt.

Abydos is a city in Upper Egypt, the cult center of Osiris and Isis. Abydos has many temple complexes including one called Temple of Set I which has clear hieroglyphs of helicopters, flying machines, and perhaps UFOs.[11]

A *nome* is an administrative division of ancient Egypt. Ati was a nome in Lower Egypt. Busiris was the capital of Ati.[12] The center of the cult of Ra in Egypt was Anu or Heliopolis.[13] The Two Halls of the Maati (Truth) was a place in the underworld.[14]

Tuat means "'Other World." It is believed to be a realm of darkness filled with lakes of fire. Supposedly it is located on the dark side of the moon[15] (also an album by Pink Floyd).

Egyptian myth refers to the Two Lands—this world and a parallel or "other" world.[16] Egyptian cosmology recognizes four worlds that interact through time and space. Manu, supposedly the horizon of the waters, was said to be the place from which time and space emerge and where every potentiality exists.[17]

Aukert is another name for underworld. The Lake of Testes is in the Temple of Aart, possibly a place in the ungodly heaven.

In the creation myth of the ancient Egyptians, the universe originated in a supposed primordial ocean called Nun. Out of this ocean was born the hill called Nu. The false Tree of Life was a plant which came from Nu; its mother was Nut—the heavens or the false sky goddess.[18]

Keb was the false Egyptian earth god whose symbol was the goose. Heliopolis was his cult center.

Ra was the false sun god, the chief of the Egyptian false deities; the Pharaoh was supposedly his manifestation on earth. Ra's symbols were the obelisk, the pyramid, and the sun. Khepera is a form of Ra whose symbol is the scarab.[19] Sebau was a huge serpent fiend who tried to devour the sun at dawn every morning. Aepep and Nak were other monster serpents.

Maat is supposedly the goddess of truth and order who works closely with Heru-khuti or the false god of justice. Ani was the royal scribe who scribed the *Book of the Dead,* which is also known as the *Papyrus of Ani.*[20] Tatun was supposedly the creator of the sun and moon.

Mut, which means mother, was thought to be the "great world mother" and was regarded as the mother of the pharaohs. Nepthys, sister of Isis and Osiris, was the false goddess of death and decay.

An, or Ani, is an ancient form of the ungodly sun god and moon god.

The Egyptians believed that the invisible man was made up of five parts. Ka is one part and represents the spirit of man.[21] Kau is the plural of Ka. Ba represents the personality.

The Uak Festival was an annual wake or feast of the dead. This is believed to be the origin of the Irish wake of the dead.[22]

Ati is an ancient Egyptian word for king. The "Atett boat" is supposedly the boat in which the sun travels across the sky in the morning. The Sektet Boat was the boat used later in the day. The Abtu and the Ant were two fish which supposedly swam in front of Ra's boat.[23]

The Urrt crown was a very old symbol of sovereignty. The White Crown, or Hedjet, is a tall, white, conical headpiece.[24] It is possible that the Ku Klux Klan headpiece originated from this. Heq means prince.

In the midst of all this, we rejoice in discovering God's marvelous purposes and kindness toward Egypt.[25]

Scholars now believe that the Great Pyramid at Giza was built much earlier than the surrounding occult pyramids.[26] Studying it uncovers its supernaturally conceived dimensions and design, massive scale, and unbelievable architectural precision. Over the years, Christians have considered that this might be a sign and wonder erected in Egypt with the help of God rather than the work of the enemy.

It has been suggested that the Great Pyramid contains a prophecy in mathematical code the redemptive plan for mankind through Jesus.[27]

Note: This research into Egyptian history brought greater clarity about the nature of the false worship in my family line that God led me to repent of through the *Book of the Dead*. I have tried to cover all the unfamiliar deities and place names mentioned in the prayer.[28] Since every family of Middle Eastern, European, and North African descent has been touched by the influence of ancient Egypt, and few have followed God wholly, it is my hope that many will find generational deliverance through it. When God called his children out of Egypt to worship him, he said, "You shall have no other gods before me." Over three thousand years later, he is saying the same thing.

The Prayer: Renunciations for Egypt

✠ Lord, on behalf of myself and all ancestors in all branches of my family line, I repent for all who said, "Homage to you, Osiris, lord of eternity, king of the gods, whose names are manifold, whose forms are holy, being of hidden form in the temples, whose Ka is holy."

✠ I repent for those who said, "You are the governor of Tattu, Busiris, and also the mighty one in Sekhem of Letopolis." I repent for those who said, "You are the lord to whom praises are ascribed in the Nome of Ati, and are the prince of divine food in Anu."

✠ Lord, I repent for all worship of Osiris. Lord, please disconnect me from Osiris, Tattu, Sekhem, Ati, and Anu.

✠ I repent for all who said, "You are the lord who is commemorated in Maati, the hidden soul, the lord of Qerrt,[29] the ruler supreme in White Wall."[30] I repent for those who said, "You are the soul of Ra, his own body, and have your place of rest in Nekhen." I repent for those who said, "You are the beneficent one, and are praised in Nart, and that you make your soul to be raised up." I repent for those who said, "You are the lord of the great house in Khemenu, the mighty one of victories in Shas-hetep, the lord of eternity, the governor of Abydos."

✠ Lord, I repent for all worship of Ra. Lord, please disconnect me from Maati, Qerrt, Memphis, Ra, Nart, Khemenu, Shas-hetep, Abydos, Ta-tcheser.

✠ I repent for all who said, "Your name is established in the mouths of men, you are the substance of two lands, your are Tem, the feeder of Kau, the governor of the companies of the gods, you are the beneficent spirit among the spirits, the god of the celestial ocean who draws from yourself the waters." I repent for those who said, "You send forth the north wind at evening and breath from your nostrils to the satisfaction of your own heart and that your heart renews itself into youth."

✠ Lord, I repent for all worship of Nu. Please disconnect me from Tem, Kau, and Nu.

✠ I repent for all who said, "The stars in the celestial heights are obedient to you, and the great doors of the sky open themselves before you." I repent for all who said, "You are the one to whom praises are ascribed in the southern heaven, and thanks are given for you in the northern heaven." I repent for those who said, "The imperishable stars are under your supervision, and the stars which never set are your thrones, and offerings appear before you at the decree of Keb."

✠ I repent for all who said, "The companies of the gods praise you, and the gods of the Tuat smell the earth in paying homage to you." I repent for those who said, "The uttermost parts of the earth bow before you, the limits of the skies offer you supplications when they see you, the holy ones are overcome before you, and all Egypt offers thanksgiving to you when they meet your majesty."

✠ Lord, please disconnect me from Keb and Tuat.

✠ I repent for all who said,

- You are a shining spirit body, the governor of spirit bodies and permanent is your rank, established is your rule.

- You are the well-doing Sekhem of the company of the gods, gracious is you face, and beloved by him that sees it.

- Your fear is set in all the lands by reason of your perfect love, and you cry out to your name making it the first of names, and all people make offerings to you.

- You are the lord who is commemorated in heaven and upon earth. Many are the cries which are made to you at the Uak Festival, and with one heart and voice Egypt raises cries of joy to you. You are the great chief, the first among your brethren, the prince of the company of the gods, the establisher of right and truth throughout the world, the son who was set on the great throne of his father Keb.

- You are the beloved of your mother, Nut, the mighty one of valor, who overthrew the Sebau-fiend.

331

- You did stand up and destroy your enemy and set your fear in your adversary.

- You did bring the boundaries of the mountains, and your heart is fixed; your legs are set firm.

✠ Lord, I repent for all worship of Keb and Nut. Please disconnect me from the Uak Festival, Keb, Nut, and the Sebau-fiend.

✠ I repent for all who said,

- You are the heir of Keb and of the sovereignty of the two lands of Egypt and Keb has seen your splendors, and he has decreed for himself the guidance of the world by your hand as long as times endure.

- You have made this earth with your hand, and the waters, and the winds, and the vegetation, and all the cattle, and all the feathered fowl, and all the fish, and all the creeping things, and all the wild animals.

- The desert is the lawful possession of the son of Nut, and the two lands of Egypt are content to crown you upon the throne of your father, Ra.

- You roll up into the horizon and have set light over the darkness.

- You send forth air from your plumes, and you flood the two lands of Egypt like the disk at daybreak.

- Your crown penetrates the height of heaven.

- You are the companion of the stars and the guide of every god.

- You are beneficent in decree and speech, the favored one of the great company of the gods, and the beloved of the little company of the gods.

✠ I repent for all who said,

- His sister, Isis, has protected him has repulsed the fiends and turned aside calamities of evil.

- She uttered the spell with the magical power of her mouth.

- Her tongue was perfect and it never halted at a word.

- The beneficent in command and word was Isis, the woman of magical spells, the advocate of her brother.

- She sought him untiringly; she wandered round and round about this earth in sorrow, and she did not stop until finding him.

✠ Lord, I repent for all worship of Isis. Please disconnect me from Isis.

✠ I repent for all who said,

- Isis made light with her feathers.

- She created air with her wings, and she uttered the death wail for her brother.

- She raised up the inactive members of one whose heart was still, and she drew from him his essence.

- She made an heir, reared the child in loneliness in the place where he was not known. He grew in strength and stature, and his hand was mighty in the House of Keb.

- The company of the gods rejoiced at the coming of Horus, the son of Osiris, whose heart was firm—the triumphant, the son of Isis, the heir of Osiris.

✠ I repent for all who said,

- Homage to you, you who has come as Khepera, Khepera the creator of the gods.

- You who are seated on your throne who rises up in the sky, illumining your mother Nut.

- You who are seated on your throne as the king of the gods.

- Your mother Nut stretches out her hands and performs an act of homage to you.

- The domain of Manu receives you with satisfaction.

- The goddess Maat embraces you at the two seasons of the day.

✠ Lord, I repent for all worship of Khepera and Maat. Please disconnect me from Khepera, Man, and Maat.

✠ I repent for all who said,

> • May Ra give glory, and power, and truth-speaking, and the appearance of a living soul so that he may gaze upon Heru-khuti, to the Ka of the Osiris, the Scribe Ani, who speaks truth before Osiris.

> • Hail, O all ye gods of the "house of the soul," who weighs heaven and earth in a balance, and who gives celestial food to the dead and who says, "Hail, Tatun, who is the one, the creator of mortals and of the companies of the gods of the south and of the north, of the west and of the east."

✠ Lord, I repent for all worship of Ra, Heru-khuti, Ani, and Tatun. Please disconnect me from these gods.

✠ I repent for all who said,

> • Give thanks to him in his beneficent form which is enthroned in the Atett boat.

> • Thoth and the goddess Maat mark out your course day by day and every day.

> • Your enemy, the serpent, has been given over to the fire. The serpent-fiend, Sebau, has fallen headlong, his forelegs are bound in chains, and his hind legs has Ra carried away from him.

✠ Lord, I repent for all worship of Thoth. Please disconnect me from Atett, Thoth, and Sebau.

✠ I repent for all who said,

> • The sons of revolt will nevermore rise up.

> • The house of the aged one who keeps a festival and the voices of those who make merry are in the "great place." The gods rejoice

when they see Ra crowned upon his throne, when his beams flood the world with light.

• The majesty of this holy god, Ra, sets out on his journey, and he goes onwards until he reaches the land of Manu.

• The earth becomes light at Ra's birth each day.

• He proceeds until he reaches the place where he was yesterday.

✠ I repent for all who said, "Let me gaze upon your beauties. Let me journey above the earth. Let me smite the ass. Let me slit apart the serpent-fiend, Sebau. Let me destroy Aepep at the moment of his greatest power. Let me behold the Abtu fish at his season and the ant fish with the ant boat as it pilots it in its lake. Let me behold Horus when he is in charge of the rudder of the boat of Ra with Thoth and the goddess Thoth on each side of him."[31]

✠ Lord, I repent for all worship of the Abtu fish, the ant fish, and Horus. Please disconnect me from Aepep, the Abtu fish, the ant fish, and Horus.

✠ I repent for all who said, "Let me lay hold of the towrope of the Sektet boat and the rope at the stern of the Matett boat. Let Ra grant to me a view of the disk, the sun, and a sight of Ah, the moon, each day. Let my Ba-soul come forth to walk about hither and thither and wherever it pleases. Let my name be called out. Let it be found inscribed on the tablet which records the names of those who are to receive offerings. Let meals from the sepulchral offerings be given to me in the presence of Osiris as to those who are in the following of Horus. Let there be prepared for me a seat in the boat of the sun on the day when the god sails. Let me be received in the presence of Osiris in the land of truth-speaking, the Ka of Osiris Ani."

✠ Lord, please disconnect me from the Sektet boat, the Matett boat, and the Ka of Osiris Ani.

✠ I repent for all who said,

• Homage to thee, O thou glorious being, you who are covered with all sovereignty.

- O Tem-Heru-Khuti, Tem-Harmakhis, when thou rise in the horizon of heaven a cry of joy goes forth to you from all people.

- O thou beautiful being, you did renew yourself in your season in the form of the disk within your mother Hathor, and therefore in every place every heart swells with joy at thy rising forever.

✠ Lord, I repent for all worship of Tem-Heru-Khuti and Hathor. Please disconnect me from these gods.

✠ I repent for all who said,

- The regions of the south and the north come to you with homage and send forth acclamations at your rising on the horizon of heaven.

- You light the two lands with rays of turquoise-colored light.

- O Ra, you are Heru-Khuti, the divine man-child, the heir of eternity, self-begotten and self-born, king of the earth, prince of the Tuat, the other world, and the governor of Aukert.

- You did come from the water-god.

- You did spring from the sky-god, Nu, who does cherish you and order your members.

✠ Lord, I repent for all worship of Heru-Khuti. Please disconnect me from Heru-Khuti, Tutat, and Hukert.

✠ I repent for all who said,

- O god of life, you lord of love, all men live when thou shine.

- You are crowned king of the gods.

- The goddess Nut embraces you and the goddess Mut enfolds you in all seasons.

- Those who are in your following sing to you with joy, and they bow down their foreheads to the earth when they meet you, the lord of heaven, the lord of the earth, the king of truth, the lord of eternity, the prince of everlastingness, sovereign of all the gods.

• You are a god of life, you, the creator of eternity, maker of heaven where you are firmly established.

✠ Lord, I repent for all worship of Mut. Please disconnect me from Mut.

✠ I repent for all who said,

• The company of the gods rejoices at your rising; the earth is glad when it beholds your rays.

• The people who have been long dead come forth with cries of joy to behold your beauty every day.

• You go forth each day over heaven and earth, and you are made strong each day by your mother, Nut.

• You pass over the heights of heaven.

• Your heart swells with joy, and the lake of Testes, the great oasis, is content there.

• The serpent-fiend has fallen, his arms are broken off, and the knife has severed his joints.

✠ I repent for all who said,

• Ra lives by Maat, the law, the beautiful.

• The Sektet boat advances and comes into port. The south, the north, the west and east turn to praise you.

• You are first, great god, Pauta, who came into being of your own accord.

• Isis and Nephthys salute you, they sing to you songs of joy at your rising in the boat, and they stretch out their hands to you.

• The souls of the east follow thee, and the souls of the west praise you.

• You are the ruler of all the gods.

337

- You who are in your shrine have joy for the serpent-fiend Nak has been judged by the fire, and your heart will rejoice forever.

- Your mother, Nut, is esteemed by your father, Nu.

�֍ Lord please break all ungodly connections to the south, north, west, and east. I repent for all worship of Nepthys. Please disconnect me from Nephthys, Nak, and Nu.

✖ I repent for all who said,

- A hymn of praise to Osiris Un-Nefer, the great god who dwells in Abtu, the king of eternity, the lord of everlastingness, who travels millions of years in his existence.

- You are the eldest son of the womb of Nut.

- You were born of Keb, the Erpat.

- You are the lord of the Urrt crown.

- You are he whose white crown is lofty.

- You are the king, Ati, of gods and men.

- You have gained possession of the scepter of rule, the whip, the rank, and dignity of divine fathers.

- Thy heart is expanded with joy, you who are in the kingdom of the dead.

✖ I repent for all who said,

- Your son, Horus, is firmly placed on your throne.

- You have ascended your throne as the lord of Tetu and as the Heq who dwells in Abydos.

- You make the two lands to exist through truth-speaking in the presence of him who is the lord to the uttermost limit.

- You draw on that which has not yet come into being in your name of "Ta-her-sta-nef."

✠ Lord, I repent for all worship of the lord of Tetu, Heq and Ta-her-sta-nef. Please disconnect me from these gods.

✠ I repent for all who said,

- You govern the two lands by Maat in your name of Seker.

- Your power is widespread.

- You are he of whom the fear is great in your names of Usar and Asa.

- Your existence endures for an infinite number of double henti periods in your name of Un-Nefer.

- Homage to you, king of kings, lord of lords, and prince of princes.

- You have ruled the two lands from the womb of the goddess Nut.

- You have governed the lands of Akert.

✠ Lord, I repent for all worship of Seker, Usar, Asar, and Un-nefer. Please disconnect me from these gods.

✠ I repent for all who said,

- Your members are of silver-gold, your head is of lapis-lazuli, and the crown of your head is of turquoise.

- You are of millions of years.

- Your body is all-pervading, O beautiful face in Ta-tchesert.

- Grant to me glory in heaven, power upon earth, truth-speaking in the divine underworld, and power to sail down the river to Tetu in the form of a living Ba-soul.

- Grant to me the power to sail up the river to Abydos in the form of a Benu bird and the power to pass through and pass out from, without obstruction, the doors of the lords of the Tuat.

- Let there be given to me bread cakes in the house of refreshing, sepulchral offerings of cakes and ale, propitiatory offerings in

Anu, and a permanent homestead in Sekhet-Aaru, with wheat and barley therein—to the double of the Osiris.

✠ Lord, I repent for all worship of the lords of the Tuat. Please disconnect me from these gods and from Abydos and Sekhet-Aaru.

✠ Lord, I repent for all worship of the gods whom you judged by sending the plagues against Egypt—Anuket, goddess of the Nile, Khnum, the guardian of the Nile, Hapi, the spirit of the Nile, Osiris, who had the Nile as his bloodstream, Heqt, the frog-goddess of fertility, Geb, god of the earth, Hathor, a cowlike mother goddess, Qadshu, goddess of sexuality, Imhotep, the god of medicine, Serapis, protector from locusts, Shu, god of the air, Nut, the sky goddess, and Set, god of the desert, storms, darkness and chaos. Please disconnect me from these gods.

Notes:

1. E. A. Wallis Budge, trans., *The Egyptian Book of the Dead* (Whitefish, MT: Kessinger Publishing, 2003). Translations of *The Egyptian Book of the Dead* are freely available in several places on the Internet.

2. David L. Carrico, *The Egyptian, Masonic, Satanic Connection* (Evansville, IN: Followers of Jesus Christ Ministries, 2006, 1994).

3. George H. Steinmetz, *Freemasonry: Its Hidden Meaning* (Richmond, VA: Macoy Publishing and Masonic Supply Company, reprinted 1982).

4. Manly P. Hall, *Freemasonry of the Ancient Egyptians* (Los Angeles, CA: Philosophical Research Society, 2000).

5. Isaiah 14:13–14.

6. *See* chapter 40. "Renunciations for Babylon" (Hesperia, CA: Aslan's Place, December, 2007).

7. E.A. Wallis Budge, *Egyptian Ideas of the Future Life* (Charleston, SC: BiblioBazaar,1903; repr., 2007).

8. Manly P. Hall, *The Lost Keys of Freemasonry* (New York: Tarcher, 2006).

9. David L. Carrico, *The Egyptian, Masonic, Satanic Connection* (Evansville, IN: Followers of Jesus Christ Ministries, 2006, 1994).

10. William Henry, "Place of the Gods–The Stargate at Abu Ghurab, Egypt," http://www.bibliotecapleyades.net/stargate/stargate10.htm.

11. Bill Alford, "The Abydos Egypt Temple Glyphs," http://netowne.com/historical /egyptology/.

12. *Wikipedia*, s.v. "Nome (Egypt)", http://en.wikipedia.org/wiki/Nome_(Egypt).

13. E.A.Wallis Budge, *Tutankhamen: The Cult of Aten, the God and Disk of the Sun, Its Origin, Development and Decline* (Cheshire, CT: Biblo-Moser, 1992).

14 I. M. Oderberg, "The Twin Halls: Egyptian Myths," *Sunrise*, April/May 1986. http://www.theosophy-nw.org/theosnw/world/med/my-imo4.htm.

15. H.P.Blavatsky and William Judge, "Ancient Landmarks XX: Egyptian Immortality," *Thesophy* 15, No. 11, September 1927. http://www.wisdomworld.org /additional/ancientlandmarks/EgyptianImmortality.html.

16. Moustafa Gadalla, *Egyptian Cosmology: The Animated Universe*, 2nd ed. (Greensboro, NC: Tehuti Research Foundation, 2001).

17. Rosemary Clark, *The Sacred Tradition in Ancient Egypt: The Esoteric Wisdom Revealed*, (Woodbury, MN: Llewellyn Publications,2000).

18. Audrey Fletcher, "The Osiris Legend and the Tree of Life," Ancient Egyptians and the Constellations: Part 6," http://ancientegypt.hypermart.net/treeoflife/index.htm.

19. April McDevitt, *Ancient Egypt: The Mythology*, http://www.egyptianmyths.net /khepera.htm.

20. Ernest Alfred Wallis Budge, *The Papyrus of Ani: The Egyptian Book of the Dead* (Sioux Falls, SD: NuVision Publications, 2007).

21. E.A.Wallis Budge, *Osiris and the Egyptian Resurrection*, vol. 2 (Mineola, NY: Dover Publications, 1973).

22. Gerald Massey, *Book of the Beginnings,* vol. 1 (Whitefish, MT: Kessinger Publishing, 2002).

23. E. A. Wallis Budge, trans., *The Egyptian Book of the Dead.*

24. Egyptology Online, http://www.egyptologyonline.com

25. Isaiah 19:18–25; Jeremiah 32:20.

26. Chuck Missler, "Monuments From Prehistory," *The Book of Isaiah: A Commentary*, (Coeur d'Alene, ID: Koinonia House, 2001), MP3 CD-ROM.

27. Peter Lemesurier, *Decoding the Great Pyramid* (Boston, MA: Element Books, Ltd., 2000).

28. Quotations in the following prayers are reversals and renunciations of the *Book of the Dead.*

29. Elephantine.

30. Memphis.

31. *Book of the Dead*, chapter 1.

Renunciation
for Hinduism

SARAH VICTOR

My family had been under a fairly intense series of witchcraft attacks for about two years. We would petition God to break the curses and God would graciously help us, but every couple of weeks a fresh batch of curses[1] were released against us. Many of these curses were landing. Every person in my family experienced attacks—accidents, traffic accidents, serious illness, broken finances and relationships. We continued to wait on the Lord.

Then the Lord led us to Aslan's Place and started cleansing our generational lines. He led us to repent specifically for all the roots of Hinduism in our generational lines. When we renounced and repented for these Hindu beliefs and practices, we experienced strong deliverance. Amazingly, the curses launched against us were no longer effective. We were no longer falling sick all the time, and the accident rate dropped off abruptly.

We started studying the roots of Hinduism and trying to understand its effects on our bodies, minds, and spirits, as well as its influence on our approach to life, our reactions to our circumstances, and our engagement with community and society. God had graciously disconnected us from many of these roots, but the process of rebuilding and restoration took time. Hoping to help others, here is background information about Hinduism and some of the issues we discovered that those seeking freedom from Hinduism may need to work through in the restoration process.

Hinduism is a set of religious traditions, beliefs, and practices that have been established in India over thousands of years. The goal of Hinduism is to reach salvation, a union between man's eternal soul and the world soul that supposedly frees a soul from karma—the cycles of cause and effect—and samsara—the cycles of death and rebirth. We discovered that essentially, the union between the world soul and a human soul is the union of a human being with the demonic realm—to such an extent that it is hard to separate the divine creation of God from the profane.

This is described in a tract published by Pathlights:[2]

> The Hindu heaven is Nirvana, which is the "quiet slipping of the dewdrop into the silent sea." Everything around them is god, and they are also. Someday, in some unexplained way, they will become part of what they are now already part of!—god! And that is what it means to arrive at the Hindu heaven. It is not peace; it is not happiness; it is just slipping quietly into the silent hole. Nirvana sounds like that which takes place at eternal death.

There is nothing like the Hindu ideas about Nirvana in Judeo-Christian beliefs. The resurrection of Jesus Christ demonstrates the reality of life after death. The Bible affirms individual personhood, both in this life and after death.

Both Hinduism and Buddhism see the personality as an enemy that is finally destroyed by absorption into Brahman;[3] Hinduism and Buddhism both work to suppress our identity, personality, and individuality, not recognizing the way in which God uniquely designed and created every one of us. Their goals are to first suppress the human spirit and then to unite our spirits with demons so that demons can control men and ultimately the world.

Hinduism uses the way God made us to seduce us into a counterfeit. We are wired to crave intimacy with God. We will move in the direction of this craving, using whatever path is within our reach. The great Christian saints and mystics passionately pursued union and intimacy with God.[4] The Church has left us easy prey by watering down the reality of intimacy with God and minimizing his plan for us to be partakers of his divine nature. Has the true and staggering meaning of Scriptures about us being one with God[5] been too overwhelming for us to comprehend or accept?

Restoration from the effects of Hinduism includes recognition of our unique design, identity, gifting, and birthright.[6]

The Caste System, Passivity, and Loss of Identity

The ancient Hindu religious texts, the *Vedas*, recognize inequalities of birth and family circumstances and codify them into the caste system. The word for caste is *varna* or color. The four castes are white, red, brown, and black. Essentially the caste system is institutionalized racism.

The caste system divided Hindu society into four rigid classes that restricted a person's occupation, marriage, and social participation. People in the lowest castes were called untouchables because they were believed to pollute the higher castes. They were oppressed and exploited, without access to education or opportunities to change their social position or status.

Unfortunately, because of Hindu karmic law,[7] Hindus accept their castes and economic positions as the inevitable result of deeds performed in previous lives and don't resist them. Christians believe in the principle of sowing and reaping,[8] and we also believe that the actions of past generations will release blessings or curses into our lives.[9] However, we know that the power of the cross redeems us and annuls all curses from previous generations—when the cross is appropriated and brought into the unredeemed places in our lives. Hinduism has no such provision.

The religious practices of fatalistic renunciation in both Hinduism and Buddhism foster dissociation from life and its events in ways that are diametrically opposite to the way God wants us, as human beings, to walk in dominion[10] actively engaging with the world around us. God calls us to overcome obstacles, to fight our battles, to walk in dominion, and to receive his blessings as we extend and establish his Kingdom here on this earth. In the parable in Luke 19:13 Jesus said, "Occupy till I come." (KJV)

One of the four objectives of Hinduism is called *dharma*. In Hindu belief, *dharma* is both a principle that orders the universe as well as a moral code of behavior that conforms to this law. It emphasizes doing one's duty as a way to salvation. Unfortunately, dharma is not about doing good deeds like helping someone cross the street, but is a fairly rigid set of prescribed rules or duties which vary for gender, for different castes, and for stages of a person's life. For example, according to dharma, a "lower caste" street sweeper is obliged by duty to accept his place in society and sweep streets without hope for reward or change. In fact, seeking reward or change would be wrong and bring negative consequences in future lives.

This produces a strong religious spirit. Most Hindus worship daily at their home shrines, repeating rituals before sculptures and images of their gods. Some visit temples every day to worship. Vivekananda said, "Here in India, it is religion that forms the very core of the national heart."[11]

In restoration from the effects of Hinduism, it is essential to recognize the love of our Father; when we turn to him, his kindness and grace[12] restores our righteousness, a righteousness that comes from him[13] alone and restores our awesome birthright.

Restoration of Women

Unequal status for women is coded into the Hindu scriptures in many ways. A woman is not allowed to study the scriptures, but service to her husband is equivalent to it. Even if her husband has no virtue, he must constantly be worshipped as a god by his wife. A woman may not even mention the name of another man after her husband has died, but a man may marry again. Women are not fit to be independent; they are to be protected through their lives by their father, their husband, and their son. No woman is allowed to do anything independently even in her own home but must be kept dependent upon the male members in her family.[14]

Traditionally men controlled property. A woman's inheritance was given to her as a dowry at marriage, thus disinheriting women from their parents' estates because all dowry went to their husband's families. Because women were disinherited, daughters became liabilities,[15] and female infanticide is still common in India. The (now outlawed) practice of *sati* or self-immolation of a widow on the funeral pyre of her husband illustrates a woman's subordination to men and imitates a similar act by a Hindu goddess.

Restoration from effects of Hinduism for both men and women must include the recognition that on the cross, Christ restored the equal status of women.

Tantra or Ritual Acts

The ritual acts or practices of the Hindu theology are written in the Tantras or scriptures.[16] Among these are astrology, ayurveda—a system of traditional Hindu medicine, and yoga, which is an occult spiritual discipline developed to help people to achieve the Hindu salvation or union with their god. Hindu scriptures and traditional Vedic medicine teaches that the physical human body is divided in chakras. They believe that these chakras are invisible organs, in the form of wheels of light in man's spiritual body, each with its own color and frequency.[17] Practicing Kundalini and chakra rituals opens people up to dissociation[18] and to entry by demonic beings, facilitating the perpetration of mind control on the generations of these practitioners.

Drawing *mandalas* is another form of tantric ritual and meditation. The mandala is an occult circle. It means container of essence. Drawing a mandala seems to act as a portal to bring demonic beings to that place. Mandalas can break the boundaries between the human spirit and outside demonic energies, thus permitting an entry point for demons into the human spirit. A mandala can be used personally or corporately. It can be used to transmute demonic forces into the earth, into running bodies of water, and through the air, giving demons a legal right to interfere with weather patterns. The Tibetan masters are famous for the defilement of land and waterways using sand mandalas. Land that has been defiled by a mandala needs to be cleansed of demonic influence, healed, and restored.

Tantric ritual also involves sound. Hinduism recognizes that the universe was created by sound. The primary auditory symbol of Hinduism is a sound called *om*, which Hindus say is the sound of the universe or the sound of light. Restoration from the effects of Hinduism will also include the restoration of our body's frequencies and vibrations to resonate with the sound of the Lord.[19]

The concept of eternal and cyclical time lies at the heart of the Hindu worldview. The Kalachakra is the Hindu wheel of time—eight spokes ruled by eight deities indicate the directions of a compass. The wheel represents both creation and cycles of existence in the fabric of space-time. Restoration from the effects of Hinduism includes breaking all associations and links with ungodly time and its deities and renouncing all counterfeit prophesies about time. Restoration brings believers out of the ungodly wheel of time and into God's time.

The Prayer: Renunciation for Hinduism

✠ Heavenly Father, I ask you to forgive me and all members of my ancestral line for all ungodly beliefs in Hinduism and its philosophies, for all Hindu idolatry, and for all ungodly practice of Hinduism and its disguised offshoots; forgive us for obtaining knowledge illegally through ungodly Hindu sources, for practicing sorcery and witchcraft, and for making ungodly sacrifices to the false gods of Hinduism.

✠ Heavenly Father, I repent for and renounce the worship of and all covenants that my ancestors or I made with the ungodly trinity—Brahma the creator, Vishnu the preserver, and Shiva the destroyer.

✠ On behalf of myself and my family line, I repent for believing or saying that in whom reside all beings and who resides in all beings, who is the giver of grace to all, the supreme soul of the universe, the limitless being—I am that.[20]

✠ On behalf of myself and my family line, I repent for believing or saying, "I am the supreme divinity which, like space, fills all things completely from within and without, changeless, perfect, with no attachment, stain or motion. I am eternal, pure and free, one, indivisible."[21]

✠ On behalf of myself and my family line, I repent for believing or saying, "Brahma, primal motive force is my womb; in that I place the seed; thence, O Arjuna, is the birth of all beings! Whatever forms are produced, in all the wombs, the great Brahma is their womb, and I am the seed-giving father."[22]

✠ Lord, please disconnect me from the heart and womb of Brahma and from ungodly seed and seed-giving entities. I repent for all who allowed ungodly incarnations of gods within the human consciousness within me. Lord, please disconnect me from all ungodly avatars.

✠ On behalf of myself and my family line, I repent for believing or saying, "The knower catches in the ecstasy of his heart the full light of that Brahman which is indescribable . . . all pure bliss, incomparable, transcending time, ever free, beyond desire."[23]

� Lord, please disconnect us from the light of Brahman and from all ungodly light sources.

✖ On behalf of myself and my family line, I repent for using the Hindu sacred texts as our source and direction. I renounce all ungodly invitations from, guidance by, and connections to the ungodly spiritual realities behind these texts.

✖ On behalf of myself and my family line, I repent for all believing or saying, "Oh mind, the greatest bird, play in the cage of the two lotus feet of Sankara, in the tree with the Vedas as branches, with the Upanishads as the top, with fruits which destroy pain and whose juice is nectar."[24]

✖ Lord, please remove us and our minds from ungodly trees, birds, fruits and cages. Please disconnect us from the Vedas, Upanishads, Puranas and from Sankara.

✖ On behalf of myself and my family line, I repent for and renounce all beliefs in the repeated cycles of creation, preservation, and destruction of this universe. I renounce the cyclic worldview represented by the ungodly wheel of time or *Kalachakra*.

✖ Please forgive us for believing that: "This wheel of life that is associated with [*sic*] pairs of opposites and devoid of consciousness . . . that man who always understands accurately the motion and stoppage of this wheel of life, is never seen to be deluded, among all creatures. Freed from all impressions, divested of all pairs of opposites, released from all sins, he attains to the highest goal."[25]

✖ On behalf of myself and my family, I repent for believing or saying, "Know the self who alone is to be known, he in whom the sixteen parts rest, the spokes of the hub of the wheel of life, lest death should hurt you."[26]

❖ I renounce the belief that the supreme self is at the center of the wheel of life and that achieving this self is the goal that goes beyond death. Lord, please disconnect me and my family from the Kalachakra, the ungodly wheel of time and its cycles.

❖ I repent for and renounce all beliefs in karma, the law of cause and effect by which each individual creates his own destiny by his thoughts, words, and deeds.

❖ I repent for and renounce all false beliefs in karma as the deeds related to the cycle of cause and effect, action and reaction, that my future and my destiny is determined by all my actions in this life and my previous lives. I repent for striving through self-effort to free myself of negative karma and trying to make my destiny better through mantra, meditation, and positive deeds.

❖ On behalf of myself and my family line, I repent for believing or saying, "As blazing fire reduces wood to ashes, O Arjuna, so does the fire of self-knowledge reduce all Karma to ashes."[27]

❖ Lord, please forgive us for believing that shaping ourselves to circumstances according to our karma is the only way to acquire happiness.

❖ On behalf of myself and my generational line, I repent for and renounce all false beliefs in the principle of reincarnation or *samsara*, that after death my soul transmigrates into a new body and I come back to earth.

❖ I also repent for believing that through our individual choices, we can resolve karma, attain *moshka* or liberation, and realize God, thus ending this cycle of death and rebirth. I repent for believing that my soul is on a cosmic journey meant for its purification and that it manifests a body again and again 8.4 million times until it is purified.

❖ I repent for everyone in my family line who said or believed that our desires for earthly objects chained us to rounds of births and deaths and that *moshka*, or freedom from this cycle, comes from renunciation of desires.

✠ On behalf of myself and my family, I repent for all who believed and said, "As man casts off worn-out garments and puts on others which are new, similarly the embodied soul, casting off worn-out bodies, enters into others which are new."[28]

✠ I repent for myself and all in my family line who accepted the cycle of death and rebirth as inevitable for us.

✠ I repent for and renounce all beliefs in, worship of, service to, and covenants made with the Hindu celestial beings—the devas, the ungodly sons of God, the mahadevas, and the evil trinity or Trimurti. Lord, please disconnect me from these.

✠ I repent for believing that an enlightened master or *satguru* is essential to guide my soul to self-realization.

✠ On behalf of myself and my family, I renounce, "[Bowing] before the sacred footwear of my teacher, who taught me the meaning of *om*."

✠ I repent for and renounce any ungodly practices of noninjury to all creatures—*ahimsa*—that reveres creation above the true Creator.

✠ I repent for and renounce the belief that there is not a single way to salvation and that all spiritual paths are acceptable.

✠ I repent for and renounce the belief that dharma is the aim of existence and that observing dharma will lead to attainment of *jnana*, or higher religious knowledge and to *bhakti*, or union with God through devotion.

✠ I repent for and renounce the belief that *moksha* is achieved by the observation of dharma, fulfilling one's assigned duty and moral obligation to society according to one's position in life. I renounce all belief that I am obliged by duty to accept my current place in society without hope for reward or change. I renounce all belief that men attain salvation by faithfully following predetermined paths of duty. Lord, please remove the effects that these constraints had on me that I may enter into my birthright and inheritance in you.

✠ I repent for and renounce all the practices of *bhakti*, or devotion to god and the gods of Hinduism, so that the atman, or individual soul and spirit, can merge with *Brahman*, or universal consciousness, and allow the realization of *moksha*.

✠ On behalf of myself and my family line, I repent for believing or saying, "One who serves me with unfailing devotional service, at once transcends creation, preservation and destruction and becomes fit to become one with Brahman."[29]

✠ Lord, please forgive me and my ancestors for all practices of the four main denominations associated with Hinduism: for Saivism and the worship of Shiva; for Shaktism and the worship of Shakti; for Vaishnavism and the worship of Vishnu; and for Smartism and the worship of one of the six deities, Ganapati, Surya, Vishnu, Shiva, Shakti, and Kumara. Lord, please disconnect me from these entities.

✠ I renounce and repent for all worship of and covenants made with Shiva as the highest supreme self or Brahman, the all and in all, the destroyer and transformer of the trinity, and as father god, who causes the continuous cyclic process of creation, preservation, dissolution, and recreation of the universe. I repent for worship of Shiva and the phallic Shiva Lingam as the source of the universe, as static, unmanifested consciousness in the transcendental plane. I repent for believing that Shiva is within and for all striving to be one with the Shiva within.

✠ Lord, I repent for all worship of and covenants made with Shiva in any and all manifestations including the following:[30] Nataraja, lord of the dance; Dakshinamurthy, Shiva facing south and teacher of yoga, music, and wisdom; Sadashiva, eternal Shiva; Parameswara; Shiva on Mount Kailash; Paramasiva, the highest; Maheswara, lord of the manifest universe; Saguna Brahman, cosmic lord of creation, maintenance, and destruction; Iswara or Rudra, the destroyer; Shankara, the doer of good; Nilakantha, blue necked; Bholenath, innocent god; Hanuman, monkey god; Dakshinamurthy, guru; Pashupati, lord of the animals; Indra, regent of the East; Vishveshwara, lord of the universe; Sarveshwara; Shiva Lingam; Prajapati, lord of creatures. Lord, please disconnect me and my family from all these entities.

Lord, I repent for all worship of and covenants made with Shiva in his various tantric manifestations such as Bhairava, the wrathful, the fierce manifestation of Shiva, the embodiment of fear; Virabhadra, the wrath of Shiva; Mahakaleswar, lord of time and death; Tripurantaka, the archer; Vastospati, the guardian of the dwelling; Agni, the fire god; Vayu, the wind god; Ardhnarishwara, half Shiva and half Shakti; Ganesha, lord of obstacles; Murugan, god of war; Subramanian, the god of war. Lord, please declare these covenants broken and disconnect me and my family from all these forms of Shiva. Lord, please annul any marriage covenants between my family line and Shiva.

On behalf of myself and my family, I repent for believing or saying, "He alone at the proper time, is the guardian of this world, the lord of all, hidden in all beings, in him are united the gods and knowers of Brahman alike. He who knows him cuts the fetters of death asunder. He who knows Shiva, the blessed, hidden in all beings like the subtle film that rises from out the clarified butter, alone enveloping everything, he who knows the god is freed from all fetters."[31]

On behalf of myself and my family, I repent for believing or saying, "Lord Shiva is seated on Mount Kailash; his forehead is adorned with the moon and the king of serpents as a crown. The lord is the ocean of mercy and the remover of illusion. Shiva is the only protector. I surrender myself to such great Lord Shiv-Shankar."[32]

I repent for and renounce the mantra Aum Namah Sivaya, Sadyojata, Vamadeva, Aghora, Tatpurusa, Isana. Lord, please disconnect me from its sounds.

Heavenly Father, on behalf of myself and my family line, I repent for and renounce all false worship of and covenants made with the entity Shakti—the supreme energy of Shiva, the ungodly feminine, creative, and dynamic energy in the physical plane and all other planes. Lord, I repent for those who tapped into the matrix of energy, the goddess Power. Lord, please disconnect me from ungodly matrices.

✠ Lord, I repent for and renounce all worship of and covenants made with Shakti in her various manifestations: divine mother, goddess, supreme mother of the universe; Adi Parashakti, original source of the universe; Devi, goddess; Lalitha, goddess of bliss; Tripura Sundari, goddess who is beautiful in three realms; Parvati or Uma, divine Shakti, consort of Shiva; Saraswati, goddess of knowledge; Lakshmi, goddess of wealth; Gayatri, mother of mantras; Ganga, goddess as Divine River; Sita, Rama's consort and goddess of marital relations; Radha, Krishna's consort; Sati; Meenakshi, avatar of Parvati; Bhuvaneshwari, world mother; Kumari, virgin; Bagalamukhi, hypnotic power of the goddess who paralyzes enemies; Kamala, the lotus goddess. Lord, please disconnect me from all these.

✠ Lord, for myself and my family line, I repent for and renounce all worship of and covenants made with Shakti in her various tantric manifestations such as Shakti Kali, goddess of cosmic destruction and eternal night; Bhadrakali, auspicious Kali; Bhavani, source of creative energy; Chinnamasta, goddess who cuts off her own head; Durga or Ambika, the invincible; Bhairavi, fierce goddess of decay; Dhumavati, who widows herself; Matangi, the outcast goddess, the goddess of pollution; Tara, the protector and guide.

✠ Lord, please disconnect us from Kali as mother-goddess, Black Time, devourer of time, personification of manifest time and the color black. Lord, please disconnect me from the ten forms of Kali known as Mahavidyas. Lord, please disconnect me from the ungodly timeline of Kali. Lord, please remove all ungodly connections between Kali and my timeline, between me and Kali Yuga or Age of Kali. Lord, please remove all dakinis and other tantric consorts from me and my family line. Lord, please destroy all ungodly Kali time rifts connected to me and my generational line. Lord, please annul any marriage covenants between my family line and Kali.

✠ I repent for all agreement with goddess power, for saying that the feminine is the dominant power of the universe, and for all goddess-focused spiritual practices, mantras, yantras, nyasa, mudras, and yogas.

✠ Lord, in the name of Jesus of Nazareth, on behalf of me and my family, I renounce the aspect of Shakti called Kundalini, serpent power, ungodly mystic fire. I repent for all ungodly contact with this spirit. I repent for and renounce all practices that would awaken, invite, or allow the presence or activity of the sleeping goddess Kundalini in any way. I renounce and repent for accepting the ungodly blessing of a Siddha-guru, for all tantric sexual rites and for all tantric practices of Shakta yoga and Kundalini yoga that awaken this serpent power and make it ascend through the psychic centers, the chakras that lie along the axis of the spine as consciousness centers.

✠ Lord, please disconnect me from union of Shakti and Shiva above the crown or sahasrara chakra of my head. I repent for everything to do with any fusion of the ungodly absolute, attempting a union of the individual with the universe. Lord, please remove from me all ungodly cosmic vibrations and radiant energies. Lord, please restore godly chemistry and righteous elements of my body. Lord, please separate me from Kundalini and from all ungodly coiled serpents.

✠ Lord, on behalf of myself and my family line, I repent for practicing *kundalini* as a translocal vibration allowing Shakti to change the space-time continuum of my body-mind. I repent for bartering for and seeking the vibration to change our body-minds, to create a *chinmaya* or light body endowed with transcendent and supernatural powers. Lord, please remove all abilities from my family line which came to us through ungodly sources.

✠ Father, for myself and my family line, I renounce all declarations, affirmations, proclamations, and beliefs about Shakti as divinity. I repent for identifying Shakti in any pantheistic way with any aspect of your creation. Please forgive us for confusing Creator with creation and thinking that Shakti could ever encompass any aspect, good or evil, of your creation. Please cleanse us of her influence.

✠ Lord, on behalf of myself and my family, I repent for and renounce believing or saying, "This whole universe is interwoven in Shakti." I renounce believing and saying that Shakti is the supreme controller in causal bodies. I renounce believing and saying that Shakti is the stream of consciousness and the golden womb in subtle bodies. I renounce believing and saying that Shakti is the universal soul in external bodies. I renounce believing and saying that Shakti is Brahma, Vishnu, and Shiva, and is Brahma, Vaishnavi, and Raudri Shaktis. I renounce believing and saying that Shakti is the sun, the moon, and the stars, the beasts, birds, and outcasts. I renounce believing and saying that Shakti is the thief and the cruel hunter; that Shakti is the virtuous, high-souled person. And I renounce believing and saying that Shakti is female, male, and hermaphrodite."[33]

❊ Lord, I repent for use of the Shaktism symbol Shri Chakra Yantra, the tantric symbol of cosmic unity as the junction point between the physical universe and its unmanifest source.[34]

❊ Lord, please disconnect me and my family from the Shri Chakra Yantra and all its mantras, rituals, and sounds; disconnect us from all metaphysical and geometrical constructs that correspond to the psychic centers of the subtle body. Lord, please disconnect us from ungodly lotus flowers, instruments, machines, geometries, swastikas, from ungodly circles as the energy of water, ungodly squares and the energy of earth, ungodly triangles and the energy of fire, ungodly lines and the energies of air, water, fire, and all ungodly points and ungodly energy of ether. I repent for and renounce all shamanic Shaktism and the use of magic, trance, mediumship, fire walking, and animal sacrifice for healing, fertility, prophecy, and power.

❊ Lord, please disconnect me from ungodly positioning of planets, precious stones, metals, and alloys. Lord, please remove anything in me born of Shakti and any ungodly union of Shiva and Shakti in me or in anything godly connected to me. Lord, please cleanse all the connectors in my body.

❊ For myself and my family, I repent for believing or saying, "Only when united with Shakti has Lord Shiva the power to create the universe; without her, he cannot even move."[35]

✠ On behalf of myself and my family, I repent for all who believed or said, "At the dissolution of things, it is Kala who will devour all, and by reason of this he is called Mahakala, and since thou devourest Mahakala himself, it is thou who art the supreme primordial Kalika. Because thou devourest Kala, thou art Kali, the original form of all things, and because thou art the origin of and devourest all things thou art called the Adya Kali. Resuming after dissolution thine own form, dark and formless, thou alone remainest as one ineffable and inconceivable. Though having a form, yet art thou formless; though thyself without beginning, multiform by the power of Maya, thou art the beginning of all, creatrix, protectress, and destructress that thou art."[36]

✠ For myself and my family, I repent for and renounce the mantra Aum Chandikayai Namah. Lord, please disconnect us from its sounds.

✠ On behalf of myself and all in my family line, I repent for and renounce all worship of and covenants made with Vishnu and his various manifestations: Vishnu as the supreme god; preserver of the universe; all-pervading essence of all beings; the master of—and beyond—the past, present, and future; the creator and destroyer of all existences; one who supports, sustains and governs the universe and originates and develops all elements within.

✠ Father, I ask you to forgive us—for you alone are God, our Creator, and you alone uphold the universe by the word of your power. Father, I repent for attributing to Vishnu anything of your character or attributes and anything of the person, purpose, and authority of your only son, Jesus Christ.

✠ On behalf of myself and my family, I repent for all who believed that in each age, whenever evil prevails over good, Vishnu comes down to earth in some mortal form to save righteousness. I repent for all practice of *prapatti*, single-pointed surrender to Vishnu or his ten or more incarnations, called avatars. Lord, I repent for all worship of the avatars: Matsya the fish; Kurma the tortoise; Varaha the boar; Narasimha, half lion, half man; Vamana the dwarf; Parashurama or Rama with the axe; Rama the perfect man; Krishna the lover; Balarama the brother of Krishna; and the coming avatar, Kalki, as eternity or time.[37]

✠ On behalf of myself and my family, I repent for believing or saying, "I am the goal, the sustainer, the lord, the witness, the abode, the refuge, the friend, the origin, the dissolution, the resting-place, the storehouse and the eternal seed."[38]

✠ On behalf of myself and my family, I repent for believing or saying, "I bow to lord Vishnu, the master and controller of the universe, identical with the sun; destroyer of all-destroying time itself; he that upholds the earth in space; he is the food which supports the life of living creatures; he that has incarnated on earth a hundred times to rescue the good, destroy the wicked, and establish righteousness; he that leads us safely across the ocean of life."[39]

✠ Lord, please disconnect us from Vishnu, Seshnaga, Narayana, Matsya, Kurma, Varaha, Narasimha, Vamana, Parashurama, Rama, Krishna, Balarama, Kalki, Adinath, Hrishikesh, and Badrinath.

✠ I repent for and renounce the mantra Aum Namo Narayanaya. Lord, please disconnect me from its sounds. Father, I renounce all beliefs and practices regarding the saints, scriptures, and temple worship connected to Vishnu and his incarnations. Father, cleanse me completely of Vaishnavism.

✠ Father, on behalf or myself and my family, I repent for all worship of Adi Shankara. I repent for belief in and practice of the philosophies of Advaita Vedanta.[40]

✠ On behalf of myself and my family, I repent for believing or saying:

• Brahman is the one, the only reality, that this universe is unreal and that the individual soul is the same as Brahman.

• The atman or soul is self-evident and cannot be denied because it is the very essence of the one who denies it.

• Brahman is not an object, as it is beyond the reach of senses or intellect. It is infinite, imperishable, impersonal, self-existent, self-delight, self-knowledge, self-bliss and essence—the essence of the knower. It is the silent witness, always the witnessing subject, never an object as it is beyond the reach of the senses. Brahman is non-dual and has no other beside it.

• Brahman has neither form nor attributes. The essence of Brahman is existence, consciousness, and bliss or *sat-chit-ananda*.

• The world is not absolutely false but is relatively false compared to Brahman who is absolutely real. The world is a superimposition of non-self or objects on self or Brahman.

• The individual soul is only relatively real. There are not several atmans or souls. The one soul appears as multiple souls in our bodies because of illusion.

• Samsara or duality exists due to ignorance; knowledge alone can make an individual realize his true nature.

• Knowledge of Brahman is not about acquiring external knowledge, as Brahman cannot be known, but about removing the ignorance and illusion. When these are removed there is no difference between soul and Brahman.[41]

✠ I repent for the belief that to be saved I have to be able to discern between the real substance (Brahman) and the substance that is unreal.[42]

✠ I repent for the belief that to be saved I have to renounce enjoyments of objects in this world and the other worlds.

✠ I repent for the belief that to be saved I have to have the six-fold qualities of tranquility of the mind, control of external sense organs, focusing on meditation and refraining from actions, endurance of suffering, faith in gurus and the Vedas, and the concentration of the mind.

✠ I repent for the belief that to be saved I must have the firm conviction that the nature of the temporary world is misery and that I need an intense longing to be liberated from the cycle of births and deaths.

✠ For myself and my family, I repent for believing or saying, "A particle of its bliss supplies the bliss of the whole universe. Everything becomes enlightened in its light. All else appears worthless after a sight of that essence. I am indeed of this supreme eternal self."[43]

✠ Lord, please remove me from all that is not me and reestablish my godly boundaries. Lord, please remove me from the ungodly depths and seat me with Jesus Christ in your heavenly places.

✠ In the name of Jesus Christ, I renounce and repent for all belief in and connections to ungodly Vedic cosmology. Lord, please remove all parts of me that are trapped in the seven lower lokas or worlds and please disconnect me from Sutala, Vitala, Talatala, Mahatala, Rasatala, Atala, and Patala—deepest hell and the serpents, or nagas, and demons there.

✠ On behalf of myself and my generational line, I repent for believing or saying, "The four chakra triangles of Shiva, the five chakra triangles of Shakti are the nine of the primal energy of the universe all apart from the circle center with a lotus of eight petals, one of sixteen petals, the three circles and three lines, remains a total of forty four—the angles of your sacred abode of the wheel."[44]

✠ Lord, please disconnect us from all the ungodly wheels, petals, circles, lines, and angles of the Sri Chakra Yantra. Please disconnect us from ungodly Mount Meru. Please disconnect us from the ungodly union of the masculine and feminine divine and all ungodly webs of the universes and wombs of creation. Lord, please disconnect us from ungodly geometries and portals.

✠ Lord, please disconnect us from the cosmic dance of Shiva, the tandava that is the source of the cycles of creation, preservation and dissolution, salvation and illusion, and the rhythm of birth and death. Lord, please remove us from the rhythms, violence, grief, and anger associated with these ungodly cycles.

✠ On behalf of myself and my family, I repent for those who meditated on the goddess Kalika in the trikona, in the six petals the six limbs, in the navel the Shaktis of the directions, in the heart the twelve suns, in the throat the sixteen kalas of the moon, in the two-petaled lotus Kala and Kali together.[45] Lord, please would you disconnect us from ungodly trikonas, suns, phases of the moon, and lotuses.

✠ On behalf of myself and my family, I repent for worshipping the Hindu deities of time and for believing or saying, "I worship you, Shani—you are the essence of time! The universe and time itself dissolves in you! You are the body of time, the self, the source of happiness, the soul that regulates time, the planetary guardians!"[46]

✠ Lord, please disconnect us from the ungodly Shani[47] and its cycles. Please remove the destruction associated with Shani. Lord, please restore to us godly time, space, and dimensions. Lord, please remove ungodly time locks and time references. Please restore my timeline and restore my origin to you.

✠ In the name of Jesus of Nazareth I forgive anyone who released curses connected to Hinduism against me or my family. Lord, please remove all curses, backup curses, time curses, reempowerment of curses and negative consequences that may come against me or my family line for breaking covenant with Hindu entities.

✠ On behalf of myself and my family line, I repent for and renounce all beliefs in and participation of the ungodly division of society into four social classes and castes.[48] I repent for and renounce the historical exclusion from the caste system of the untouchables or *dalits*.

✠ On behalf of myself and my family line, I deeply repent for and renounce all discrimination, oppression, and abuse that we have practiced on our fellow men because of the caste system.

✠ I repent for and renounce the belief every person is born into and must marry, live, and die within their caste. Lord, please remove the effects in my life of the rigid limitations of the caste rules in determining my food, occupation, marriage, and association with people in other castes. Lord, please remove all ungodly boundaries, barriers, and ceilings in my life.

✠ On behalf of any ancestors who were oppressed because of the caste system, I forgive those who discriminated against us and oppressed us because of the color of our skin and our caste. Lord, please disconnect us from all victim spirits related to discrimination due to caste or gender.

✠ I repent for and renounce all practices of child marriage, dowry, and sati, or the self-immolation of a woman on her husband's funeral pyre.

✠ Lord, for myself and my family, I renounce and repent for all ungodly gender inequalities we have agreed with. I repent for those in my generational line who have degraded, oppressed, suppressed, humiliated, murdered, and raped women. Father, will you please break off the ungodly consequences of domination and victimization and restore the women in my family to their equal status in the family of God. Please restore the inheritance, property, position, status, and gifting of all the women in my generational line.

✠ On behalf of myself and my family line, I repent for believing or saying, "The syllable *Om* is the highest and also the lower Brahma. He who meditates on it . . . comes to the light and the sun. And as a snake is freed from its skin, so is he freed from evil and led to the world of Brahma."[49]

✠ On behalf of myself and my family line, I repent for and renounce all ungodly uses of our bodies in and during false worship, including all forms of idol worship: dedication to idols, bowing to idols, icon worship, daily *darshan* or viewing of idols, eating food sacrificed to idols as well as eating *prasada* or food offered to idols. I repent for maintaining home shrines for idols, visiting and worshipping in temples of idols, participating in festivals, making temple offerings, viewing or participating in ungodly processions, pilgrimages, dramas, and storytelling associated with idols. I also repent of ungodly fasting, self-mutilation, whipping, singing, dancing, wearing special clothing, and chanting that is linked to idolatry.

✠ On behalf of myself and my family line, I repent for and renounce other ungodly uses of our bodies during false worship including: temple prostitution, yoga, fornication, ritual sex, sex with animals, sex with demons, sex with the dead, ungodly masturbation, pedophilia, same-sex relations, and viewing of sexual imagery in sculptures, books, dance, or movies.

✠ On behalf of myself and my family line, I repent for and renounce all ungodly uses of my soul during false worship including being in ecstatic states, reading and studying the false scriptures, and false meditation.

✠ On behalf of myself and my family line, I repent for and renounce all ungodly use of my spirit during false worship including astral travel, inhabiting the bodies of other people, all shamanic practices, shape-shifting, and forming ungodly communications and ties with the second heaven and with false deities, false priests, and other people.

✠ I repent for and renounce all ungodly openings of the eye of my spirit, my pineal gland, my third eye. I pray that you will shut down any ungodly opening of my third eye and seal it with your Holy Spirit.

✠ On behalf of myself and my family line, I repent for and renounce all false worship of the elements including stone, wood, water, fire, air, and ether. I repent for and renounce all ungodly worship of the sun, moon, and any other heavenly bodies. I repent for all witchcraft, animal sacrifices, people and child sacrifices, all necromancy, blood covenants, drinking of blood, eating of flesh, mingling of blood, and communication with the dead.

✠ I repent for and renounce ungodly use of ungodly Vedic calendars based upon illegal mystical knowledge of equinoxes and solstices. I repent for and renounce the use of Vedic astrology to determine decisions and propitious times for public and personal ceremonies and events.

✠ On behalf of myself and my family line, I repent for and renounce all ungodly vegetarianism, celibacy, monasticism, and asceticism practiced as Hindu religious acts. I repent for and renounce the use of all herbal medicines in the ayurvedic tradition that have been made by knowledge gained from the enemy.

✠ Lord Jesus, please cleanse all pathways of my mind, my will, and my emotions. Align my body, soul, and spirit to you and you alone. Lord, please restore all parts of me that were lost to other dimensions. Lord, please unite all parts of me in you. Lord, please join me to you and to your body which is the Church. Lord, I ask that you will fill me with your Holy Spirit and guide me as I continue to walk in the healing that you have provided for me.

Notes:

1. See chapter 11, Renunciation of Curses: Deuteronomy 28:15–68 (pages 79–86), for a discussion of the word *curse* in the Old Testament.

2. "Hindu Origins of the New Age—Supplement to Lesson 31," tract 31d (Altamont, TN: Pathlights), http://www.pathlights.com/theselastdays/tracts/tract_31d.htm.

3. One of the deities in the Hindu trinity.

4. Romans 8:1, 10, 16; Galatians 2:20; 3:27; 1 John 1:3; Ephesians 1:13; 2:13; 3:17; John 14:23; Colossians 1:27; John 15:5. Joseph Stump, *The Mystical Union, The Christian Faith* (New York: The Macmillan Company, 1932).

5. John 6:56; 14:17–20, 23; 1 Corinthians 6:17; 2 Peter 1:4; Ephesians 5:30.

6. Psalm 139:13–17; Jeremiah 1:5; 29:11; Proverbs 18:16; Romans 12:6.

7. Karma is the law of cause and effect.

8. Galatians 6:7.

9. Paul L. Cox, *What's All This Generational Stuff?* (Hesperia, CA: Aslan's Place, 2007).

10. Genesis 1:28–30.

11. Swami Vivekananda, "Lectures from Colombo to Almora/Reply to the Address of Welcome at Madras," in *The Complete Works of Swami Vivekananda*, vol 3. http://en.wikisource.org/wiki/Author:Swami_Vivekananda.

12. Romans 2:4; Ephesians 2:7; Titus 3:4.

13. Romans 9:30; 1 Corinthians 1:30; Philippians 3:9.

14. *Manusmriti, the Laws of Manu*, George Büller, trans., Max Müller, ed. Sacred Books of the East, vol. 25 (Oxford University Press Warehouse, Amen Corner, E.C.) 2:67; 5:154, 168, 157; 9:2, 3. http://www.sacred-texts.com/hin/manu.htm. Hindu texts about Hindu dharma or duty.

15. Donald Johnson and Jean E. Johnson, eds., *Through Indian Eyes*, 5th rev. ed. (New York: Council on International and Public Affairs/APEX Press, 2008).

Notes (continued):

16. *Tantra* in Sanskrit means *woven*. It is the practice and application of theoretical wisdom. Most of the time *tantra* means *rituals*.

17. See chapter 29, "Rescinding the Evils of Buddhism" (pages 230–243), for more information on *chakras*.

18. *Dissociation* is: "A psychological defense mechanism in which specific, anxiety-provoking thoughts, emotions, or physical sensations are separated from the rest of the psyche. . . . so that they lead an independent existence, as in cases of multiple personality." *The American Heritage® Dictionary of the English Language*, 4th ed. (Boston, MA: Houghton Mifflin Company, 2009).

19. Paul L. Cox, *The Sound of the Lord* (Hesperia, CA: Aslan's Place, 2004).

20. Amritbindu Upanishad, AP. Nisargadatta Maharaj, *I Am That: Dialogues of Sri Nisargadatta Maharaj*, http://www.docstoc.com/doc/11697512/I-Am-That.

21. Adi Sankaracharya, *Atma Bodha* in Sir Monier Monier-Williams, *Indian Wisdom*, 3rd ed. (London: Wm H. Allen & Co., 1876), 122, vs. 35-36. Available through books. google.com.

22. The Bhagavad Gita 14:3–4, Swami Swarupananda, *Srimad-Bhagavad-Gita*, (Mayavati, Himalayas: Advaita Asharama, 1909), http://www.sacred-texts.com/hin /sbg/sbg19.htm.

23. Quote from *Vivekachudamani* in *The Spirit of the Upanishads* (Chicago, IL: The Yogi Publication Society, 1907), 79.

24. Adi Sankaracharya, *Shivananda Lahari*, P.R. Ramachander, trans., from sloka 45. http://www.celextel.org/adisankara/shivanandalahari.html.

25. "Aswamedha Parva," *Mahabharata*, Book 14, Sri Kisari Mohan Ganguli, trans., http://www.sacred-texts.com/hin/m14/m14045.htm.

26. Prashna Upanishad, Question 6:2–6, Friedrich Max Müller, trans., The Sacred Books of the East, vol. 15. (Oxford: The Clarendon Press, 1880), http://www .sacred-texts.com/hin/sbe15/sbe15111.htm.

27. Bhagavad Gita 4:37, Swami Swarupananda, ed., *Srimad-Bhagavad-Gita* (Mayavati, Himalayas: Advaita Asharama, 1909), http://www.sacred-texts.com/hin/sbg/sbg09.htm.

28. Bhagavad Gita 2:22, Swami Paramananda, ed., *Srimad-Bhagavad-Gita*, (Mayavati, Himalayas: Advaita Asharama, 1909), http://www.sacred-texts.com/hin/sbg/sbg07.htm.

29. Bhagavad Gita, 14:26, Swami Paramananda, ed., *Srimad-Bhagavad-Gita*,(Mayavati, Himalayas: Advaita Asharama, 1909), http://www.sacred-texts.com/hin/sbg/sbg19.htm.

30. Hindu children are very often named after the deities. These deity names may sound unusual to Western ears but are common in practically every Hindu home. Much deliverance may result in asking God to separate ungodly connections with these deities using their individual names.

31. Svetasvatara Upanishad (4:15–16), Max Müller, trans. [1879], http://www.sacred-texts.com/hin/sbe15/sbe15103.htm.

32. Shiva Sloka. Sloka is a verse of praise. (Several versions are available in many places on the Internet.)

33. *Srimad Devi Bhagavatam*, VII.33.13-15 Adapted from translation by Swami Vijnanananda, (1921-1922), http://www.sacred-texts.com/hin/db/bk07ch33.htm.

34. *Wikipedia*. s.v. "Sri Yantra," http://en.wikipedia.org/wiki/Sri_Yantra.

35. Adi Shankara, *Soundarya Lahari*, sloka 1. Many translations are available on the Internet.

36. *Mahanirvana Tantra: Tantra of the Great Liberation*, Arthur Avalon, trans., (Sir John Woodroffe), 1913. 4:30–34. http://www.sacred-texts.com/tantra/maha/maha04.htm.

37. *Wikipedia*. s.v. "Dasavatara of Vishnu," http://en.wikipedia.org/wiki/Dasavatara _of_Vishnu.

38. Bhagavad Gita, 9:18. Swami Paramananda, ed., *Srimad-Bhagavad-Gita*, (Boston, MA: The Vedanta Centre, 1913), 75. Available through books.google.com.

39. "Vishnu Sahasranama, The Thousand Names of Vishnu," in *Mahabharata*, Kisari Mohan Ganguli, trans. (published between 1883 and 1896), 13:149, http://www.sacred-texts.com/hin/m13/m13b114.htm.

40. *Wikipedia*. s.v. "Advaita Vedanta," http://en.wikipedia.org/wiki/Advaita_Vedanta.

41. Advaita Info website, http://www.advaita.info/ and "Sankara," http://www.rationalvedanta.net/bios/vedantists/sankara.

42. *Tattva Bodha*, Adi Sankaracharya, http://www.sacred-texts.com/hin/cjw/cjw17.htm.

43. Ramacharaka, *The Spirit of the Upanishads* (Chicago, IL: The Yogi Publication Society, 1907), 18, http://www.archive.org/details/spiritupanishad00unkngoog.

44. Adi Shankara, *Soundarya Lahari*, sloka 11. Pandit S. Subrahmanya Sastri and T.R. Srinivasa Ayyangar, trans. (Adyar, Madras, India: The Theosophical Publishing House, 1948), 64. http://www.archive.org/details/SaundaryaLahari. Sloka 11 describes the Sri Chakra Yantra—a tantric instrument representing the union of the masculine and feminine divine.

45. Mike Magee, trans., "Shri Mahakala Deva," http://www.religiousworlds.com /mandalam/mahakala.htm.

46. "Hymn to Mahakala Shani Mrityunjaya," attributed to *Martandabhairava Tantra*, Mike Magee, trans., http://www.shivashakti.com/mahakala.htm.

Notes (continued):

47. Planet Saturn.

48. The four castes are Brahmins or priests, Kshatriyas or warriors and professionals, the Vaishya class of business people, and the Sudra class of laborers.

49. Prashna Upanishad, Question 5:2–5, Robert Ernest Hume, *The Thirteen Principal Upanishads* (London: Oxford University Press, 1921), 387–88, http://www.archive.org /details/thirteenprincipa028442mbp.

Renunciation
for Babylon

SARAH VICTOR

In April, 2007, God led us to construct a prayer of renunciation and repentance for Hinduism. This removed many roots of idolatry and witchcraft from my generational lines and closed many open doors which the enemy had used to attack my family.

At the same time, God directed us to go further back in time to Babylon. Babylon is the fountainhead of all false religion in the post-Flood world. All paganism, idol worship, mystery religions, and secret societies are thought to have their roots in the Babylonian legends of Nimrod, Semiramus, and Tammuz.

Babylon, the city in present-day southern Iraq, was founded by Nimrod,[1] who was Noah's great-grandson. Nimrod was a mighty ruler and empire builder who rebelled against God[2] and led men into idolatry. He built the city of Babel, which is translated as "gateway of the gods." This phrase captures a lot of what Babylon is about.

Centuries later, a spirit of world dominion similar to Nimrod's was resurrected in Nebuchadnezzar. He brought Babylon from a little obscure city-state into prominence as a world empire that the Bible describes as the greatest empire of this world.

Nimrod is associated with the Tower of Babel, which was built to reach heaven—essentially as a gateway of the gods. The ancient Babylonian religion is thus an ascension religion, corresponding to Lucifer's ambition, as described in Isaiah 14:13–14:

*For you have said in your heart: "I will ascend into heaven, I will
exalt my throne above the stars of God; I will also sit on the mount
of the congregation on the farthest sides of the north; I will ascend
above the heights of the clouds, I will be like the Most High."*

It is interesting to note that the context of this verse is a prophecy against
the king of Babylon. These verses capture the essence of the spirit of
Babylon, its rebellion against God, its ascension nature, and its astral
nature. Lucifer[3] in Hebrew means "morning star." It is a religion that tries
to reach the heavens. It is an astral religion, that is, a religion that identifies
the gods with the stars.

Although the gateway to the gods may not have succeeded in helping
man ascend to the heavens, unfortunately for the earth, it does appear
that portals may have been opened which allowed ungodly entities in the
second heaven to come to the earth.[4] Some controversial interpretations
of cuneiform tablets relate stories of the Sumerians interacting with their
gods.

These controversial theories say that in Sumerian times, "stargate"
devices, or portals, were used by the Nephilim (who were known as
Anunnaki by the Sumerians) to travel between the heavens and the earth.[5]
Modern attempts at opening such interdimensional gates to allow aliens
through started in 1918.[6]

The story of the Annunaki and the Nephilim is also the story of genetic
engineering and the mixing of the seed of Satan with the seed of man.[7] The
race was on to produce a being that is fully man and fully fallen angel; this
being will be called the Antichrist.

All of these schemes and devices are related to the end-time battle for
dominion of this world. The Day of the Lord is near. In these end times,
as the conflict between God and his enemies escalates, God calls us to
work with him to defeat the devices of his enemies and to establish the
dominion of Jesus Christ on earth.

Idolatry is thought to have originated in Babylon. What is idolatry?
What are the effects of idolatry? Is idolatry relevant in this day and age?
Evidence points that way: one of the most popular shows on television is
called *American Idol.* It mirrors a culture that values stardom, success,
physical beauty, fortune, and the pursuit of the American dream.

Who or what are the true objects of our trust, our hopes, our dreams, our comfort, our security, our fulfillment, and our worship?[8] Are they our retirement accounts, the security and fulfillment in our careers, happiness with our spouses or families? God has spoken of idolatry as a matter of the heart.

We look briefly at two key passages of Scripture regarding idolatry. The first is Psalm 115:4–8, which says that we become like the idols we worship.

> *Their idols are silver and gold, the work of men's hands. They have mouths, but they do not speak; eyes they have, but they do not see; they have ears, but they do not hear; noses they have, but they do not smell; they have hands, but they do not handle; feet they have, but they do not walk; nor do they mutter with their throat. Those who make them are like them; so is everyone who trusts in them.*

The same passage is echoed in Psalm 135:15–18 and in Isaiah 6:8–20 where, immediately after Isaiah's commissioning, his first mission was to expose the effects of idolatry on the hearts of the people. Isaiah 6:8–10 says,

> *Also I heard the voice of the Lord, saying: "Whom shall I send, and who will go for Us?" Then I said, "Here am I! Send me." And He said, "Go, and tell this people: 'Keep on hearing, but do not understand; keep on seeing, but do not perceive.' Make the heart of this people dull, and their ears heavy, and shut their eyes; lest they see with their eyes, and hear with their ears, and understand with their heart, and return and be healed."*

Idolatry can make us hard-hearted, insensitive, and calloused to sin. It can block our senses from perceiving God and his ways and the spiritual world that we live in. It can be a block to our healing.

We worship God with our spirits.[9] The Bible says that we become like the idols we worship. What happens to the spirit of man when he worships many gods and becomes like the gods that he worships? Do his soul and spirit become fractured into several identities? Is idolatry perhaps one of the spiritual roots of difficult deliverance issues such as dissociative identity disorder?

It is easy enough to say a renunciation prayer for the mystery religion of Babylon and ask God to remove the occult roots and consequent curses from our family lines. However, it can take some time to truly displace the idols in our hearts and align our hearts to God so that he is truly our first love. When we study Scripture on Babylon, it is clear where God's focus is—it is on the attitudes and motives of our hearts!

In teaching our family about Babylon, God led us to the book of Jeremiah where there is more about Babylon than in any other book of the Bible. Jeremiah was called to minister in Judah in its last days as an independent nation. The fall of Jerusalem, the destruction of the Temple, and the subsequent exile to Babylon were perhaps the most significant events of the stay of the children of Israel in the Promised Land.

God used Babylon as an instrument of justice against Judah for specific sins, in particular, the sin of idolatry.[10] In essence, they had broken covenant with their God and the covenant curse came upon them. On page after page in Jeremiah, God details the sins that caused the brutal hand of Babylon to come upon the land and the people.

Jeremiah pours out his heart in great distress and anguish at the suffering this judgment brought upon the Lord's beloved people and his own pain at the destruction of the defiled land. Today we hear familiar echoes of this suffering in our lives, our families, our nation, and the world around us.

The consequences of sin continue to be played out in our world today—one has only to look at the wars in the world—the young men cut down in their prime, the tragedies of famine, death, and destruction that touch every family, every society and every country. God feels the same anguish when he sees our suffering today that he felt centuries ago, when his people suffered the consequences of their iniquity.

Woven through God's complaint about his people in the book of Jeremiah, God also pleads with his people to return to him, to repent and be restored. We heed his voice in Jeremiah, confessing our sins and those of our ancestors, pleading with him to restore us and our families, our nation, and our land. We cannot resist the cry of his heart in Jeremiah calling us to return to the passion and intimacy of our first love for him. Time and time again in Jeremiah he examines our hearts closely, searching our motives, our attitudes, and our thoughts. He reassures us about his plans for our lives, for our restoration.

This prayer can be used for personal and corporate purposes.

The Prayer: Renunciation for Babylon

✠ Heavenly Father, I ask you to forgive me and all members of my ancestral line for the spirit of rebellion that was in Nimrod, who set himself to oppose you[11] and revolted against you.

✠ On behalf of myself and my ancestors, I repent for and renounce the tyranny and despotism that Nimrod practiced and the evil of the empire that he established. I repent for the lust for power that the empire was founded on and for Nimrod's hunting of the souls of men.

✠ I repent for the trading of the souls of men in Babylon.[12] Forgive me and my family line for the spirit of rebellion in which the city of Babel or Babylon was founded.[13]

✠ Heavenly Father, I ask you to forgive me and all members of my ancestral line for all the beliefs and attitudes that caused the building of the religious ziggurat which was the Tower of Babel and was the motivation behind other ungodly buildings and structures. We repent for the arrogance and presumption that holds that men could by themselves build the gateway to God.[14]

✠ We repent for the astral worship and astrology practiced at the Tower of Babel. We repent for the fear that the people lived in, the fear that they would be scattered abroad to live in isolated communities—exposed to danger, unknown, and without honor and standing.

✠ We repent for the fear behind building a religious tower to "make a name for ourselves." We repent for misusing the power of religion to share the glory of God, to make a name for ourselves, and to try to control our lives and our futures. We repent for all agreement with the spirit of Babylon, which uses religious authority to gain earthly power and prestige. We repent for our rebellion, pride, and self-will—the arrogance that makes us want to make a name for ourselves and to believe that we can accomplish anything we want on our own without you.[15]

✠ Lord, help us not to avoid the risks of establishing new frontiers but to embrace them; help us to be fruitful and replenish the earth,[16] to bring your dominion to bear in places where your Kingdom has not been established, and to partner with you to fulfill the birthrights and callings that you have for our lives.

✠ Lord, we repent for being aligned with Babylon, the city of man. Please help us to be citizens of and aligned with the city of God, the New Jerusalem.[17] Lord, help us to enter into your inheritance for us by faith, looking for a city which has foundations, whose builder and maker is you.[18]

✠ Lord, we repent for the state religion Nimrod established to deify and worship himself as emperor. We repent for the worship of Satan and his demons, and for star worship.

✠ We repent for the worship of Nimrod that is connected to the planet Jupiter, and for worshipping Nimrod as Zeus in Greece, as Jupiter in Rome,[19] and as Marduk or "bull calf of the sun," god of magic and incantations, god of the agricultural people.

✠ We repent for the worship of this entity as the god associated with the planet Mars, as the patron deity of the city of Babylon, also known as Bel or "lord," and as the "bull of Utu."[20]

✠ We repent for the worship of this entity as the "Bull of Heaven" and for worshipping the crescent moon as a symbol of the horns of the bull. We repent for the worship of the bull in Egypt as Apis, embodiment of Ptah and later of Osiris. We repent for the worship of the bull in Greece as the "bull of Crete," the Minotaur.

✠ We repent for the worship of Nimrod as Ninus in Babylon, Kronos, "Bull-Horned One" or Saturn in Rome, Zeus in Greece, Osiris in Egypt, or as Zoroaster in Chaldea. We repent for his worship as Hercules or Atlas in Greece.

✠ We repent for the worship of Semiramis, wife of Nimrod, queen of Babylon. We repent for the worship of the queen of heaven, also known as Ammas or mother of the gods and Ge or Gaia the earth goddess. As the Madonna in Italy, as Juno, Cybele, or Rhea in Rome, as Athena, Minerva, or Hera in Greece, as Shing Moo or Ma Tsoopo in China, as Astarte or Ashtoreth in Phoenicia. We repent for the worship of Semiramis as Aphrodite of Greece, Venus of Rome, and Vesta or Terra of Rome.

✠ We repent for the worship of the unholy trinity in the Babylonian mysteries—Nimrod, his consort Semiramis and their posthumous son, Tammuz, who was proclaimed as the reincarnation of Nimrod. We repent for all the paganism and idol worship that had their roots in the legends having to do with Nimrod, Semiramis, and Tammuz.[21]

✠ We repent for the worship of Semiramis and Tammuz as Ashtoreth and Tammuz of Phoenicia, Isis and Horus of Egypt, Aphrodite and Eros of Greece, Venus and Cupid of Rome, Cybele and Deoius of Asia, and Parvati and Iswara of India.

✠ We repent for the system of mysteries of Babylon that was set up when this false worship went underground in Babylon at the time Nimrod was killed. We repent for the intended purpose—glorifying the dead Nimrod. We repent for the sacrifices to the dead that this worship involved.[22] We repent for the ritual of lamenting his early death at the summer solstice.

✠ We repent for the use of seals of secrecies, oaths, initiation ceremonies, and magic used to continue this idolatry in secret. We repent for spreading this secret mystery religion through the earth.

✠ We repent for Freemasonry, which promulgates the mysteries of the Egyptian Isis, the goddess-mother, wife of Osiris. We repent for the practice of other mystery and false religions, such as Satanism, Luciferianism, Illuminati, Gnosticism, the Knights Templar, Rosicrucianism, the Theosophical Society, the New World Order, New Age, and Lucid Trust. Lord, please disconnect us from all these false cults.

✠ Lord, on behalf of ourselves and our ancestors, we repent for the worship of Tammuz, posthumous son of Semiramis, who was claimed to be Nimrod resurrected. We repent for the false legend that he was the promised "seed of the woman" who would deliver mankind.

✠ We repent for the association of the worship of Tammuz with the winter solstice when the days are the shortest and for the legend that the winter solstice is the sun dying and being reborn. We repent for burning the Yule log on the winter solstice[23] and replacing it with a trimmed tree the next morning to represent his resurrection. We repent for continuing this pagan tradition during Christmas celebrations. We repent for the worship of Tammuz as the sun god and as the Assyrian fertility deity. We repent for the worship of Tammuz as Horus in Egypt, Bacchus in Rome, Adonis in Greece, Baal-berith or Lord of the Covenant,[24] and as Vishnu in India.

✠ Lord, we repent for the worship of all heavenly bodies—the sun, the moon, and the planets—and for the association of false gods with planets. We repent for the development of astrology, which focuses on a study of the zodiac that originated in Babylon. We repent for trying to find and manipulate our birthrights and callings by locating the section of the sky that we were born under. We repent for the association of astrology with demonism or Satanism where Satan and his hosts have been worshipped in the guise of signs or planets.

✠ Forgive us for the worship of the moon god of the Chaldeans, the god of nomadic people. Forgive us for using the crescent moon as the symbol of the moon god and for establishing the lunar calendar around this ungodly worship. Forgive us for worshipping the black meteorite stone as the Ka'aba, for calling the moon god the Lord of the Ka'aba and for its worship and the worship of 360 other idols. Forgive us for the worship of the moon god as Sin in Syria and as Al-Ilah in Arabia.

✠ Forgive us for the establishment of Islam as a religion built around the worship of the moon god Al-lah. Forgive us for the establishment of cities such as Jericho or Beth-Yerah (house of the moon god) around this false worship of the moon god. Forgive us for the establishment of centers of worship of the moon god at Ur and Harran and building temples to this god throughout Babylonia and Assyria. Lord, please disconnect us from the principalities of the land of Babylon, including all astral worship and worship of the moon.

✠ Lord, would you deliver us from all curses of insanity that have come upon us as a result of the worship of the moon.[25] Forgive us for all rituals and practices associated with the different cycles of the moon, including rituals done at new moon, full moon, and all shape-shifting.

✠ We repent for all worship of the sun and sun deities such as Helios or Titan and Apollo in Greece, Shamash or Tammuz in Mesopotamia at Sippar and Larsa, the Germanic Sol, the Vedantic Surya and Adityas, the Incan Inti and Aztec Huitzilopochtli, the Egyptian Ra, Amaterasu in Japan, and the Slavic Dazhbog.

✠ We repent for the use of the symbol of the snake, serpent, or dragon that is associated with Nimrod/Marduk. We repent for all worship of snakes, use of snakes in rituals, and worship of deities associated with snakes.

✠ We repent for the use of the caduceus or Rod of Asclepius,[26] that is, the winged staff with two snakes wrapped around it, the ancient astrological symbol of commerce associated with the Greek god Hermes, as the symbol of medicine based upon the astrological principles of using the planets and stars to heal the sick. We repent for all worship of Asclepius, Chiron, Hermes and all association of these false deities with the practice of medicine. We repent for the use of magic and hermetic arts in the practice of medicine.

✠ We repent for the worship of other false deities associated with the snake such as Poseidon, Hydra, and Triton, Gorgons and Medusa, Shiva, Naga, Auslavis in Lithuania, the rainbow serpent of the Aboriginal people of Australia, the Minoan snake goddess, Zombi in West Africa and Haiti, and Degei in Fiji. Lord, please disconnect us from all these snake deities. Lord, please disconnect us from Leviathan, the sea monster. Lord, please disconnect us from the ancient serpent, the dragon.

✠ We repent for the worship of An, the god of heaven at the E'anna temple at Uruk.

✠ We repent for the worship of Enlil, the god of the air and storms, associated with the planet Jupiter, at the E'kur temple in Nippur.

✠ We repent for the worship of Enki, the god of water and fertile earth, associated with the planet Mercury, at the E'abzu temple.

✠ We repent for the worship of Eridu or Ea, the god of magic, wisdom, and intelligence.

✠ We repent for the worship of Ki or Nirhursag, the mother-goddess representing the earth, at the E'saggila temple at Kish.

✠ We repent for the worship of Ashur, the sky god, the main god of Assyria, at Assur.

✠ We repent for the worship of Ninlil or Nillina, the goddess of the air, the south wind, and wife of Enlil, at the E'kur temple in Nippur. We repent for the worship of Nergal, god of death, associated with the planet Mars, son of Enlil and Ninlil.

✠ We repent for the worship of Inanna, the goddess of love and war, associated with the planet Venus, at the E'anna temple at Uruk.

✠ We repent for the worship of Marduk, son of Ea, the god of light, the main god of Babylon (Babylonian), at the E'saggila temple in Babylon.

✠ We repent for the worship of Nanna or Suen or Sin, god of the moon, at the E'hursag temple of Ur and Harran.

✠ We repent for the worship of Utu Tutu or Shamash, god of the sun, at the E'barbara temple of Sipparand in Babylonia.

✠ We repent for the worship of Ninurta at the E'Girsu temple at Lagash.

Lord, please disconnect us from all these ungodly entities.

Heavenly Father, on behalf of my ancestors and myself, I repent for coveting[27] the things of Babylon or the world system and being seduced by the things of the world into disobeying your commandments and going against your ways. On behalf of myself and my ancestors who were part of the Babylonian system, I repent for agreeing with the seductive spirit of Babylon and for anything we did in this spirit to seduce your people away from you.

We repent for trying to find our legitimacy by displaying to the world the power, wealth, influence, gifts, talents, and treasures that you gave us and for using them in the world when they were meant to be dedicated to you[28] and be used in your service. We repent that we found our legitimacy in looking for admiration and favor from the world instead of deriving our legitimacy from our relationship with you. Lord, we repent for being found wanting when you tried us to know what was in our hearts.[29] We pray that you would align our hearts with your heart.

On behalf of our ancestors, we repent for allowing curses into our generational lines so that generational blessings and treasures were stolen from our families and our generational lines and sold to the Babylonian system.[30] Lord, please restore to us these generational treasures.

Lord, we pray for our own deliverance from Babylon and the deliverance of many people from this system. On behalf of ourselves and our ancestors from Babylon, we humble ourselves before you, pray, seek your face, and repent of our wicked ways,[31] our evil, our iniquity, our pride, arrogance, and haughtiness.

Forgive us for not listening to or obeying the words of your servants, the true prophets, for not turning from our evil ways and living in the land and inheritance that you have given to us. Forgive us for going after other gods to serve them and worship them and for provoking you to anger with the works of our hands.

✠ Lord, please set your eyes upon us for good; bring us into our land and into our inheritance; build us up and plant us. Give us a heart to know you—to know that you are the Lord and that we are your people. We return unto you with our whole hearts.

✠ Please remove the destruction, the desolation, the scorn and shame that have come upon us. Please restore to us the sounds of joy, singing, laughter, the sounds of marriage festivities, and the sound of the workmen; please give us light for our activities. Please remove the barrenness of our land. Please take away the sword and the wine cup of your fury. Please deliver us from our oppression, for we put our trust in you alone.[32]

Notes:

1. Genesis 10:9–10.

2. Genesis 10:9. The Hebrew word *pânîym* which is translated "before" in some translations can also mean "against." Commentators such as Keil and Delitzsch, Clarke, and Matthew Henry have described him as being a tyrant in rebellion against the Lord.

3. *Hêylêl.*

4. Michael E. Salla, "An Exopolitical Perspective on the Preemptive War against Iraq," *Exopolitics*, February 3, 2003, http://www.exopolitics.org/Study-Paper-2.htm.

5. William Henry, "Saddam Hussein, the Stairway to Heaven and the Return of Planet X," based on *Ark of the Christos* by William Henry, http://www
.bibliotecapleyades.net/exopolitica/esp_exopolitics_k_1.htm.

6. Thomas Horn, "Stargates, Ancient Rituals, and those Invited through the Portal," http://www.bibliotecapleyades.net/stargate/stargate06.htm.

7. Genesis 6:1–4; Numbers 13:33; Deuteronomy 2:11, 20; 3:11, 13; 2 Samuel 21:16–22; 1 Chronicles 20:4–8; Daniel 2:43.

8. Elyse Fitzpatrick, *Idols of the Heart: Learning to Long for God Alone,* (Phillipsburg, NJ: P&R Publishing, 2002).

9. John 4:23–24.

10. Jeremiah 1:15–16.

11. Genesis 10:8–9.

12. Revelation 18:13.

13. Genesis 10:10.

14. Babel is composed of two words: *baa* meaning "gate" and *el* meaning "god."

15. Genesis 11:4–6.

16. Genesis 1:28.

17. Revelation 3:12.

18. Hebrews 11:8–10.

19. Powerful spirits can take on many names depending on the culture that manifest in.

20. For the association of Marduk with Mars, see Bryce Self, "Nimrod, Mars and the Marduk Connection," http://www.ldolphin.org/Nirmord.html and Gerald Massey, *A Book of the Beginnings*, vol.2 (New York: Cosimo, 2007). For information on Marduk with Bel, see http://www.ldolphin.org/Nimrod.html, *Wikipedia*, s.v. "Marduk," http://en.wikipedia.org/wiki/Marduk, and Joseph Eddy Fontenrose, *Python: A study of Delphic Myth and Its Origins* (Cheshire, CT: Biblo-Moser, 1959); for the association of Marduk with Bull of Utu, see: *Wikipedia*, s.v. "Bull (mythology)." http://en.wikipedia.org/wiki/Bull_(mythology) and Gwendolyn Leick, *Historical Dictionary of Mesopotamia* (Lanham, MD: Scarecrow Press, Inc., 2003).

21. Alexander Hislop, *The Two Babylons*, (1858; repr., Stilwell, KS: Digireads.com Publishing, 2007).

22. Psalm 106:28.

23. The word in Chaldean for "infant" is *yule*.

24. Judges 8:33.

25. Lunacy is from *luna* or the Latin word for moon. *Merriam-Webster's 11th Collegiate Dictionary*, s.v. "Lunatic."

26. Greek god of medicine and healing.

27. Joshua 7:21.

28. 2 Kings 20:15.

29. 2 Chronicles 32:31.

30. 2 Kings 20:17–18.

31. 2 Chronicles 7:14.

32. Jeremiah 25:4–7, 25:9–16, 25:38.

Prayer for Release into Emotional Healing

AMYBETH BERNER

As a therapist for twenty years, I have been searching for wisdom and revelation to increase the potential for healing. On one search the Lord brought me back to the Garden of Eden, "Then the eyes of both of them were opened, and they knew that they were naked; and they sewed fig leaves together and made themselves loin coverings."[1] (NASB) I heard the question, "What eyes were those?" Whenever the Lord asks me questions, I begin to get excited because he is teaching me something new.

I didn't think the Lord was talking about eyes that were already open in Genesis—the physical eyes Adam used to name the animals[2] and to receive Eve,[3] and the spiritual eyes that communed with God.[4] I also crossed off the eyes that were opened at the Fall, the eyes that discerned good and evil,[5] perceived nakedness,[6] felt emotions,[7] and developed self-protection and defense mechanisms related to emotions,[8] the eyes that ultimately ushered in sin.

After the fall, man was left with a dilemma; he was able to discern good and evil but lacked wisdom. He didn't know how to resolve issues and emotions that came with this new awareness. Also, because of their emerging emotions, Adam and Eve no longer trusted themselves, each other, or the Lord. Their relationship attachment was broken. Man was now forced to find solutions that would relieve his pain.

What eyes were those? What was the Lord pointing me toward? From my study of Jim Wilder's[9] material on maturity and brain development,

I began to see a correlation between the eyes that "were opened" and the function of the amygdala. The amygdala is sometimes named the "guard shack" of the brain; it is the organ that decides if incoming information is good, bad, or scary. This organ also holds memories of every negative emotion, keeping them on file for protective reference. When a current event overwhelms our capacity to handle an emotion and we are unable to return to our prefrontal cortex or "joy center," the mind will often choose self-defensive strategies.[10] For example, Adam who was afraid and ashamed when he heard the Lord coming, hid himself.[11] Every generation of people since Adam has devised escape plans, defense mechanisms, and survival techniques to help them cope with the intense reactions of the amygdala. We have attached ourselves to behaviors, events, experiences, people, and substances to escape or subdue internal pain.[12] To attach fully to the Lord, we must first repent and release old patterns of comfort and self-protection.

Recently, as I was teaching a class in Nashville, the Lord brought me again to Genesis—to see Cain's reaction at the rejection of his offering.

So Cain became very angry, and his countenance fell. Then the Lord said to Cain, "Why are you angry? And why has your countenance fallen? If you do well, will not your countenance be lifted up? And if you do not do well, sin is crouching at the door; and its desire is for you, but you must master it."[13] (NASB)

We see that Cain displays his rejection as anger and that the Lord instructs Cain, telling him how to find way out of this emotion. The Lord explains that "doing well" is the way of escape. In exploring this word, *yatab*, we see that it means to be glad, to be cheerful, to be pleasant, to be good.[14] The theme of joy is repeated with the phrase "will not your countenance be lifted up" from *se eth* which figuratively means cheerfulness or elation.[15] The way out of pain for Cain is through returning to joy. The Lord's desire is for Cain to rejoice, to be cheerful, and to remain in relationship with him. Instead, Cain entertained his anger and murdered his brother.

Because I have participated in creating some of the prayers in this book with Paul Cox and know their effectiveness, I began asking the Lord to release a prayer to dissolve the bondage of old attachments, cover the iniquity of being lead by emotions, and eliminate relying on the tree of the knowledge of good and evil for wisdom.

In this prayer, we are repenting for destructive patterns and immaturity in our responses to pain, hurt, fear, shame, and hopeless despair. We are declaring that our Lord has prepared a way of escape, and his way is through the joy of our relationship with him.[16] The Lord wants us to take dominion over our emotions, walk in the Spirit, and rejoice in him always.

It is time for us to claim our inheritance, drop our fig leaves, and walk again in the garden with naked hearts and minds. It is my petition that he will use this prayer to strengthen your desire to seek him during emotional storms, to run to him for joy, and to rest in love.

The Prayer: Release into Emotional Healing[17]

✠ I repent for all those in my generational line, beginning with Adam and Eve, who, in their desire to know good and evil, opened a door of fear and shame. Lord, please close the portal and cleanse the neural pathways of the brain to reestablish your joy.

✠ I repent for myself and for all those in my family line who have hidden themselves from their own emotions and from the Lord when he has come to help. I choose to remove all fig leaves of self-protection and to come into the place of intimacy that the Lord Jesus provided by his redemption.

✠ I repent for all those in my generational line who exchanged the glory of the Lord for the fruit of the knowledge of good and evil. Lord, I declare that all wisdom and knowledge are hidden in Christ, and I choose to set my mind on things above.[18]

✠ I repent for all those in my generational line who denied their emotions and projected their fear and shame onto those around them. Lord, please repair the attachment patterns in our brains and restore them to the perfection that existed when Adam and Eve walked with you in the garden.

✠ I repent for all those in my generational line who refused to rejoice in the Lord, who allowed their countenances to fall, thus allowing sin to enter their doors.[19]

✠ Lord, please remove the iniquity and pattern in my family line that flowed from Cain's choice to remain in pain and not return to joy. I choose to count it all joy, believing that endurance and maturity are gifts from above.[20]

✠ I repent for myself and all those in my generational line who did not acknowledge you as the "I Am." I repent for all those who, not seeing your love, turned to false attachments to comfort themselves. Lord, would you cleanse the attachment center of my brain and wash over the DNA in my family with your precious blood?

✠ I repent for those who rejected you as Loving Father, Provider, and Sustainer of all life.

✠ I repent for those who gave their hearts to idols, worshipping and serving them in place of the Lord.

✠ I repent for everyone in my family line who rebelled against parents and authority figures in an effort to escape shameful emotions.

✠ I repent for all in my generational line who became thieves and refused to see you, Lord, as the source of all provision. I repent for all those who lied and deceived out of fear or greed.

✠ I repent for all those in my generational line who coveted things and for all who attached themselves to the belongings of others.

✠ I repent for all those in my generational line who became drunk with alcohol, seeking to escape painful emotions rather than seeking your face.

✠ I repent for all those in my family line who used or provided others with drugs to exit from this world and enter into the second heaven. Lord, please call back any parts of my spirit or my generational inheritance from the second heaven and seal the door with your blood.

✠ I repent for those in my generational line who did not forgive the sins against them and who held onto anger as a protection. Lord, would you release all debts and debtors that have been held by my generational line, and would you remove the tormentors that have come against my life?

� I repent for all those who boasted in chariots, horses, and the might of men for their deliverance and protection.

✖ I repent for all in my generational line who sought mediums, witchcraft, fortune-tellers, necromancers, or Satan's representatives as a source of comfort in times of fear or loss.

✖ I repent for all in my generational line who demanded life for life, eye for eye, tooth for tooth, hand for hand, foot for foot, burn for burn, wound for wound, bruise for bruise, and who did not love and pray for their enemies.[21]

✖ I repent for myself and all those in my family line who, not mastering their emotions, turned to their flesh, committing sins of immorality, impurity, sensuality, idolatry, sorcery, enmities, strife, jealousy, outbursts of anger, disputes and dissensions, factions, envying, drunkenness, and carousing.[22]

✖ I repent for myself and all those in my generational line who have refused to crucify the flesh with its passions and desires. Lord, I ask that you would release your holy fire and burn off the iniquity that has passed through the generations.

✖ I repent for all those in my generational line who devised man-made rules, legalistic guidelines, and spiritual laws to control emotions and behavior. Lord, I choose to live and walk by your Spirit, relying on your voice to direct my path.

✖ I repent for all those in my generational line who have tried to live by bread alone. Lord, would you interrupt the pathway to the pleasure center in my brain and form new connections to your heart.

✖ I declare that I am a new creature in Christ and that old things have passed away. I believe that when I walk by the Spirit I will not gratify the desires of my flesh.

✠ Lord, would you strengthen the pathway of the Spirit in my mind so that I might enter your gates with thanksgiving and your courts with praise? Lord, would you remind my spirit that it is seated with you in heavenly places far above all powers, rulers, and authorities? Lord, would you judge every spiritual force connected to this iniquity and restore everything that has been stolen from my generational line?

Notes:

1. Genesis 3:7, NASB.
2. Genesis 3:20.
3. Genesis 2:23.
4. Genesis 2:16.
5. Genesis 3:5, 22.
6. Genesis 3:7, 10–11.
7. Genesis 3:7–8, 10.
8. Genesis 3:7–8, 10, 12–13.
9. For more information on Jim Wilder, see http://www.lifemodel.org.
10. E. James Wilder, *The Complete Guide to Living With Men* (Pasadena, CA: Shepherd's House Inc., 2004).
11. Genesis 3:10.
12. For information about BEEPS and addictions, see http://www.thirvingrecovery.org.
13. Genesis 4:5–7, NASB.
14. James Strong, *Strong's Exhaustive Concordance of the Bible*, Hebrew word no. 3190.
15. James Strong, *Strong's Exhaustive Concordance of the Bible*, Hebrew word no. 7613.
16. 1 Corinthians 10:13.
17. Amybeth Brenner.
18. Colossians 2:3; 3:2.
19. Genesis 4:6–7.
20. James 1:2–5.
21. Deuteronomy 19:21; Matthew 5:38–39.
22. Galatians 5:19–21.

CHAPTER FORTY-TWO

Prayer of Agreement to Bless the Jewish People

DENA GEWANTER, MD

Few Christians understand what the Bible actually says about Israel and the Jewish people. Most ignore or overlook the fact that Jesus was a Jewish man, who quoted from the Tanach (Old Testament) in almost everything he said, observed Jewish laws, celebrated all the Jewish feasts, and used examples in his teachings from Jewish history. Jesus said people would be judged according to how they treated "these brothers of mine," the Jews.[1] He said he "did not come to destroy [the Law] but to fulfill [it]."[2] Paul said that Jesus was "a servant of the Jews on behalf of God's truth, to confirm the promises made to the patriarchs so that the Gentiles may glorify God."[3] (NIV) The gates of heaven have the names of the twelve tribes of Israel on them.[4] In the light of these biblical truths, why do most Christians have such a disconnect with Hebraic traditions and the people who are the blood relatives of the Lord they serve and believe in?

Christians who do not understand the covenantal promises of God to Israel and his final plan for the Jewish people are missing an opportunity to see the amazing fulfillment of prophecies spoken thousands of years ago. The reemergence of the State of Israel after almost two thousand years is a complete miracle! Jewish people from over one hundred twenty different countries have returned to Israel in fulfillment of multiple prophecies in the Bible; "In that day the Lord will reach out his hand a second time to reclaim the remnant that is left of his people. . . . He will assemble the scattered people of Judah from the four quarters of the earth."[5] He banished the sons of Jacob from the land he covenanted to their forefathers, but promised to bring them back in the last days, a promise that he is fulfilling at this very moment as a testimony to his own faithfulness and the veracity of his Word! In Jeremiah we read that only if God breaks his covenant with day and night will the descendants of Israel ever cease to be a nation before him[6] and that God would plant the Jewish people in their land with "all his heart and soul."[7] How amazing to read that God planted them in Israel with *all his heart and soul!*

The land of Israel is the place where God dwells, and Jerusalem is the city where the Lord chose to put his name.[8] The Jewish people are called his people. "For the sake of his great name the LORD will not reject his people, because the LORD was pleased to make you his own."[9] (NIV)

Should we care about what is happening in Israel and with the Jewish people if we are Christians? Those who hate, reject, or even dismiss what the Bible says about Israel and the Jewish people may actually be bringing a curse upon themselves. If we hate the Jews or the nation of Israel, we are under God's curse until we repent and are cleansed of this sin. Did you know that it is written, "I [God] will bless those who bless you [Abram/Israel], and whoever curses you [Abram/Israel] I will curse"?[10] (NIV) Joel clearly states that God will gather **all** the nations who scattered his inheritance, his people Israel, and divided up his land and he will come into judgment against them.[11] This should concern all Americans and those from the nations whose governments are trying to force Israel to divide the land that God covenanted to give the Jewish people.

While most committed Christians believe that we are living in the "last days" before the return of the Messiah, few think seriously about the *place* of his return. We are told in Acts 3:21 (NIV) that "He [Jesus] must remain in heaven until the time comes for God to restore everything, as he promised long ago through his holy prophets." The Bible clearly states that he will come to fight against the nations who surround Jerusalem, standing on the Mount of Olives.[12] This means that there must be Jewish believers living in Jerusalem who are praying for the Messiah to appear, as there are today.

God's Word says, "Indeed, he [God] who watches over Israel will neither slumber nor sleep,"[13] and that the Jewish people are "the apple of his eye."[14] "Pray for the peace of Jerusalem: 'May those who love you be secure. . . . For the sake of my brothers and friends, . . . For the sake of the house of the Lord, I will seek your prosperity."[15] (NIV) We see here that there is a blessing for those who pray for Jerusalem, both personally and corporately.

> *I have posted watchmen on your walls, O Jerusalem; they will never be silent day or night. You who call on the LORD, give yourselves no rest, and give him no rest till he establishes Jerusalem and makes her the praise of the earth.*[16] (NIV)

Apparently, those who call upon God are supposed to give him no rest until he makes Jerusalem the praise of the earth. Is this happening in your church and your personal prayer life?

The first believers were almost exclusively Jewish and incorporated all the Jewish feasts and ceremonies in their lives as followers of Yeshua (Jesus). After the destruction of the temple in AD 70, the Jewish people were expelled from Israel and scattered throughout the Roman Empire. Then, after the Roman Emperor Constantine was converted to Christianity in AD 312, he started to separate and isolate the Jews through physical expulsion, legal discrimination, and death sentences. Augustine wrote in AD 400, "the true image of the Jew is Judas Iscariot, who sells the Lord for silver . . . and forever will bear the guilt for the death of Jesus."[17] When there were unexplained epidemics, like the Black Death plague, the Jews were often blamed and hundreds were murdered.

Between AD 1100 and 1270, the Crusaders murdered thousands of Jewish people on the way to Jerusalem; streets ran with the blood of their victims. During the Spanish Inquisition, starting in AD 1230, many thousands were tortured and killed, or forced to convert. The first Jewish ghettos were started in Italy in 1516; Jewish men were forced to wear horned hats and badges to distinguish themselves from Christians. Thomas Aquinas, a Catholic priest, said that the Jewish people should always live in servitude. Martin Luther wrote in the fifteen hundreds that "God's anger with the Jew is so intense that Christians should . . . burn their synagogues, destroy their homes, deprive them of their prayer books, forbid them to teach, travel, own land, and all their money should be taken from them."[18] Popes, kings and religious leaders in Europe all joined together in their persecution and discrimination against the Jewish people through the eighteen hundreds.

It is estimated that from the time of Christ until the time of the holocaust of Hitler, over seven million people had been killed simply because they were religiously and ethnically Jewish.

During the time leading up to World War II, the world paid scant attention to the increasing persecution of the Jewish population of Europe. False publications like "The Protocols of the Elders of Zion" stating that Jews used the blood of Christian children to make matzoh for Passover were widely distributed, and in fact, "The Protocols of the Elders of Zion" is still a best seller in the Muslim world.

In the nineteen thirties, Hitler quoted Martin Luther in *Mein Kampf*, saying that he was "acting in accordance with the will of God by defending himself against the Jews." In the United States, Henry Ford published a book defaming the Jewish people that was in agreement with Nazi ideology. North American universities made quotas against employing and enrolling them. Muslim leaders also cooperated with Hitler in the attempt to exterminate the Jewish people, and the Grand Mufti was a guest in Berlin during World War II. Jewish people in Arab countries such as Syria, Iraq, Yemen, Tunisia, Morocco and Libya were labeled *dhimmi*, (outcasts) and suffered religious persecution, beatings, rape, and forced conversions. Anti-Semitism was a milder problem in the Arab countries prior to World War II, but during the time of Hitler's "Final Solution," propaganda spread throughout the Arab territories, and life for Jewish people in the Arab countries that had been their homes for centuries became intolerable. Records show that the U.S. government knew about the Nazi concentration camps but did nothing to stop the cattle cars full of Jewish Europeans who were taken to the gas chambers. Canada even turned away a boat full of Jewish refugees; they were forced to return to Europe, where most of the passengers were sent to their deaths in concentration camps. England, the occupying ruling country over what was then called Palestine, did everything in its power to prevent Jewish refugees fleeing from the Nazis from immigrating to Israel, yet actively encouraged Arab migration to the region. Thanks to the obsessively accurate record keeping of the Nazis, it is known that at least six million Jewish people were exterminated from 1939–1945. Of that number, one and one-half million were children. Hitler's goal was to seek out every member of the Jewish race from all countries dominated by Nazi Germany and to "wipe the race off the face of the earth." The words and desires of Iran's President Ahmadinejad and other radical Muslim clerics today echo the spirit behind Hitler's demonic ideology.

In 1948, on the day after Israel was given statehood by the League of Nations, seven Arab nations attacked Israel. With no army, weapons, or air force, the Israelis miraculously beat back the Arabs from all sides and began to rebuild their homeland. "Can a country be born in a day or a nation be brought forth in a moment? Yet no sooner is Zion in labor than she gives birth to her children."[19] (NIV) All the wars fought by Israel have been won through the miracle of God's intervention. To this day, many soldiers who fought in these wars tell of God's invisible hand turning battles in Israel's favor. Many do not realize that the constant clamor for a Palestinian state is a thinly veiled plan to ultimately destroy the State of Israel; its very existence is an insult to the tenets of Islam. The Koran states that the land of Israel, once lived on by Muslims, must always belong to a Muslim.[20] Sharing land and peaceful coexistence is unheard of in Islam. The Koran requires that Islam to be the dominant ruling power, and Muslims are required by the Koran's teachings to fight a jihad (holy war) to overthrow any country that is not controlled by Islam. This is why although there are twenty-two Islamic states and more than enough room to settle the Palestinian refugees in other Muslim countries, they continue to fight to overthrow Israel and refuse to accept one Jewish state; it is an abomination to their religious beliefs.

Israel is a desert land that has come to life in fulfillment of the prophecy in Isaiah 27:6 (NIV): "In days to come Jacob will take root, Israel will bud and blossom and fill all the world with fruit." Yet the United Nations has made more pronouncements against Israel than all the other countries of the world combined! One has to be reminded of the passage,

Why do the nations conspire and the peoples plot in vain? The kings of the earth take their stand and the rulers gather together against the LORD and against his Anointed One.[21] (NIV)

All Jewish people, and particularly those in Israel, desperately want to live in peace and not in the middle of so much conflict and hatred. Israel and the Jewish people are not at center stage because of righteousness or good works, nor because they are particularly evil or bad. It is simply because of election, something God **chose** to do. In Romans 11:2 (NIV) it clearly states, "God did not reject his people, whom he foreknew." Today, Some Christian leaders and groups are coming out in support of a Palestinian state and against "Israeli occupation of Arab land." The age-old anti-Semitism that was dormant after World War II is rising up again, and now it is directed not only against the Jewish race, but also against their homeland. In God's eyes, there is no separation of the Jewish people and the land of Israel. Anti-Zionism (opposition to the State of Israel) is the same entity as anti-Semitism.

Dear friends, if you want to keep yourselves from deception and from being used as an instrument against God's purposes in these last days, be sure to align yourself with God's plans as described in the Bible. Do not be deceived by the clamor of the masses. Search God's Word and read what it says about Israel and the Jewish people; then pray for his will to be accomplished. You will surely be blessed and amazed as you watch God bring you into a deeper level of intimacy and revelation about his very heart and soul.[22]

The Prayer: Agreement to Bless the Jewish People[23]

Lord, I come to you now asking your forgiveness for anything I have said or done that cursed the sons of Israel (name specific sins if known). I understand your righteous decree that you will bless those who bless them and curse those who curse them. I now ask you to break any curses on my family that fell on us because of our sins against the Jews. I plead the blood of Jesus and asked to be cleansed from all sin and unrighteousness. Lord, I submit to your plan for my life and ministry in any way that will bless the Jews. I also agree with your plans and purposes for the nation of Israel. Lord I want to receive your heart for your people and the courage to do your will, no matter what the opposition may be. Lord, help me to humble myself and pray for the Jewish people. Lord, release to me provisions and favor to bless and protect the Jews. Lord, confirm your message in me with signs and an inner witness of the Holy Spirit. In Yeshua's name, Amen.[24]

Notes:

1. Matthew 25:40 (NIV).

2. Matthew 5:17.

3. Romans 15:8–9 (NIV).

4. Revelation 21:12.

5. Isaiah 11:11–12 (NIV).

6. Jeremiah 31:35–36; 33:19–27.

7. Jeremiah 32:41.

8. 2 Chronicles 12:13.

9. 1 Samuel 12:22 (NIV).

10. Genesis 12:2–3 (NIV).

11. Joel 3:2.

12. Zechariah 14:3–4.

13. Psalm 121:4 (NIV).

14. Zechariah 2:8.

15. Psalm 122:6, 8–9 (NIV).

16. Isaiah 62:6–7 (NIV).

17. Alexander Kimel, "Source of Hatred, Anti-Semitism," *Holocaust Understanding and Prevention*, http://kimel.net/antisem.html

18. Donald K. McKim, ed., *The Cambridge Companion to Martin Luther* (New York: Cambridge University Press, 2003), 58.

19. Isaiah 66:8 (NIV).

20. *The Qur'an*, chapter 5:20–21.

21. Psalm 2:1–2.

22. Thanks to Miriam Rodlyn Park of Eagles' Wings Ministries for her manual, *Watchmen on the Wall* (Clarence, NY: Kairos Publishing, 2005), which contains much of the historic data on anti-Semitism.

23. Prayer written by Dr. Earbin Stanciell.

24. Genesis 12:3.

Prayer for Releasing
the Gift of Discernment

PAUL L. COX

After the Lord gave me the gift of discernment,[1] he continued to develop it. As I matured in the gift, I began training others in discernment. This opportunity to train others in the gift of discernment has been rewarding, but also challenging. It has not been unusual in a group of trainees for over 75 percent of those present to begin to discern? There are, however, many who do not discern. Why is this so? It is possible that not everyone is able to discern.[2] I have noted that those who operate in the redemptive gift of teaching find it difficult to discern. I believe this is true because the teacher is to observe what is happening and evaluate it according to the Word of God. But could there be other reasons why some do not discern?

I had been introduced to a couple who had been missionaries from Japan and who walked in the gift of discernment. As we talked, they shared how the Lord showed them that a spirit of autism inhibited discernment. Autism is a disorder that affects the physical senses, so it would make sense for an ungodly spirit of autism to affect the spiritual senses. I had an idea. The next time I was training a group in the gift of discernment, I would have them pray to break off any ungodly spirits of autism. The results were amazing! Several who could not discern immediately began discerning.

The Lord then revealed that often, in a family line, some have either denied the gift of discernment or have used it in an ungodly way. This ungodliness limits the gift of discernment so that the current generation either cannot discern or discerns in a diminished capacity. Repenting and renouncing for this sin opens up the possibility for increased discernment. Prayer does make a difference!

The following prayer was formulated by the Kingdom Glory Church of Singapore.

The Prayer: Releasing the Gift of Discernment[3]

✠ Father, for myself and my generational line, I renounce and repent for all sins, iniquities, and transgressions that have blocked the gift of discerning of spirits from being activated and used in a way that is godly and anointed for the glory of God. I renounce and repent for all wrong uses of the gift of discernment for selfish, manipulative, personal gain. I also renounce and repent for using the gift of discernment with help from the power of darkness.

✠ Father God, would you forgive me even as I ask for your forgiveness? I receive your forgiveness and I choose to forgive myself for all misuse and abuse of the gift of discernment.

✠ Father God, I pray that you will release the gift of discernment so that I can grow up and be on the cutting edge and listen sharply and clearly to the voice of your Spirit.

✠ Lord, right now I repent and renounce all spirits assigned against the gift of discernment: deaf and dumb spirits, passivity, unbelief, accusation, intimidation, religious spirits, torment, greed, doubts, blockages, condemnation, destruction, fears, unforgiveness, pride, shame, control, deception, uncertainty, dullness, distractions, procrastination, laziness, victimization, legalism, timidity/intimidation, mockery, oppression, repression, suppression, rebellion, inferiority, inadequacy, limitation, failure, double binding, double-mindedness, confusion, rejection, abuse, loss, stupidity, occult, lust, insecurity, seduction, jealousy, envy, malice, anger, murder, pain, resistance, rebellion, disobedience, poverty, unworthiness, sabotage, criticalness, wanting, helplessness, spirit of death, violence, mistrust, gossip, lying, slander, infirmity, manipulation, dissension, and spiritual autism.

✠ Give me ears to hear you and words from you to speak; help me be proactive, believing, trusting, encouraging, courageous, bold, spirit-filled, peace-filled, quiet, generous, content, open and flowing in your Spirit, praiseworthy, edifying, forgiving, humble, pure, innocent, not controlling, honest, without guile, true, sure of the truth, alert, clear, bright, resonant, quickened, focused, quick to obey, hardworking, diligent, overcoming, grace giving, merciful, real, authentic, free, obedient, adequate, unlimited in your resources, successful, single-hearted and single-minded for you, filled with understanding, rightly ordered and aligned, coherent, connected, accepted, loved, cared for, provided for, wise, accurate, self-controlled, secure, loving, joyful, vulnerable, rich, worthy, trustworthy, helpful, life filled, strong, stable, sound, direct, awake, and alert.

✠ Lord Jesus, I renounce and repent for all activities that have opened up my third eye to deceptive vision and opened all the different chakras. Would you blind all powers of darkness that have utilized my third eye in all its various dimensions and in all my different parts that are trapped, lost, and enslaved in the dimensions?

✠ Lord, would you cut off all demonic connections that demonic watchers have with my third eye to gain information and monitor my movements? Lord, please remove all evil powers associated with my third eye.

✠ And Lord, please assign angels to remove the third eye from all parts of my being, in all its various dimensions, in the past, in the present, and in the future.

✠ Lord, please fill me with your presence and replace evil with good. I remove all occult influences and pressures over my life to try to attempt to plant and to activate the third eye from now until forever.

✠ Lord Jesus, I receive the eyes of your Spirit and ask that I will only see what you want me to see. I ask that all the strategies of the enemy will be exposed by divine revelations of your will.

✠ Lord, please open my eyes to see your power and glory and all your glories in heaven.

✠ Father God, thank you for giving me the gift of discernment so that I can have complete knowledge of your will in all manners of life. Thank you for spiritual wisdom and understanding to apply all that you've shown me. Thank you for teaching me how to live a life that will always honor and please you. And Father God, thank you for giving me the discernment to produce a good harvest, every time, in all my investments and in every manner of life.[4]

✠ Father God, thank you for showing me how to receive your resources in all situations with all kinds of people. Father, thank you for letting me know your divine timing, your opportunities, and your open doors to supply all that is necessary in my life—in all spiritual, physical, and emotional abundance, so that all I do and all I say will be a sweet-smelling aroma and sacrifice that is acceptable and pleasing to you.[5]

✠ Father God, I thank you. You help me to begin to understand the incredible greatness of your power to all who believe in you, the same mighty power that raised Christ from the dead and seated him at God's right hand in the heavenly realms.[6]

✠ God, thank you for giving us a way to access your incredible wealth of grace and kindness even as we walk in unity.[7]

✠ Father God, thank you for showing by discernment how to walk in love, joy, peace, patience, kindness, goodness, faithfulness, gentleness, and self-control. Father God, thank you that there are no limitations to all you have called me to do.[8]

✠ Father God, thank you for showing me the lust of the flesh, the lust of the eyes, and the pride of life, so that I will be able to flee from temptation and live in spiritual truth and freedom.[9]

✠ Father God, I want to know what you want me to do. I am asking you now for your wisdom. I thank you that you will gladly give me what I ask for and will never resent my asking.[10]

✠ Father God, thank you for teaching me how to submit to my leaders and to fellow believers, biblically and spiritually. Give me the attitude and faith that produces breakthrough, healing miracles, growth, and fruitfulness so that I will reach the full potential of my birthright. Teach me how to live in the harmony of the unity of faith that will glorify you.[11]

✠ Father God, thank you for giving me the ability to discern all the spiritual gifts and callings that you have given to me. Thank you for teaching me how to develop, use, and maximize all you have given me to the fullest potential—to bring your glory into all aspects of my life and to the people round about me.[12]

✠ Father God, please give me the discernment to receive the right spiritual impartation from the specific people that you have sent into my life. Give me the wisdom to flee, escape, avoid, and refuse any wrong impartation from the servants of Satan. Please teach me to recognize all false servants from afar, even at the sound of their voices. Will you protect my ears, my eyes, and my five spiritual senses from the assault of the enemy camp? Lord, surround me with the songs of deliverance, with the presence of your Holy Spirit, so that even when darkness comes, it shall not come near me.

✠ Father God, you have given me the ability to hear the voice of your Spirit. I will not follow the voice of the stranger, but I will follow you all the rest of my life. Thank you that I have the ability to hear your voice in all my decision making—for my family, for my work, my ministry, investments, business, studies, relationships, marriage, and church. May all I that I do and say pertain to life, be filled with life, release life, and be life-giving. Lord, thank you that I can hear your voice clearly and sharply like the prophets of old.[13]

✠ Father God, thank you for showing me the crisis of the land rather than letting me become a victim to it. I will become a protector and encourager of those in need. Help me flee from all works of darkness upon the land and the economy. Secure my properties and all my possessions by your Spirit.[14]

✠ Father God, will you teach me how to live in peace and harmony with all people to bring about your will? Teach me how to walk with tenderness, mercy, kindness, humility, gentleness, and patience. Teach me how to forgive every fault and how to walk in love and perfect harmony.[15]

✠ Father God, thank you for teaching me how to give and receive counsel perfectly, with all the wisdom of heaven, so that I can be whole in spirit, soul, and body.[16]

✠ Father God, thank you for teaching me how to receive all your provisions so that I will have everything that I will ever need. Teach me how to share all that I have received. Father God, thank you for teaching me how to increase the resources that you have provided to produce a great harvest of generosity in my life.[17]

✠ Father God, thank you for teaching me how to share your work in my life effectively with the people I love in ways that demonstrate your mercy, kindness, and goodness. Thank you for teaching me how to walk in your peace at all times.[18]

Notes:

1. See *Unwrap the Gifts* by Paul L. Cox (Lake Mary, FL: Creation House, 2009) for a full description of the gift of discernment. Discernment is the use of five physical senses to discern in the Spirit.

2. Although Hebrews 5:14 may indicate otherwise: "But solid food belongs to those who are of full age, that is, those who by reason of use have their senses exercised to discern both good and evil."

3. Prayer written by Kingdom Glory Church (originally Destiny Center), Singapore.

4. Colossians 1:9.

5. Philippians 4:19.

6. Ephesians 1:19.

7. Ephesians 1:7.

8. Galatians 5:22–23.

9. 1 John 2:16.

10. James 1:5.
11. Matthew 8:9.
12. 2 Timothy 1:6–7.
13. John 10:27.
14. Matthew 28.
15. Colossians 3:12–14.
16. Colossians 3:16.
17. 2 Corinthians 9:8.
18. Mark 5:19.

Scripture Index

Genesis 1:1; 43
Genesis 1:26–28; 218
Genesis 1:28; 184, 379
Genesis 1:28–30; 363
Genesis 2; 35
Genesis 2:9; 107
Genesis 2:16; 385
Genesis 2:23; 385
Genesis 2:24; 92
Genesis 3; 194
Genesis 3:5; 385
Genesis 3:1–7; 146
Genesis 3:7; 380, 385
Genesis 3:7–8, 10; 385
Genesis 3:10–11; 385
Genesis 3:12; 260
Genesis 3:12–13; 385
Genesis 3:14; 86
Genesis 3:16; 168, 173, 260
Genesis 3:18; 185
Genesis 3:20; 385
Genesis 3:22; 385
Genesis 4:1–16; 212
Genesis 4:5–7; 381, 385
Genesis 4:6–7; 385
Genesis 4:7; 168
Genesis 4:11; 86
Genesis 6:1–4; 378
Genesis 6:1–6; 200
Genesis 7:11; 43
Genesis 8:21; 86
Genesis 8:22; 146
Genesis 10:8–9; 378
Genesis 10:9; 378
Genesis 10:9–10; 378
Genesis 10:10; 379
Genesis 11:4; 58
Genesis 11:4–6; 379
Genesis 12; 146
Genesis 12:2–3; 387, 392

Genesis 15; 129
Genesis 12:3; 392
Genesis 24:40–41; 86
Genesis 26:28; 86
Genesis 27:29; 86
Genesis 34:1–3; 93
Genesis 38:21; 110
Genesis 44:5; 30–31
Genesis 44:5, 15; 32

Exodus 4:2; 119
Exodus 4:20; 120
Exodus 14:16; 125
Exodus 16:33; 184
Exodus 17:8–16; 120
Exodus 20:1–17; 218
Exodus 20:5–6; 86, 201,
   204–205
Exodus 24:1–11; 78
Exodus 33:12; 229
Exodus 34:7; 212

Leviticus 10:10; 194
Leviticus 17:11; 78
Leviticus 17:1–12; 78
Leviticus 17:3–14; 78
Leviticus 19:14; 86
Leviticus 19:19; 229
Leviticus 19:26; 35
Leviticus 19:28; 78
Leviticus 19:31, 20:6; 31
Leviticus 26:40–42; 206

Numbers 13:33; 378
Numbers 17:10; 184
Numbers 18; 184
Numbers 20:8; 120
Numbers 22:6–12; 86
Numbers 30:2; 94

Deuteronomy 2:11, 20; 378
Deuteronomy 2:13; 146
Deuteronomy 3:11, 13; 378
Deuteronomy 4:15–20; 35
Deuteronomy 8; 212
Deuteronomy 8:18; 146
Deuteronomy 9:1–2; 17
Deuteronomy 10:16; 146
Deuteronomy 11:26–29; 86
Deuteronomy 14:1; 78
Deuteronomy 15:7–8; 146
Deuteronomy 18:9–14; 35
Deuteronomy 18:11; 31
Deuteronomy 19:21; 385
Deuteronomy 27:12–13; 86
Deuteronomy 27:15–26; 86
Deuteronomy 28; 146, 164,
   212
Deuteronomy 28:13; 165
Deuteronomy 28:15–68;
   79, 81–86
Deuteronomy 28:15; 81, 86
Deuteronomy 28:20; 81
Deuteronomy 28:23; 260
Deuteronomy 28:33; 260
Deuteronomy 29:12; 86
Deuteronomy 29:29; 165
Deuteronomy 30:1; 86
Deuteronomy 30:4–5; 17
Deuteronomy 30:19; 86
Deuteronomy 31:26; 184
Deuteronomy 33:26: 43

Joshua 1:2–3; 5, 6
Joshua 6:20; 260
Joshua 6:26; 86
Joshua 7:21; 379
Joshua 9:22; 86
Joshua 24:14–15; 229

403

Key Word Index

About the Author

Paul L. Cox was born in Wellington, New Zealand. Paul received his BA in history and English from Pepperdine University. He went on to graduate from the American Baptist Seminary of the West and the California Graduate School of Theology. Paul has served as a senior pastor in four different churches. He has also served in a number of leadership positions, such as president of a ministers' council in the Pacific Southwest and president of a denominational evangelism committee .

Paul and his wife, Donna, live in Hesperia, California, and are the co-directors of Aslan's Place, a ministry dedicated to bringing freedom and wholeness to the wounded and captive. Aslan's Place equips the body of Christ in the ministry of spiritual warfare and in the exercise of the gift of discernment. Paul and Donna have ministered around the world. They have three children and seven grandchildren.

For additional information on Aslan's Place ministry, please visit their Web site at www.aslansplace.com. Additional books written by Paul L. Cox are available for purchase at the Web site:

Guidelines for Deliverance
Heaven Trek
Prayers for Generational Deliverance

Contributors

I would like to acknowledge the wonderful contributions to the text and prayers contained in this book by the following list of people:

Jeffrey Barsch, EdD
Amybeth Berner
David Brown
Kelsey Budd
Lewis Crampton
Dena Gewanter, MD
Terry Johnson
Alice Mills
Annemie-Joy Munnik
Nigel Reid
Richard Sicheneder
Dr. Earbin Stanciell
Joanne Towne
Mary Upham
Patti Velotta
Sarah Victor

Many others who are not named have prayed and contributed to the prayers from our Advanced Discernment Training and Exploration Schools held around the world. I am so grateful for all that the Lord teaches us through our extended family in Christ.